EUROPEAN JUDICIAL SYSTEMS AS A CHALLENGE FOR DEMOCRACY

EUROPEAN JUDICIAL SYSTEMS AS A CHALLENGE FOR DEMOCRACY

Edited by
Elżbieta Kużelewska
Dariusz Kloza
Izabela Kraśnicka
Franciszek Strzyczkowski

intersentia
Cambridge – Antwerp – Portland

Intersentia Ltd
Sheraton House | Castle Park
Cambridge | CB3 0AX | United Kingdom
Tel.: +44 1223 370 170 | Email: mail@intersentia.co.uk

Distribution for the UK:
NBN International
Airport Business Centre, 10 Thornbury Road
Plymouth, PL6 7 PP
United Kingdom
Tel.: +44 1752 202 301 | Fax: +44 1752 202 331
Email: orders@nbninternational.com

Distribution for the USA and Canada:
International Specialized Book Services
920 NE 58th Ave. Suite 300
Portland, OR 97213
USA
Tel.: +1 800 944 6190 (toll free)
Email: info@isbs.com

Distribution for Austria:
Neuer Wissenschaftlicher Verlag
Argentinierstraße 42/6
1040 Wien
Austria
Tel.: +43 1 535 61 03 24
Email: office@nwv.at

Distribution for other countries:
Intersentia Publishing nv
Groenstraat 31
2640 Mortsel
Belgium
Tel.: +32 3 680 15 50
Email: mail@intersentia.be

European Judicial Systems as a Challenge for Democracy
Elżbieta Kużelewska, Dariusz Kloza, Izabela Kraśnicka and Franciszek Strzyczkowski (eds.)

Review: Prof. Dr. Paul De Hert, Vrije Universiteit Brussel and Tilburg University

Cover illustration: *General Illustration of the Court of Justice of the European Union* © Court of Justice of the European Union

ISBN 978-1-78068-316-4
D/2015/7849/90
NUR 828

GPRC
Guaranteed
Peer Reviewed
Content

British Library Cataloguing in Publication Data. A catalogue record for this book is available from the British Library.

FOREWORD

BY PROF. MACIEJ SZPUNAR, ADVOCATE GENERAL AT THE COURT OF JUSTICE OF THE EUROPEAN UNION

The role of European Judiciary in the process of European integration cannot be overestimated. The achievements of European integration after the second world war are usually analysed from the perspective of political decisions that were made, initially, by the Founding Fathers and, subsequently, by the political leaders of the European countries. However, in the public debate we very often forget how much we owe to the two supreme jurisdictions of Europe, that is the Court of Justice of the European Union and the European Court of Human Rights.

One cannot deny that without some "revolutionary" decisions of the Court of Justice, the process of European integration would never come to the place where we are now. We would have never achieved the level of integration that, despite some shortcomings, still remains unique in comparison to all other initiatives of economic and political integration in the rest of the world. The Court of Justice takes the mission of ensuring that "law is observed" seriously and continues to assure that it is the rule of law which is at the heart of the European Union. The strength of the European Union comes essentially from the fact that it constitutes an autonomous legal order which rests on the concepts of direct effect and supremacy. These latter concepts were not only developed by, but – and this must be emphasized – originated in the case law of the Court of Justice. The landmark decisions of the Court of Justice gave life to and strengthened the internal market that still remains the cornerstone and the main achievement of the European integration. One would not exaggerate by saying that political initiatives would remain "wishful thinking" if they were not supported by the historic decisions of the Court of Justice.

The contribution of the European Court of Human Rights is equally significant. It assured that the protection of human rights on our continent became effective and universal. The limits of human rights are no longer restricted to national boundaries nor exposed to the danger of national authorities abusing their discretionary competences.

I am very happy that the group of young scholars, under the auspices of Elżbieta Kużelewska and Dariusz Kloza, has taken the initiative to explore the challenges for the European Judiciary that have emerged in recent years. It seems clear that despite its evident achievements, the process of European integration is, if not at a crossroads, at least at a moment where important choices have to be made. It is impossible to enumerate all these challenges. They stem not only from internal changes and developments of the European Union, but also from external threats.

The authors of the contributions to the book decided to concentrate their research on the response of the European Judiciary to the problems of modern democracy. The problem of the so-called democratic deficit has been present in the academic debate for many years. It has been discussed by political scientists, lawyers and economists. The continuing extension of the competences of the European Union, especially in the field economic and monetary policy, calls for the new assessment of the nature of the decision making process at the European level. Is this process sufficiently democratic? If not, what are alternative solutions? To what extent can one accept a possible shift from the traditional model of a democratic decision making process towards new models? These kinds of questions will have to be dealt with by the Court of Justice of the European Union as well as by the European Court of Human Rights. Clearly, the mere existence of judicial review does not make a decision making process democratic. It does, however, strengthen the accountability of decision making bodies. Moreover, it is for the European judiciary to shape the democratic framework of the decision making process. Will the response of the European judiciary to the new challenges be as brave and effective as in the past?

Maciej Szpunar
Luxembourg, March 2015

PREFACE

EUROPEAN INTEGRATION, DEMOCRACY AND THE COURTS

Toutes ces institutions pourront être modifiées et améliorées à l'expérience
Jean Monnet[1]

The process of European integration is "evolving and the form it finally takes still cannot be predicted".[2] The European judiciary – i.e. the Court of Justice of the European Union (CJEU), the European Court of Human Rights (ECtHR) and national courts interpreting and applying European law *sensu largo* – have shaped this process actively, alongside the Founding Fathers, European nations, European states and their citizens. The involvement of judiciary raises its own wide range of questions concerning the very nature of democracy. Much ink has been already spilled over issues such as democratic legitimacy, subsidiarity and accountability, the rule of law or judicial activism. But it was the recently celebrated 50th anniversaries of *Van Gend en Loos* (1963)[3] and *Costa v ENEL* (1964)[4] judgements that gave us further impetus to ponder about the place of the European judiciary in the democratic life in the Old Continent and their role in the process of its integration.

Therefore, under the auspices of the Centre for Direct Democracy Studies (CDDS) at the Faculty of Law, University of Białystok, in March 2014 we issued a call for papers and seventeen scholars from across Europe, predominantly young researchers, have kindly responded thereto and shared their views on the European judiciary as a challenge for democracy.

The present book constitutes the third fruit of our academic interest in the questions posed by European integration and democracy. In 2012 the Centre established a dedicated, peer-reviewed book series that produced, up-to-date, two volumes.[5] It is edifying that from this volume onwards, the reputable

1 J. Monnet, *Les États-Unis d'Europe ont commencé*, Robert Laffont, Paris 1955, 141 pp.
2 K.-D. Borchardt, *The ABC of European Union law*, Publications Office of the European Union, Luxembourg 2010, p. 32.
3 Case 26/62, *NV Algemene Transporten Expeditie Onderneming van Gend en Loos v Nederlandse Administratie der Belastingen* [1963] ECR 1.
4 Case 6/64, *Flamino Costa v ENEL* [1964] ECR 585.
5 The two previous books were: E. Kużelewska and D. Kloza (eds.), *The Challenges of Modern Democracy and European Integration*, European Integration and Democracy Series, Vol. 1,

Belgian-based international publishing house *Intersentia* has decided to publish this series.

The various contributions to the present volume have been split into two parts. The first provides ten chapters on the judicial systems of the European Union (EU), discussing, *inter alia*, recognition of democratic principles in the case law of the CJEU, contribution thereof to the democratisation of the Union and reception of EU law in the Member States. The second part discusses the judicial means to protect human rights in Europe, consisting of three chapters devoted to the promise of advisory opinions of ECtHR as well as to democratic standards for voting and for fair trial.

The authors of this collection of papers have done an excellent and outstanding job illuminating – as Advocate General Maciej Szupnar, who kindly provided this book with a foreword, puts it – "the response of the European judiciary to the problems of modern democracy". The series editors, the reviewers and the peer-reviewers helped us ensuring academic quality of this volume. We have been fortunate to work with *Intersentia* and our editor Tom Scheirs. Further invaluable assistance was received from Michał Czerniawski, Valentin Gros, Władysław Jóźwicki and Monika Kokštaitė. We thank them all. Finally, each of us, editors, undersigned, thank each other for this piece of teamwork.

We gratefully acknowledge financial and intellectual support of the Faculty of Law, University of Białystok, the Faculty of Law and Administration, University of Łódź as well as of the Institute for European Studies, Vrije Universiteit Brussel.

The corresponding editors welcome any comments and suggestions at *ekuzelewska@gmail.com* and *dariusz.kloza@interia.pl*, respectively.

Elżbieta Kużelewska
Dariusz Kloza
Izabela Kraśnicka
Franciszek Strzyczkowski
Białystok – Łódź – Brussels, March 2015

Aspra-JR: Warsaw-Białystok 2012, 249 pp.; E. Kużelewska and D. Kloza (eds.), *Elections to the European Parliament as a Challenge for Democracy*, European Integration and Democracy Series, Vol. 2, Aspra-JR: Warsaw-Białystok 2013, 371 pp.

CONTENTS

Foreword by Prof. Maciej Szpunar v
Preface vii
List of Abbreviations xv

PART ONE
THE COURT OF JUSTICE OF THE EUROPEAN UNION

1. Democracy in Constitutional Politics of European Courts: An Overview of Selected Issues
Bogusia PUCHALSKA 3

1. Introduction 3
2. The ECJ and national courts: power struggle or cooperation? 6
   2.1. European Court of Justice: its own master? 6
   2.2. The main tenets of ECJ's constitutional politics 7
   2.3. The enduring attraction of the concept of sovereignty in relations between the ECJ and NCs 10
   2.4. Beyond 'sovereignty': power struggle, or power-posturing? 14
3. The supremacy of EU economic policy 16
   3.1. What is the model of economic policy entrenched in the Treaties? . . . 17
   3.2. The ECJ and the EU's 'democratic deficit' 18
   3.3. Entrenchment of the EU economic policy, TTIP, and the role of the courts 20
      3.3.1. Democratic deficit of economic policy and the courts 20
         a. Investor-state dispute settlement 21
4. Conclusions 22
Bibliography 23

2. The Institutional Balance as CJEU's Contribution to Democracy in the Union: Selected Issues
Tomasz DUBOWSKI 25

1. Introduction 25
2. The CJEU and the traces of institutional balance in the Treaties 26
3. Institutional balance as a general principle of EU (EC) law? The Court's role 29

4. Institutional balance and democracy in the EU – visible links 32
5. Conclusion 35
Bibliography 36

3. From Judicial Dialogue Towards Constitutional Spill-Over? The Economic Analysis of Preliminary Reference Procedure and the Application of the EU Charter of Fundamental Rights
Mariusz J. Golecki 37

1. Introduction 37
2. Constitutional courts and the preliminary reference procedure: judicial dialogue and judicial spill-over 41
3. Towards an economic analysis of breach of the EU Charter of Fundamental Rights by the national constitutional court 45
4. Tentative conclusion 53
Bibliography 54

4. Towards the Democratization of the EU? Strengthening prerogatives of the European Parliament in the case law of the Court of Justice of the European Union
Agnieszka Piekutowska 57

1. Introduction 57
2. The defence of the prerogatives of the European Parliament before the CJEU. Pre-Lisbon case-law 59
3. Post-Lisbon judgments of the CJEU on the EP's prerogatives 63
4. Conclusion 67
Bibliography 69

5. Democratic Values in the Court of Justice Adjudication on the Private Enforcement of the European Union Competition Law
Franciszek Strzyczkowski 73

1. Introduction 73
2. The influence of the American experience on private enforcement of the European antitrust law 75
3. The importance of the reform of the EU competition law enforcement. . . . 76
   3.1. Towards fostering private damages actions – proposals of the European Commission 77
4. The position of the European Courts 78
5. *Locus standi* to claim damages under European Union competition law . . 83
6. Concluding remarks 85
Bibliography 85

6. **Judicial Control of Monetary and Fiscal Decisions in the European Union**
Filip Křepelka 87

1. Introduction 87
2. Traditional and emerging roles of judiciary 88
3. Rules and institutions for monetary and fiscal policy 90
4. A single currency for the integration in the European Union 94
5. Original legal framework for the euro 95
6. Onset of the debt crisis and its causes 96
7. Alleviation of the crisis and prevention of its escalation 98
8. Political consequences of the crisis 100
9. Legal aspects of remedies and reinterpretation of rules 102
10. Judicial involvement in the crisis 104
11. Conclusions 108
Bibliography 109

7. **How CJEU's "Privacy Spring" Construed the Human Rights Shield in the Digital Age**
Gabriela Zanfir 111

1. Introduction 111
2. The relationship between individuals and the state in the digital world: *Digital Rights Ireland* 112
   2.1. Preliminary observation: there is a wide societal interest in protecting human rights against the bulk collection and retention of metadata 113
   2.2. Bulk retention of metadata touches on the freedom of expression, not only on privacy 113
   2.3. Clarification on the differences in content between Articles 7 and 8 of the Charter 115
   2.4. Requirements for data retention legislation to comply with fundamental rights 117
3. The relationship between individuals and private bodies in the digital world: *Google v. Spain* 119
   3.1. Internet search engines are data controllers and their activity involves processing of personal data 120
   3.2. "Global" territorial scope of Directive 95/46/EC 121
   3.3. The right to erasure applies when the processing does not comply with the provisions of Directive 95/46/EC 122
   3.4. Criteria for the balance of rights 123
4. Conclusion 123
Bibliography 124

8. The Supremacy of the EU Law as Interpreted by the Polish Constitutional Tribunal
Elżbieta Kużelewska and Dariusz Kużelewski 127

1. Introduction 127
2. Specificity of the constitutional review in Poland 128
3. The primacy of the EU law over national law 129
4. The principle of supremacy in the light of the Polish Constitutional Tribunal's judicature 131
5. Conclusions 137
Bibliography 139

9. Reception of EU Law in Polish Courts – A Case of "Teddy Bear" Law
Izabela Kraśnicka 143

1. Introduction 143
2. The principle of supremacy, the principle of direct effect and the principle of indirect effect of EU law 144
3. "Working time" under the Polish law and EU law 148
4. Czesław Miś' arguments in the light of the ECJ case law 150
5. Arguments of the Polish courts 152
6. The final decision and its consequences 154
7. Closing remarks 156
Bibliography 157

10. Enforcing Europe's Foundational Values in Central and Eastern Europe: A Case in Point
Tine Carmeliet and Georgia Christina Kosmidou 159

1. Introduction 159
2. Shortcomings of the EU's institutional framework 162
   2.1. Article 7 TEU 162
      2.1.1. Procedural obstacles 162
      2.1.2. Substantive obstacles 164
      2.1.3. Conclusion 166
   2.2. Legal creativity to protect the European foundational values 167
      2.2.1. Infringement actions by the European Commission 167
      2.2.2. Social pressure and issue linkage 169
3. Policy recommendations 171
   3.1. In search for a definition of liberal democracy 171
   3.2. A stronger role for the CJEU 173
4. Concluding observations 175
Bibliography 177

PART TWO
THE EUROPEAN COURT OF HUMAN RIGHTS

11. Protocol 16 to the ECHR: A Convenient Tool for Judicial Dialogue and Better Domestic Implementation of the Convention?
Władysław Jóźwicki 183

1. Introduction 183
2. Protocol 16 – background 184
3. The new advisory opinion mechanism – basic characteristics 187
3. Protocol 16 and the chances it opens 191
   3.1. A step towards enhancing domestic implementation of the ECHR . . 192
   3.2. A step towards more harmonious and up-to-date interpretation of the Convention 193
4. Protocol 16 and its drawbacks 197
   4.1. ECtHR – victim of its success revisited? 197
   4.2. The optional and nonbinding character of the AOs and some practical concerns 199
   4.3. Protocol 16 and the EU 201
5. Conclusion 205
Bibliography 206

12. The EU's Parliamentary Representation in the Light of the Strasbourg Court's *Sejdić* and *Zornić* Standards: Is there Tendency for a New Parliamentary Order in the EU?
Fisnik Korenica and Dren Doli 211

1. Introduction 211
2. EU's constitutional architecture with regard to parliamentary representation 214
3. A note on the concept of parliamentary representation in the light of *Sejdić* and *Zornić*: European Parliament of the EU people or European Parliament of the EU Member States *peoples* 217
4. Thresholds on EU Parliament and 'regressive proportionality' model of electoral system: is there an objective system of electoral criteria? 225
5. Concluding remarks and a general forthcoming outlook 229
Bibliography 231

13. The European Concept of a Fair Trial and the Legal Admissibility of Assessors in the Polish Judicial System
Karol Pachnik and Jakub Krajewski 233

1. Introduction 233
2. The position of an assessor in Polish common courts 233
3. Standards of a fair trial 236
4. Amending the organisation of courts 239
5. Regulations on assessors in Polish administrative courts – possible solutions 241
6. Conclusion 242

Bibliography 243

LIST OF ABBREVIATIONS

AG	Advocate General
AO	Advisory Opinion [ECtHR]
BVerfG, FCCG	Federal Constitutional Court [Germany] (Bundesverfassungsgericht)
CC	Constitutional Court
CCP	Code of Criminal Procedure [Poland]
CE	Central Europe
CFR	Charter of Fundamental Rights of the European Union
CFSP	Common Foreign and Security Policy
CJEU	Court of Justice of the European Union
CoE	Council of Europe
CoM	Committee of Ministers [CoE]
EAW	European Arrest Warrant
EC	European Community
EC, Commission	European Commission
ECB	European Central Bank
ECHR	European Convention on Human Rights
ECJ	European Court of Justice
ECtHR	European Court of Human Rights
EEC	European Economic Community
EFSF	European Financial Stability Facility
EFSM	European Fiscal Stabilisation Mechanism
ELA	Emergency Liquidity Assistance
EP, Parliament	European Parliament
ESM	European Stability Mechanism
EU	European Union
GCh	Grand Chamber [ECtHR]
GDP	Gross Domestic Product
ISDS	Investor-State Dispute Settlement
MEP	Member of European Parliament
MS	Member State
NC	National Court
NCA	National Competition Authorities
OMT	Outright Monetary Transactions
SMP	Securities Markets Programme

SRM	Single Resolution Mechanism
SSM	Single Supervision Mechanism
TEAEC, TAEC	Euratom Treaty, Treaty establishing the European Atomic Energy Community
TEC	Treaty establishing European Community
TECSC	Treaty establishing the European Coal and Steel Community
TEEC	Treaty establishing the European Economic Community
TEU	Treaty on European Union
TFEU	Treaty on the Functioning of the European Union
TTIP	Transatlantic Trade and Investment Partnership
UK	United Kingdom of Great Britain and Northern Ireland

PART ONE

THE COURT OF JUSTICE OF THE EUROPEAN UNION

1. DEMOCRACY IN CONSTITUTIONAL POLITICS OF EUROPEAN COURTS

An Overview of Selected Issues

Bogusia PUCHALSKA*

Lancashire Law School, University of Central Lancashire, Preston, UK

1. INTRODUCTION

One of the principal constitutional functions of the European Court of Justice (ECJ)[1] is to secure legitimacy[2] of the European Union (EU) system of governance by protecting the fundamental values on which this system is said to rest.[3] This role of the ECJ – as a guardian of democracy, fundamental rights and the rule of law – is complicated by the multi-layered nature of the EU's sources of legal authority: the EU institutions and the law-making bodies of Member States (MSs), and by the heavy reliance on the co-operation of National Courts (NCs) in building up and maintaining the EU's legal system.[4] I focus on providing an overview of selected problems that are directly related to the ECJ's legitimising role, and I will do so from the perspective of the ECJ's constitutional politics.[5]

---

* Email: bapuchalska@uclan.ac.uk.

1 The current name under the Treaty of Lisbon is the Court of Justice of the European Union (CJEU). I prefer to stay with the old name – ECJ. I also do not include the General Court in my discussion since its role is much less constitutionally salient than that of the ECJ.

2 This idea is partially inspired by the writings of T. Parsons, 'The professions and social structure' (1939) *Social forces*, 17(4), pp. 457–467.

3 The ECJ has been credited with paying increasing attention to effective application of the principle of democracy in its case law, but as is widely known, this has not always been the case. What still remains problematic is the judicial treatment of democracy and other substantive constitutional principles or values in the high plane of constitutional politics of the EU.

4 According to de Waele, there is a suggestion that the ECJ is legally obligated to steer pro-integration course: H.D. de Waele, 'The Role of the Court of Justice in the European Integration Process. A Contemporary and Normative Assessment' (2010) *Hanse Law Review* Vol. 6 No 1.

5 This is a huge topic of which a number of aspects warrant a more in-depth investigation that can be provided here. Also, I will not cover issues related to the infamous 'democratic deficit', i.e., the well-recognised problems with popular political participation and representation,

First, I will consider whether the alleged prioritising – by the ECJ – of the principles of integrity of the EU legal system and economic regulations over constitutional values – such as fundamental rights and democracy – amounts to an ideological project that undermines the legitimacy of the EU law. I will focus on instances where the ECJ failed to recognise concerns of the NCs related to the standard of protection of these values in the EU law for the sake of protecting its own authority and the uniformity of the EU law. Historically, these concerns were most famously identified in the so-called 'supremacy' challenges, but there was also a string of other cases where the protection of market freedoms clashed with fundamental rights and other constitutional principles.[6] This period of the ECJ jurisprudence took a more rights-friendly turn in cases such as *Omega* and *Schmidberger*.[7] The more recent NCs challenges yet again put the ECJ under pressure, this time because of its reluctance to recognise the higher standards of fundamental rights protection related to criminal trials in national constitutions over those existing in the EU law. The string of the European Arrest Warrant (EAW) cases[8] seems to suggest that the ECJ yet again entered a path of prioritising the supremacy of the EU law over substantive constitutional objectives.

Secondly, I will consider if the ECJ can be said to preside over a process of entrenching a particular model of economic policy across the EU – in contradiction with the core principles of constitutional transparency and contestation. These issues relate directly to the fundamental nature of the EU Treaties as international agreements, which were negotiated by the governments and imposed top-down on the electorate, hence lack popular legitimacy.[9] Since the ECJ and the national courts play key roles in interpreting

---

and the functioning of the European Parliament *vis-à-vis* the Commission and the Council. The sources on this topic are too numerous to cite here.

6 Compare with Lenaerts, who argued that the ECJ's interpretation of the principle of democracy is respectful of national traditions as well as supranational regime of the EU; K. Lenaerts, 'The Principle of Democracy in the Case Law of the European Court of Justice' (2013) *ICLQ* vol 62, April, pp. 271–315. There is obviously, a whole string of cases where the ECJ directly recognised and supported fundamental rights. See for instance D Chalmers, G. Davies & G. Monti, *European Union Law: Text and Materials* (CUP: Cambridge), 2014, 3rd ed. ch.6. See also J. Weiler & N. Lockhart, 'Taking Rights Seriously' "Seriously": The European Court and its Fundamental Rights Jurisprudence' (1995) 32 *CMLRev.* 51.

7 Cases C-36/02, *Omega* [2004] I-9609; and C-112/00, *Schmidberger* [2003] I-5659. Cases such as *Laval* C-341/05 [2007] ECR I-11767 and *Viking: International Transport Workers' Federation, Finish Seamen Union v Viking Line ABP* [2007] ECR I-10779 led to renewed concerns about the ECJ's priorities, but did not undermine the overall trend.

8 See for instance: C-399/11, *Melloni* [2013].

9 This is a rather sweeping claim, but, I believe it should be accepted, as it captures a key tension at the heart of EU constitutional settlement. The simple fact is that all the basic provisions of the Treaties were decided with the exclusion of the electorates of the MSs – due to the international nature of the EU Treaties. The negotiations of the Treaties on accession, and accession referenda could not be reasonably considered as capable of rectifying this shortcoming. See for instance: J. Zielonka, 'Europe as empire: the nature of the enlarged

and enforcing treaty provisions and by-passing national parliaments in this process, it can be argued that the courts contribute to further shrinking of the scope for democratic scrutiny and contestation, deepening the already weak legitimacy of the EU law.[10] Arguably, this problem is particularly acute in areas of economic policy, as illustrated in cases where the courts enforce seemingly technical rules that in reality are democratically salient – such as those created by administrative agencies – under the non-legislative procedure regulated by article 290 TFEU.[11]

In the last section, I briefly outline the most disturbing aspects of the Transatlantic Trade and Investment Partnership (TTIP) between the US and the EU currently being negotiated, that is the Investor-State Dispute Settlement (ISDS) – a judicial process of doubtful constitutional legitimacy.

Overall, I argue that the ECJ's constitutional politics might be seen as amounting to a type of ideological project that the ECJ uses as a way to legitimise the EU legal system which, on balance, prioritises the maintenance of efficient jurisdictional order across the EU over substantive principles of democratic governance – despite challenges from national constitutional courts (CC).[12] Furthermore, I suggest that the ECJ's persistence in promoting such ideology might have created a self-reinforcing dynamics; by defining NC challenges as threats to EU law uniformity, the ECJ concentrates on dispelling such threats and fails to refocus its attention towards substantive constitutional concerns. Additional challenges to democracy and constitutionalism in the EU comes from specific choices of economic policy enshrined in the EU Treaties and the way these are interpreted and developed by the ECJ and NCs. With some exceptions[13] these choices amount to a particular model of economic policy that has been entrenched without much popular or parliamentary debate, and which depends on the active and essential support of the courts.

European Union' (2006) *Central European Review of International Affairs*, *27*, 135. G. Ivaldi, 'Beyond France's 2005 referendum on the European constitutional treaty: Second-order model, anti-establishment attitudes and the end of the alternative European utopia' (2006) *West European Politics*, *29*(1), 47–69.

10 Conflicting national law is to be 'set aside' or disapplied according to *Simmental II*, Case C-106/77 [1978] ECR I-629.

11 Lenaerts uses the term 'other forms of governance' to describe the process of administrative agencies rule-making function. See note 6 above, p. 271.

12 Weiler famously stated: '[t]his need for a successful market not only accentuates the pressure for uniformity, but also manifests a social (and hence ideological) choice which prizes market efficiency and European-wide neutrality of competition above other competing values' in: J. Weiler, 'The Transformation of Europe' (1991) 100 *Yale Law Journal*, p. 2478.

13 See n. 6.

2. THE ECJ AND NATIONAL COURTS: POWER STRUGGLE OR COOPERATION?

2.1. EUROPEAN COURT OF JUSTICE: ITS OWN MASTER?[14]

The preliminary reference procedure contained in Article 267 TFEU[15] has been hailed as the 'jewel in the Crown of the ECJ jurisdiction'.[16] It is undoubtedly a cornerstone of the EU legal system, the very survival and development of which – according to the ECJ's discourse developed in the early constitutional cases – crucially depend on its smooth operation. Article 267 is also the main mechanism determining important aspects of the relationship between the ECJ and NCs. More recently, this relationship has moved from *horizontal* and *bilateral* to more steadily vertical and *multilateral*.[17] This is mainly due to two factors: the doctrine of *acte clair*, which, in effect, makes it very difficult for the national courts to avoid making a reference under threat of *Francovich* action for damages or Article 258 TFEU infringement action, and, also, the fact that ECJ judgements under Article 267 have become binding on all courts across the EU, even retrospectively.[18] Yet, the normal function that it is ascribed to any court hierarchy, that of appeals and reviews of judgements, is limited in relation to ECJ, and not available at all under Article 267 TFEU.

This lack of availability of appeals against the ECJ's preliminary ruling is coupled with the weak mechanism of control over the ECJ power *per se*. It is clear that the Council and the European Parliament can overrule the ECJ by legislating against its decisions, but this is not the most effective system of constitutional checks and balances over the court. Caldeira and Gibson suggested that the ECJ is the 'least accountable EU institution'.[19] Alter[20] outlined two approaches to understanding the ECJ's position: legal and neo-functionalist scholars consider the ECJ as enjoying a significant autonomy, as it can, in principle, overrule the interest of MSs, whereas neo-realist claim that in fact, the political control over the court exercised by the MSs means that ECJ is dependent on the governments of the powerful MSs and must heed their interests. The neo-realist positions seem only weakly applicable; the early interference of politicians attempting to instruct the NCs to ignore the ECJ's jurisdiction should be seen as consigned to the past – the national judges have proved to be much too keen to enforce the

14 For an overview of the debates and literature on the ECJ's activism, see e.g. de Waele, note 4.

15 Treaty on the Functioning of the European Union, OJ C 83, 30 Mar. 2010.

16 P. Craig & G. De Búrca, '*EU Law: Text, Cases and Materials*' (2008) (OUP), p. 460.

17 P. Craig & G. De Búrca, p. 461, note 42.

18 Case C-2/06 *Kempeter v. Hauptzollant Hamburg-Jonas* [2008] ECR I-411, para. 39.

19 G.A. Caldeira & J.I. Gibson, 'The legitimacy of the Court of Justice in the European Union: Models of institutional support' (1995) 89 *American Political Science Review*, No. 2, 356–376.

20 K.J. Alter, 'Who are the "Masters of the Treaty?": European Governments and the European Court of Justice' (1998) 52 *International Organization* 1, pp. 121–147.

ECJ decisions even if that went against their governments.[21] The other type of political control over the ECJ is the system of judicial appointments: one judge from each MS. But this type of oversight is only partly effective, which is due mainly to the different time horizons of the judges and the politicians whose term of office is limited and whose re-election can never be assumed. In contrast, the ECJ judges enjoy relative security of tenure.[22]

The issue of democratic legitimacy of the ECJ itself is an important one, given the court's immense power: its judgements affect more than 500 million EU citizens. Probably the best way to provide such legitimacy would be to subject the court to some form of higher judicial control. I suggest that the national constitutional courts might be best placed to provide the necessary system of checks and balances over the ECJ, to ensure that its claims to legitimacy rest on firmer foundations. If, as the evidence over the years suggests, the NCs are more ready to respect the higher authority of the law, often against political pressure, such a set-up would strengthen the legitimacy of the EU legal system in more than just formal sense – as evidenced by the NCs' attachment to substantive constitutional values in 'supremacy' and the EAW challenges.[23] Nor should we forget that constitutional courts already enjoy supreme legal status in their domestic environment, which means that their authority and legitimacy might be resting on more solid grounds than that of ECJ's.[24] However, it is clear that the ECJ would be very reluctant to accept such arrangements as potentially threatening the uniformity of the EU law, and its own position as its guardian.

2.2. THE MAIN TENETS OF ECJ'S CONSTITUTIONAL POLITICS

There is an emerging body of literature claiming that the ECJ has been focussing disproportionately on safeguarding the legal foundations and integrity of the EU at the expense of substantive constitutional values and fundamental rights, as well as principles of democratic governance: their standard has been less than satisfactory over the years.[25] This is particularly visible on the high plane of the

---

21 That was the case in the UK. See for instance: *McCarthy v Smith* [1979] 3 All ER 325; *Secretary of State for Transport, ex parte Factortame Ltd (UK no 2)* [1991] 1 AC 60.

22 Article 254 TFEU.

23 See later.

24 This idea goes against the mainstream position that treats the NCs challenges as potentially destructive to the EU legal order. The complexities and challenges of such an arrangement are numerous. For a start, there would need to be agreed set of constitutional principles and rules to refocus the jurisdictional objectives of the EU. See also Komarek's idea of 'constitutional democracy' in the EU, note 15.

25 The ECJ has developed the rights of individuals under EU law in a way that can only be described as respectful of fundamental values of democracy and liberty, particularly in its jurisprudence expanding the meaning of citizenship under the EU law. This, however, does not negate the main argument of this paper that the type of relationship that developed

ECJ's constitutional politics in the way the ECJ managed the NCs' challenges in the so-called 'supremacy' cases – and other type of legal challenges – where the ECJ claimed to have identified a threat to jurisdictional integrity of the EU law. According to the ECJ, the only way to avert such a threat is by the NCs' unconditional acceptance of the priority of judicial co-operation rooted in the acceptance of limited sovereignty of national legal orders. Most recently, Albi asked if such priorities of the ECJ might be damaging substantive constitutional values:[26]

> [...] the somewhat simplistic focus on sovereignty and co-operation, we are inadvertently discarding a whole set of other intrinsic values embodied by national constitutions, such as limiting power to ensure the protection of the individual against undue arbitrary interferences by the authorities, the protection of constitutional rights and civil liberties, the rule of law and separation of powers with due checks and balances, and judicial review by courts to safeguard these values.

Albi placed her concerns in the area of the relationship between the ECJ and domestic courts, or, rather, in the bi-dimensional framework of 'Euro-friendliness' or 'Euro-hostility' within which this relationship seemed to have developed. She blames European scholarly and public discourse for reinforcing this duality which results in a displacement of concerns with substantive constitutional values articulated by the national constitutions and CCs of Member States in relation to the developments in EU law. The bi-dimensional framework that Albi criticised is in fact very familiar to me as a seminar tutor in EU law – and most likely many colleagues who teach this subject – both from readings of the mainstream textbooks and academic papers, but also from the approach taken to the way this part of the EU syllabus has been taught in my law school and probably in other law schools as well.

The focus on the confrontational nature of the challenges of MSs constitutional courts[27] to supremacy of the EU law represents the seductively

---

between the ECJ and NCs has been far from conducive to developing a joint unifying platform aimed at protecting the basic values of democracy and human rights in the case-law that belong to the 'supremacy' type of challenges. See A.T. Williams, 'Taking values seriously: towards a philosophy of EU Law' (2009) 29 *OJLS* (3), pp. 549–577; A. Albi, 'Erosion of constitutional rights in the EU: A call for substantive co-operative constitutionalism' *Paper presented at the IACL IXth World Congress*, 12–16 June 2014 in Oslo.

26 See, for instance, case C-345/06, *Henrich* [2009] ECR I-1659, which raised the issue of secret EU rules; European Arrest Warrant system does not allow the scrutiny of the circumstances on which the accusation is based, hence clashing with the core principle of *Habeas Corpus*; and perhaps the best known *Solange* series of cases, followed by *Banana* judgement, where the ECJ clearly prioritised single-market regulations over concerns with human rights – Case C-280/93 [1994] ECR I-4973. See also: W. Sadurski, 'Solange, chapter 3': Constitutional Courts in Central Europe – Democracy – European Union, (2008) *European Law Journal*, Vol. 14, No. 1, January 2008, pp. 1–35.

27 J. Weilee, 'Community, Member states and European integration: is the law relevant?' (1982) 21 *JCMS: Journal of Common Market Studies* no. 1: 39–56; J. Weiler, 'The Community system: the dual character of supranationalism'(1981) 1 *Yearbook of European law*, (1), 267–306.

simple dynamics of a relationship between the two sides, as it draws clear lines of struggle for power referred to by some sources as the 'clash of the titans' or 'clash of absolutes'[28] between the EU and national constitutional orders. The use of expressions such as the threat of 'limiting' sovereignty by the ECJ, and the national courts' defences against such threats, feeds into this dynamics. The deceptive attraction of this type of discourse has been clearly visible in my classroom – it proved excellent in shaking young minds out of tutorial lethargy. However, that also meant that the students were much less receptive to any ideas that disturbed this clarity: any mention of fundamental rights or democracy in the context of 'supremacy' cases usually resulted in a return to indifferent slumber.

Albi's argument plunges the debate on the state of the EU constitutionalism straight back into this messy realm as she attempts to refocus it on the principles that should have been placed in its heart long ago.[29] She pitches ECJ's focus on 'sovereignty' and 'cooperation' against the relative neglect of substantive constitutional values. Such a construction suggests that in the relationship between the ECJ and national constitutional courts, both cooperation and sovereignty have been construed as opposing rather than complementary. The existing evidence suggests that this has largely been the case both historically and contemporarily. Crucially, it seems that the nature of 'cooperation' was mainly of a procedural type, emphasising a hierarchy of legal authority, rather than the protection of substantive principles. This omission is surprising given that the level of commitment to constitutional principles is strong both in the EU Treaties and in national constitutions. Why is it, then, that such commitments do not translate into a substantive platform of cooperation between the ECJ and NCs? I suggest that this might be due, at least in part, to the ECJ's ideologically driven agenda of protecting its own legal authority by constructing a unifying doctrine of the supremacy of EU law.[30]

The firm stance taken by the ECJ in early 'constitutional' cases on supremacy confirms that this might have been the case. It was obvious, then, that the ECJ's objective was to create an effective hierarchy of legal authority between the ECJ and domestic courts, despite the rhetoric of partnership and co-operation. This was demonstrated by the ECJ's claim that the imperative to protect the legal integrity of the EEC's still budding legal system could only have been secured by setting clear rules for resolving conflicts of laws in a way that ensures its uniform, coherent interpretation and application. Another strand of this argument was the famous *effet utile* of the common-market regulatory framework. In contrast, values such as democracy, respect for fundamental rights and the rule of law

---

28 M. Kumm, 'The Jurisprudence of Constitutional Conflict: Constitutional Supremacy in Europe before and after the Constitutional Treaty' 2005) 11 *European law Journal*, No. 3, pp. 262–307.

29 See also M. Kumm p. 290.

30 Compare with M. Kumm p. 287.

– now articulated in article 2 TEU – were only gradually introduced into the text of the Treaties, and only relatively recently found their way into the ECJ's jurisdiction.[31] These are notoriously contested concepts, which means that, understandably, their meaning and legal interpretation has been often less than coherent.[32] This absolves the ECJ only to some degree, as it is clear that it declared itself to be on the side of rule of law as applied to economic rules and policy, but less inclined to show a similar commitment where democratic values were decoupled from economic concerns.[33]

2.3. THE ENDURING ATTRACTION OF THE CONCEPT OF SOVEREIGNTY IN RELATIONS BETWEEN THE ECJ AND NCs

Sovereignty is a highly fluid and contested concept, and engaging in the lively debate over how its meaning evolves in today's globalised world[34] is outside the scope of this paper.[35] What is certain, and experientially verifiable, is the long endurance of this term in the language of politics and academia. The huge body of academic literature defining the EU as a supranational organisation largely refers to 'divisibility of sovereignty', 'transfer of sovereignty', 'divided sovereignty' and many other variations on this theme. It seems that there is no getting away from this concept despite growing number of scholars questioning its usefulness in explaining political dynamics of contemporary world.[36] I suggest that sovereignty had lost part of its currency in the early days of the first European Communities, as even then it appeared misaligned with the character

31 There is a string of cases that confirm this suggestion. For an analysis of the most representative ones see for instance A.T. Williams, note 25, above, and J. Komarek, 'The Place of Constitutional Courts in the EU' (2013) 9 *European Constitutional Law Review*, pp. 420–450.

32 Williams p. 552, note 25 above; D. Kochenov, 'EU Enlargement and the Failure of Conditionality: *Pre-accession Conditionality in the Fields of Democracy and the Rule of Law*', Wolters Kluwer: Austin 2007.

33 There are various cases that illustrate this point. See C-159/90 *Grogan* [1991] ECR I-4685; C-584/10 *Kadi and Al Barakaat* [2013] ECR I-6351; *Laval* [2007] ECR I-11767; *International Transport Workers' Federation, Finish Seamen Union v Viking Line ABP* [2007] ECR I-10779. Cases where the ECJ showed more willingness to recognise fundamental rights were mainly those of EU citizenship-related rights. See e.g. *Grzelczyk* C-184/99 [2001] ECR I-6193; *Zhu and Chen* C-200/02 [2004] ECR I-9925. The cases of *Mangold* C-144/04 [2005] ECR I-9981, and *Kücükdeveci* C-55/07[2010] ECR I-00365 elevated the principle of anti-discrimination on the ground of age to new jurisprudential heights.

34 See e.g. M. Koskieniemi, 'What Use for Sovereignty Today?' (2011) *Asian Journal of International Law* 1, pp. 61–70 and sources quoted there.

35 See also A. Albi, *'EU enlargement and the constitutions of Central and Eastern Europe'*, Cambridge: Cambridge University Press 2005.

36 See Albi's overview of the most vocal of scholars who propose new ways of looking at sovereignty, or express doubts about the explanatory potential of this term, pp. 122, 198–199, note 25.

of the Communities governance structure. The 'transfer or limitation of sovereignty' in support of the supranational governance require relinquishing it or ceding it to an autonomous site of power that is discreet and self-contained. Yet, none of the EU law-making bodies entirely fit this description: both Councils (of Ministers and the European) and the Commission are populated by representatives of the MSs who are seasoned politicians. Only the occasional MEP might be elected from the general public, by then the European Parliament is not the primary agenda shaper in the EU. This confirms the existence of a firm link between the decisions taken in Brussels, Luxemburg and Strasburg and national capitals, despite the Treaties' provisions requiring 'independence' from the Commissioners.[37] There does not have to be a contradiction between the duty of independence from one's government, and recognising the best interest of the majority of the MSs comprising the Union, especially if the best interest of one's own country also happen to belong to this category.

The clear lines defining the 'best interests' and 'authority' under the ECJ's sovereignty-determined logic, on the other hand, would require the EU institutions, particularly the Commission, to be completely alienated from national sites of political authority – a depiction which is difficult to accept as realistic. An alternative explanation should be created, one that would escape the confines of the 'sovereignty' discourse and be better suited to reflect the true nature of the nuanced and complex relations between the EU institutions and the MSs. There are few signs of this happening any time soon. Yet, the centrality of 'sovereignty' has many complex, and mostly negative implications, most serious perhaps in relation to integration politics, as it clashes with the original imperative to curb the sovereign power of the nation state that was one of the strongest political drivers behind the very idea of the European project.[38]

It must therefore have been seen as disappointing that soon after the signing of the first Treaties, the ECJ actively resurrected 'sovereignty' as the central plank of its legal integration discourse in the *Van Gend en Loos (1963)* and *Costa (1964)* cases. That also meant that ECJ placed the sovereignty-centred narrative at the very heart of the two constitutional principles that these cases created – supremacy and direct effect. The member states were told that only by limiting their sovereignty, albeit within limited fields, could the legal integrity of the EU law be sustained and protected. The ECJ failed to elaborate on the essence of the

37 Article 17(3) TEU.

38 After all, the key steps taken in the Treaties of Paris and Rome amounted to a serious assault on sovereignty: the transfer of control over strategic resources such as coal and steel, and later atomic energy to the collective entity, i.e., community of states and its supranational institutions (mainly then the High Authority) was aimed at removing such control from the sovereign prerogative of nation states. Such strategy was to lead to a new model of international co-operation, one that would protect Europe from military aspirations of states such as Germany that were blamed for the devastation of past conflicts, particularly the World War II.

concept of 'legal integrity of the EU law', but it was clear that this was the court's choice of the legitimising principle rather than fundamental rights, democracy or the rule of law.

The ECJ's emphasis on limiting national sovereignty in those early years is surprising, but to a degree understandable, since sovereignty has been associated with all sorts of anti-communal, anti-cooperative, qualities,[39] hence tempering such tendencies was rightly seen as a priority for the budding 'community' of states. The ECJ's strategy, however, might be seen as partly rebounding – the overreliance on sovereignty – even when deployed to limit or control it – suffused the ECJ's discourse with negative semantics associated with this concept.

The narrative of 'sovereignty' created by the ECJ in the early 'supremacy' judgements is proving remarkably persistent, and remains strong in shaping the ECJ's, and the EU's constitutional politics. The relationship between the ECJ and national courts continues to revolve largely around this concept. Hence, we seem to be stuck with the narrative of 'limited sovereignty' that defined the terms of reference within which the relationship between the ECJ and NCs was to be conducted and made sense then and in the future. This kind of phrasing, as argued above, decisively defined this relationship as one focussing mainly on protection of the EU legal system by adherence to the ECJ-created doctrines of supremacy and direct effect.[40] This was to be achieved by what the ECJ projected as 'co-operation', yet, what in reality turned out to be the expectation of subservience from the NCs, and unquestioning support for the objectives chosen by the ECJs.[41] Arguably, this demonstrates the ideological nature of the discourse of supremacy and direct effect[42] which is also visible in the way the ECJ rebuked the NCs challenges to supremacy, regardless of their substantive grounds.[43]

In contrast to NCs' concerns in relation to substantive values raised in supremacy cases, the ECJ was much more ready to protect only those values that it deemed essential for the construction and successful operation of the common

39 M. Koskieniemi, p. 61, note 34.

40 Yet, as pointed out by a number of scholars, these two doctrines have been known in International Law. See, for instance, de Waele, note 4. Hence, this strong justification based on limits to sovereignty may not have been needed, as the MSs were likely to accept both anyway.

41 Compare with Komarek, p. 420, note 31.

42 Komarek, stated: 'National Constitutional Courts [...] are gradually marginalised by the ECJ's decisions, which follow a rather dogmatic approach to the principle of primacy and direct effect', p. 420, note 31.

43 There is no need to rehearse here the well-known saga from the Solange I & II, through *Brunner*, *Carslen* to the Polish and Czech challenges. See also *Gauweiler* 2 BvE 2/08 [2010] 3 *C.M.L.R.* 13 & *Re Honeywell* 2 BvR 2661/06 [2011] 1 *C.M.L.R.* 33. The common thread connecting these case is the questioning of EU commitments to democracy, fundamental rights and constitutionalism.

market – a long-term objective of the EU.[44] Prioritising those values contributed, in some degree at least, to the displacement of concerns with democracy and fundamental rights.[45] There was a strong rationale behind this: on a practical level, any weakening of the uniform application and interpretation of the EU law could potentially weaken the common market regulations – by giving rise to distortions of competition and discriminations between economic operators.[46] From a theoretical perspective, such an incursion would have been likely to weaken the legitimising strategy of the ECJ, who assumed the role of seemingly neutral enforcer and guardian of the Treaties, which, after all represent a political and constitutional settlement between the MSs.

The type of legal stance taken by the ECJ on supremacy, described by Allott[47] as 'self-serving and self-referential,' had not been well suited to encourage a frank exchange of views and challenges that could help clarify the law and foster mutual learning between the European court and the NCs. It also largely failed to steer the relationship between the courts towards tempering the early hostility of national courts to preliminary reference procedure.[48] In other words, the focus was predominantly on quashing the potential dissent that could threaten the hierarchy of judicial power and legal integrity of the EU, at the expense of what should have been the substantive concerns of the courts.[49] Simply, this can be taken as if the ECJ was saying to the national courts 'We could not trust you to co-operate on raising the level of substantive rights protection, as we suspect that you would abuse such co-operation for your own domestic ends.' This stance of the ECJ also suggests the limited nature of the EU's legal integrity promoted by the ECJ as mainly one of a procedural variety, in areas other than common market.

Could matters have taken a different turn? I suggest that they could have. This is obviously a purely speculative argument, but developing some relevant points should help to seek a more productive way of promoting the core constitutional principles in the EU through the judicial process, while preserving the

---

44 See note 33 for a selection of cases illustrating this point. See also Wiliams's analysis of some of the most recent cases in note 25.

45 Williams p. 570, note 25.

46 Williams, p. 562, note 25.

47 P. Allott, 'Globalisation from Above' in *The Health of Nations: Society and Law Beyond the State*, CUP, Cambridge 2002.

48 On this point see for instance: K.J. Alter, 'Who are the "Masters of the Treaty?": European Governments and the European Court of Justice' (1998) 52 *International Organization* 1, pp. 121–147.

49 In this sense, the challenges focussed more on establishing the 'ultimate [legal] authority' in the EU. Compare with Poiares Maduro, 'Contrapunctual Law: Europe's Constitutional Pluralism in Action', in N. Walker (ed), *Sovereignty in Transition* Hart, 2003, 501, at 502; N. Walker, 'Late Sovereignty in the European Union', in Walker (1999: 3–32); N. MacCormick, *Questioning Sovereignty* Oxford University Press, Oxford 1999; M. Kumm, 'The Jurisprudence of Constitutional Conflict: Constitutional Supremacy in Europe before and after the Constitutional Treaty' (2005) 11 *European Law Journal* 262.

imperatives of EU legal integration and protecting the foundations of common market.

In order for this to happen, however, the legitimising role of the ECJ, NCs and national constitutions should be more openly accepted. But equally, the principle of co-operation between the courts must be recast in line with a different organisational approach. Mutual trust and respect should replace the emphasis on sovereignty to make way for mutual learning and rallying around substantive values and principles. Most of all, however, this would require the legitimising ideology promoted by the ECJ to be more balanced and more receptive to the concerns raised by the NCs in 'supremacy' cases.[50]

2.4. BEYOND 'SOVEREIGNTY': POWER STRUGGLE, OR POWER-POSTURING?

A closer look at the way in which supremacy and direct-effect doctrines have operated over the years reveals a slightly different picture than the sovereignty-focussed analysis allows. Instead of a full-on confrontation, the so-called power struggle never amounted to more than mere posturing between the ECJ and NCs – that is, in essence, closer to full co-operation and acceptance of the supremacy of the ECJ and the EU law by the national courts, although, seemingly, on their own terms.[51] The Treaty of Lisbon Declaration 17; the EU Charter of Fundamental Rights (CFR); the Opinion of the Council Legal Service[52] – these all reinforce the perception that the MSs' senior courts accept the primacy of EU law.[53] A number of new provisions of the Lisbon Treaty offer conflict-diffusing clauses by stressing mutual respect and sincere co-operation.[54] Still uncertain, though, are the types of value-choices and policy priorities that will underpin this type of co-operative framework.

A dark shadow of doubt about such value-choices of the ECJ has been cast in a number of ECJ decisions in the following areas:[55] secret and unpublished legislation,[56] EU Data Retention Directive 2006/24[57] cases related to market

50 Albi 2014, note 25.

51 Chalmers, Davis and Monti concluded that the 'primacy [of the EU law] now represents the political consensus as to the status of EU law', p. 188, note 6. They further consider three approaches that have emerged in relation to the internal authority of the EU law: European constitutional sovereignty, unconditional national constitutional sovereignty and constitutional tolerance which dominates. On this point, see also Kumm, p. 285, note 29.

52 *EU Council Doc. 11197/07*, 22 June 2007.

53 See also A. Dyevre European Integration and national Courts: Defending Sovereignty under Institutional Constraints? (2013) 9 *European Constitutional Law Review* pp. 139–168.

54 Articles 4(2) and 4(3) of the TEU 2009.

55 Albi, n. 25.

56 For instance, Case C-345/06 *Heinrich* [2009] ECR I-1659.

57 C-594/12 *Seitlinger and Others*.

regulations where substantive rights clashed with common market imperative[58] and the European Arrest Warrant (EAW).[59] Let me briefly discuss the last example.

A number of concerns have been raised by several NCs in relation to the EAW. Some of the most serious concerns focused on the potential breaches of the right to a fair trial, presumption of innocence, retroactivity, double jeopardy, judgements in absentia.[60] The common thread discernible in the ECJ's responses is a tendency to avoid directly addressing the issue,[61] or to reject the possibility to grant a due level of protection guaranteed under national constitutions – as in the case of *Melloni v. Ministerio Fiscal*. That is despite Article 53 of the EU CFR guarantee: 'Nothing in this Charter shall be interpreted as restricting or adversely affecting human rights and fundamental freedoms as recognised [...] by [...] the Member States' constitutions.'[62]

Can the NCs trust the ECJ to find a more viable balance between democratic and constitutional principles and the EU law integrity? The Treaty of Lisbon adoption of the EU Charter of Fundamental Rights and the promise of accession to the European Convention on Human Rights (ECHR) contained in Article 6(2) TEU[63] seem to suggest that this might indeed be the case. However, new concerns have been raised by the ECJ's *Opinion 2/13* on the compatibility with the EU law of the draft agreement for EU accession to the European Convention of Human Rights, delivered on 18 December 2014. In this document, the ECJ concluded that the accession agreement is not compatible with the EU law. The reasons for this incompatibility given by the Court relate almost entirely to the alleged special nature and autonomy of the EU law, and the position of the Court itself, as the only judicial body authorised to interpret the EU law – a role that could be threatened by the binding nature of the European Court of Human Rights interpretation of the ECHR. The ECJ's concerns in relation to the draft agreement might be resolved and accession could be achieved. However, by focussing so strongly on preserving its own position of power as the highest arbiter of the EU legal order and by stressing the special nature and position of EU law, the Court, once again, placed its priorities on the wrong side of constitutional politics: in preservation of judicial power as a key factor in safeguarding the unity of the EU, rather than on upholding substantive standards of fundamental rights. Is seems, then, in light of *Opinion 2/13*, that the prospects for development of the ECJ-led

58 See n. 34.
59 See the case of *Melloni*, n. 8.
60 See V. Mitsilegas, '*General Report: The Area of Freedom, Security and Justice from Amsterdam to Lisbon. Challenges of Implementation, Constitutionality and Fundamental Rights*' (FIDE: 2012). Available at: www.fide2012.eu/index.php?doc_id=90; See also Albi, n. 25.
61 D. Sarmiento, 'European Union: the European arrest warrant and the quest for constitutional coherence' (2008) 6 *International Journal of Constitutional Law* 1, 177–178.
62 Charter of Fundamental Rights (2007/C 303/02), 14 December 2007.
63 See also: *CoE Final Report to the CDDH* 47+1(2013)008 rev2.

substantive constitutionalism appears to have diminished even further. This is particularly unfortunate in the current climate of growing Euro-scepticism and the potential paralysis of the European Parliament, which has been populated by a sizable fraction of MEPs representing political formations on the far-right political spectrum, and also hostile to the very idea of European integration.

3. THE SUPREMACY OF EU ECONOMIC POLICY

In this section I suggest that part of the ECJ's legitimising strategy is to deploy a particular type of ideology which projects the economic common market regulations as coherent and consistent, hence well serving the overall objective of EU integration. Such a strategy, however, might be hiding the underlying policy choices and protecting those from democratic scrutiny and oversight[64] as they could be smuggled into the body of EU law under the guise of technical rules contained in secondary legislation, known as 'non-legislative acts'.[65] Since such rules, supposedly, do not entail policy choices (as they are only 'supplementary', or amending the 'non-essential elements of the legislative acts') they are not subjected to the same scrutiny as the legislative acts. A number of reforms over the years partly addressed this concern – those culminated in the European Parliament's power of veto, both stopping the adoption of such an act and revoking delegation.[66] Still of concern, however, are rules that are not very likely to register on the EP's radar, such as those presented as purely technical and created by administrative agencies. Despite these shortcomings in the democratic oversight, those rules have the same binding power in domestic law as 'legislative acts' through the doctrines of supremacy and direct effect.

Let us recall that one of the most significant effects of the doctrines of supremacy and direct effect was the opening up of national jurisdictions to the reception of EU law. The operation of these two doctrines is supported and complemented by the preliminary reference procedure. These three legal devices combined place the national courts in position of enforcers of the EU law over and above conflicting national law, under the supervision of the ECJ.[67] Since internal-market law is by far the widest in scope and impact of all the types of EU legal regulations,[68] and since its main aim is to integrate national markets

64 The best-known examples where such inconsistencies are visible are the CAP and the bail-outs of the banks across the EU in the wake of financial crisis. Discussion of these two phenomena is outside the scope of this paper.

65 Article 290 TFEU.

66 Article 290 TFEU.

67 Compare with D. Nicol *The constitutional protection of capitalism*, Oxford, Oregon, Hart Publishing 2010.

68 A. Follesdal and S. Hix 'Why there is a democratic deficit in the EU: A response to Majone and Moravcsik' (2006) 44 *JCMS: Journal of Common Market Studies* no. 3 pp. 533–562, at 11.

into a single EU one, it follows that the national courts were placed in a position to play a key role in transforming and integrating the economies of the Member States in line with the policy choices of the EU institutions, and, even more crucially, under the control of the ECJ.

The key role that the national courts play in protecting the integrity of the EU legal system and in enforcing the individual rights under EU law gives the courts the power to override their own parliaments, particularly in cases when domestic provisions fall short of, or conflict with, the EU standard of legal protection. What is more, national courts are empowered to create rights and obligations not available under domestic law, including domestic constitutions.[69] Since most of such instances are, either directly or indirectly, related to economic law and policy, this activity of the courts amounts to assisting in the entrenchment of certain tenets and ideas underlying the EU Treaties regulation of that nature.[70] Such entrenchment raises a number of important questions related to constitutional and democratic standards of economic law- and policy-making in the EU, since it commits the national courts to act as guardians of an economic model that has in effect been placed outside democratic control, contestation and debate of the MSs' electorates.[71] The key role in this process is played by the ECJ,[72] which has the ultimate authority in the interpretation and application of the Treaties.[73]

3.1. WHAT IS THE MODEL OF ECONOMIC POLICY ENTRENCHED IN THE TREATIES?

Article 3(3) TEU commits the EU internal market to be based on 'highly competitive social market economy'. Both in law and in practice this broad commitment translates into priority of competition and privatisation. These two objectives underpin the vast majority of policies that can be described as core within the EU Treaties: the four freedoms provisions within the internal market and competition law, rules governing state aid and public procurement. These objectives are often described as 'neoliberal'.[74] (Common Agricultural Policy is the one glaring exception here, its persistence often explained by the power-

69 Caldeira & Gibson, note 19.
70 See Article 48 TEU, which in effect entrenches the Foundation Treaties.
71 See also n. 9.
72 According to Article 225(3), the General Court also has the power of hearing article 267 TFEU preliminary references, but this has not yet been made operational.
73 Article 19 TEU.
74 I am using this concept in a theoretically unsophisticated way, as denoting the possibility of extracting commercial value from any type of human endeavour. See also Nicol, note 67. The exceptions are the interventionist policies of the CAP, and the recent bail-out of the banks in some MSs. But, these can be understood as an unorthodox application of neoliberalism, which is used to promote certain type of private interest, even if this goes against the free-

politics in the EU, particularly in the early years after the signing of the Treaty of Rome.)[75] There are, obviously, a number of Treaty provisions and ECJ case-law examples where objectives other than of the free-market nature are, at least theoretically, permitted to shape the law and policy. But, even those are relatively few. All in all, it would be difficult to dispel the suggestion that the pursuit of economic objectives in EU law and policy 'outweighs the taking into account of social concerns'[76]

3.2. THE ECJ AND THE EU'S 'DEMOCRATIC DEFICIT'

The issues identified above relate directly to the EU's infamous 'democratic deficit'.[77] However, a serious weakness of the democratic-deficit debate is the narrow focus on standards of democracy considered within the traditional divide of public/private, in line with the dominant neo-liberal views, which exclude market economy – considered as private – from democratic scrutiny.[78] Following Nicol and Stupiot,[79] among others, I argue that such an exclusion is no longer viable. There are a number of factors that justify this suggestion. The following two are probably the most pertinent: the traditional problem of technocratic bias in EU law making, particularly under article 290 TFEU; and the Eurozone crisis, which led to the ousting from power of democratically elected governments in Italy and Greece, driven by the need to implement economic austerity measures by technocrats.[80] The latter provided a shocking reminder that economy and politics – even when relating to the governance of MSs, hence of constitutional nature – must be seen as closely interwoven;

---

market principles of limited intervention in the economy, as suggested by D. Harvey, *A brief history of neoliberalism*, Oxford, Oxford University Press 2005.

75 Mainly the French leverage.

76 Lenaerts, n. 6, p. 274.

77 Sources on this topic are too numerous to mention here. The most famous is the debate between A. Moravcsik, 'Reassessing legitimacy in the European Union' (2002) *JCMS: Journal of Common Market Studies*, 40(4), 603-624, and A. Follesdal & S. Hix, 'Why there is a democratic deficit in the EU: A response to Majone and Moravcsik' (2006) *JCMS: Journal of Common Market Studies* 44(3), 533–562. I will not engage in this debate, as its focus is mainly on procedural standards of democratic oversight, which still remain problematic, but have been considerably strengthened under the Treaty of Lisbon, through empowering further the National Parliaments via the enhanced regulations of subsidiary and proportionality.

78 See e.g. F.A. Hayek *The Road to Serfdom: Text and Documents: The Definitive Edition*. Routledge 2014; Nicol (2010), n. 68.

79 A. Supiot, 'The public-private relation in the context of today's refeudalization' *International Journal of Constitutional Law* (2013) Vol. 11, No. 1, pp. 125–145.

80 According to Supiot, at stake here is much more than the 'familiar practice of privatizing profits and having taxpayers bear the losses. What we are witnessing, rather, is an undisguised challenge to a people's right to self-government' Supiot, n. 79, p. 125. See also 'Eurozone turmoil: Enter the technocrats' in the *Financial Times*, 11 November 2011, available at: www.ft.com/cms/s/0/93c5cb36-0c92-11e1-a45b-00144feabdc0.html#axzz2ztWNegpu (accessed 25 Apr. 2014).

the powerful effects of the EU law on shaping not just the economic, but also political orders of the MSs became clearly visible. In the case of the former, the very nature of the market-regulation measures, including those enacted under Article 290 TFEU, illustrate the impossibility of separating economic and non-economic considerations from the broader objectives of public policy.[81]

It is therefore necessary to extend the democratic-deficit debate to the whole of EU law and policy-making, including internal-market regulation, against the current position which prevents market regulation from being 'politicised', in line with the assertion that scientific and economic issues involved in market regulation 'are a matter of technical competence more than political choices'.[82] An outcome of such an approach is that the technical, science-based rationales are often prioritised over ethical, environmental, or public health concerns, which cannot be backed by hard scientific data either because such data is not yet available, or because the nature of such concerns makes it impossible to express them in strictly scientific terms. As illustrated by the *Austrian GMOs* case, this often results in the marginalisation of this type of legitimate 'non-scientific' concerns.[83]

The reasons for this are complex. According to Chalmers et al.:

> 'the adoption of the distinction between the questions of fact (what is the risk?) and value (what should be done about it?) has led to the exclusion of the vast majority of public concerns from the most influential stage of the decision-making model: the process of risk framing.'[84]

This is partly the result of the key role played by the technocratic agencies in both framing the issues under consideration and influencing actual policies by supplying expert advice and scientific data. Yet, those agencies are not always neutral and objective,[85] hence, their advice might be biased. In fact, there is evidence to suggest that the agencies might be seen as conduits for private interests not always subjected to sufficient political control:

> Charged with market entry/exit regulation and more general, informal, information-gathering and policy-informing duties, the new European agencies apparently meet

81 The Treaty itself demands such a fusion in Article 7 TFEU, which states that 'the Union shall ensure consistency between its policies and activities, taking all of its objectives into account.' Articles 8–17 & 114 TFEU identify most of those objectives. The Transatlantic Trade and Investment Partnership (TTIP) which is currently negotiated, arguably, blurs such division even further.

82 Chalmers, n. 6, p. 704.

83 Joined cases C-439/05 P and C-454/05 P *Land Oberösterreich & Austria v Commission* [2007] ECR I-7141.

84 Chalmers, n. 6, p. 703. See also M. Kriticos, Traditional Risk Analysis and Releases of GMOs into the European Union: Space for Non-Scientific Factors (2009) *44 European Law Review*, p. 405.

85 K. Kanska 'Wolves in the clothing of sheep? The case of European Food Safety Authority' (2004) *E.L. Rev.* 29(5), 711–727, p. 727.

> a purely technical demand for market-corrective and sector-specific regulation. This seemingly technocratic and semi-autonomous status implicitly provides market interest with a voice [...] Notwithstanding their placement under the Commission's institutional structure [...] varying degree of budgetary autonomy and direct networking with national administrations largely shields these agencies from explicitly political processes.[86]

Given that the Commission is duty-bound to seek and to follow the advice of the agencies,[87] this places the agencies in a position to shape EU policy and law-making without much political scrutiny.[88, 89] It means that large areas of law and policy-making are, indeed, excluded from political debate and contestability, indicating a critical shortfall in democratic credentials. Moreover, as argued earlier, the scope and focus of existing debate on the EU democratic-deficit is too narrowly oriented at issues not directly linked to this particular aspect of the EU functioning.

3.3. ENTRENCHMENT OF THE EU ECONOMIC POLICY, TTIP, AND THE ROLE OF THE COURTS

3.3.1. Democratic deficit of economic policy and the courts

These weaknesses of political scrutiny over some key areas of EU law and policy-making, particularly related to the internal-market regulations, are not satisfactorily addressed by the Courts. In fact, the opposite might be the case: for instance, the ECJ's interpretation of exceptions under Article 114 TFEU in the *Austrian GMOs* case suggests that the court allowed the parties to rely on exceptions within this article only under very strict conditions, one of which is 'new scientific evidence'. According to the ECJ, no sufficient new scientific evidence was provided for the existence of unique ecosystems in this case.

Even if the court's textual interpretation was correct, it failed to take into account that phenomena such as ecosystems are not easily quantifiable, and that there is no hard scientific evidence to support the claim of their uniqueness. That is partly due to the fact that the judgement of what is and what is not a unique ecosystem is also closely bound to ethics and social values. Yet, by adopting its position, the court found itself endorsing the limited understanding of complex

---

86 C. Joerges, 'The Law's Problem with the Governance of the Single European Market' in C. Joerges and R. Dehousse (eds.) *Good Governance in Europe's Integrated Market* Oxford, Oxford University Press 2002, p. 17.

87 The Commission has, in practice, always followed agencies' advice, as the conditions for suggesting an alternative are almost impossible to satisfy.

88 Chalmers, n. 6, p. 274.

89 K. Lenaerts, 'The Principle of Democracy in the Case Law of the European Court of Justice' (2013) *ICLQ* vol 62, April, p. 274.

phenomenon, one that is based on the only available, narrowly defined 'scientific evidence'.

One of the most complex challenges within the EU internal-market law is how to achieve a balance between the free-market imperative and public-policy goals and interests. Arguably, the ECJ struggles to get this balance right, as demonstrated in a string of cases within this field, including public procurement, and state-aid rules.[90] This might be seen as reflecting the ECJ's narrow and predominantly economic approach to harmonisation of EU internal market law.

a. Investor-State Dispute Settlement

The Transatlantic Trade and Investment Partnership (TTIP) between the United States and the EU, which is currently being negotiated, might contribute to further tipping the balance towards prioritising purely economic objectives (at the expense of the public interest ones) in the way that EU and national law is interpreted and enforced. Its Investor-State Dispute Settlement (ISDS)[91] allows businesses and corporations to sue governments when their commercial interests are threatened by public-interest regulation. Moreover, the ISDS enables foreign investors to circumvent domestic legal processes and sue host governments in third-party arbitration tribunals for unfair or discriminatory treatment, bypassing domestic laws and regulations, and hence, domestic parliaments. Yet the need to protect the commercial interests of companies means that the hearings are held in secret by panels of corporate lawyers, without the usual safeguards provided by an open trial in domestic courts. Citizens and communities affected by decisions have no legal standing to challenge such decisions.[92]

The details of the ISDS under the TTIP are still being negotiated. However, what is clear is that the main challenge of running this mechanism will be to find a way of reconciling public-interest-driven objectives and the commercial interests of the investors. If the ISDS will be based on a strict application of contractual agreement in a black-letter, legalistic manner, which demands equality in the eyes of the law, and objective, neutral application of the rules, the public interests regulation will almost certainly be vulnerable to be trumped by commercial interests. The democratic underpinnings of state regulation will be immaterial in this type of proceedings. On the other hand, it is difficult to

90 See for instance Chalmers et al. n. 6, and sources listed there.

91 For more see European Commission Factsheet on Investor-State Dispute Settlement, 3 Oct. 2013.

92 See for instance Open Democracy Centre comment available at: www.opendemocracy.net/ourkingdom/thomas-mc-donagh/allowing-corporations-to-sue-governments-for-changing-their-laws-may-be- (accessed 27 April 2014); Stigliz on the dangers of bilateral investment agreement, 2013, available at: www.project-syndicate.org/commentary/joseph-e--stiglitz-on-the-dangers-of-bilateral-investment-agreements (accessed 27 April 2014).

imagine open-ended clauses being accepted by corporations in their contractual agreements with governments that would protect democratically legitimate, but commercially unviable solutions.

All in all, this new development including the ISDS in the TTIP will create a new layer of judicial authority in the EU, which might prove the most controversial to date when it comes to deepening the democratic deficit in enforcement of economic law and policy.

In the light of the above, it can be argued that the ECJ, the national courts and the panels under the ISDS mechanism all contribute, in some measure at least, to the enforcement of a particular model of the economic order where increasing areas of (mainly) economic regulations are de facto entrenched and, as a result, placed beyond the democratic control of the national parliaments and the electorate. This contributes to the wider process of 'inverting the relation between public and private' which leads to the 'privatization of legal rules',[93] and amounts to the shrinking of the public sphere and a corresponding shift of power towards the private sphere of market-driven interests.[94] From this perspective, it can be argued that the ECJ and the constitutional courts of the MSs enforcing EU law appear more as challengers to democracy than as its defenders, at least on the level of constitutional legal politics in the EU.

4. CONCLUSIONS

The main purpose of this paper was to present an overview of some key challenges in the constitutional politics of the European courts that pitch constitutional principles such as democracy, fundamental rights and rule of law against the ECJ-created ideology of legal integrity of the EU. More specifically, I show that in performing its role as the guardian of the EU legal order, the ECJ is largely guided by the imperative to provide legitimacy for the EU legal system, resting on its uniformity and clear hierarchy of judicial authority, often to the detriment of substantive constitutionalism. Such a perspective brings into focus the way in which the ECJ used the concept of 'sovereignty' in structuring its relationship with the national and constitutional courts, diverting attention from substantive concerns raised by the NCs in the 'supremacy' challenges and the EWA cases. This discussion also suggested that the ECJ used the alleged threat of national 'sovereignty' to the unity of the EU, as an excuse to protect its own position of power and authority *vis-à-vis* the NCs. It seems that by doing this,

93 Supiot, n. 79, p. 134.

94 According to Koskieniemi: the process of power being shifted towards private economy and finance might already dominate. He noted: 'Corporate executives and hedge fund managers do not consult the populations whose fate they determine...sometimes with the assent of the state, more often in complete independence': M. Koskieniemi 'What Use for Sovereignty Today?' (2011) *Asian Journal of International Law* 1, pp. 61–70.

the ECJ continues in its failure to develop a more balanced approach towards the twin objectives of preserving the integrity of EU law and paying attention to substantive constitutional principles.

This suggests that the democratic credentials and legitimacy of the ECJ might be questioned from at least two perspectives: its commitment to substantive values in the face of market imperative and the perceived threats to the uniformity of EU law, and as a body that is its own master, due to an almost non-existent system of oversight of its 'constitutional' jurisdiction.

BIBLIOGRAPHY

Albi, A., *EU enlargement and the constitutions of Central and Eastern Europe*, Cambridge University Press, Cambridge 2005

Albi, A., 'Erosion of constitutional rights in the EU: A call for substantive co-operative constitutionalism' *Paper presented at the IACL IXth World Congress, 12–16 June 2014 in Oslo.*

Allott, P., 'Globalisation from Above' in *The Health of Nations: Society and Law Beyond the State*, CUP, Cambridge 2002.

Alter, K.J., 'Who are the "Masters of the Treaty?": European Governments and the European Court of Justice'(1998) *International Organization*, vol. 52 issue 1, pp. 121–147.

Caldeira, G.A. and J. L. Gibson, 'The legitimacy of the Court of Justice in the European Union: Models of institutional support'(1995) *American Political Science Review*, 89(02), 356–376.

Chalmers, D., G. Davies and G. Monti, G. 2nd ed. *European Union Law: Text and Materials*, CUP, Cambridge 2010.

Chalmers, D., G. Davies and G. Monti, G. 3nd ed. *European Union Law: Text and Materials*, CUP, Cambridge 2014.

Craig, P., 'Formal and substantive conceptions of the rule of law: an analytical framework' (1997) *Public Law*, (3), pp. 467–487.

de Waele, H., 'Role of the European Court of Justice in the Integration Process: A Contemporary and Normative Assessment' (2010) *Hanse L. Rev.*, vol. 6, no.1.

Dyevre, A., 'European Integration and national Courts: Defending Sovereignty under Institutional Constraints?' (2013) *European Constitutional Law Review*, 9: 139–168.

Harvey, D., *A Brief History of Neoliberalism*, Oxford University Press, Oxford 2005.

Hayek, F.A.,*The Road to Serfdom: Text and Documents: The Definitive Edition*, Routledge, 2014.

Follesdal, A. and S. Hix, 'Why there is a democratic deficit in the EU: A response to Majone and Moravcsik' (2006) *JCMS (Journal of Common Market Studies)* 44, no. 3: 533–562.

Ivaldi, G., 'Beyond France's 2005 referendum on the European constitutional treaty: Second-order model, anti-establishment attitudes and the end of the alternative European utopia' (2006) *West European Politics*, *29*(1), 47–69.

Joerges, C., 'The Law's Problem with the Governance of the Single European Market' in C. Joerges and R. Dehousse (eds.) *Good Governance in Europe's Integrated Market*, Oxford University Press, Oxford 2002.

Kanska, K., 'Wolves in the clothing of sheep? The case of European Food Safety Authority' (2004) *E.L. Rev.* 29(5), 711–727.

Kochenov, D., *EU enlargement and the failure of conditionality: pre-accession conditionality in the fields of democracy and the rule of law*, Wolters Kluwer, Austin 2007.

Komarek, J., 'The Place of Constitutional Courts in the EU' (2013) *European Constitutional Law Review*, 9: 420–450.

Koskieniemi, M., 'What Use for Sovereignty Today?' (2011) *Asian Journal of International Law* 1, pp. 61–70

Kriticos, M., 'Traditional Risk Analysis and Releases of GMOs into the European Union: Space for Non-Scientific Factors' (2009) *3 European Law Review* pp. 405–432.

Kumm, M., 'The Jurisprudence of Constitutional Conflict: Constitutional Supremacy in Europe before and after the Constitutional Treaty' (2005) *European law Journal*, vol.1, No. 3, pp. 262–307.

Lenaerts, K., 'The Principle of Democracy in the Case Law of the European Court of Justice' (2013) *ICLQ*, vol. 62, April, pp. 271–315.

Nicol, D., *The constitutional protection of capitalism*, Hart Publishing, Oxford, Oregon 2010.

Parsons, T., 'The professions and social structure' (1939) *Social forces*, 17(4), pp. 457–467.

Sadurski, W., 'Solange, chapter 3': Constitutional Courts in Central Europe – Democracy – European Union' (2008) *European Law Journal*, Vol. 14, No. 1, January 2008, pp. 1–35.

Supiot, A., 'The public-private relation in the context of today's refeudalization' (2013) *International Journal of Constitutional Law* Vol. 11, No. 1, pp. 125–145.

Zielonka, J., 'Europe as empire: the nature of the enlarged European Union' (2006) *Central European Review of International Affairs, 27*, 135

Weilee, J., 'Community, Member States and European Integration: Is the Law Relevant?. (1982) *JCMS (Journal of Common Market Studies) 21*(1), 39–56.

Weiler, J. and N. Lockhart, 'Taking Rights Seriously' "Seriously": The European Court and its Fundamental Rights Jurisprudence', (1995) 32 *CMLRev.* 51.

Weiler, J., 'The Community system: the dual character of supranationalism' (1981) *Yearbook of European law, 1*(1), 267–306.

Weiler, J., 'The Transformation of Europe' (1991) 100 *Yale Law Journal*, p. 2478.

Williams, A.T., 'Taking values seriously: towards a philosophy of EU Law' (2009) 29 *OJLS (Oxford Journal of Legal Studies)* no.3 pp. 549–577

2. THE INSTITUTIONAL BALANCE AS CJEU'S CONTRIBUTION TO DEMOCRACY IN THE UNION

Selected Issues

Tomasz Dubowski*
Department of European Law, Faculty of Law, University of Bialystok

1. INTRODUCTION

What is an institutional balance in the European Union (EU) law? An idea, a proposal, a mental shortcut or an empty formula?[1] There are many controversies referring to its nature. They are connected, for example, with the way of its introduction onto the plane of the European Union law. It has not been directly expressed in any of the Treaty provisions. Simultaneously, it is certain sets or groups of these provisions read in a systemic way, that allowed the Court of Justice of the European Union (the Court, CJEU) to formulate and embed it in the EU legal order. This is a quite typical operation in reference to the so-called general principles of law.[2] Institutional balance, although not without controversies, seems to fit this category.[3]

Since institutional balance has not been directly expressed in any Treaty provisions, its embedding in the European Union legal order had to be based on the Court's creative interpretation of the Treaties. It is one of the cases where the Court seems to exceed the framework of its literally understood function and

---

* Email: t.dubowski@uwb.edu.pl.

1 R. Bieber refers in that respect to the term *Leerformel*, see: R. Bieber, 'Institutionen' in R. Schulze, M. Zuleeg (Hrsg.), *Europarecht. Handbuch für die deutsche Rechtspraxis*, Baden-Baden 2006, pp. 51–52.

2 See: J.A. Usher, *General Principles of EC Law*, London 1998, p. 12.

3 What might be interesting in that context is the relation between institutional balance and separation of powers principle (doctrine) which itself is linked to democracy. For interesting analysis see: G. Conway, 'Recovering a Separation of Powers in the European Union', (2011) 17 *ELJ (European Law Journal)*, pp. 304–322.

competence determined by the Treaties.[4] It is one of the examples of the Court's active affecting the development of the whole of EU law.

However, the question arises if, in the context of institutional balance, the Court "creating" a certain general principle contributed to strengthening the democratic nature of the Union as an exceptional integration structure. Has the Court's "law-making" activism contributed in this case to consolidation of the democratic foundations of the Union?

In order to answer these questions it is, firstly, necessary to find out whether the introduction of institutional balance as a general principle into the EU legal system required the Court's real adjudicating activity, an activity close to legislation. Secondly, it is important to establish the content of the principle of institutional balance – prohibitions and prescripts it generates and to demonstrate in what way the maintenance of institutional balance affects or may affect the state of democracy within the European Union – what is the link between this principle and democratic values.

The analysis of the aforementioned elements will allow us to formulate a conclusion referring to the connections between the Court's activity, institutional balance as its effect and the state of democracy within the Union: the value strongly emphasized in the Treaties.

2. THE CJEU AND THE TRACES OF INSTITUTIONAL BALANCE IN THE TREATIES

As indicated in the Introduction, institutional balance has not been directly expressed and defined in Treaty provisions. In reference to general principles of a certain legal order it is not, however, anything exceptional. These principles are relatively often derived from a set of interconnected provisions, which, read in a systemic context, allow us to formulate a norm of a more general nature: a principle.[5] In this context, it is possible to meet opinions that general principles are derived not as much from a particular provision as from the content and meaning of certain groups of provisions, and even from the system and "the spirit"[6] of the Treaties. This, however, assumes an active role of the authority applying the law: in the case of the European Union it is the Court.

---

4 Article 19(1) TEU: *The Court of Justice of the European Union shall include the Court of Justice, the General Court and specialised courts. It shall ensure that in the interpretation and application of the Treaties the law is observed.*

5 J.A. Usher, *supra* note 2.

6 The Court referred to *the spirit, the general scheme and the wording of the Treaty* in famous *van Gend & Loos* case: ECJ 05.02.1963, 26/62, *NV Algemene Transport- en Expeditie Onderneming van Gend & Loos v Netherlands Inland Revenue Administration*, ECR 1963, English Special Edition, p. 1.

Taking into consideration the evolution of legal foundations of the European Union functioning, it seems that institutional balance since the beginning has been connected with the present Article 13 TEU.[7] This regulation contains a catalogue of the EU institutions and (paragraph 2) the following provision:

> Each institution shall act within the limits of the powers conferred on it in the Treaties, and in conformity with the procedures, conditions and objectives set out in them. The institutions shall practice mutual sincere cooperation.

The provision quoted replaced Article 7 TEC[8] (formerly Article 7 TEEC),[9] and this one, in turn, Article 3 TECSC.[10] The substance of these regulations was not and is not identical. They have always remained, however, especially Article 7 TEC and Article 13 TEU, regulations generally defining the institutional structure of the Community and the Union, as well as the rules of operating of its elements.[11] Adjudicative examples of references to institutional balance indicate, however, that the Treaty sources of institutional balance are not reduced to the aforementioned provisions only.

As early as in the 1950s, the Court referred to institutional balance. In the judgment in case C-9/56 (*Meroni*)[12] it explicitly referred it to inter-institutional relations and the question of delegation of powers. It asserted that passing the discretional powers to the institutions other than those authorized to exercise and control such powers would be against the balance of powers[13] established by the Treaty. In this judgment the Court referred clearly to Article 3 TECSC. The presented interpretation of institutional balance required, however, a broader perspective and reading the general provision in the light of subsequent provisions referring to particular institutions, their powers and the rules of their exercising.

As long as in the *Meroni* judgment the institutional balance became a criterion enabling to repeal a decision contrary thereto, in case C-138/79[14] (*SA Roquette*

7 *Consolidated version of the Treaty on European Union*, OJ C 326, 26.10.2012.

8 *Treaty establishing European Community*, for the consolidated version from 2006 see: OJ C 321E, 29.12.2006.

9 *Treaty establishing European Economic Community*.

10 *Treaty establishing the European Coal and Steel Community*.

11 Article 3 TECSC was of a little different nature. It did not determine the catalogue of the Community institutions but determined their tasks, with a reservation that the institutions accomplish the tasks *within the limits of their powers and in the common interest*.

12 ECJ 13.06.1958, 9–56, *Meroni & Co Industrie Metallurgiche SPA vs. High Authority of ECSC*, ECR 1957–1958, English Special Edition, p. 133.

13 In this case it referred to Article 3 TEEC (read in the context of the nature and competences of particular institutions) discussing the tasks of the Community, not defining, however, the institutional balance. Moreover, in the *Meroni* judgment, the term "institutional balance" was not used yet. Nevertheless, later the Court referred to it consistently. The convergence of the provisions referred to by the Court in this context suggests an identity of what in the case *Meroni* was called a balance (division) of powers and the term of institutional balance used afterwards.

14 ECJ 29.10.1980, C-138/79, *SA Roquette Frères v. Council*, ECR 1980, 3333.

Frères v. Council) it was treated as an interpretative guidance. For in this case the point was the interpretation of the then Article 43 para 2 sentence 3 TEEC (later Article 37 TEC; they both assumed adopting the act by the Council on the proposal from the Commission and after consultation with the European Parliament – EP).[15] The sense of this – seemingly clear – provision turned out to be disputable in the situation where the Council adopted the regulation without a prior opinion of the Parliament for which it had unsuccessfully applied. The lack of the EP's opinion resulted from the lengthy internal procedure: the Parliament failed to present the opinion before the end of its term. In this situation the Council adopted the act independently, maintaining that the requirement of consultation had been fulfilled.

The main objection to the act of the Council was the infringement of essential procedural requirements. The Council, in general categories, did not intend to question the importance of consultation with the Parliament as a formal requirement. However, it pointed out that it was the Parliament itself which, through its action, made its fulfilment impossible. Thereby referring to its infringement is groundless.[16] In this light, the interpretation of a relevant Treaty provision turned out to be necessary indeed. It was the only way to explain the doubts concerning the decision which appeared clear. The clarification was made on the basis of the concept of institutional balance and references thereto are essential here.

The Court asserted foremost that the procedural requirement in the form of the EP consultation is fulfilled the moment the Parliament really expresses its opinion. The fact of application for an opinion itself is not sufficient.[17] In this way the primary doubt generated by the facts described above was explained. The Court stated namely as follows:

> (…) The consultation provided for in the third subparagraph of article 43 (2), as in other similar provisions of the Treaty, is the means which allows the Parliament to play an actual part in the legislative process of the Community, such power represents an essential factor in the institutional balance intended by the Treaty (…)

The adopted solution, except Article 4 TEEC (Article 7 TEC) again required referring to a broader context determined by regulations on powers of particular institutions and procedures of the EU law making.

Thus, it turns out that the provisions of Articles 13 TEU, 7 TEC (4 TEEC) and Article 3 TECSC were relatively general, constitutional. Embedding institutional

---

15 At present it is Article 43(2) TFEU: *The European Parliament and the Council, acting in accordance with the ordinary legislative procedure and after consulting the Economic and Social Committee, shall establish the common organisation of agricultural markets provided for in Article 40(1) and the other provisions necessary for the pursuit of the objectives of the common agricultural policy and the common fisheries policy.*

16 Deeper analysis of this judgment: T. Dubowski, *Zasada równowagi instytucjonalnej w prawie Unii Europejskiej*, Warszawa 2010, p. 107–108.

17 ECJ 29.10.1980, C-138/79, *SA Roquette Frères v. Council*, ECR 1980, 3333, para. 34.

balance in the EU legal order required a broader perspective and connecting the aforementioned provisions with more specific rules concerning the nature of particular institutions, their mutual relations, competences and procedural issues. This indicates the active role of the Court in forming the principle in point. For it is worth underlying that the provisions in question (both those more general and those more specific) in no case referred to the term of institutional balance and all the more they did not define it. Reading the Communities and the Union's tasks, as well as the values accompanying their setting in the light of Treaty objectives, made it possible to formulate a concept of institutional balance. In the face of the framework nature of the Treaties which constitute the bases of the Union, the concept of institutional balance has become useful in reference to the evaluation of legality of certain actions of institutions and the interpretation of Treaty provisions.[18] Simultaneously, the role of the Court in its reconstruction from the whole of the Treaty matter and its placement in the Union order is undisputable.

Despite this fact the judgments quoted do not provide fundamental evidence of the creative role of the Court in the process of shaping institutional balance as a general principle of EU law. Literature, relatively consistently, presents the view that the Court fully defined it and raised to the rank of a principle only in the early 1990s[19] along with the judgment in the *Chernobyl* case.[20]

3. INSTITUTIONAL BALANCE AS A GENERAL PRINCIPLE OF EU (EC) LAW? THE COURT'S ROLE

As stated previously, the adjudicative references to institutional balance have not been so frequent and coherent that its nature, especially its status as a general principle, raises no doubts and controversies. The judgments quoted above may not fully reflect the nature of institutional balance in the EU legal order. From this perspective, the judgment in the *Chernobyl* case remains fundamental.

In short, in this case the matter of argument was the EP bringing an action for annulment against the regulation of the Council. The Parliament questioned the selection of the legal basis of the act, which the Council based on the

18 It is important to note that these functions are typical of the categories of general principles of a particular legal system.

19 See: S. Prechal, 'Institutional Balance: A Fragile Principle with Uncertain Content' in T. Heukels, N. Blokker, M. Brus (eds.), *European Union after Amsterdam. A Legal Analysis*, The Hague/London/Boston 1998, p. 275; B. de Witte, 'Institutional Principles: A Special Category of General Principles of EC Law' in U. Bernitz, J. Nergelius (eds.), *General Principles of European Community Law. Reports from a Conference in Malmö, 27–28 August 1999*, The Hague-London-Boston 2000, pp. 151–152.

20 ECJ 22.05.1990, C-70/88, *Parliament v. the Council of the EC*, ECR 1990, I-2041.

provisions of TEAEC.[21] These provisions reduced the role of the EP in the procedure of adopting the act to consultation only.[22] The Parliament challenged the regulation of the Council, referring, among others, to Article 173 TEEC (now Article 263 TFEU), raising an objection to the invalidity of the act. Under then existing legal status, the provision referred to by the EP did not provide the EP a right to bring this type of action.[23] It was assumed, and reflected in judicial decisions,[24] that the interests of the EP are guarded by the Commission, which in the case of a threat is entitled to bring a relevant action. The EP itself, however, did not have such right.[25] Thus, the Council naturally raised objection to the action as unacceptable. It is this question to which the Court expressed its opinion in the judgment of 22 May 1990.[26]

In the proceedings the Parliament argued that the Commission having selected the legal grounds for the act against the Parliament's demand had lost the status of the guarantor of its prerogatives. It is all the more difficult to expect the Council to bring an action against the invalidity of its own act – the act at which legal basis it pointed itself, and this turned out to be the basis of the conflict. It is also difficult to expect that other entities entitled to bring the action for annulment take up the protection of the rights of the Parliament.[27]

The Court admitted that the role of the Commission as an institution protecting the powers of the Parliament turns out dubious. It is difficult to force the Commission to recognize the position of the Parliament as its own and to bring an action which it clearly considers as groundless.[28] In this situation the Court recognized the lack of possibility of independent bringing an action for annulment by the Parliament as a procedural gap preventing the EP from the protection of its own prerogatives. This gap should have been simultaneously completed and the Court recognized, as an accurate solution in this matter, the acceptance of the Parliament's right to bring an action for annulment.[29] The reasoning of the Court was as follows:

---

21 *Treaty establishing the European Atomic Energy Community.*

22 The Parliament demanded previously from the Commission submitting the project in TEEC cooperation procedure. The Commission failed to comply with the demand and consequently the Council adopted the act on the grounds of the provisions of TEAEC, marginalizing the role of the Parliament.

23 In accordance with the current legal status, the Parliament has this right, see: Article 263 TFEU.

24 See: ECJ 27.09.1988, C-302/87, *European Parliament vs. the Council of European Communities*, ECR 1988, p. 5615.

25 Deeper analysis on the strengthening the European Parliament's prerogatives is presented by A. Piekutowska in this volume.

26 ECJ 22.05.1990, C-70/88, *Parliament vs. the Council of the EC*, ECR 1990, I-2041. The judgment referring to the substance of the case was passed on 4 October 1991. See: ECR 1991, p. 4529.

27 ECJ 22.05.1990, C-70/88, *Parliament vs. the Council of the EC*, ECR 1990, I-2041, para. 7.

28 ECJ 22.05.1990, C-70/88, *Parliament vs. the Council of the EC*, ECR 1990, I-2041, paras. 16–17.

29 Within the scope in which it would serve the protection of its prerogatives.

> (...) it is the Court' s duty to ensure that the provisions of the Treaties concerning the institutional balance are fully applied and to see to it that the Parliament's prerogatives, like those of the other institutions, cannot be breached without it having available a legal remedy, among those laid down in the Treaties, which may be exercised in a certain and effective manner.
>
> The absence in the Treaties of any provision giving the Parliament the right to bring an action for annulment may constitute a procedural gap, but it cannot prevail over the fundamental interest in the maintenance and observance of the institutional balance laid down in the Treaties establishing the European Communities.

In this way the Court, against the literary content of the Treaties, recognized the EP's right to bring an action for annulment. The basis for the acceptance of this right of the Parliament became the institutional balance, in this case treated as a general principle of EU law, derived from the system of the Treaties, the substance and sense of its provisions. In the case, this systemic interpretation of the Treaty turned out far-reaching. It exposed the Court to the accusation of law making.[30] However, not evaluating this issue, it is important to assert that the judicial decision in point is an example of a creative contribution of the Court in the development of EU law. Institutional balance has become a permanent element of the EU *acquis* introduced into its legal order by the Court. The case *Chernobyl* clearly proves that institutional balance was treated here as a principle decoded from the EU legal system and not explicitly expressed in one of the provisions. The role of the Court turned out to be the reconstruction or decoding of institutional balance as a principle derived from the essence of the Treaty – its constitutional interpretation. As such this principle is rooted in the system of EU law and constitutes one of the fundaments of the EU legal order.[31]

Thus, institutional balance remains the work of the Court itself. To this day it has not been directly expressed in any of the provisions of the Treaty and its "presence" in the EU law seems to be the achievement of the Court and its interpretative activity. It is the Court that derived this rule from "the spirit" of the system of the Treaty, from the substance and meaning of its provisions. In this way it becomes an example of the contribution of the Court to the development of the whole of EU law.

However, did the Court, by "creating" institutional balance as a principle, connect it in any way with democratic principles? Can it be perceived as a factor enhancing democracy in the EU?

---

30 There are, however, opinions stating, that the Court, in fact, did not rule against the Treaties. General principles find their source in the Treaty provisions, consequently, in case of the institutional balance, what the Court did was just a full interpretation of EU (Community) constitutional charter without exceeding area of principles and values of EU (Community) law – area where the institutional balance was in such a way uncovered. For more see: T.T. Koncewicz, *"Sędziowski aktywizm" czyli wspólnotowe czynienie sprawiedliwości*, "Palestra", Vol. 1–2/2007, p. 236.

31 T. Dubowski, *supra* note 16, pp. 114–117.

4. INSTITUTIONAL BALANCE AND DEMOCRACY IN THE EU – VISIBLE LINKS

Already a quick analysis of judgments quoted in the previous section suggests that institutional balance was relatively clearly bound with democratic values. Although in various ways (and with different intensity), the Court underlined this connection. Of course, what seems to be the most explicit in that respect are direct references to the connection between institutional balance and democracy. We have to, however, bear in mind that the judgments analysed above, even those which do not directly connect the institutional balance with democracy, gave a basis for establishment of certain prohibitions and prescripts (normative character) which arise from the institutional balance principle. They seem to guarantee the possible minimum degree of the Union's democracy. This perspective should put more light on the Court's judgments on institutional balance as it will be described below.

Already in the *Meroni* judgment it was clearly indicated that institutional balance supports the protection of entrepreneurs, citizens. In this way the analysed principle became an element of democratic character of the Union (Community). It should be reminded that in this judgment the unhampered delegation of discretionary powers by the EU institutions turned out to be contrary to the institutional balance according to the following way of reasoning:

> (...) there can be seen in the balance of powers which is characteristic of the institutional structure of the community a fundamental guarantee granted by the treaty in particular to the undertakings and associations of undertakings to which it applies. To delegate a discretionary power, by entrusting it to bodies other than those which the treaty has established to effect and supervise the exercise of such power each within the limits of its own authority, would render that guarantee ineffective.

Institutional balance, typical for institutional framework of the Union, cumbers in this way the arbitrary delegation of discretionary powers in the EU – protects private parties against such practices and becomes a guarantee of cutting them. At the same time, a distinct prohibition resulting from institutional balance principle takes shape here – a ban towards EU institutions precluding unhampered delegation of their own powers on other bodies. This prohibition has no absolute character. Delegation of powers is, however, subject to quite strict requirements.[32]

In the *Roquette Frères* judgment, which was also quoted above, the connection between institutional balance and democratic values becomes even more visible. In this judgment, the Court – in principle – interpreted procedural provisions of the Treaties. What is however interesting, the Court, by interpreting particular

32 *Supra* at p. 126.

Treaty provision, namely Article 43(2) TEEC (later Article 37 TEC) "revealed" the other side of its argumentation. This provision has been interpreted in the light of institutional balance principle. And this principle itself has been strongly related to the demand of democracy. The Court ruled as follows:

> (...) The consultation provided for in the third subparagraph of article 43 (2), as in other similar provisions of the Treaty, is the means which allows the Parliament to play an actual part in the legislative process of the Community, such power represents an essential factor in the institutional balance intended by the Treaty (...)

And then added:

> (...) Although limited, it reflects at Community level the fundamental democratic principle that the peoples should take part in the exercise of power through the intermediary of a representative assembly. Due consultation of the Parliament in the cases provided for by the Treaty therefore constitutes an essential formality disregard of which means that measure concerned is void.

As a result, the institutional balance became an important hint for interpretation[33] – a proper context in the light of which the significance of the EP's consultation, as an procedural requirement in the EU decision-making, should be perceived. What is more important, the institutional balance was treated here as one of the guarantees of democratic rules in the EU – in this particular case – as an instrument protecting the principle of citizens' participation in the exercise of power. At the same time, the role of the European Parliament as a representative body was stressed, which – considering the shape of EU institutional framework of that time (and also of today) – causes no objections.[34] Preservation of institutional balance seems to remain a *sine qua non* condition for the EP's prerogatives protection. This body, in turn, secures the individual interests as a representative assembly, an institution composed of directly elected members. The relation between institutional balance and democratic fundamentals of the EU – also on the level of the interpretation of law – is thus evident. What is important, the argumentation given by the Court seems to prove, that the institutional balance has a kind of "prescriptive (order) content" and certain obligations might be derived from it. In this case this content amounts to an order to respect other institutions' prerogatives. It is clear, that in this case these are EP's prerogatives which deserve observance. It may be, however, assumed, that the other institutions may benefit from that order as well.

---

33 It is also a typical function of general principles of EU law, cf. T. Dubowski, *supra* at pp. 78–80. See also: T. Tridimas, *The General Principles of EC Law*, Oxford 2006, pp. 29–35.

34 The role of the Court in enhancing the EP as an EU representative institution is analyzed in one of other contributions to that volume.

Finally, despite the fact that *Chernobyl* judgment lacks wide direct references to the democratic values and the necessity of observance thereof, undeniably it was the EP's powers protection this judgment was mostly about. The core problem was to enable the Parliament to undertake individual and efficient action securing its prerogatives. Without any doubts, such strong references to the institutional balance as a principle guaranteeing inviolability of the EP's powers once again prove that there exists a strict link between this principle and democratic values.

Once again it seems that invoking the institutional balance the Court emphasized the obligation (order) of (mutual) respect of the powers of the EU institutions. In that case the Court applied creative interpretation of Treaty provisions in order to give the EP an instrument to protect its powers in case they are violated. In this way, due to institutional balance, the order to respect institutions' prerogatives has a chance to become even more efficient. In relation to the EP, it enhances unquestionably the democratic foundation of the Union.

The above, necessarily concise, analysis of judicature indicates, that institutional balance is clearly connected to the democratic features of the European Union. It becomes, in a quite unique way, one of the elements securing the desired level of democracy in the EU. The judgments quoted above confirm that this relation manifests itself not only in the wording of separate rulings and terms used therein (for example: institutional balance as a reflection of a "fundamental democratic principle that the peoples should take part in the exercise of power through the intermediary of a representative assembly"[35]), but also on the level of prohibitions and orders resulting from the principle of institutional balance. The obligation to refrain from unhampered delegation of own powers and to respect the powers of other institutions – both accepted also in literature[36] – seems to serve the preservation of desired degree of democracy in the EU – the degree possible to achieve on the level of an international (supranational) organization.

It should be noted at the same time that the guarantees resulting from institutional balance secure not only the position of European Parliament, but also the position of other institutions. It becomes clear particularly in the light of Article 13 TEU ("(...) Each institution shall act within the limits of the powers conferred on it in the Treaties, and in conformity with the procedures, conditions and objectives set out in them. The institutions shall practice mutual sincere cooperation (...)"), which today might be perceived as a Treaty "inspiration" for the principle under consideration. There are no doubts, however, that the institutional balance shows the largest "democratic load" in cases where it enhances the position of the EP and its prerogatives. This enhancement of the EP's

35 ECJ 28.10.1980, C-139/79, *Maizena GmbH v. Council of the European Communities*, ECR 1980 I-3393, p. 3394.

36 K. Lenaerts, P. van Nuffel, *Constitutional Law of the European Union*, London 2005, p. 560. In Polish literature see: M.M. Kenig-Witkowska (red.), *Prawo instytucjonalne Unii Europejskiej*, Warszawa 2004, p. 155.

role is at the same time worth reading in the context of Article 10 TEU, stating that "the functioning of the Union shall be founded on representative democracy". What is more – "citizens are directly represented at Union level in the European Parliament" and have a right to participate in Union's democratic life.

5. CONCLUSION

On the basis of the above considerations, the following remarks might be presented. Firstly, it has been proved that institutional balance as a principle of the European Union (Community) law is to a large extent a "product" of the Court's creative interpretation of the Treaties. The principle in question is not (and was not) directly expressed in any of the Treaty provisions. Traces of that principle were however found by the Court in the process of wide, systemic interpretation of the Treaties. Certain groups of provisions – relating mostly to the institutional structure of the Union, institutions' prerogatives, their mutual relations, decision-making process and the system of connections between them, let the Court establish a particular principle – principle of institutional balance. It is also important to mention in that context that the principle of institutional balance – as quoted judgments indicate – was used in a way typical for general principles of law, namely as an interpretative guide, a general norm enabling the fulfilment of lacunae in the Treaties and as a criterion for evaluating the legality of Union acts. Summing up – it seems clear that the Court's role in decoding the principle of institutional balance and introducing it into the EU legal order is crucial.

Secondly, it has been also proved that there exist strong links between institutional balance and the degree of democracy in the Union. These links are quite visibly reflected in the judicature and present themselves in two models. First model would be the approach of the Court in which it directly binds the institutional balance with democratic values in the EU. It happened for example in the *Roquette Frères* judgment, where the Court stated that institutional balance "reflects at Community level the fundamental democratic principle that the peoples should take part in the exercise of power through the intermediary of a representative assembly". Second model would consists of more concrete obligations resulting from the principle of institutional balance – obligation to refrain from unhampered delegation of own powers and to respect the powers of other institutions. If we relate those obligations to the system of Treaty provisions on institutions' competences and decision-making process, it becomes clear that institutional balance may contribute to the protection of democracy in the EU. It concerns mostly the protection of prerogatives of the EP. In fact, in most cases, this principle was used by the Court just in order to enhance the position of the EP as a representative assembly, the main institutional foundation for democracy in the European Union.

Consequently, it may be confirmed that in case of institutional balance, the Court's activity setting this principle in the EU legal order has simultaneously contributed to the enhancement of the EU democratic character.

BIBLIOGRAPHY

BOOKS

Bernitz, U. and Nergelius, J. (eds.), *General Principles of European Community Law. Reports from a Conference in Malmö, 27–28 August 1999*, The Hague-London-Boston 2000

Dubowski, T., *Zasada równowagi instytucjonalnej w prawie Unii Europejskiej*, Warszawa 2010

Heukels, T., Blokker, N. and Brus, M. (eds.), *European Union after Amsterdam. A Legal Analysis*, The Hague/London/Boston 1998

Kenig-Witkowska, M.M. (red.), *Prawo instytucjonalne Unii Europejskiej*, Warszawa 2004

Lenaerts, K. and Van Nuffel, P., *Constitutional Law of the European Union*, London 2005

Schulze, R. and Zuleeg, M. (Hrsg.), *Europarecht. Handbuch für die deutsche Rechtspraxis*, Baden-Baden 2006

Tridimas, T., *The General Principles of EC Law*, Oxford 2006

Usher, J.A., *General Principles of EC Law*, London 1998

ARTICLES

Conway, G., 'Recovering a Separation of Powers in the European Union' (2011) 17 *ELJ (European Law Journal)*

Koncewicz, T.T., *„Sędziowski aktywizm" czyli wspólnotowe czynienie sprawiedliwości*, „Palestra", Vol. 1–2/2007

EU CASE-LAW

ECJ 05.02.1963, 26/62, *NV Algemene Transport- en Expeditie Onderneming van Gend & Loos v. Netherlands Inland Revenue Administration*, ECR 1963

ECJ 13.06.1958, 9–56, *Meroni & Co Industrie Metallurgiche SPA v. High Authority of ECSC*, ECR 1957–1958

ECJ 29.10.1980, C-138/79, *SA Roquette Frères v. Council*, ECR 1980

ECJ 29.10.1980, C-139/79, *Maizena GmbH v. Council of the European Communities*, ECR 1980

ECJ 27.09.1988, C-302/87, *European Parliament v. the Council of European Communities*, ECR 1988

ECJ 22.05.1990, C-70/88, *Parliament v. the Council of the EC*, ECR 1990

3. FROM JUDICIAL DIALOGUE TOWARDS CONSTITUTIONAL SPILL-OVER?

The Economic Analysis of Preliminary Reference Procedure and the Application of the EU Charter of Fundamental Rights*

Mariusz J. Golecki**
Department of Theory and Philosophy of Law, Faculty of Law and Administration, University of Lodz

1. INTRODUCTION

The construction of governance structure based on judicial activism of the Court of Justice of the EU (European Court, ECJ, CJUE) has been explained as judicial *coup d'état*, where the European Court created the doctrine of the primacy of the European Communities law.[2] The question arises whether the spill-over effect may play an adverse role of an obstacle in integration since the Member States, and especially their courts, may adopt a similar set of doctrines, reasoning, concepts and legal instruments in order to diminish the effect and scope of the primacy of the EU law doctrine.[3] This position has been taken by some intergovernmentalists, who claimed that states remained principal actors on the European scene and remained ultimate decision makers. This position has

* Acknowledgment: The paper has been prepared within the framework of the FOCUS research project of the Foundation for Polish Science.
I'd like to thank Prof. Arno Várnay, Dr Marton Varju and Dr Emese Szilágyi for inspiring and invaluable remarks on the application of the EU law in Hungary and the Hungarian constitutional reform.

** Email: MGolecki@wpia.uni.lodz.pl.

2 A. Stone Sweet, The Juridical Coup d'État and the Problem of Authority, *German Law Journal* 8 (2007), pp. 915–926.

3 A. Arnull, "Me and My Shadow: The European Court of Justice and the Disintegration of European Union Law", *Fordham International Law Journal*, 31 (2007), pp. 1174–1211.

been unsuccessfully defended by different authors.[1] It has been suggested that the discretion enjoyed by the ECJ has not in fact been curbed by any successful strategy adopted by any Member State.[2]

It seems, however, that things have been changed with the enlargement and the creation of platform for the horizontal judicial discourse and coordination of state driven policy concerning the minimization of the discretion successfully having been controlled by the ECJ. W. Sadurski has been successfully demonstrating how the constitutional courts in Central Europe (CE) have limited the application of the EU law by rejection of the full application of the doctrine of the primacy of the EU law.[3] The enactment of the Treaty on Functioning of the European Union resulted with many judgments of constitutional courts in Member States in which the concept of sovereignty and the doctrine of sovereign powers played an important role. The paper will thus concentrate on two issues, namely on the difference in the meaning of the concept of sovereignty and its application by the constitutional courts in Poland and Hungary and the position of the constitutional courts within the dynamic constitutional setting, embracing the legislature and the other courts.

Two waves of judgments by the national courts in CE seem to be conspicuous in this respect. The first wave concerned judgments of some constitutional courts containing the doctrines on the relationship between the national constitutional law and the European law. This wave of judgments resulted with the adoption of different versions of the principle of primacy or autonomy between the law of European Union and the national constitutional law in different CE states. In Poland the doctrine of the constitutional supremacy of the Polish Constitution has been adopted whereas the position adopted by the Hungarian Constitutional Court was based on the doctrine of absolute separation between the Hungarian Constitution and the EU law. Later on the doctrines adopted by these courts apparently converged under the shadow of the judgments of the German Constitutional Court concerning the constitutionality of the enactment of the Treaty on Functioning of the European Union.[4]

1 A. Moravcsik, "Preferences and Power in the European Community: A Liberal Intergovernmentalist Approach", *Journal of Common Market Studies*, 31(1993): 473–524, C.J. Carrubba and L. Murrah L., "Legal Integration and Use of the Preliminary Ruling Process in the European Union", *International Organization*, 59(2005), pp. 399–418; C.J Carrubba, M. Gabel, and C. Hankla, "Judicial Behavior under Political Constraints: Evidence from the European Court of Justice", *American Political Science Review*, 102(2008), pp. 435–452.

2 A. Stone Sweet and T.L. Brunell, "The European Court of Justice, State Noncompliance, and the Politics of Override", *American Political Science Review*, 106(2012), p. 204.

3 W. Sadurski, *Constitutionalism and the Enlargement of Europe*, Oxford, Oxford University Press 2012, pp. 99–142.

4 According to A. Dyevre, the most important factor influencing the position of the constitutional court is just the power to review the legislation. In the CE all relevant constitutional court generally have this prerogative. Cf. A. Dyevre, "European Integration and National Courts: Defending Sovereignty under Institutional Constraints?", *European Constitutional Law Review*, 9(2013), pp. 165–168.

It should be noted that the solutions to this problem might be found through the interactive process, transforming the monologue of the European Court of Justice into more refined and complex version of judicial discourse leading to genuine judicial dialogue. This kind of dialogue taking place between Member States and the European Courts seems to be a new and powerful tool shaping division of labour between the European Courts and courts in Member States. Two types of judicial dialogue may be distinguished.

Firstly, the vertical dialogue between the ECJ and the supreme and other courts of the Member States. The institutional framework for this kind of dialogue is based on the preliminary reference procedure based on Article 267 TFEU.[5] The other type of judicial dialogue is rather informal and based on observation, adjustment and coordination of the judicial practice of different judicial institutions in Member States. This kind of judicial dialogue may take different forms, varying form explicit references to other courts' decisions to implicit references to some concepts and doctrines applied by other courts in Member States.[6]

Two ways of setting the problem of apparent conflict between democratic participation and primacy of the EU law have been marked by the Polish and German Constitutional Tribunals. In three judgments the Polish Constitutional Tribunal established a refined doctrine of constitutional supremacy and its limits. In judgment of 27 April 2005 (P 1/05) the Polish Constitutional Tribunal found the European Arrest Warrant (EAW) Framework Decision unconstitutional, since the Polish Constitution explicitly prohibited extradition of Polish citizen, whereas the European Arrest Warrant Framework Decision was based on the cooperation requiring "surrender" of the offender to the other Member State. The Tribunal, however, suspended for 18 months the annulment of Article 607t(1) of the Code of Criminal Procedure, itself allowing to extradite a Polish national to another EU Member State under the EAW framework. Meanwhile, in 2006 the Polish Constitution was amended, enabling the full operation of the EAW in Poland. The same decision has been taken by the German Federal Constitutional Court, which also found the framework decision unconstitutional in Germany. However, the immediate annulment of the European Arrest Warrant Framework Decision put Germany in a difficult situation.[7] German Constitutional Court observed that states remain sovereign as possessing control over the degree of

---

5 A. Łazowski (ed.), "The Application of EU Law in the New Member States: Brave New World", T.M.C. Asser Press, The Hague 2010.

6 M. Kumm, "The Jurisprudence of Constitutional Conflict: Constitutional Supremacy in Europe before and after the Constitutional Treaty", *European Law Journal*, 11(2005), pp. 262–307.

7 J. Komárek, J., "European constitutionalism and the European arrest warrant: in search of the limits of "contrapunctual principles". *Common Market Law Review*, 44(2007), pp. 9–40; J. Komárek, "Czech constitutional court playing with matches: the Czech constitutional court declares a judgment of the court of justice of the EU ultra vires; judgment of 31 January 2012, Pl. ÚS 5/12", *European Constitutional Law Review*, 8(2013), pp. 323–337.

participation, the content of participation or lack thereof, in a similar way in which the Constitutional Court possesses the control over constitutionality of the EU law in Germany, even if it represents an astonishing compliance with the EU law and only very rarely decides against the validity of the EU law or its applicability in Germany.

In order to explain the process, two potential theories will be confronted. The first one presented by W. Sadurski suggests that the protection of human rights (*Solange strategy*) and the internal conflict between political actors together constitute a vehicle for the empowerment of the constitutional courts in CE.[8] This strategy seems to be strictly connected with the process of transition from communism to liberal democratic constitutionalism. Sadurski's theory ("Solange Chapter 3 theory") competes with other potential explanations that emphasize the internal dynamics of the judicial empowerment process, such as constitutional incompleteness, political transaction costs or hegemonic preservation.[9] In this context, it seems that the change in the position of the Hungarian Constitutional Court in the new Hungarian constitutional framework could usefully be compared to the creeping evolution of the judicial constitutional adjudication in Poland. Two major arguments for and against the specific nature of these processes will be investigated.

Firstly, unlike the Solange chapter 3 story, the later judgments of the CE constitutional courts have been based on the present, unconditional criticism and open rejection of the primacy doctrine by the German Constitutional Court in 2010. It seems that in this case, the spill-over effect led to the adverse direction that is to the fragmentation of the primacy principle, understood and applied in different ways in different Member States.

Secondly, the argument about the domestic game of power which led the constitutional courts in CE to the declaration of the sovereignty principle and implied doctrine of the constitutional superiority does not seem to be satisfactory given the fact of differences in political situation between Poland and Hungary. The Polish Constitutional Tribunal in fact declared the need to shift some of its competences to the lawmaker,[10] meanwhile nothing of this kind took place in Hungary. Hungarian Constitutional Court has never declared its position concerning the primacy of the EU law or of the Hungarian Constitution, observing the separation doctrine according to which, the Court revised the Hungarian law exclusively. Additionally, the references to the European law became a source of additional Court's power in its struggle

8 W. Sadurski, "Solange, Chapter 3': Constitutional Courts in Central Europe", *European Law Journal*, 14(2008), pp. 1–35.

9 A. Stone-Sweet, *Governing with Judges*, Oxford 2000. R. Hirschl, *Towards Juristocracy. The Origins and Consequences of the New Constitutionalism*, Cam. Mas. 2004, pp. 1–31, R. Posner, *How Judges Think*, Cam. Mas. 2008, pp. 269–324.

10 Judgment of the Polish Constitutional Court, P 1/05, 27 April 2005.

against the Hungarian lawmaker recently amending the Fundamental Law and narrowing the Constitutional Court's competences.[11]

It seems that the application of the EU Charter of Fundamental Rights in the post-Lisbon Treaty institutional landscape creates a new vehicle for judicial cooperation and competition between the EU Court of Justice and the national constitutional and supreme courts on the constitutional level. Economic analysis of these complex interactions concentrates on two problems: the spill-over effect of the judgments of national constitutional and supreme courts and the potential application of the so called "Köbler strategy" based on tort remedies for breach of the EU law by national court.

2. CONSTITUTIONAL COURTS AND THE PRELIMINARY REFERENCE PROCEDURE: JUDICIAL DIALOGUE AND JUDICIAL SPILL-OVER

The phenomenon of "judicialization" of the European Union plays an important role in the discourse pertaining to the theory of the European integration. It seems that the integration through the judicial activism of the European Court of Justice and the so called "constitutionalization" of the European integration gives strong arguments in favour of the Neofunctionalism as a theory which explains the integration as process based on the spill-over effect. According to the classical definition proposed by L.N. Lindberg:

> "'spill-over' refers to a situation in which a given action, related to a specific goal, creates a situation in which the original goal can be assured only by taking further actions, which in turn create a further condition and a need for more action, and so forth. (...) the initial task and grant of power to the central institutions creates a situation or series of situations that can be dealt with only by further expanding the task and the grant of power. Spill-over implies that a situation has developed in which the ability of a Member State to achieve a policy goal may depend upon the attainment by another Member State of one of its policy goals."[12]

This mechanism may play an important role in case of application of the EU law by national courts. It is not strange then that the unique position and role played by the ECJ as an initiator of judicial multilevel dialogue led some theorists to the proposition according to which the Court plays central role, initiating the integration on the legal level, where the political discourse is blocked by lack of

11 Decision of the Hungarian Constitutional Court, II/00648/2013, 23 April 2013.

12 L.N. Lindberg, *The Political Dynamics of European Economic Integration*, Stanford, CA, Stanford University Press 1963, p. 10.

unanimity or power of major players on both the EU and the national levels.[13] The construction of governance structure based on judicial activism of the ECJ has even been explained as judicial *coupe d'état*, where the European Court created the doctrine of the primacy of the European Communities law.[14]

The spill-over effect may however play an adverse role of an obstacle in integration since the Member States, and especially their courts, may adopt a similar set of doctrines, reasoning, concepts and legal instruments in order to diminish the effect and scope of the primacy of the EU law doctrine.[15] This position has been taken by some Intergovernmentalists, who claimed that states remained principal actors on the European scene and remained ultimate decision makers. This position has been defended by different authors.[16] The failure of Intergovernmentalism lies probably in the fact that it has not been successful in explaining the integration process through the lens of intergovernmental cooperation shaped by the states on legal level. It seems that the discretion enjoyed by the ECJ was not in fact curbed by any successful strategy adopted by any Member State.[17]

It seems however that things have been changed with the enlargement and the creation of platform for the horizontal judicial discourse and coordination of state driven policy concerning the minimization of the discretion successfully having been controlled by the ECJ. This approach has been recently reinforced by the Austrian Federal Constitutional Court. In its decision on the constitutionality of the Charter of Fundamental Rights, the Court established an a posteriori review jurisdiction over the application of the Charter of Fundamental Rights of the European Union. The Court observed that:

---

13 J.H.H. Weiler, "A Quiet Revolution: The European Court of Justice and its Interlocutors", *Comparative Political Studies*, 26(1994), pp. 510–534.

14 A. Stone Sweet, "The Juridical Coup d'État and the Problem of Authority", *German Law Journal*, 8(2007) pp. 915–926.

15 A. Arnull, "Me and My Shadow: The European Court of Justice and the Disintegration of European Union Law", *Fordham International Law Journal*, 31(2007), pp. 1176–1182.

16 A. Moravcsik, "Preferences and Power in the European Community: A Liberal Intergovernmentalist Approach", *Journal of Common Market Studies*, 31(1993): 473–524, C.J. Carrubba and L. Murrah L., "Legal Integration and Use of the Preliminary Ruling Process in the European Union", *International Organization*, 59(2005), pp. 399–418; C.J Carrubba, M. Gabel, and C. Hankla, "Judicial Behavior under Political Constraints: Evidence from the European Court of Justice", *American Political Science Review*, 102(2008), pp. 435–452, L. Blutman and N. Chronowski (2011), "Hungarian Constitutional Court: Keeping Aloof from European Union Law", *Vienna Journal on International Constitutional Law*, 5(2011), pp. 329–348; Broberg M. and Fenger N. (2013), "Variations in Member States' Preliminary References to the Court of Justice – Are Structural Factors (Part of) the Explanation?", *European Law Journal*, 19(2013), pp. 488–501.

17 Cf. J.H.H. Weiler, "The Transformation of Europe", *Yale Law Journal*, 100(1991), pp. 2403–2483 and more recently: A. Stone Sweet and T.L. Brunell, "The European Court of Justice, State Noncompliance, and the Politics of Override", *American Political Science Review*, 106(2012), pp. 204–2013.

"For the scope of application of European law, the Charter of Fundamental Rights has now enshrined (ensuing) rights as they are guaranteed by the Austrian Constitution in a similar manner as constitutionally safeguarded rights. (...)

(T)he Constitutional Court, after having referred a matter for a preliminary ruling to the Court of Justice of the European Union according to Article 267 TFEU as appropriate, takes the Charter of Fundamental Rights in its scope of application as a standard for national law (Article 51(1) CFR) and sets aside contradicting general norms according to Article 139 and/or Article 140 Federal Constitutional Act (B VG). In this manner, the Constitutional Court fulfils its obligation to remove from the domestic legal order provisions incompatible with Community law, which is also postulated by the Court of Justice of the European Union".[18]

A similar position seems to be adopted quite recently by the Hungarian Constitutional Court. The references to the European law and the obligations resulting from the Hungarian membership in the EU became a source of additional power in its struggle for power against the Hungarian lawmaker recently amending the Fundamental Law and narrowing the constitutional court's competences. In its recent judgment concerning the constitutionality of the Fourth amendment to the Hungarian Fundamental Law, the Hungarian Constitutional Court referred openly to the EU law and the necessity of applying the rules conferred by the supranational institutions as the argument in favour of its control over the amendments to the Constitution, stipulating that:

"The power of the Constitutional Court is a restricted power in the structure of division of powers. Consequently, the Court shall not extend its powers to review the constitution and the new norms amending it without an express and explicit authorization to that effect. (...) The Constitutional Court shall moreover consider the obligations Hungary undertook in its international treaties or those that follow from membership in the EU, along with the generally acknowledged rules of international law, and the basic principles and values reflected therein. All of these rules – with special regard to their values that are also incorporated into the Fundamental Law – constitute such a unified system (of values), that shall not be disregarded neither in the course of constitution-making or legislation, nor in the course of constitutional review conducted by the Constitutional Court."[19]

The Court simply stated that it had to take the international obligations of Hungary into account and thus it had to maintain the control over the process of the constitutional amendments set out by the 2/3 parliamentary majority. It seems that within the context of the Hungarian constitutional law, the primacy doctrine may potentially serve as the argument of last resort in favour of the wider scope of control exercised by the Hungarian Constitutional Court.

18 Judgment of the Austrian Federal Constitutional Court, U 466/11-18, 14 March 2012.

19 The Constitutional Court of Hungary, Press release regarding the constitutional review of the Fourth Amendment of the Fundamental Law of Hungary, 23 May 2013.

Certainly those challenges and new directions towards a wider application of the Charter and the usage of the preliminary reference procedure also by the national constitutional courts do not affect every Member State to the same degree, since the applicability of the Charter is to some extent limited e.g. in the UK, Poland and the Czech Republic. Nevertheless, the emerging doctrine of sovereignty understood as the power to ultimate control over the constitutionality of legal acts will be seriously weakened by the prospect of harmonization of the application of the EU Charter of Fundamental Rights through the Member States. The Austrian Federal Constitutional Court has concluded that the Charter may be enforced in front of the Constitutional Court as if it contained 'constitutionally guaranteed rights' and, furthermore, that the Charter may serve as a standard of review of constitutionality of domestic law.

This position has recently been reinforced in the provisional decision of the German Federal Constitutional Court pertaining to the validity of the Decision of the Governing Council of the European Central Bank of 6 September 2012 concerning the Outright Monetary Transactions (OMT) and the continued purchases of government bonds on the basis of this Decision and of the predecessor program for Securities Markets (SMP), where the Court repeated that the protection of constitutional identity remains its exclusive prerogative and this doctrine has been commonly accepted in other EU Member States, referring to the respective judgments of national constitutional and supreme courts. It seems that the German Federal Constitutional Court treats the doctrine of constitutional identity and a special concept of sovereignty in respect of the participation in the EU as a consolidated doctrine shared by many other constitutional courts and belonging to the common constitutional identity of these Member States.[20] The Court has referred to the concept of constitutional control exercised by national constitutional courts, emphasizing procedural aspects of constitutional sovereignty. The Court thus reinforced the doctrine and commented on the practice of different supreme and constitutional courts in other EU Member States, considering these judgments as reflecting common constitutional principles and practices of the EU Member States. The Court observed that:

> "The above-mentioned principles concerning the protection of the constitutional identity and of the limits of the transfer of sovereign powers to the European Union can also be found, with modifications depending on the existence or non-existence of unamendable elements in the respective national constitutions, in the constitutional law of many other Member States of the European Union (…).[21] This applies to all

20 BVerfG, 2 BvR 2728/13, 14 January 2014.

21 The German Federal Constitutional Court explicitly referred to the following judgments: the Kingdom of Denmark: Hojesteret, Judgment of 6 April 1998 – I 361/1997 –, para. 9.8.; for the Republic of Estonia: Riigikohus, Judgment of 12 July 2012 – 3-4-1-6-12 –, sec. no. 128, 223; for the French Republic: Conseil constitutionnel, Decision no. 2006–540 DC of 27 July

> constitutional organs, authorities and courts. It results from the constitutional principles of democracy (Art. 20 sec. 1 and sec. 2 GG) and the rule of law (Art. 20 sec. 3 GG), as well as from Art. 23 sec. 1 GG, and is safeguarded under European Union law by the principle of conferral (Art. 5 sec. 1 sentence 1 and sec. 2 TEU) and the obligation of the European Union to respect the national identities of the Member States (Art. 4 sec. 2 sentence 1 TEU).
>
> Besides the institutions of the European Union, German constitutional organs are also responsible to make sure that the programme of integration is observed".

On the other hand the Court decided to suspend the case and to refer questions for a preliminary ruling on the interpretation of various provisions of the EU law to the Court of Justice of the EU, in accordance with Article 267 section 1 b TFEU. Concurringly, the control over the decision and the content of the decision remain two separate issues.

This development towards further exchange of views between the EU Court of Justice and the national constitutional courts seems to play an important role in constructing the framework of the EU legal order. It seems that the application of the Charter could, at least to some extent, bring more coherence and participatory judicial dialogue into increasingly polarized conflict on the competence-competence issue. Alternatively it may predict the final chapter of this never-ending story, namely the chapter entitled the ultimate constitutionalisation of the European Union as federal legal order.

3. TOWARDS AN ECONOMIC ANALYSIS OF BREACH OF THE EU CHARTER OF FUNDAMENTAL RIGHTS BY THE NATIONAL CONSTITUTIONAL COURT

Within a hierarchical judicial system, the coherence of adjudication is preserved by virtue of appeals and – by the same token – by the control of cases exerted by higher courts such as court of appeal or supreme/constitutional court. Since each judge tends to avoid overruling, the judicial system usually sustains the

2006, 19th recital; Decision no. 2011–631 DC of 9 June 2011, 45th recital; for Ireland: Supreme Court of Ireland, *Crotty v. An Taoiseach* <1987>, I.R. 713 <783>; *S.P.U.C. (Ireland) Ltd. v. Grogan*, <1989>, I.R. 753 <765>; for the Italian Republic: Corte costituzionale, Decision no. 183/1973; Decision no. 168/1991; for the Republic of Latvia: Satversmes tiesa, Judgment of 7 April 2009 – 2008–35–01 –, sec. no. 17; for the Republic of Poland: Trybunal Konstytucyjny, Judgments of 11 May 2005 – K 18/04 –, n. 4.1., 10.2., of 24 November 2010 – K 32/09 –, n. 2.1. et seq.; of 16 November 2011 – SK 45/09 –, n. 2.4., 2.5., with further references; for the Kingdom of Sweden: Chapter 10 Art. 6 sentence 1, Form of government; for the Kingdom of Spain: Tribunal Constitucional, Declaration of 13 December 2004, DTC 1/2004; for the Czech Republic: Ústavni Soud, Judgment of 31 January 2012 – 2012/01/31 – Pl. ÚS 5/12 –, para. VII.

cohesion and diminishes the number of judicial errors. Nevertheless, the question arises what would happen if the constitutional or supreme court within some jurisdiction had no virtual possibility to review cases from lower instances? Alternatively, what would happen if, instead of one court on the top of the centralized hierarchical structure, there would be many different courts and each of them would have the power to review the cases and all of them would be allowed to rely on the preliminary reference set out by the specialized court responsible for the efficacy and coherency of the whole adjudicative practice? Such a situation takes place in the EU law, where the EU Court of Justice has no power to review the cases concerning the application of the EU Charter of Fundamental Rights by the national courts in Member States *ex propio vigore*.

The relationship between the CJEU and national courts, especially in regard to the courts of last instance, cannot be described as a hierarchical structure. The CJEU does not revise or control verdicts of national courts. Concurringly, the European Courts do not have power to overrule judgments given by national courts. This situation is somehow puzzling for many commentators for it requires a completely new approach to standardization and unification of judicial activity. As it has been suggested by the Austrian Federal Constitutional Court,[22] this approach could be developed on the basis of the preliminary reference procedure under Article 267 of the Treaty on the Functioning of the European Union".[23] The strategy is based on the assumption that under Article 267 the TFEU imposes a duty on the court of last instance to make references to the CJEU. This means that "a court or tribunal of a Member State against whose decisions there is no judicial remedy under national law" shall bring also questions of mere interpretation of the European law before the CJEU, including the constitutional court applying the relevant provision of the EU Charter. This approach is additionally supported by the recognition of the principle of state liability and might be derived from Joined Cases C-6/90 and C-9/90 *Francovich and Bonifaci v Italy*, where the CJEU held that a Member State was liable to make good the loss and damage caused to individuals as a result of breaches of EU law for which

22 Judgment U 466/11-18, 14 March 2012.

23 Article 267 (ex Article 234 TEC): The Court of Justice of the European Union shall have jurisdiction to give preliminary rulings concerning: (a) the interpretation of the Treaties; (b) the validity and interpretation of acts of the institutions, bodies, offices or agencies of the Union; Where such a question is raised before any court or tribunal of a Member State, that court or tribunal may, if it considers that a decision on the question is necessary to enable it to give judgment, request the Court to give a ruling thereon. Where any such question is raised in a case pending before a court or tribunal of a Member State against whose decisions there is no judicial remedy under national law, that court or tribunal shall bring the matter before the Court. If such a question is raised in a case pending before a court or tribunal of a Member State with regard to a person in custody, the Court of Justice of the European Union shall act with the minimum of delay.

it was responsible.[24] The rulings of the CJEU in *Köbler* and *Traghetti* cases have created the normative framework for the application of the improved *strategy of privatization*.[25]

The *privatization strategy* thus relies upon the fact that private individuals may bring suits against their states in case of infringement of the EU law because, according to the assumptions commonly accepted by the adherents of the law and economics movement, adjudication should be treated in an analogous way to production activity.[26] The single effect of this activity is encapsulated within the national court's decision. The suit should be brought in front of a national court, which in majority of cases has the obligation to make a preliminary reference. Thus, the activity of national courts throughout the European Union should be standardized, leading to a greater homogeneity of judicial rulings concerning the application of the EU law in different Member States. But the strategy of privatization does much more than that. As A. Somek once again observes:

> "No recourse to legal theory is needed here, merely the ordinary principles of tort law, the application of which requires the existence of harm, causality and, where applicable, some standard of fault."[27]

As such, A. Somek seems to express the view according to which the privatization strategy will inevitably lead to some deplorable results, namely it will blur the concept of law and will melt the remnants of traditional approach to the activity of the EU legal institutions due to the spill-over effect. It seems however, that this allegation is based on misunderstanding. In fact, the application of the privatization strategy will not lead to the deterioration of the Rule of Law in the EU law. Certainly the application of the privatization strategy calls for new descriptive tools and new methodology of legal theory.

Given the fact that the courts in Member States have to balance between different costs, the courts tend to minimize redundant costs of investigation of a

24 The functions of public liability have recently been investigated in G. Dari-Mattiacci N. Garoupa and F. Gómez-Pomar, *State Liability, ACLE* (1) 2010, pp. 15–23. For the assessment of *Francovich* principle cf. p. 12. M. Golecki and B. Wojciechowski "The Application of Law within a Multicentric Legal System. Economic Analysis of Köbler and Traghetti" [in:] *Multicentrism as an Emerging Paradigm in Legal Theory*, M. Zirk-Sadowski, M. Golecki and B. Wojciechowski (eds.), Peter Lang Publishing Group, Frankfurt am Main, 2009; DIA-LOGOS. Schriften zu Philosophie und Sozialwissenschaften- Studies in Philosophy and Social Sciences, vol. XI, p. 171–174; M. Golecki and B. Wojciechowski, "Cyberspace as a Precondition of Application of Law within a Multicentric Legal Area", *Masaryk University Journal of Law and Technology*, 1(2017), pp. 9–17.

25 A. Somek, "Inexplicable Law. Legality's Adventure in Europe", *Transnational Law & Contemporary Problems*, 15(2006), p. 108.

26 W.M Landes and R.A Posner, "Adjudication as a Private Good", *Journal of Legal Studies*, 8(1979), pp. 235–284.

27 A. Somek, "Inexplicable Law. Legality's Adventure in Europe", *Transnational Law & Contemporary Problems*, 15(2006), p. 110; W.M. Landes and R.A. Posner, "Adjudication as a Private Good". *Journal of Legal Studies*, 8(1979), pp. 235–284.

given case and maximize the value of the case. This could well lead to the strong correlation between the *ex ante* complexity of a given case in front of the court and total expected costs, including the cost of judicial error.

Some recent developments of the application of the EU law by national courts are symptomatic in this respect. Quite recently the English Court of Appeal applied the *Köbler* doctrine in a way strikingly different from what could be expected from a well-informed national court. In *Cooper v. Attorney General* the Court decided that although, in general, domestic law could not excuse a breach of EU law, in a given case the standard of *Köbler* has not been met, since the plaintiff has been unsuccessful in demonstrating that the court acted in breach of the EU law in such a way the breach was manifest or sufficiently serious.[28] In deciding on the issue the Court referred to the necessity of taking all relevant considerations into account including whether the national court was deliberately intended to cause a breach of EU law and whether the court's decision was in accordance with other decisions in its domestic law. Certainly, additional conditions narrowing the *Köbler* doctrine to its application to the cases in which the national court would have intentionally violated or misapplied the EU law, constitutes in itself a manifest infringement of the EU law, since it is thoroughly obvious from the ECJ's ruling in *Köbler* that a state liability in case of judicial error cannot be limited to cases of intentional misapplication of the EC law. Actually it seems that the state liability in *Köbler* must, at least to some extend, correspond with a general principle of state liability in the EU law as established in *Francovich and Bonifaci v Italy*. This kind of liability could be either strict or based on negligence. Certainly it could be inadmissible to narrow the state liability in the EC law to cases of intentional torts, even if it could be acceptable in reference to English law. Moreover, the reference to the well-established practice of domestic courts seems to be based on misunderstanding of the EC law. Actually, the practice of national courts in this respect has not much to do with the evaluation of the application of the EU law. The case law of the CJEU could be regarded as a point of reference and certainly in case of any doubt, the national court could initiate the preliminary reference procedure.

It is quite obvious that the operation of the complex legal system such as the EU law as applied by courts in Member States can no longer be explained by purely normative analysis of the relationship between different rules within a legal system. It seems that the economic analysis of remedies could become a potential candidate for such an endeavour. According to R. Coase, commodities should be defined as bunches of rights transferred between parties.[29] These transfers may be either voluntary or involuntary. Voluntary transfers are carried out in the relevant market and under the condition that rights to

28 *Cooper v. Attorney General* [2010] WLR (D) 122.

29 R.H. Coase, The Problem of Social Cost. In: R.H. Coase (ed.), *The Firm, The Market and the Law* Chicago: The University of Chicago Press. 1988, pp. 95–156.

commodities are well defined and adequately protected. This could be achieved by the application of the property rules which effectively deter the potential trespasser and thus fully protect the entitlements. The scope of the market exchange is however limited by the fact that, in many cases, transaction costs are prohibitively high. In those cases the exchange could be channelled through the court system, where involuntary exchanges of rights for a given sum of money take the form of compensations awarded by the courts. Involuntary transfers play an important role in case of takings and expropriations by Member States, as well as in a wider area of tort liability.

This model has been extended by Calabresi and Melamed who proposed the concept of *transactional framework*.[30] This idea dates back to the seminal article of G. Calabresi and A.D. Melamed on *Property Rules, Liability Rules and Inalienability: One View of the Cathedral* where the Authors distinguished three different types of legal rules.[31] Property rules are protection oriented, for they exclude everybody, except the holder, from interfering with entitlement. Liability rules are compensation oriented, rewarding the owner with the value of an entitlement, determined by the state. Inalienability rules are intended to deter both potential parties from the transfer of entitlement, regardless of the consent of the holder of entitlement. There is no cost to be determined between parties or damage to be assessed. These three types of rules have evolved creating a characteristic framework for legal institutions across different branches of any legal system.[32] The detailed shape of this framework is however determined by specific national traditions or the peculiarities of civil law and common law systems. It is important that the distinction between different types of legal rules, as originally proposed by Calabresi and Melamed, rests upon the assumption that property and liability rules are protected by different sanctions.[33] On the one hand, property rules are deterrence oriented. The application of such a rule has to make the infringement of the right protected by a given property rule unprofitable. In a simple formula, costs faced by the potential defendant for the infringement of the protected entitlement should be set at $D > vD$ so that the defendant has no incentive to infringe a given right as the sum he has to pay always exceeds his own valuation of the entitlement. On the other hand, liability rules operate by rewarding the owner with some externally determined compensation that is usually set by a court, a legislator, or an administrative agency. In case of the infringement of the EU law, the amount of compensation is to be determined by the national court according to the national rules. Under a liability rule, the goal is to compensate the entitlement's holder while allowing a non-consensual taking. The defendant would appropriate the entitlement if its

30 G. Calabresi and A.D. Melamed, "Property Rules, Liability Rules, and Inalienability: One View of the Cathedral", *Harvard Law Review*, 85(1972), pp. 1089–1128.

31 *Ibidem*, pp. 1106–1115.

32 *Ibidem*, pp. 1108–1109.

33 *Ibidem*, pp. 1123–1125.

own valuation was higher than the compensation determined by the court, it is if $vD > D$, where vD denotes the defendants valuation of an entitlement and D denotes amount of damages awarded by the court. Concurringly, the goal of liability remedies is quite complex: they compensate the entitled party through the officially determined payment of a compensation usually in form of damages and additionally, they somehow allow a non-consensual access to the entitlement for the potential defendants who have a valuation of it relatively higher, at least, than the amount of damages. In the context of the EU law, if a Member State decides to infringe the individuals' entitlement protected by the EU law, then it has to pay damages. Accordingly, damages should equalize individual's (i.e. plaintiff's) valuation according to the equation: $D = Pv$. where D denotes amount of damages awarded by the court and Pv denotes the defendants valuation of the entitlement.

Given the universal application of the remedies, it is striking that among sanctions listed by Calabresi and Melamed, the sanction of invalidity or voidness has not been taken into account. It seems that this kind of sanction is all but a provisional one, leading to the application of one of virtually two sanctions: compensation or punishment.[34] The alleged deficiency of the Calabresian scheme of remedies does not, however, play any important role, as far as the application of the scheme to the EU law is concerned. Since it is impossible for the CJEU to reverse the verdict of the national court, the choice of the remedy concerns the punishment or the compensation exclusively, which means that, depending on the strategy deployed in a given case, the wrongful misapplication of the EU law could be sanctioned by property or liability rule.

The first is the case if the procedure of Article 258 and 260 TFEU is being implemented by the European Commission or the Member State. The second holds in case of the individual's claim against the state, according to the rule set out in *Francovich* and elaborated in *Köbler*. It could accordingly be stated, that the *public strategy* based on Article 250 TFEU implements the property rule, whereas the privatization strategy expressly adopted in *Köbler*, deploys the *liability rule*.

Figure 1. The matrix of property rules and liability rules (based on G. Calabresi and A.D. Melamed 1972, pp. 1111–1115)

Initial Entitlement	Property Rule	Liability Rule
Individual A	Rule 1	Rule 2
Member State B	Rule 3	Rule 4 (?)

Nevertheless, the possibility of application of liability rules in the EU law goes far beyond that if the recent development of the theory of *transactional framework* is

34 R. Cooter, "Prices and Sanctions", *Columbia Law Rev.* 84(1984), pp. 1537–1550.

to be taken into account.[35] According to the theory of optional law, the number of liability rules could be increased. The theory suggests that the liability rule rewarding damages to the potential injured party might be interpreted through the lenses of option theory as a rule granting the injurer the right to acquire an entitlement for a given price equal to the damage assessed by the court. Such a state of affairs resembles a situation in which the injurer (defendant) owns a *call option* over the entitlement. Such an option can be exercised at the price set equal to damage. Concurringly, two different liability rules are to be discernible. The rule according to which the holder keeps the entitlement subject to the condition, that the defendant would not exercise the option to acquire the entitlement, and the opposite rule giving the entitlement to the defendant subject to the fact that the plaintiff would not exercise the *call option*. Additionally, property rules may also be incorporated into this optional scheme. One may say that the difference between liability and property rules is quantitative instead of qualitative one. In case of property rules the price of the option is so high that the option is very unlikely to be exercised and this could be regarded as an equivalent of the sanction whose main purpose is deterrence. Under this perspective, property rules could be regarded as a special kind of liability rules with an exuberant price for the option. Additionally, the optional theory of remedies has enabled scholars to multiply the framework of remedies. Assuming that liability rule may be stylized as a *call option* (granted to plaintiff or defendant, hence, there are two rules), it is possible to propose an option to sell, namely the *put option*. The *put option* rule would grant an entitlement to one party and at the same time, it would confer the conditional right to sell the entitlement to the other party, the other party being under obligation to acquire the entitlement at will of the option holder. The extended matrix of the optional law remedies can be illustrated by the following figure:

Figure 2. Possible combinations of different optional rules (based on I. Ayres 2005, p. 17)

Type of rule	Individuals' options	Member State's options
Rule 1	Asset	0
Rule 2	Asset – Call	Call
Rule 3	0	Asset
Rule 4	Call	Asset – Call
Rule 5	– Put	Asset + Put
Rule 6	Asset + Put	– Put

35 I. Ayres, *Optional Law: The Structure of Legal Entitlements*, Chicago, Chicago University Press 2005, pp. 16–21.

Thus, one can consider the possibility of styling the liability rule set out against the background of the optional theory of law. Referring to the other figure (Figure 1) one should remark that the set of remedies could be much extended as illustrated on Figure 2. The liability rules of type 1 (pro plaintiff) and 2 (pro defendant) could now be divided in four types; call pro defendant, put pro defendant, call pro plaintiff and put pro plaintiff.

The main normative hypothesis presented by the theory of optional law concerns the choice between property and liability rules. There is no unanimity as far as such a choice between two types of rules is concerned. Additionally, there is no *opinio communis* about the set of factors that should determine the choice of the appropriate type of rule. For G. Calabresi and D. Melamed it seemed obvious that property rules were superior in low transaction cost settings, while liability rules were more efficient in high transaction cost settings. This initial position has given way to many contradictory theories and hypotheses. L. Kaplow and S. Shavell, for example, focus on the costs of administering litigation and conclude that liability rules are superior under many circumstances.[36] L. Bebchuk focuses on the incentive to invest *ex ante* in front of property or liability rules.[37] He comes to the conclusion that property rules give a stronger *ex ante* incentive to invest and are more efficient in this respect. I. Ayres presents the opposite solution. He claims that liability rules mitigate the risk of strategic behaviour and information asymmetry due to their "harnessing effect".[38] H. Smith occupies a contrary position when he supports the relative efficiency of property rules based on their intelligibility and respect for parties' "idiosyncratic valuations".[39] Summarizing, one may state that whereas property rules promote voluntary exchanges, liability rules enable involuntary transfers in cases of high transaction costs. Those involuntary transfers play an important role in cases of appropriations and expropriations by Member States, as well as in a wider area of tort liability. Empirical surveys show that the average compensation in the EU varies greatly from state to state. If liability rules are superior and privatization strategy expressed in deployment of the liability rules is going to supersede the public strategy based on protection of property rules, then couple of questions arise.

Firstly, what would be the actual reason for the superiority of the liability rules and what would be the potential result of that? According to the theory of optional law in a form proposed by I. Ayres, the main argument for liability rules and against property rules relays heavily on the concept of harnessing effect

---

36 L. Kaplow and S. Shavell, "Property Rules Versus Liability Rules", *Harvard Law Review*, 109(1996), p. 713.

37 L.A. Bebchuk, "Property Rights and Liability Rules: The Ex Ante View of the Cathedral", *Michigan Law Review*, 100(2001), p. 601.

38 I. Ayres, *Optional Law: The Structure of Legal Entitlements*, Chicago, Chicago University Press 2005, pp. 152–165.

39 H. E. Smith, "Exclusion Versus Governance: Two Strategies for Delineating Property Rights", *Journal of Legal Studies*, 31(2002), p. 453.

and the alleged information asymmetry. The liability regime is virtually more effective because it forces the potential plaintiff to reveal private information about the valuation of the entitlement. The courts may also more accurately divide the costs of application of the EU law, relaying on the doctrine of the manifest infringement. Thus, the court in place may still have a choice between the application of the pro liability or pro plaintiff remedies, which would be very difficult in case of property rules and public strategy.

The choice between property and liability rules reveals also some deeper relevant considerations. It is quite obvious that the application of the property rule enhances the protection of the entitlement. The application of the liability rules provides with much a weaker remedy although of a much more flexible and discretional character. If this line of reasoning is a proper one, then it seems that the protection of the individual's rights bestowed by the EU law is not regarded as a fundamental aim of the CJEU. The much more convincing explanation is that the CJEU tends to strengthen the efficacy of the EU law, applying the concept of the protection of the rights of individuals as a kind of pretext. If this allegation is correct, the future of the EU court system will heavily depend on the level of administrative costs and a coherency of judicial practice in different national courts.

The complex liaisons between the CJEU and national courts give rise to two additional problems. The first one concerns the negative externalities arising in case of non-standardized, heterogeneous or even contradictory practices of national courts applying the EU law. The second issue is a typical agency problem. National courts, especially courts of the last instance, are supposed to act as agents of the CJEU. However, the judicial independence and a relative autonomy of national legal systems do not offer a firm ground for a proper principal-agent relationship. On the one hand, the TFEU provides the CJEU with the exclusive competence to interpret the EU law; on the other hand, it lacks the power to maintain an effective control over the national courts. This paradoxical nature of the EU law has led the CJEU to produce various methods of coordination, such as the state liability for judicial error in the application of the EU law. It seems that the application of liability rules could enhance the coherence of the application of the EU law, since the national courts would adjudicate under the shadow of the appropriate liability rule. Nevertheless, this result is not obvious and it would be attained only in a case of coherent application of the liability rule as proposed in *Köbler* in different Member States. The result depends heavily on the level of administrative costs, and on accuracy of verdicts of the courts.

4. TENTATIVE CONCLUSION

In two recent cases, the Austrian and the German Federal Constitutional Courts suggested a proper application of the mixed *Köbler* doctrine to the EU

Charter. The paper offers a positive analysis of these propositions and some recommendations within the light of the economic analysis of judicial two-stage decision-making process under uncertainty, where the liability standard for breach of the EU law is treated as an exogenous and continuous variable. The courts seem to be accepting the CJEU doctrine provided the standard of liability have been weakened aligning the rise of potential costs of application of the EU law with decreasing costs of judicial error and the probability of damages in these cases. This attitude may of course lead to the spill-over effect and the "race to the bottom" was actually already started by the English Court of Appeal and some other courts in the EU Member States.

The practice of domestic courts such as this reflected in *Cooper v. Attorney General* proves the need of the existence of the *public strategy* based on the activity of the European Commission rather than on the practice of the domestic courts. It seems that the application of liability rules could enhance the coherence of the application of the EU law, since the national courts would adjudicate under the shadow of the appropriate property rule. Nevertheless, this result is not obvious and it would be attained only in a case of coherent application of the liability rule as proposed in *Köbler* in different Member States, based on the spill-over effect. On the other hand, the national courts might be even more eager to weaken the liability standard applied to the breach by the constitutional court, which may lead to the negative spill-over effect.

BIBLIOGRAPHY

Arnull, A., 'Me and My Shadow: The European Court of Justice and the Disintegration of European Union Law' 31 *Fordham International Law Journal*, (2007) 1174–1211.

Blutman, L., Chronowski, N., 'Hungarian Constitutional Court: Keeping Aloof from European Union Law' 5 *Vienna Journal on International Constitutional Law* (2011) 329–348.

Broberg, M. and Fenger, N., 'Variations in Member States' Preliminary References to the Court of Justice—Are Structural Factors (Part of) the Explanation?' 19 *European Law Journal*, (2013) 488–501.

Carrubba, C.J. and Murrah, L., 'Legal Integration and Use of the Preliminary Ruling Process in the European Union' 59 *International Organization* (2005) 399–418.

Carrubba, C.J., Gabel, M. and Hankla, C., (2008), 'Judicial Behavior under Political Constraints: Evidence from the European Court of Justice', 102 *American Political Science Review* 435–452.

Komárek, J., 'European constitutionalism and the European arrest warrant: in search of the limits of 'contrapunctual principles' 44 *Common Market Law Review* (2007) (1) 9–40.

Komarek, J., 'Czech constitutional court playing with matches: the Czech constitutional court declares a judgment of the court of justice of the EU ultra vires; judgment of 31 January 2012, Pl. ÚS 5/12' 8 *European Constitutional Law Review* (2013) 323–337.

Kumm, M., 'Who is the Final Arbiter of Constitutionality in Europe?: Three Conceptions of the Relationship Between the German Federal Constitutional Court and the European Court of Justice', 36 *Common Market Law Review* (1999) 351–386.

Kumm, M., 'The Jurisprudence of Constitutional Conflict: Constitutional Supremacy in Europe before and after the Constitutional Treaty', 11 *European Law Journal* (2003) 262–307.

Lindberg, L.N., *The Political Dynamics of European Economic Integration*, Stanford University Press 1963.

Łazowski, A. (Ed.) *The Application of EU Law in the New Member States: Brave New World*, T.M.C. Asser Press 2010.

Moravcsik, A., 'Preferences and Power in the European Community: A Liberal Intergovernmentalist Approach', 31 Journal of Common Market Studies (1993) 473–524.

Sadurski, W., 'Solange, Chapter 3': Constitutional Courts in Central Europe - Democracy - European Union', 14 *European Law Journal* (2008) 1–35.

Sadurski, W., *Constitutionalism and the Enlargement of Europe*, Oxford University Press 2012.

Sajo, A. 'Learning Co-operative Constitutionalism the Hard Way: the Hungarian Constitutional Court Shying Away from EU Supremacy', 3 *Zeitschrift für Staats- und Europawissenschaften* (2004) 351–371.

Stone Sweet, A., 'Judicialization and the Construction of Governance', 32 *Comparative Political Studies* (1999) 147–184.

Stone Sweet, A., *The Judicial Construction of Europe*, Oxford University Press 2004.

Stone Sweet, A. 'The Juridical Coup d'État and the Problem of Authority', 8 *German Law Journal* (2007) 915–926.

Stone Sweet, A. and Brunell, T.L., 'The European Court of Justice, State Noncompliance,and the Politics of Override', 106 *American Political Science Review* (2012) 204–2013.

Weiler, J.H.H., 'The Transformation of Europe', 100 *Yale Law Journal*, (1991) 2403–2483.

Weiler, J.H.H., 'A Quiet Revolution: The European Court of Justice and its Interlocutors', 26 *Comparative Political Studies* (1994) 510–534.

4. TOWARDS THE DEMOCRATIZATION OF THE EU?

Strengthening prerogatives of the European Parliament in the case law of the Court of Justice of the European Union

Agnieszka PIEKUTOWSKA*

Department of European Law, Faculty of Law, University of Bialystok

1. INTRODUCTION

Individuals conceptualize the term *democracy* in a variety of ways. While in the 19th century democracy was associated with a direct form of government in Athenian style, a major breakthrough with the development of nation-states and the prevalence of representation was the foundation for the development of representative democracy.

Representation means transformation of the individuals' will to the will of the political institutions. Thus, in a representative democracy, public authorities should have democratic legitimacy following citizens' choice. This statement is a starting point for the reflection in terms of democratic legitimacy, reflection transposed on the ground of the integration processes in Europe. As a result of the creation of the European Community and the European Union, there has been a further relocation of the part of public power. Therefore, public powers exercised by the EU institutions must have democratic legitimacy.

There is a consent that mainstream theories of state democratization are ill-equipped to explain EU democratization as they are bonded to the nation-state context.[1] The issue of democratic deficit in the EC yielded a vast, heterogeneous literature, notably after the publication of the Tindemans report in 1975, in which, for the very first time, the distance between citizens and the institutions

---

* Email: piekutowska@uwb.edu.pl.

1 F. Schimmelfennig, The Normative Origins of Democracy in the European Union: Towards a Transformationalist Theory of Democratization, (2009) *Challenges to Democracy in the 21st Century National Centre of Competence in Research Working Paper*, No 39, p. 7.

of the EC was acknowledged.[2] Thus, a wide debate on political reforms so as to achieve a more democratic EU has been started, bringing numerous potential solutions to this problem that vary in range and scope. In the debate on democratic deficit in the EU, it is argued that the EU policy is dominated by unelected bodies and directly elected EP plays a secondary role. As a result, the claims on greater power of parliamentary assembly arose such as – for instance – a proposal that the EP should have an independent power of legislative initiative. Majone finds such an argumentation as based on the analogy with national institutions.[3] Moravcsik adds that political decision-making should not always be majoritarian and this could be the case in Europe.[4] Still, the Community's 50-year trajectory "from an international organization with very limited traits of democracy to one that has the major institutional trappings of a democratic polity" is marked by the enhancement of the European Parliament's prerogatives.[5]

With the introduction of direct elections to the European Parliament in the institutional structure of the Community, a directly legitimated body appeared.[6] The first, direct elections to the EP gave rise to the process of strengthening the position of the European Parliament. Representative character of this institution was the starting point for justifying the need for the defence of its competencies. Such argumentation was used by the Court of Justice in its judgments.

Participation of the European Parliament in the legislative process, as the Court of Justice of the European Union (CJEU) stated in its judgments, reflects, at Community level, "fundamental democratic principle that the peoples should take part in the exercise of power through the intermediary of a representative assembly".[7] In the same spirit, the Court of First Instance stated that at Community level, the fundamental democratic principle assumes that "the people must share in the exercise of power through a representative assembly".[8] Thus, democratic principle is reflected by the participation of the European

---

2 O. Ruchet, Cultural diversity, European identity and legitimacy of the EU: A review of the debate, in D. Fuchs, H-D. Klingemann (eds), *Cultural Diversity, European Identity and the Legitimacy of the EU*, Edward Elgar 2011, p. 3.

3 G. Majone, Democracy and Constitutionalism in the European Union, (2000) *ECSA Review* Vol 13, No 2, p. 4.

4 A. Moravcsik, Democracy and Constitutionalism in the European Union, (2000) *ECSA Review* Vol 13, No 2, p. 6.

5 F. Schimmelfennig, The Normative Origins of Democracy in the European Union: Towards a Transformationalist Theory of Democratization, (2009) *Challenges to Democracy in the 21st Century National Centre of Competence in Research Working Paper*, No 39, p. 3.

6 Sz. Pawłowski, Zasada legitymizacji władzy, in Z. Brodecki (ed), *Europa Sędziów*, LexisNexis Warszawa 2007, p. 335.

7 The Judgment of the Court of Justice of 29 October 1980, Case 138/79, (*SA Roquette Frères v Council of the European Communities*), ECLI:EU:C:1980:249, paragraph 33.

8 The Judgment of the Court of First Instance of 17 June 1998, Case T-135–96, (*Union Européenne de l'artisanat et des petites et moyennes entreprises (UEAPME) v Council of the European Union*), ECLI:EU:T:1998:128, para. 88.

Parliament in the Community legislative process. Therefore, the respect for the principles of democracy at the European level has been provided, *inter alia*, through the participation of the European Parliament in the legislative process.

First, direct elections to the European Parliament raised high expectations, as to legitimize European policies through the electoral process. As Tindemans said "the election of your Assembly by universal suffrage would undoubtedly set the seal on the authority of Community democracy".[9]

Recognizing that the representative character of the European Parliament is based on the democratic mandate of the representatives elected in direct elections reflects – albeit to a limited extent – the principle of democracy – this article seeks to explore the role of the Court of Justice of the European Union in the field of protecting the EP's prerogatives as well as the role of the CJEU in their development. The main hypothesis of this article is as follows: by teleological, dynamic interpretation of the provisions of the Treaties, the CJEU has played an important role in the development of the prerogatives of the EP, using as a premise the EP's democratic legitimacy. Acting with "the spirit of the Treaties", through its line of jurisprudence, the Court follows the changes resulting from the integration processes, setting also its directions.

Recognizing that in the institutional structure of the EU it is the EP that sets "the seal on the authority of Community democracy", in the context of the democratization process in this structure, disputes on its competencies are of great importance.

2. THE DEFENCE OF THE PREROGATIVES OF THE EUROPEAN PARLIAMENT BEFORE THE CJEU. PRE-LISBON CASE-LAW

The analysis of the CJEU's role in the field of the protecting EP's prerogatives starts with an issue of *légitimation passive* and *légitimation active* of the European Parliament. In the following part of this paper the most meaningful CJEU judgments in that respect will be presented. To show the evolution of the Court's standpoint, a chronological approach was used.

It must be borne in mind that before the amendments were introduced by the Maastricht Treaty, the former Articles 173 EEC Treaty and 146 the Euratom Treaty[10] did not provide for *locus standi* of the European Parliament. Due to the fact that

9 L. Tindemans, Debates of the European Parliament 1975–1976 Session. Report of Proceedings from 7 to 11 July 1975 (Sitting of Wednesday, 9 July 1975), OJ, p. 129.

10 Article 173 of the EEC Treaty and Article 146 of the EAEC Treaty provided that: 'The Court of Justice shall review the legality of acts of the Council and the Commission [...]. It shall for this purpose have jurisdiction in actions brought by a Member State, the Council or the Commission [...]'.

the Parliament strove for a role in the decision-making process of the Community commensurate with its ambitions, in the absence of Treaty amendments, it became inevitable that the CJEU needs to resolve the issue.[11] Analysing the Court's case law on the *locus standi* of the EP it is essential to recall: Case 230/81 (*Luxembourg v European Parliament*), Case 294/83 (*Les Verts*) and Case 70/88 (*Chernobyl*). Those judgments were broken by Case 302/87 (*Comitology*).

In Case 230/81 (*Luxembourg v European Parliament*) the CJEU acknowledged that EP was not entitled to appear either actively or passively in proceedings, according to the EEC Treaty and EAEC Treaty. However the Article 38 of the ECSC Treaty[12] applied in this case, thus the EP could be a party to proceedings.[13]

The issue of *légitimation passive* of the EP was also raised in Case 294/83 (*Les Verts*), the subject of which were two decisions of the Bureau of the EP concerning the allocation of funds related to preparations for the next European elections. An applicant – political party – brought an action for annulment under Article 173 EEC Treaty recognizing that the Court's power to review the legality of measures adopted by the institutions under this article cannot be limited only to acts of the Council and the Commission "without giving rise to a denial of justice".[14] The EP stated likewise. In the opinion of the Parliament the list of potential defendants in Article 173 EEC Treaty was not exhaustive.

In its judgment the CJEU made momentous statements on the nature of the system established by the Treaty and the importance of judicial review.[15] Firstly, the Court emphasized that the EEC is based on the rule of law, therefore, its institutions cannot avoid considering the question whether the measures adopted by them are in conformity "with the basic constitutional charter, the Treaty". Although Article 173 refers only to acts of the Council and the Commission, the system established by the EEC Treaty is to make a direct action available against all measures adopted by the institutions. This system of legal remedies and procedures was designed to permit the CJEU to review the legality of measures adopted by the institutions. Thus, CJEU stated that "an action for annulment may lie against measures adopted by the European Parliament intended to have legal effects *vis-à-vis* third parties".[16]

---

11 A. Arnull, *The European Union and its Court of Justice*, Oxford EC Law Library, New York 1999, p. 34.

12 Art 38 of the ECSC Treaty stated that: 'The Court may, on application by a Member State or the High Authority, declare an act of the Assembly or of the Council to be void'.

13 The Judgment of the Court of Justice of 10 February 1983 – Case 230/81, (*Grand Duchy of Luxembourg v European Parliament*), ECLI:EU:C:1983:32, para. 17, para. 20.

14 The Judgment of the Court of Justice of 23 April 1986 – Case 294/83, (*Les Verts v Parliament*), ECLI:EU:C:1986:166, para. 21.

15 A. Arnull, *The European Union and its Court of Justice*, Oxford EC Law Library, New York 1999, p. 35.

16 The Judgment of the Court of Justice of 23 April 1986 – Case 294/83, (*Les Verts v Parliament*), ECLI:EU:C:1986:166, para. 25.

The judgment in *Les Verts* Case plays an important role in the scope of developing the EP prerogatives, underlying the dynamic character of the EP competencies. According to the CJEU, the EP was not mentioned in Article 173 of the EEC Treaty, since the original version of the Treaty of Rome conferred powers of consultation and political control on it. Over time, the position of the EP has been changing, including the right to adopt measures that would influence third parties.

When the Court departed – in *Les Verts* Case – from the literal interpretation of Article 173 EEC Treaty (recognizing the Parliament's *légitimation passive*), the question of the Parliament's *légitimation active* arose. As the EP raised in the *Les Verts* Case, such a departure from the strict wording of Article 173 EEC Treaty should in turn lead to the capacity of the EP to bring an action against measures adopted by the Council and the Commission. To resolve this issue the volte-face was needed.[17] In the Case 302/87, known as *Comitology*, the EP's attempt (the action for annulment brought against the Council's decision, generally known as the 'comitology' decision) failed due to the procedural question of its standing to bring annulment actions. The European Parliament was a long standing enemy of comitology, possessing a suspicion that its arcane procedures had been placed to subvert parliamentary competences.[18] The EP argued that if it had no power to bring actions for annulment, it could not defend its prerogatives against the other institutions.[19] Even though the EP argued that the decision infringes the institutional balance due to lack of *locus standi*, the Parliament was nonetheless to continue its campaign against the regulatory committee procedure.[20] The Court asserted that the EP had no power to bring actions for annulment relying purely on literal interpretation[21] of Article 173 EEC Treaty. This decision is characterized as unconvincing.[22] As the Court argued, responsibility for ensuring that the Parliament's prerogatives are respected were provided for in the Treaty. By virtue of Article 155 EEC Treaty, this responsibility was conferred on the Commission.

---

17 A. Arnull, *The European Union and its Court of Justice*, Oxford EC Law Library, New York 1999, p. 36.

18 M. Everson and F. Rodrigues, A crisis of governance. Can comitology theory help legitimise ECB/ESCB operations? in E. Chiti, A.J. Menéndez and P.G. Teixeira (eds), *The European Rescue of the European Union? The existential crisis of the European political project*, Centre for European Studies, University of Oslo, Oslo 2012, p. 195.

19 The Judgment of the Court of Justice of 27 September 1988 – Case 302/87, (*European Parliament v Council of the European Communities*), ECLI:EU:C:1988:461, paragraph 25.

20 E. Vos, The Rise of Committees, (1997) *European Law Journal*, Vol 3, No. 3, p. 213.

21 Literal interpretation is characterized by limited usefulness, for example, due to multilingualism. Furthermore, the dynamic nature of integration processes in Europe (and difficulties with amending the treaties) requires the Court to ensure that the right corresponds to the constantly changing reality; T.T. Koncewicz, *Zasada jurysdykcji powierzonej Trybunału Sprawiedliwości Wspólnot Europejskich*, Oficyna a Wolters Kluwer business, Warszawa 2009, p. 147.

22 V. Georgiev, 'Comitology and Parliamentarisation: Strong Causality and Weak Interaction', (2012) *Journal of Contemporary European Research* Volume 8, Issue 1, p. 113.

In May 1990, (i.e. less than two years after the judgment in the *Comitology* Case), such reasoning could not be upheld. As the EP was dissatisfied with the Court's statement that the defence of its prerogatives could be left in the Commission's hands, it continued in another case (Case 70/88, *Chernobyl).* In this case, the EP brought an action for annulment of a Council regulation (adopted under Article 31 of the Euratom Treaty requiring consultation with Parliament). Since the Commission did not comply with the EP's request to change the legal basis (namely to Article 100a of the EEC Treaty requiring the cooperation procedure – introduced by the Single European Act, enhancing the role of the EP in the decision-making process), the Parliament argued that it could not rely on the Commission in the scope of defending its prerogatives. Hence, the Court had to acknowledge that it could not be expected from the Commission to adopt the Parliament's position and bring an action for annulment which the Commission itself considers unfounded. Thus, this measure of protecting EP's prerogatives could be ineffective.

As the Court stated in the *Chernobyl* judgment, there was "a legal vacuum which the Court must fill by recognizing that the European Parliament has capacity to bring an action for annulment",[23] although only as to safeguard its prerogatives under the legislative procedure. By the 1990 ruling the Court granted the European Parliament the right to bring before the Court actions to have decisions declared void. The judgment in the *Chernobyl* Case is a return to the *Les Verts* line: it is a departure from the literal method of interpretation, which after *Les Verts* came back with all the power in the *Comitology.*

The CJEU judgment in *Chernobyl* Case is recognized as one of the most explicit examples of judicial activism and the clearest "example of changing the law while supposedly interpreting it."[24] The *Chernobyl* Case illustrates the active role of the case law of the CJEU. The Court not only departed from literal interpretation of the law but also reinterpreted its own judgment, doing so on the basis of the institutional balance principle. How far the Court went in *Chernobyl* Case was confirmed by the Treaty of Maastricht, in which, the states decided to change Article 230 (ex 173), including *verbatim*, a fragment of the judgment (in which the Court allowed an action for annulment derived from the EP to protect its prerogatives).

The subject of numerous CJEU judgments were also prerogatives of the European Parliament in the field of: participation in the legislative process (e.g. Case C-13/83 *European Parliament v Council of the European Communities* or Case C-417/93 *European Parliament v Council of the European Union)* where the Court held that "the Parliament has to be reconsulted on each occasion on which

---

23 The Judgment of the Court of Justice of 22 May 1990 – Case 70/88, (*European Parliament v Council of the European Communities*), ECLI:EU:C:1991:373, para. 8.

24 T.C. Hartley, *The Foundation of European Union Law.* 8th ed, Oxford University Press, 2014, p. 75.

the text finally adopted, viewed as a whole, departs substantially from the text on which the Parliament has already been consulted"[25] or in the scope of budgetary powers (Case 294/83, *Les Verts*).

3. POST-LISBON JUDGMENTS OF THE CJEU ON THE EP'S PREROGATIVES

Until the Treaty of Maastricht, advisory and consultative power of the Parliament were the only "means of involving the peoples of the Community in the drafting of Community legal measures" and every attempt to "weaken participation of the peoples of the Member States in legislation" could not be accepted.[26] It seems that the CJEU has a history of ruling in favour of protecting EP prerogatives. With the entry into force of the Lisbon Treaty, the EP's legislative powers were increased. In the scope of the process of democratization of the EU it should be considered both as an achievement and as a challenge. That is why it is necessary to present an overview of the post-Lisbon CJEU judgments on EP's prerogatives. In the light of the judgments, like in Case C-130/10, it seems that the argument that "participation by the Parliament in the legislative process is the reflection, at Union level, of the fundamental democratic principle" is still used by the CJEU.[27]

To some extent, it could be regarded as natural that the changes introduced by the Treaty of Lisbon could give rise to certain ambiguities with regard to the new practice of the functioning of the EU institutions, affecting also the institutional balance. Such ambiguities appeared in the scope of the process of the budgetary procedure in 2010, by which the European Union general budget was adopted for the financial year 2011. The manner in which this procedure was conducted (for the first time based entirely on the basis of Article 314 TFEU) has become the subject of dispute between the Council of the European Union and the European Parliament (Case C 77/11, *Council of the European Union v European Parliament*).

By its action, the Council requested the Court to annul the act of the President of the European Parliament declaring the final adoption of the general budget of the EU. Recognizing that the Treaty of Lisbon changed the budgetary procedure significantly, the Council argued that its prerogatives were affected by the lack of adoption of a joint legislative act signed by the President of each of these two institutions that are its authors. It was also emphasized that within the framework of the budgetary function, neither of these entities is higher in the

25 The Judgment of the Court of Justice of 10 May 1995 – Case C-417/93, (*European Parliament v Council of the European Communities*), ECLI:EU:C:1995:127, paragraph 17.

26 The Opinion of the Advocate General – AG Reischl of 18 September 1980 in Case 138/79, (*SA Roquette Frères v Council of the European Communities*), ECLI:EU:C:1980:213, p. 3375.

27 The Judgment of the Court of Justice of 19 July 2012 – Case C-130/10, (*European Parliament v Council of the European Union*), ECLI:EU:C:2012:472, paragraph 81.

hierarchy. Thus, the Council alleged a failure to observe institutional balance, noting that both branches of the budgetary authority are henceforth on an equal footing, with the same privileges and no institution can have the last word on the act which has to be agreed jointly.

The President of the Parliament had a contrary view and acknowledged that the Treaty of Lisbon did not change the fact that the President of the Parliament declares that the budget has been finally adopted and that doing so, he signs the budget in accordance with Article 314(9) TFEU.[28] Justifying his attitude, the Parliament found that the assertion of the Council, stating that no institution has the last word on the joint legislative act, is erroneous. In this regard, the EP argued that TFEU envisages a situation when the Parliament (after the fulfilment of the essential requirements) may state that the budget has been adopted even if only the Parliament approves the joint text whilst the Council rejects it. Hence, the signing of a joint act by the European Parliament and the Council seems to be illogical procedure. In the opinion of the Advocate General – Yves Bot, considering this situation, it is difficult to argue that the authors of the Treaties were going to make the adoption of the budget dependent on the signature of the President of the Council, even when this institution has rejected a joint text.[29]

The Court dismissed the action. In the opinion of the Court, the introductory paragraph of Article 314 TFEU[30] states that the budget is to be adopted in accordance with a special legislative procedure.[31] Therefore, the argument of the Council underlying its allegations, which equates budgetary procedure with the ordinary legislative procedure, must be rejected.[32]

Another case (C-658/11, *European Parliament v Council of the European Union*) also indicates that the entry into force of the Treaty of Lisbon may give rise to vagueness with regard to the new roles and power of the EU institutions (in this case in the framework of Common Foreign and Security Policy, CFSP, which, as this case reveals, is not immune to the EP's advances).[33]

---

28 Article 314(9) TFEU provides that: 'When the procedure provided for in this article has been completed, the President of the European Parliament shall declare that the budget has been definitively adopted'.

29 The Opinion of the Advocate General – Yves Bot of 28 May 2013 in Case C-77/11 (*Council of the European Union v European Parliament*), ECLI:EU:C:2013:330, point 74.

30 Article 314(1) TFEU is worded as follows: 'The European Parliament and the Council, acting in accordance with a special legislative procedure, shall establish the Union's annual budget…'.

31 In accordance with Article 297(1) TFEU: 'Legislative acts adopted under the ordinary legislative procedure shall be signed by the President of the European Parliament and by the President of the Council. Legislative acts adopted under a special legislative procedure shall be signed by the President of the institution which adopted them'.

32 The Judgment of the Court of Justice of 17 September 2013 in Case C-77/11, (*Council of the European Union v European Parliament*), ECLI:EU:C:2013:559.

33 J. Larik, Democratic scrutiny of EU Foreign Policy: from pirates to the power of the people, available at: http://europeanlawblog.eu/?p=2469, retrieved: 25 August 2014.

The EP brought an action for annulment of the decision adopted without its involvement. The first plea in law concerned the infringement of Article 218(6) TFEU.[34] In the opinion of the EP, the absence of the participation of the EP can take place only in cases 'where agreements relate exclusively to the [CFSP]'. The Parliament argued that the fact that the contested decision and the agreement assumed – albeit only incidentally – purposes other than those covered by the CFSP, is sufficient to rule out that decision is only covered by the CFSP.

The Court did not accept such interpretation of the provision, noting that if the analysis of the measure shows that it pursues two goals and one of these objectives can be identified as the main, then the act must be founded on a single legal basis – the one that is required by main purpose. According to the CJEU, the procedure in Article 218(6) TFEU takes into account the specific features which the Treaties lay down in each field of action of the Union, in particular as regards the powers of the institutions. Nevertheless, the role that the Treaty of Lisbon has entrusted to the Parliament in the CFSP area remains limited. Ultimately, the Court held that the contested decision could be adopted without the consent or consultation of the EP.[35]

While this could satisfy the Council, it still lost the case on the second plea in law. As much as the "special" status of the CFSP was a basis for Court's findings in the first plea in law, "democratic legitimacy" governed the second,[36] which is especially interesting as the CFSP has been criticized for its lack of democratic legitimacy.[37]

In the second plea in law, the Parliament stated that the Council sending the Parliament the text of the decision and of the agreement more than three months after the adoption of this decision and the signing of the agreement and seventeen days after their publication in the Official Journal of the European Union – infringed Article 218(10) TFEU.[38]

The Court has acknowledged that the failure to satisfy the information requirement led to the nullity of the contested decision. The Court could have concluded at that stage, but instead it continued expounding the democratic credentials of the EP. As the Court stated, the aim of the requirement to inform

---

34 Article 281(6) TFEU provides that: '[...] Except where agreements relate exclusively to the common foreign and security policy, the Council shall adopt the decision concluding the agreement:
(a) after obtaining the consent of the European Parliament [...]
(b) after consulting the European Parliament in other cases [...]'.

35 The Judgment of the Court of Justice of 24 June 2014 in Case C-658/11, (*European Parliament v Council of the European Union)*, ECLI:EU:C:2014:2025, para. 62.

36 J. Larik, Democratic scrutiny of EU Foreign Policy: from pirates to the power of the people, available at: http://europeanlawblog.eu/?p=2469, retrieved: 25 August 2014.

37 M. Romaniello, The international role of the European Parliament: the SWIFT Affair and the 're-assessed' European institutional balance of power, (2013) *Perspectives on Federalism* Vol 5, issue 1, p. 98.

38 Article 218(10) TFEU states that: 'The European Parliament shall be immediately and fully informed at all stages of the procedure'.

the EP is to ensure that the Parliament is able to carry out 'democratic scrutiny of the European Union's external action' and verify if its powers are respected. Once again (recalling, *inter alia*, the judgment in Case 138/79, *Roquette Frères v Council*) the Court in its ruling regarding the EP's prerogatives appealed to the democratic legitimacy of this institution, evoking once more that 'the Parliament's involvement in the decision-making process is the reflection, at EU level, of the fundamental democratic principle that the people should participate in the exercise of power through the intermediary of a representative assembly'.

The amendments introduced by the Treaty of Lisbon in the field of the EP's competence also resulted in the changes in the organization of its work. As far as the Parliament's competence to decide on their internal organization conferred on the EP under Article 232 TFEU[39] is concerned, it is reasonable to evoke the judgment in joined Cases C-237/11 and C-238/11 *(French Republic v European Parliament)*. The subject of dispute was the votes of the European Parliament on the calendar for the EP plenary sessions for the years 2012 and 2013. According to the calendar, two two-day plenary part-sessions in the same week of October were fixed, which was considered by the French Republic as contrary to the protocols concerning the seats of the institutions,[40] and an action for annulment was brought.

The French Republic argued that the contested votes show a paradox: the duration of parliamentary plenary sessions is being limited, whereas the tasks of this institution are constantly increasing.

The Parliament argued that the protocols on the seats of the institutions do not specify the duration of monthly plenary sessions, and the determination of their duration is the task of the EP, falling within the EP's power to adopt rules for its own internal organisation. The Parliament also argued that the protocols on the seats of the institutions should be interpreted in such a way so as not to deprive the effectiveness of its prerogatives with regard to its internal organisation. This effectiveness would mean that the EP has the right – with two plenary sessions in the same week – to minimize the economic, transport and environmental burdens arising from the plurality of its working places. The Parliament also stressed that as a result of the entry into force of the Treaty of Lisbon, the budgetary procedure was simplified and only one reading is required, hence the budget session mentioned in the protocols is unnecessary.

According to the CJEU, the contested votes resulted in a significant reduction in the time that the Parliament could devote for its debates in October 2012 and October 2013. In the light of the expansion of the Parliament's areas of competence, the Parliament did not provide reasons to justify the limitation of the duration of sessions. In particular, the Court emphasized that the exercise

39 Article 232 TFEU provides that: 'The European Parliament shall adopt its Rules of Procedure, acting by a majority of its Members'.

40 Protocol no 6 on the location of the seats of the institutions and of certain bodies, offices, agencies and departments of the European Union annexed to the EU Treaty and to the Treaty on the Functioning of the European Union.

by the Parliament – in plenary session – its budgetary power is 'a fundamental event in the democratic life of the European Union',[41] therefore, must be carried out with all diligence and commitment.

In the opinion of the Advocate General Paolo Mengozzi, it becomes reasonable to assume that the planned meetings of the EP in October 2012 and October 2013 was artificially split into two in order to meet the formal requirements. The Court held that the contested votes must be annulled to the extent that they do not provide twelve monthly plenary sessions in Strasbourg in the years 2012 and 2013.[42]

European Parliament found the action of the French Republic as an attempt to declare a failure to fulfil the EP's obligations. Such legal remedy has not been provided for in the Treaties. The Court's judgment, however, contains certain threads pointing to the need for careful execution of tasks belonging to the Parliament, which, during the proceedings, itself justified its reasons by the circumstance that the EP 'is the only institution which is directly elected by the citizens'.[43]

4. CONCLUSION

It is clear from the judgments of the Court that Parliament's prerogatives are part of the institutional balance (and the protection of these prerogatives is justified, even in the absence of a specific provision, which simply would give the Parliament the right to bring an action for annulment).[44]

The Court in its judgment in the *Chernobyl* Case once more referred to institutional balance principle. For the Court, this principle is a substitute for the principle of the separation of powers which, in Montesquieu's original exposition of his philosophy, aimed to protect individuals against the abuse of power.[45] Although the issue how far the principle of institutional balance can be associated with one of the fundamental principles characteristic of modern democratic countries (namely the principle of separation of powers) is disputable, one of the arguments in this discussion seems to have great significance in the considerations over the issue of 'towards the democratization of the EU'. Bearing

---

41 The Judgment of the Court of 13 December 2012 in joined Cases C-237/11 and C-238/11, (*French Republic v European Parliament*), ECLI: EU:C:2012:796, paragraph 68.

42 The judgment of the Court of 13 December 2012 in joined Cases C-237/11 and C-238/11, (*French Republic v European Parliament*), ECLI: EU:C:2012:796.

43 The Opinion of the Advocate General – Paolo Mengozzi of 6 September 2012 in joined Cases C-237/11 and C-238/11, (*French Republic v European Parliament*), ECLI: EU:C:2012:545, point 43.

44 The Judgment of the Court of 22 May 1990 – Case 70/88 (*European Parliament v Council of the European Communities*), ECLI:EU:C:1991:373.

45 J.P. Jacqué, The principle of institutional balance, (2004) *Common Market Law Review* Vol 41, p. 383.

in mind that the degree of the impact of EU regulations on the legal status of the individuals is significant (as a consequence of, *inter alia*, the principle of the primacy of EU law over national law) and the preservation of institutional balance would be a manifestation of maintaining the traditional separation of powers, it is a kind of the guarantee which respects the rights of individuals.

Furthermore, the principle of institutional balance has a dual nature: a strictly legal and political one. Speaking in legal terms, the principle of institutional balance implies that the EU institutions and the Member States act within the limits of their spheres of competence as provided for by the treaties. The concept is conceived in a static way, aimed at protecting the legal prerogatives and safeguarding the interests of institutions and the rights of individuals. Speaking in political terms, the principle of institutional balance is perceived as the relative power position of EU institutions regarding also institutional behaviour. Such a point of view has a dynamic application.[46] The political element assumes that the principle of institutional balance will be interpreted in the light of evolution that is inevitable in the Community. In the *Chernobyl* Case, the principle was not used by the Court in a static manner, but on the contrary, the Court relied on it to supplement the Treaty in a dynamic way.[47] Although the Court was consistently referring to the institutional balance "introduced by the Treaty"[48] (i.e. under a static aspect), it is evident that the balance established by the Treaties has developed radically through the history of the Community. Incidentally, as far as relations within the institutional triangle are concerned, the history of the Community is marked by the progressive growth of the powers of the Parliament.[49]

The EP power has increased dramatically through the successive Treaty reforms which are followed by certain ambiguities (also in the scope of new institutional balance). These ambiguities raise doubts about the meaning of the provision hence a need for interpretation arises and the CJEU can play its role here.

Assessment of the role of the CJEU in the European integration process is performed mainly around two opposing perspectives. In the first one, the CJEU, which pursues purposive (teleological) approach while interpreting the Treaties, is considered as the motor of this integration. The supporters of the other perspective recognize that the CJEU going beyond the interpretation of the text of the Treaty established by the treaty-makers "makes law" and is therefore guilty of judicial activism.[50]

---

46 M. Romaniello, The international role of the European Parliament: the SWIFT Affair and the 're-assessed' European institutional balance of power, *Perspectives on Federalism* (2013), Vol 5., issue 1, pp. 100–101.

47 J.P. Jacqué, The principle of institutional balance, (2004) *Common Market Law Review* Vol 41, pp. 383–387.

48 T. Dubowski, *Zasada równowagi instytucjonalnej w prawie Unii Europejskiej*, EuroPrawo, Warszawa 2010, p. 151.

49 J.P. Jacqué, The principle of institutional balance, (2004) *Common Market Law Review* Vol 41, p. 387.

50 D. Edward, Foreword to "*Zasada jurysdykcji powierzonej Trybunału Sprawiedliwości Wspólnot Europejskich*" by T.T. Koncewicz, Oficyna Wolters Kluwer business, Warszawa 2009, pp. 21–22.

Understanding the role of the CJEU requires identification of certain basic principles, concepts and values that lie behind and are the foundation of its judicial activity. Using teleological (purposive) interpretation the Court refers not only to the wording of the provision but also to the purpose of provision which is the subject to interpretation. In the case of the Treaties – at the top of the hierarchy of EU law – this purpose should be sought in the preamble, having the nature of a specific compass for the interpretation of subsequent provisions.[51] And the Preamble of the TEU clearly indicates "attachment to the principles of democracy (...)" and desire "to enhance further the democratic and efficient functioning of the institutions".[52]

As the Court of Justice of the European Union clearly indicates, "where there are several possible interpretations of Community law, it is appropriate to choose the one which best enables the full attainment of the democratic values of the Union."[53] Thus, the representative character of the European Parliament acknowledged as reflecting – albeit to a limited extent – the principle of democracy, comprises durable premise in CJEU rulings in the field of protecting the EP's prerogatives (as well as in their development).

Concluding, the strengthening of the role of the European Parliament was the result of, *inter alia*, judicial activity of the CJEU using as a premise EP's democratic legitimacy. However, the recent case-law indicates interesting direction. This democratic legitimacy of the EP could not only be a premise in the field of protecting the EP's prerogatives but also a circumstance which could constitute a reference point while alluding to the need for sound execution of tasks belonging to the European Parliament.

BIBLIOGRAPHY

BOOKS AND ARTICLES

Arnull A., *The European Union and its Court of Justice*, Oxford EC Law Library, New York 1999.

Dubowski T., *Zasada równowagi instytucjonalnej w prawie Unii Europejskiej*, EuroPrawo, Warszawa 2010.

Everson M. and Rodrigues F., A crisis of governance. Can comitology theory help legitimise ECB/ESCB operations? in Chiti E., Menéndez A. J. and Teixeira P.G. (eds.),

51 T.T. Koncewicz, *Zasada jurysdykcji powierzonej Trybunału Sprawiedliwości Wspólnot Europejskich*, Oficyna Wolters Kluwer business, Warszawa 2009, p. 150.

52 Consolidated version of the Treaty on European Union, Preamble, points 4 and 7.

53 The Judgment of the Court of First Instance of 2 October 2001 in joined Cases T-222/99, T-327/99 and T-329/99, (*Jean-Claude Martinez, Charles de Gaulle, Front national and Emma Bonino and Others v European Parliament*), ECLI:EU:T:2001:242, paragraph 196.

The European Rescue of the European Union? The existential crisis of the European political project, Centre for European Studies, University of Oslo, Oslo 2012.

Georgiev, V., 'Comitology and Parliamentarisation: Strong Causality and Weak Interaction', (2012) *Journal of Contemporary European Research* Vol. 8, Issue 1, pp. 109–127.

Hartley T.C., *The Foundation of European Union Law.* Eighth ed, Oxford University Press 2014.

Jacqué J.P, The principle of institutional balance (2004), *Common Market Law Review* Vol 41, pp. 383–391.

Koncewicz T.T, *Zasada jurysdykcji powierzonej Trybunału Sprawiedliwości Wspólnot Europejskich,* Oficyna a Wolters Kluwer business, Warszawa 2009.

Larik J., Democratic scrutiny of EU Foreign Policy: from pirates to the power of the people, available at: http://europeanlawblog.eu/?p=2469, last accessed August 25, 2014.

Majone G., Democracy and Constitutionalism in the European Union, (2000) *ECSA Review* Vol 13, No 2.

Moravcsik A., Democracy and Constitutionalism in the European Union, (2000) *ECSA Review* Vol 13, No 2.

Pawłowski Sz., Zasada legitymizacji władzy, in Z. Brodecki (ed), *Europa Sędziów,* LexisNexis, Warszawa 2007.

Romaniello M., The international role of the European Parliament: the SWIFT Affair and the 're-assessed' European institutional balance of power, (2013) *Perspectives on Federalism* Vol 5., issue 1.

Ruchet O., Cultural diversity, European identity and legitimacy of the EU: A review of the debate, in Fuchs D., Klingemann H-D (eds), *Cultural Diversity, European Identity and the Legitimacy of the EU,* Edward Elgar 2011.

Schimmelfennig F., The Normative Origins of Democracy in the European Union: Towards a Transformationalist Theory of Democratization, (2009) *Challenges to Democracy in the 21st Century National Centre of Competence in Research Working Paper,* No 39.

Schmitter P.C., How to Democratize the European Union... And Why Bother?, Rowman&Littlefield Publishers, 2000.

Tindemans L, Debates of the European Parliament 1975–1976 Session. Report of Proceedings from 7 to 11 July 1975 (Sitting of Wednesday, 9 July 1975), Official Journal of the European Communities, Office for Official Publications of the European Communities, Luxembourg 1975.

Vos E., The Rise of Committees, (1997) *European Law Journal* Vol 3, No. 3, pp. 210–229.

LEGAL ACTS

Consolidated versions of the Treaty on European Union and the Treaty on the Functioning of the European Union, OJ C 326, 26.10.2012.

Treaty establishing the European Atomic Energy Community, OJ C 84, 30.03.2010.

CASE-LAW

The Judgment of the Court of Justice of 29 October 1980 in Case 138/79, (*SA Roquette Frères v Council of the European Communities*), ECLI:EU:C:1980:249.

The Judgment of the Court of Justice of 10 February 1983 in Case 230/81, (*Grand Duchy of Luxembourg v European Parliament*), ECLI:EU:C:1983:32.

The Judgment of the Court of Justice of 23 April 1986 in Case 294/83, (*Les Verts v Parliament*), ECLI:EU:C:1986:166.

The Judgment of the Court of Justice of 27 September 1988 in Case 302/87 (*European Parliament v Council of the European Communities*), ECLI:EU:C:1988:461.

The Judgment of the Court of First Instance of 17 June 1998 in Case T-135–96, (*Union Européenne de l'artisanat et des petites et moyennes entreprises (UEAPME) v Council of the European Union*), ECLI:EU:T:1998:128.

The Judgment of the Court of Justice of 22 May 1990 in Case 70/88, (*European Parliament v Council of the European Communities*), ECLI:EU:C:1991:373.

The Judgment of the Court of Justice of 10 May 1995 in Case C-417/93, (*European Parliament v Council of the European Communities*), ECLI:EU:C:1995:127.

The Judgment of the Court of First Instance of 2 October 2001 in joined Cases T-222/99, T-327/99 and T-329/99, (*Jean-Claude Martinez, Charles de Gaulle, Front national and Emma Bonino and Others v European Parliament*), ECLI:EU:T:2001:242.

The Judgment of the Court of Justice of 19 July 2012 in Case C-130/10, (*European Parliament v Council of the European Union*), ECLI:EU:C:2012:472.

The Judgment of the Court of Justice of 13 December 2012 in joined Cases C-237/11 and C-238/11, (*French Republic v European Parliament*), ECLI: EU:C:2012:796.

The Judgment of the Court of Justice of 17 September 2013 in Case C-77/11, (*Council of the European Union v European Parliament*), ECLI:EU:C:2013:559.

The Judgment of the Court of Justice of 24 June 2014 in Case C-658/11, (*European Parliament v Council of the European Union),* ECLI:EU:C:2014:2025.

Opinion of Advocate General – AG Reischl of 18 September 1980 in Case 138/79, (*SA Roquette Frères v Council of the European Communities*), ECLI:EU:C:1980:213.

Opinion of Advocate General – Paolo Mengozzi of 6 September 2012 in joined Cases C-237/11 and C-238/11, (*French Republic v European Parliament*), ECLI: EU:C:2012:545.

Opinion of Advocate General – Yves Bot of 28 May 2013 in Case C-77/11, (*Council of the European Union v European Parliament*), ECLI:EU:C:2013:330.

Opinion of Advocate General – Yves Bot of 30 January 2014 in Case C-658/11, (*European Parliament v Council of the European Union),* ECLI:EU:C:2014:41.

5. DEMOCRATIC VALUES IN THE COURT OF JUSTICE ADJUDICATION ON THE PRIVATE ENFORCEMENT OF THE EUROPEAN UNION COMPETITION LAW

Franciszek Strzyczkowski*
Department of Theory and Philosophy of Law, Faculty of Law and Administration, University of Lodz

1. INTRODUCTION

Democracy and equality of citizens are the fundamental values of the European social and economic order. This axiological assumption is generally reflected in extensive legal regulations organizing the social and economic life in the European Union (EU). For the purposes of this chapter, a detailed analysis of those foundations intend to be limited to the manifestations of the democratic values in the Court of Justice of the European Union (CJEU) adjudication in the selected issues of the European antitrust law where, under private enforcement against practices violating the prohibitions of the European antitrust law, equal participation and citizen's access to the proceedings before the courts, based on the principle of freedom of choice of all concerned, are ensured.

Competition, understood as an ideal position equilibrium, which confirms the optimal allocation of recourses and the protection of consumer's interests, is essential for the social welfare. Yet the conditions for optimal competition and its further functioning are not guaranteed only by the free market and economic mechanisms. Historically, there were two ways of dealing with competition law regulation. Looking at the gradual transformation of the European law in the field of competition law, both dominant approaches, that is the Anglo-American one, following the case-by-case logic, and the European (continental) one, that takes more policy-based attitude, were adopted.

* Email: fstrzyczkowski@wpia.uni.lodz.pl.
Acknowledgement: the paper has been prepared within the framework of the FOCUS research project of the Foundation for Polish Science.

The foundation of the European antitrust law can be identified in Articles 101 and 102 of the Treaty on the Functioning of the European Union (TFEU),[1] which respectively address the issue of "undertakings" distorting the internal market by agreements, decisions of associations of undertakings or by concerted practices,[2] and the abuse of their "dominant position". Whenever both prohibiting agreements and abuses of dominant position affect the trade between EU Member States under the Treaty, they are enforced by the European Commission and by the National Competition Authorities (NCA). Both EU highest courts as well as national courts can adjudicate the EU competition law.

In the context of the private litigation, Articles 101 and 102 TFEU (until the 2003 reform of the European antitrust law) were rarely invoked by private parties to claim damages and injunctions. It was for the legal systems of the Member States to provide for appropriate remedies and procedures for bringing actions. The realization of the democratization paradigm, the assertion of the principle of equality within EU economic law and related thereto private enforcement of EU competition law, has rested upon the CJEU adjudication. Nevertheless, fundamental in this respect, the reform of European competition law, although largely procedural in nature, has been set forth through Regulation 1/2003.[3] Introduction of this legislation has resulted in the establishment of a new enforcement scheme and a significant change in the application of European competition law in relation to agreements and practices restricting competition. Since Regulation 1/2003 entered into force, such agreements have no longer been a subject to the preventive notification system, but entrepreneurs (citizens) pursuing their own interests assess themselves whether the agreement they enter to complies with European competition law, i.e. Articles 101(1) and 101(3) TFEU. Thus, this reform includes a new, decentralized application system of EU competition law, as a combination of both private and public actions. Through decentralization, the European legislator aimed to achieve a higher level of compliance to the European substantive norms by the way of better coordination of complementary private and public interests. As it was pointed out and proposed by the European Commission in the prior White Paper[4] on modernisation of the rules implementing Articles 101 and 102 TFEU (Articles 85 and 86 of the EC Treaty, at that time), Regulation 1/2003 laid down that exemptions from Article 101(3) TFEU have a direct effect. In result, both NCAs and national courts can apply them directly, thus making the enforcement of EU

1 Consolidated Version of the Treaty on the Functioning of the European Union [2008] OJ C115/47.

2 For the reasons of simplicity, all those are further referred to as anticompetitive or restrictive agreements.

3 Council Regulation (EC) No. 1/2003 of 16 December 2002 on implementation of the rules on competition laid down in Articles 81 and 82 of the Treaty [2003] OJ L1/1.

4 White Paper on modernisation of the rules implementing Articles 85 and 86 of the EC Treaty [1999] OJ C132/1.

competition law stronger. The above-mentioned reform to protect competition was particularly important for the democratization of the available private enforcement measures in the context of European antitrust law application, allowing – at the same time – for the Commission to concentrate on the most serious infringements of Articles 101 and 102 TFEU.

The significant character of a decision to facilitate the enforcement mechanism against practices restricting competition through the initiative of private parties, by means of actions brought by the victims of violation of the prohibition, relies on the change from prior situation when such practice among the Member States was not, at least to say, widely used.

2. THE INFLUENCE OF THE AMERICAN EXPERIENCE ON PRIVATE ENFORCEMENT OF THE EUROPEAN ANTITRUST LAW

The American system of antitrust rules enforcement has been regarded as a stimulus for EU antitrust law. In fact, it is still considered to be a kind of paradigm for the so-called private rules for the implementation of competition law. Undoubtedly, comparing the American experience to European antitrust law is particularly relevant due to parallels between the political structure of the United States and the European Union.

In the United States, competition law has been enforced through public and private actions since the Sherman Antitrust Act of 1890.[5] The Sherman Act authorized private parties, particularly active, to sue for triple damages when they had been harmed by a conduct violating either the Sherman Act or the Clayton Antitrust Act of 1914.[6] It further allowed obtaining a court order prohibiting the anti-competitive practice in the future. This pattern of regulation derives from even earlier English Statute of Monopolies 1623, which provided for triple compensation for damages and for double reimbursement of the process costs for the plaintiff, if a court ruled in plaintiff's favour.

At this point, it should be emphasized that the American judiciary has significantly limited the scope of the private enforcement against practices restricting competition, narrowing the scope of the entities entitled to bring actions for triple damages by setting stringent conditions for legal standing. The American doctrine argues that private antitrust proceedings based on triple damages mechanism plays an essential public function as serving the public interest.[7] Thus private parties are particularly active on the ground of American

5 26 Stat. 209, 15 U.S.C. §§1–7.

6 38 Stat. 730, 15 U.S.C. §§12–27.

7 G. Robert Blakey, *Of Characterization and Other Matters: Thoughts About Multiple Damages, Law and Contemporary Problems*, 60/1997, 121.

antitrust law. The most of private claims are independent from, or even precede, public actions. The important role played by the individuals is also reflected in the legislation. Injured persons and businesses are granted with legal standing, and furthermore class action litigation mechanisms and punitive damages available in a broad pre-trial discovery phase. Awarded plaintiffs are also able to recover attorneys' fees in the absence of the loser pays principle.

"Privatized", and as such transferring to the "hands" of the citizens in order to publicly enforce antitrust law in the United States, is an expression of the lack of confidence in the effectiveness of the exclusive competence of the public authorities responsible for the compliance with competition rules. However, the doctrine's opinions on the effectiveness of the private enforcement method are rather divided. Both its advantages and disadvantages have been emphasized. Yet, in some opinions, most of their advantages are not even moderate or there are none. In the current doctrine's opinion, it became particularly suspicious that in process interventions, actions are undertaken by the competitive companies alleging violations of antitrust law. Thus, scholarship postulates that the claim of abuse of a dominant position asserted privately by the parties suffering from restrictive business practices to have only secondary importance.[8] This is contrary to the US law, under which companies affected by such practice are actively involved in the enforcement of competition law by the means of private law. Although American inspiration remains unquestionable, the legislative initiatives presented by the European Commission discussed below proved that removing barriers for private antitrust plaintiffs is plausible without entirely mimicking the US legislation and practices.

3. THE IMPORTANCE OF THE REFORM OF THE EU COMPETITION LAW ENFORCEMENT

The necessity to facilitate private enforcement was supported by numerous reasons. Whereas the governments of the Member States, due to budgetary shortcomings and the lack of information, were not able to discover and investigate all anticompetitive practices, it was a matter of transaction costs' reduction to allow, in a greater extent, private parties to seek compensation for damages suffered from such practices, which in turn would result in a greater compliance with antitrust law. The involvement of private parties would also bring along the creation of better resources allocation, lower prices, greater innovation and efficiency, and greater democratization.

However, at this point, it should be noticed that the possibility of application of European competition law before courts in civil litigation existed long

---

8 *See*, L.J. White (eds.) *Private Antitrust Litigation; New Evidence, New Learning*, Cambridge 1988.

before the reform was introduced and before Regulation 1/2003 was passed. Safeguarding the full effect of the EU law, including competition law, was a task appointed to national remedial and procedural law of the Member States. They have exercised the so-called procedural autonomy. Due the gradually developed doctrine of effectiveness by the Court of Justice, Member States are obliged to introduce into their domestic legal systems solutions making possible to seek compensation through civil action claims for breach of competition law. In the preliminary ruling in *BRT v. SABAM* (1973),[9] resulting from the procedure of the national court before which Article 101 TFUE was invoked in judgment involving intellectual property infringement, the Court of Justice specifically underlined that the provisions of Articles 101 and 102 TFEU have a direct effect in the relations between individual entities and are a source of individual rights, which should be guaranteed by national courts. Although it would be desirable, in practice citizens as private parties are rather reluctant and rarely invoke their rights under the Treaty in cases where the EU antitrust law is applied.

3.1. TOWARDS FOSTERING PRIVATE DAMAGES ACTIONS – PROPOSALS OF THE EUROPEAN COMMISSION

The problem of private enforcement of antitrust law was addressed also by the European Commission's calling for a new system of compensation for victims of restrictive agreements. In the Green Paper of 19 December 2005,[10] accompanied by Staff Working Paper,[11] the Commission sought to identify the main obstacles preventing a more efficient system of damages actions. The Green Paper was an attempt to activate private parties, now considered as a part of the system of the competition protection, and to make a right to claim for a breach of competition law more accessible. Moreover, due to the diversity across Member States concerning antirust remedies and the threat of different outcomes generated by national judiciary in response to private plaintiffs actions, the Commission tried to find a way to harmonize national procedural and substantive rules governing competition-based damages, for instance on the costs, access to the evidence, limitation periods, legal standing, class or representative actions, fault and defences. It seems that the Commission, by issuing the Green Paper, presented a fair and comprehensive set of practical issues that would eventually be raised by national legislatives in an effort to introduce a right to recovery for damages caused by anticompetitive agreement and monopolistic abuses.

---

9 Case 127/73, BRT v SABAM [1973] ECR 51.

10 Commission Green Paper, *Damages actions for breach of the EC antitrust rules*, COM (2005) 672 final, 19.12.2005.

11 Commission Staff Working Paper, Annex to the Green Paper "Damages actions for breach of the EC antitrust rules", SEC (2005) 1732 final, 19.12.2005.

Triggered by the consultation process and a debate following the Green Paper, on 2 April 2008 the European Commission published the White Paper, accompanied by a Commission Staff Working Document,[12] on "Damages actions for breach of the EC antitrust rules".[13] Therein, the Commission, by means of European "soft law", called for the creation of better procedural rules and conditions in order to make antitrust damages actions more effective. This aimed at ensuring that all victims of infringements of EU competition law have access to effective mechanisms for obtaining full compensation for the harm suffered. In the Green Paper of 27 November 2008,[14] on "Consumer Collective Redress", regarding actions for breach of EC antitrust rules, the Commission referred to the White Paper of 2008 as well. The final EU legislation aiming at harmonization of rules for claiming damages suffered by the victims of European antitrust law infringements, is Directive 2014/104/EU.[15] Directive 2014/104 is a result of both Green and White Paper proposals, and ensures that everyone who is a victim of cartels in the EU, can exercise the right to claim compensation form such a harm. Such compensation includes an actual loss and loss of future profits with payment of interest (Article 3(2)). The importance of this legislation rests upon the creation of a system in which the enforcement of EU competition law is balanced between private and public actions. However, the legislator takes a different position than the Court of Justice on private enforcement, perceiving it as sometimes diverging form the general interest. The creation of a competition culture can be achieved by establishing complementary and coexisting private and public enforcement.

4. THE POSITION OF THE EUROPEAN COURTS

While public enforcement system was established by means of legislation, the private one originates in the jurisprudence of the CJEU. The first important step after the *BRT* case towards a wider use of the private enforcement was the decision issued by the Court of First Instance,[16] which stated that the arbitration courts are obligated to comply with EU competition law. Noticeably however, the Court at that point did not address conclusively the issue whether the direct basis for the claims of antitrust damages is European antitrust law. A great

12 Commission Staff Working Document Accompanying the White Paper on Damages Actions for Breach of the EC Antirust Rules, SEC (2008) 404 final, 02.04.2008.

13 Commission White Paper on damages actions for breach of the EC antitrust rules, COM (2008) 165 final, 02.04.2008.

14 Commission Green Paper, on consumer collective redress, COM (2008), 794 final, 27.11.2005.

15 European Parliament and Council Directive 2014/104/EU of 26 November 2014 on certain rules governing actions for damages under national law infringements of the competition law provisions of the Member States and of the European Union [2014] OJL349/1.

16 Case C-126/97 *Eco Swiss v. Benetton*, ECR [1999] I-3055.

supporter of the civil law application under antitrust law was Advocate General Van Gerven, who referred to the position of the Court of Justice in *Francovich*[17] case stating that the principles of liability for the breach of European law must be applied equally to the rules on civil liability as well. Furthermore, the European Court of Justice in its judgment in *Simmenthal*[18] case ruled that law of the EU, which has direct effect, is a direct source of rights and duties for all affected, regardless whether the Member States or private entities, who enter into legal relations being subject to European law. Moreover, according to Van Gerven, the principle of efficiency supports the character of the claims for damages, based on European law since this is the only way to ensure the full effectiveness of European antitrust law.[19] More generally, Van Gerven argued against negative harmonization as a means to facilitate private enforcement of competition law used by the Court advocating in favour of more unified approach in order to reach higher level of control over the spill-over effects.[20] In the broadest perspective, the Court's judgments indicate the possibility of direct application of Articles 101 and 102 TFEU in existing relations between individuals (citizens) in proceedings before national courts. In turn, in a narrower perspective, the Court confirmed the accessibility of redress for breaches of the Treaty competition rules.

The real breakthrough and the landmark case in private enforcement was the Court's ruling in *Courage Ltd. v. Crehan*,[21] issued in response to a question referred by the English Court of Appeal under Article 267 TFEU, in which the Court recognized private parties as being entitled to antitrust damages under the Treaty against the breach committed by other private parties, even if the claim was made by a party to the prohibited contract. The Court stressed that EU law does not prevent Member States judiciary from taking actions to ensure that litigant should not benefit from unlawful conduct. Although to deny the rights to obtain damages form the other contracting party, the court must find that the litigant bears responsibility for the competition being distorted. The expression of phenomena of the democratization is the sole fact of the existing Court's opinion according to which "any individual" is entitled to claim damages, thus pointing out on general access to the breach of Article 101(1) TFEU cause of action, so the claims may be lodged by the individuals. Justifying its position, the Court referred to its earlier jurisprudence in *van Gend en Loos*,[22] *Costa v.*

---

17 Case 9/90, *Francovich* [1991] ECR I-5357.

18 Case 106/77, *Amministrazione delle Finanze dello Stato v. Simmenthal* [1978] ECR 629.

19 Opinion of Advocate General van Gerven delivered 27 October 1993 in case C-128/92, *H.J. Banks & Co. Ltd v. British Coal Corporation*, para. 44.

20 W. Van Graven, Substantive remedies for the private Enforcement of EC Antitrust rules before national courts, in C.D. Ehlermann, I. Atanasiu, *European Competition Annual 2001: Effective Private Enforcement of EC Antitrust Law*, Hart Publishing, 2003.

21 Case 453/99, *Courage Ltd v. Bernard Crehan* [2001] ECR 1–06297.

22 Case 26/62, *van Gend en Loos v. Nederlandse Administratie der Belastingen* [1963] ECR 1.

ENEL[23] and *Francovich* stating that by the way of the European Treaties a *sui generis* legal order has been established, to which also individuals are subjected and that the European rules on competition have the direct effect regarding relations between individuals, and their protection remains the matter of the Member State courts' responsibility. According to the Court of Justice, the full effectiveness laid down in Article 101 TFEU would be compromised if a possibility to claim compensation by anyone who has suffered loss as a result of a restrictive agreement were denied to those who are injured. Moreover, the Court stressed that the full application of Article 101 TFEU would be in danger if the entitlement for compensation was restricted in scope as a result of unlawful actions (antitrust breaches) by a concluded contract or otherwise. Eventually, actions for compensation increase the effectiveness of EU competition rules and can effectively deter entrepreneurs from entering into any agreement or other practices or measures restricting or distorting competition.

However, as the Court of Justice stated, it should be noted that, in absence of a clear bright-line rules of European law, it is up to domestic legal orders of the Member States to designate the competent courts and regulate the procedural means in order to recognize the damages actions which, however, must be in compliance with the principles of equivalence and effectiveness. The *Courage* judgment has determined that there is right for compensation in respect to the activities breaching EU competition law which is derived form Treaty provisions, and affirmed its compensatory function.

Few years later, in subsequent rulings in *Manfredi*[24] and *Pfleiderer*,[25] the Court has recognized and declared private enforcement as a fundamental principle of EU antitrust law. Thus in a preliminary ruling in *Manfredi*, the Court not only referred to its views in *Courage*, but also has significantly developed its position and confirmed the standing of the individuals to claim and seek recovery of damages for harm caused by violation of Article 101 or 102 TFEU. Subsequently, in *Pfleiderer* and *Hydrogen Peroxide*,[26] the Court once again confirmed the general right for compensation from damages caused by business practices of restricting competition. Additionally, in *Otis*,[27] the Court, by a reference to the earlier rulings in *Courage* and *Manfredi*, once more recognized the right to claim damages for breach of Articles 101 and 102 TFEU.

Concerning the democratic nature of private enforcement in the aforementioned claims, Gerber commented that private enforcement of competition rules, by widening access to competition law remedies, where

---

23 Case 6/64, *Flaminio Costa v. E.N.E.L.* [1964] ECR 585.

24 Join cases C-295–298/04, *Vincenzo Manfredi v. Lloyd Adriatico Assicurazioni SpA* [2006] ECR I-6619.

25 Case C-360/09 *Pfleiderer AG v. Bundeskartellamt* [2011] ECR I-5161.

26 Case T-437/08, *CDC Hydrogen Peroxide Cartel Damage Claims v. European Commission* (CDC) [2011] ECR II-8251.

27 Case C-199/11 *Europese Gemeenschap v. Otis NV and Others*, [2012] ECR-0000.

instead of one public authority (and optionally one public authority and one or two courts) engaging their particular doctrines and concepts, private enforcement eventually transforms the whole proceeding into a forum or space that allows multiple selection of the concepts developed by other participating actors enabling them to define the objectives of the legal system.[28] Consequently, the relevant problem occurs how to define the class of persons entitled to recovery for the breach of anti-competitive restrictions. This in turn brings the question whether entitled is the one who suffered a loss from being injured directly or indirectly.

Directly injured are competitors, contractors, consumers or those engaged into businesses who infringe competition rules, if provided goods or services are directly purchased from entrepreneurs breaching the prohibition of anti-competitive behaviour. Indirectly affected are entrepreneurs associated with competitors or partners of entrepreneurs violating prohibition of competition restrictive practices. In the recent judgment of *Kone*,[29] the Court recognized the right to claim damages for loss caused by "umbrella pricing". Thus the Court once again confirmed "any individual" principle including also the so-called umbrella victims, i.e. entities that suffer from the activity of the competitors (non-cartel members) who although remain outside the business relationship with those violating anti-competitive prohibitions, but take advantage of it, for instance by charging higher prices than they would have done under normal competitive conditions.

In this regard, the legislators should settle the final position. The European Union law does not regulate the issue of standing in the matters of competition. However, the Court of Justice in the *Courage v. Crehan* case took a position in this respect, whereby any individuals may assert claims for breach of Article 101 (1) TFEU. Otherwise, effectiveness of the prohibition laid down in this Treaty provision would be in danger. The Court's position has been accepted in principle by the doctrine, albeit the Court did not intend to provide rules on the scope of *locus standi* in the matters of competition law within the Member States legal systems but rather reaffirm the general rule of direct effect of Articles 101 and 102 TFEU.[30] Some authors, however, have been questioning the wide range of entitlement and capacity for actions for damages for violation of the competition rules by excluding some classes of individuals as not having a standing in cases on the practices restricting competition.[31] The approach engaged by the Court in the *Courage* was subsequently altered both in *Manfredi* and *Pfleiderer*.

28 David J. Gerber, Private enforcement of competition law: a comparative perspective, in T. Möllers & A. Heinemann (eds.),*The Enforcement of Competition Law in Europe*, Cambridge University Press 2007, 450.

29 Case C-557/12 *Kone AG and Others v. ÖBB-Infrastruktur AG* (not reported yet).

30 A.P. Komninos, *EC private antitrust enforcement. Decentralised Application of EC Competition Law by National Courts*, Oxford/ Portland 2008, 193.

31 Ibid. at 193.

In the first one, the Court emphasized the fact that victims of antitrust law infringements may obtain compensation for the harm suffered, only if there is a causal relationship between the harm occurred and the violation. Although the direct causal link between the infringement and the harm suffered could, in turn, exclude from the subjective scope, the indirect purchasers (either other producers or final consumers) enjoy active *locus standi*. Even if there are many different categories of individuals that can be damaged by anticompetitive practices, eventually the Court advocated for a wide range of standing for infringement of Articles 101 and 102 TFEU, stating that otherwise enforcement of competition law would be undermined.

Worth noting is that the scope of *locus standi* in the antitrust proceedings was also a subject of examination by the courts of various Member States. For instance, the German judiciary, until the introduction of the 7th amendment to the German Act against Restraints of Competition (2005),[32] abolished numerous particularities of the German antitrust law, increasing its "Europeanization". Prior to the adopted amendments, the legal status of the plaintiff's claiming antitrust damages was only attributed to those entities that suffered loss from the violation. This, in turn, was excluding consumers in their capacity of redress, to those only who were directly affected by the anti-competitive conducts. Yet, in the light of the 7th amendment, a claim for damages suffered by indirect purchasers is now not precluded. Undoubtedly, the German doctrine argues along the lines of the *Courage* ruling, that the language of the paragraph 33 of the Act against Restraints on Competition should be recognized as extending the right for compensation for injuries and injunctions including apart from "competitors", the "other market participants impaired by the infringement", regardless the degree of their participation.

In the context of the decision in *Courage*, the standing for antitrust entrepreneurs that are parties to the prohibited anti-competitive agreements might be contentious. It all comes down to the question whether the principle that one ought not to take advantage of his own wrongdoings, is maintained? In this respect, the Court does not support the position that each participant has the opportunity for claiming violation of the prohibition of restrictive agreements. On the contrary, it holds that European law does not preclude the right of the Member State to refuse one of the parties the right to seek compensation from the other party's agreement, if it is proved that the party itself bears significant responsibility for the competition's distortion.[33] At the same time, according to the Court's position on the admissibility of the contractor's standing, economic and legal context should be taken into account and be conclusive, as well as the bargaining position of each of the agreement's parties.[34] In particular, the

32 Gesetz gegen Wettbewerbsbeschränkungen (GWB).

33 Case 453/99, *Courage Ltd v. Bernard Crehan* [2001] ECR 1-06297, para 31.

34 Ibid. para 32.

standing should be given if the party who claims to be the victim of the EU antitrust law infringement and of the loss suffered as a result of an agreement causing restriction or distortion of the competition, puts it in a worse position than the other party, to such an extent that its autonomy to negotiate the terms of agreements, as well as the ability to avoid the damage or reduce its size, have been severely limited or have been deprived of.[35] Additionally, in the Court's opinion, standing is likely to be allowed in the case of agreements that their anti-competitive effect appears only in the context of the network operation. Then, the co-contractor of the network holder is not liable for the breach of the prohibition of the anti-competitive agreements especially if the terms of the given agreement were somehow imposed.[36] This is much likely the instance of the vertical agreements than horizontal agreements, due to the fact that vertical agreements, unlike horizontal ones, may concern abusive practices or discrimination against dependent companies by a dominant company (e.g. manufacturer – distributor) and participation in such agreements may be economically compulsory for the parties under the threat of the exclusion from the market. The doctrine pointed out the consistency of these concepts, although it is required to indicate whether harm occurred as prerequisite for private enforcement.[37]

5. *LOCUS STANDI* TO CLAIM DAMAGES UNDER EUROPEAN UNION COMPETITION LAW

Consumers certainly have *locus standi* to claim for the breach of the anti-competitive restrictions. The European Commission's White Paper clearly indicates the support for private enforcement and a right of action against practices restricting competition being granted to the consumers, especially in an effort to regulate collective redress. The exclusion of consumers from the scope of subjects entitled to claims for breach of anti-competitive restrictions would be inconsistent with the liability principles rooted in the European legal culture. The advantages of the class action mechanism are rather clear. It facilitates governance and access to justice, reduces costs of litigation, and it plays a great deterrent function if considered that the amount of compensations will be multiplied for all the participants. The legitimacy of consumer's active *locus standi* under EU competition law is derived from the principles of effectiveness and of direct application of Articles 101 and 102 TFEU. The Court of Justice in the *Manfredi* ruling has confirmed that.

---

35 Ibid para 33.

36 Ibid para 34.

37 Clifford A. Jones, *Private Enforcement of Antitrust Law in the EU, UK and USA*, Oxford University Press 1999, 176.

Consumers are active in pursuing damage claims mainly by bringing their actions in follow-on litigation that takes place when the Commission or a NCA has previously issued a decision establishing a breach of competition law and when the damage value is estimated. Due the high costs of the consumer redress in comparison to the low value of the damage, one of the conditions for efficient use by consumers of the *locus standi* in cases for a breach of the prohibitions of the anti-competitive practices is an establishment of collective redress, which may take the form of actions representing the common interests (collective or representative actions) or class actions, which allows to combine in a single judicial proceedings to rule over the similar claims based on the same legal basis. The collectively brought actions represent private interests while representative actions are brought because of public interest and only indirectly represent the application of the competition rules.

The institution of class action finds its support and reasoning in the European Commission's Green Paper on Consumer Collective Redress (2008)[38] and in the White Paper on Damages actions for breach of the EC antitrust rules (2008).[39] The Commission has clearly indicated therein the need to create systems of collective redress in the framework of representative actions and collective actions.

Directly effective European antitrust provisions confer rights to individuals. Nevertheless, the Court has not settled yet the issue of horizontal direct effect of European law on the creation of rules on civil remedies to enforce right to compensation for the antitrust law infringement. In the *Courage* case's holding the Court does not stress that the right to claim damages for the infringement of antitrust law is a principle of European law nor specifies the conditions for the liability and remedies. Hence, much to suggest that it remains in domain of the Member States domestic regulations. This opinion is justiciable in the light of holdings in *Automec II*[40] and *Courage*, according to which it is up to national legislatives to regulate and determine the civil effects of the breach of Article 101 TFEU.

Evidently, the determination of who can seek for compensation for anti-competitive behaviour determines scope of democratization and equality in the enforcement proceedings against restrictive practices. The greater the range of individuals granted standing to bring a claim, the greater participation of citizens in the protection of competition, therefore leading to the discipline of entrepreneurs to comply with competition law. Furthermore, the precise definition of a category of persons entitled to claim for breach of the prohibitions

---

38 European Commission, *Green Paper on Consumer Collective Redress*, Brussels, 27.11.2008, COM(2008) 794 final.

39 European Commission, *White Paper on damages actions for breach of the EC antitrust rules*, Brussels, 2.4.2008 COM(2008) 165 final.

40 Case T-24/90, *Automec v. Commission of the European Communities* [1992] ECR II-2223.

of anti-competitive practices leads to equal treatment in a similar situation as a result of a breach of competition rules.

The availability of evidence of violations of the prohibitions against harmful restrictions of competition remains a fundamental problem in the private enforcement mechanism. It is still a subject of dispute and controversy in the legal discourse. In this regard the doctrine expressed deep concerns regarding simple incorporation of the characteristic of the American private enforcement of antitrust rules into European law.[41] Those concerns arise from the fundamental differences between continental legal systems and common law systems. Pre-trial discovery, as allowed in the United States with minimal court oversight, would likely contradict with civil law legal orders of the most Member States. Nevertheless, pursuing democratization requires that certain ways to disclosure for evidence, if necessary should be allowed, of course in accordance with the fair trial principle and by the judicial discretion.

6. CONCLUDING REMARKS

Entrusting citizens with enforcement powers equals to the limitation of the previously exclusive competence of a public authority. Such an approach was noticeably reflected in the jurisprudence of the Court of Justice of the European Union. The tendency that makes the involvement into the competition protection system greater is an exemplification of the democratization of the European Union polity. It is not to eliminate a public authority, still retaining its leading role, but rather to supplement it. As a conclusive point, it is essential to note the active role of the CJEU that has directly affected the initiatives of the European Commission leading to a change into more democratized enforcement. Directive 2014/104 have tried to find the balance between the stronger role of private claimants on one hand and, on the other hand, the effective public enforcement. Nevertheless, the relation between these two remains a difficult one.

BIBLIOGRAPHY

Blakey, G.R., *Of Characterization and Other Matters: Thoughts About Multiple Damages, Law and Contemporary Problems* 60, 1997

Gerber, D.J., *Private enforcement of competition law: a comparative perspective, in The Enforcement of Competition Law in Europe*, T. Möllers & A. Heinemann (eds.), Cambridge University Press, 2007

[41] V. Milutinović, "*The "Right to Damage" under EU Competition Law: from Courage v. Crehan to the White Paper and Beyond.*

Havu, K., Private Enforcement of EU (Competition) Law – Remarks and Outlooks Regarding the Intertwinement of EU and National Law, *Legal Studies Research Paper Series* Paper 29, 2014

Jones, C.A., *Private Enforcement of Antitrust Law in the EU, UK and USA*, Oxford University Press, 1999

Komninos, A.P., *EC private antitrust enforcement. Decentralised Application of EC Competition Law by National Courts*, Oxford, 2008

Milutinović, V., *"The "Right to Damage" under EU Competition Law: from Courage v. Crehan to the White Paper and Beyond*, Wolters Kluwer DV – Law & Business, 2010

Van Graven, W., Substantive remedies for the private Enforcement of EC Antitrust rules before national courts, in; C.D. Ehlermann, I. Atanasiu, *European Competition Annual 2001: Effective Private Enforcement of EC Antitrust Law*, Hart Publishing, 2003

White, L.J. (red.) *Private Antitrust Litigation; New Evidence, New Learning*, Cambridge, 1988

Wils, P.J., Should Private Antitrust Enforcement Be Encouraged in Europe?, *World Competition*, 26/3, 2003.

6. JUDICIAL CONTROL OF MONETARY AND FISCAL DECISIONS IN THE EUROPEAN UNION

Filip KŘEPELKA*
Masarykova univerzita, Brno, Czech Republic

1. INTRODUCTION

Ongoing debt crisis (since 2010) of several Member States of the Eurozone resulting from global economic slowdown (since 2007) sparked doubts about viability of single currency introduced more than 15 years ago (1999). The collapse of the Eurozone and reintroduction of national currencies has been feared since then.

The European Union and the Member States reacted with rescue measures. Heavily indebted Member States – Greece, Portugal, Ireland and Cyprus – needed massive rescue loans. The loans were provided by other Member States, international institutions and funds newly established within the European Union for this purpose. The European Central Bank alleviated with purchase of bonds of these states plus Italy and Spain on financial market, lending money to endangered banks, extremely low interest rates and quantitative easing.

Both rescue loans and unconventional monetary policy cause political skirmishes between the Member States. Mandated austerity is objected by people in the South and unexpected expenditures for rescue in the North where also inflation is feared. National politicians cannot ignore these views and push for the solutions they perceive as serving national interests. Relations between the Member States thus deteriorate. The entire existence of the European Union is questioned.

The crisis emerged due to the chronic incompliance with the rules agreed for the maintenance of the single currency two decades ago. Several measures adopted due to the crisis also compromise existing rules.

---

* Email: filip.krepelka@law.muni.cz.

The European Communities were, and the European Union is, a polity governed with law (*rule of law*), albeit with specific supranational features.[1] Judiciary plays crucial role. The above mentioned controversies are thus increasingly brought to courts of the European Union and also to the courts of the Member States, because adjudication of this supranational law is shared by supranational and national judiciary. A collection of papers addressing recent trends in judiciary in the European Union thus deserves attention to it.

Nevertheless, judicial control of fiscal and monetary decisions is rare or entirely missing in the world. Its potential, methods and limits are thus rarely discussed. Therefore, this paper must start with an overview of roles and functioning of judiciary plus an outline of nature of money and public budgets.

The crisis is a continuous political event of the highest importance. It is closely followed by media, especially in its hot phases. One such phase started in February 2015 when the cabinet formed after the victory of leftist Syriza in Greek parliamentary elections refuses austerity imposed with rescue loans. "Grexit"[2] is debated again.

Legal aspects of the crisis and measures addressing it are analysed by legal scholars with considerable delays. Attention to them varies across Europe. This reveals not only different impact of the crisis on them, but also varied authority of supranational law (and law generally) and quality of its reflection. Prominence of attention in Germany[3] will be explained.

2. TRADITIONAL AND EMERGING ROLES OF JUDICIARY

Courts have two traditional tasks. Firstly, they decide disputes among individuals (civil judiciary). Secondly, they confirm or reject guilt of perpetrators of crimes and impose punishments (criminal judiciary).

Both judiciaries suffered repeatedly from interventions of government. The courts thus developed into the third branch of government, separated from executive and legislative. The rule of law is impossible without judicial independence from political and social pressures.

---

1 The rule of law (or concept of *Rechtstaatlichkeit*) in supranational European Union is subject of continuous reflection of legal scholars in papers and monographs. Wennerström E. O., *The Rule of Law and the European Union*, Uppsala, Iustus Förlag, 2007 can be highlighted as example of the most detailed elaboration of the issue in recent English-written literature.

2 "Greek exit", portmoneau for the withdrawal of Greece from the Eurozone, coined by W. H. Buiter and E. Rahbari (Citibank) in 2012.

3 Legal aspects of debt and currency crisis of the European Union is addressed prominently in German legal literature, see among others T.M.J. Möller, F.-C. Zeitler (eds.), *Europa als Rechtsgemeischaft – Währungsunion und Schuldenkrise*, Mohr Siebeck, 2012.

Judicial control of administration developed slower. Monarchs and politicians exercising executive power opposed it. In addition, various administrative agendas are subject of judicial control to different extent.[4] Administrative judiciary is often difficult to identify. Some countries integrate it with judiciary for civil and criminal matters. Other ones established special courts. Independent tribunals and commissions exist. Experts are involved. However, the demand for the judicial control of administration can be reduced with professionalization of administrative authorities and with its protection against political interference.

The workload of national court systems differs significantly due to economic, social and political conditions, stability and quality of statutory laws, preventive effects of adjudication in general and persuasiveness of case-law of superior courts in particular. The number of judges varies significantly among countries. The amount of cases brought before courts grew significantly during the 20th century in developed countries. Attorneys and in-house counsels multiplied. Judiciaries in many countries suffer from chronic overload.[5]

New disputes brought to courts result from economic, social, political and technological development. Judges were not involved in protection of privacy in cyberspace century ago. Few anti-discrimination measures existed. However, demand for judicial interventions emerges also in spheres formerly spared. Legislation addressing industries and services, protection of environment, urban planning and land use, healthcare and education is to be applied by courts in modes and extent unseen in the past.

Misuses of legislation by totalitarian and authoritarian regimes resulted into emphasis for constitutionality. Constitutions thus acquired genuine superior position. Catalogues of fundamental rights and freedoms were attached to the outline of the government. Constitutional control of legislation and of operations of executive and judiciary was introduced. Many countries have established separate constitutional courts for this purpose.[6]

---

4 Interesting summary of tasks and organization of administrative judiciary can be found in R. Winkler, Administrative Justice in Europe: The EU *Acquis*, good practice and recent Developments – Working Paper submitted for the Twinning Project *Support to more efficient, effective and modern operation and functioning of the Administrative Court of the Republic of Croatia*, November 2007, available at www.upravnisudrh.hr.

5 Comparison of judiciaries in the Member States of the Council of Europe can be found in CEPEJ (European Commission for the Efficiency of Justice), *European Judicial Systems – Edition 2014 (2012 data): Efficiency and quality of justice – An overview*, available at www.coe.int/t/dghl/cooperation/cepej/evaluation/2014/synthese2014_en.pdf, see p. 17 (number of professional judges for 100.000 inhabitants), p. 22 (Number of 1st instance incoming and resolved civil (and commercial) litigious cases per 100 000 inhabitants in 2012), and p. (24 Clearance Rate (CR) and Disposition Time (DT) of litigious civil (and commercial) cases in first instance courts in 2012).

6 R. Wahl, *Das Bundesverfassungsgericht im europäischen und internationalen Umfeld*, Aus Politik und Zeitgeschichte, B 37–38/2001, pp. 45–54, available at www.bpb.de/apuz/26041/das-bundesverfassungs-gericht-im-europaeischen-und-internationalen-umfeld?p=all.

Numerous international treaties harmonize national laws, coordinate their application and simplify interstate cooperation. International treaties are applied together with statutes or instead of them by administration and judiciary. Specific supranational law emerged in the European Communities and grows in the European Union.

Courts thus apply more complex laws than earlier. Statutes shall be interpreted with consideration of constitutions, international treaties and entire supranational law in the Member States of the European Union.

Commentaries, papers and judgments always served both judges for their adjudication and attorneys for their argumentation. Genuine flood of information emerged with electronic databases.

Sound and fair adjudication requires understanding of political, social, psychological and economic aspects of the case. Certainly, judges can ask various experts for explanation and opinion. Nevertheless, they must understand the issue at the end.

Even laws addressing private relations and suppressing criminality do not escape entirely political consideration. Political aspects of many non-traditional judicial agendas are even more apparent.

Eventual judicial control of monetary and fiscal policy thus requires judges to interpret vaguely formulated rules and hardly identifiable principles established in various legal systems and formulated in various legal documents. In addition, they must become familiar with economic theories and practices. Fiscal and monetary measures are intensively politicized. Their eventual judicial control would be thus also politicized.

3. RULES AND INSTITUTIONS FOR MONETARY AND FISCAL POLICY

Governments steer economic, social and political activities of individuals and collectives with commands and incentives. Commands are prescriptions and prohibitions. Non-compliance is sanctioned. Incentives encourage and discourage. Commands shall be specified with law. There will be no *rule of law* without it. Most incentives are also established by laws and described with them due to their political importance.

Certainly, an individual should not be reduced to *homo economicus*. There are also incentives beyond economic stimulation which can be explained by sociologists and psychologists. Nevertheless, the most important incentives applicable by governments are undoubtedly of economic nature.

Surely, public expenditures cannot be downplayed to incentives. Governments spend money for their tasks. Administration, judiciary, police and army guarantee security from internal and external threats. Governments alleviate social inequality and risks. Intentional incentives form a thin part of public expenditures.

Money developed for easier exchange of goods, services, work and capital. Gold and silver coins were used for centuries. Attempts to replace them with banknotes failed until the 19th century. De-metallised *fiat money* emerged not earlier than in the 20th century. Electronic transactions reduce need for banknotes and coins.[7] International trade and investment are impossible without cross-border payments. Money now moves freely and easily across borders. Economists debate continuously about adequate definition of money and measurement of its amount (money supply or money stock)[8] in national economy closely integrated with other economies in the world.

Countries established central banks or agencies for creating ("printing") money and for steering its circulation. Monetary policy is, however, nothing purely technical. Price stability competes with other goals such as development, growth, employment, financing of public tasks and repayment of public and private debts.

Gradual removal of gold as intrinsic stabilizer during the 20th century resulted in inflation unexperienced in previous centuries.[9] Many countries suffered hyperinflation. Price stability was thus desirable. Independence of central banks from inherently politicized executive was a solution.[10] This independence shall be guaranteed with rules for selection and position of experts charged to formulate and realize monetary policy.

Central banking thus became comparable with judiciary as regards its independence.[11] Supreme and constitutional courts are the institutions best to compare. Being a justice of these courts is similarly excellent career for legal scholars or practitioners as being a governor, director or member of central bank board for economists. Both authorities decide issues of national importance. Competing economic theories such as Keynesian economics and monetarism can be compared with judicial activism and restraint.

---

7 Numerous books, articles, papers, presentations analyse and summarize the development of money in various historical periods for pupils, students of economics and other disciplines and for general public. Summary sufficient for understanding for purpose of this paper can be found in English Wikipedia "History of money".

8 Quantity theory of money underlines importance of money in national (international) economy. The theory developped since 16th century. Significant scholars addressing it were L. Mises and M. Friedman.

9 See B. Taylor, *Century of Inflation*, available at www.globalfinancialdata.com.

10 About recent debate on independence and responsibility of central banks K. Ullrich, *Unabhängigkeit und Verantwortlichkeit der Europäischen Zentralbank, Zentrum für Europäische Wirtschaftspolitik*, ZEW Discussion Papers, 2003, No. 03–65, available at http://hdl.handle.net/10419/23999.

11 G. Tridimas, *A comparison of Central Bank and Judicial Independence"* in A. Marciano (Ed.), *Constitutional mythologies: New perspectives on controlling the state"* Springer, Chapter 11, pp. 155–170, New York, 2011.

The differences between judiciary and central banking, however, cannot be ignored. Goals of monetary policy are formulated generally. There are several instruments available with variable effects. Economic theories shall be reflected by governors, directors and other managers of national central banks. Measures cannot be discussed in advance, if goals are to be achieved and insider trading avoided.[12]

Fiscal policy belongs inherently to sphere of public power. It culminates in periodical approvals or rejections of annual budgets and plans for longer periods by parliaments and councils. In addition, many statutes have fiscal consequences. Legislations establishing government authorities and institutions, armed forces, social security and healthcare, education and improvement and maintenance of infrastructure can be mentioned. Similarly, taxes, fees and contributions for their financing are also political topic of utmost importance.

Monetary policy is uniform for the entire territory of particular country without internal barriers for payments. On the contrary, fiscal policy is inherently decentralized. There are regional and municipal budgets. There are funds for specific tasks. Even centralized budgets need to be implemented for particular institutions and individuals. Formally separated budgets of distinct units of government are interconnected in reality.

The misappropriation of funds allocated for various purposes emerged during entire history. Expenditures were thus controlled by the government. Individual comptrollers or auditors are engaged and courts or offices of auditors were established. Their independence was later guaranteed with statutes and even with constitutions.

Many states and numerous municipalities were indebted during their entire existence.[13] Surely, many debts resulted from wars. Other causes cannot be overlooked. Politicians often prefer expenditures because this approach boosts economy and increases welfare of population or they simply serve wishes of selected groups and individuals. The burden of repayment is left for the next generations and for future politicians.

Experience with irresponsible fiscal policy leading to insolvency of particular governments resulted in demand for restrictions. Balanced budget is required or deficit is limited. Related borrowing must be authorized by elected body or by superior authorities.

These requirements are imposed foremost on municipalities, regions and public funds to avoid differentiated indebtedness and eventual insolvency compromising the fulfilling of their tasks at the expense of responsible units.

---

12 The most recent example of an entirely surprising step is the decision of the Swiss National Bank to abandon peg of the Franc to the Euro on 15. 1. 2015 (just one day after delivery of the opinion of the attorney general in the OMT case discussed below).

13 For recent reflection of sovereign debt see K. Dyson, *States, Debt and Power: Saints and Sinners in European History and Integration*, Oxford University Press, 2014.

Some autonomous governments install barriers against their indebtedness voluntarily. Most states[14] and many municipalities in the United States of America adopted them after systematic refusals of the federal government to bailout them.

The mere requirement of balanced budget and the control of indebtedness have proven inefficient in cases of sovereigns. For example, the Congress of the United States of America has enacted numerous laws limiting federal indebtedness.[15] Nevertheless, it increased them always to avoid mandatory cuts with considerable effect on government operations and economy ("fiscal cliff").[16] Nonetheless, debt brakes have become fashionable during last decade. Among European countries, Germany,[17] Switzerland,[18] Poland[19] or Spain[20] installed them. Several countries establish specific institutions for providing adequate expertise and eventually operating installed debt brakes.[21]

The independence of above mentioned authorities – central banks, courts of auditors and fiscal boards – increases their compliance of monetary and fiscal policy with broadly formulated legal requirements.

Decisions of central banks have serious and even devastating impact on particular manufactures, service providers, financial institutions, investors and individuals. Sudden changes of monetary policy spark insolvency to companies. Nevertheless, adjudication of monetary policy is missing. Probably, sporadic actions fail.

Certainly, numerous other judgments have fiscal implications. Above all, the interpretation of tax and social laws can significantly influence fiscal policies. Nevertheless, judicial control of decisions of parliaments and assemblies related to fiscal policy – approval of budgets, allocation of money for various tasks, is also rare. We can assume that politicians comply with clear rules to avoid prosecution. Otherwise, political assessment is surely respected.

---

14 For detailled overview see National Conference of State Legislatures, *NCSL Fiscal Brief: State Balanced Budget Provisions*, 2010, available at www.ncsl.org/documents/fiscal/StateBalancedBudgetProvisions2010.pdf.

15 D.A. Austin, M.R. Levit, *The debt limit: history and recent increases*, Congressional Research Service Report for Congress, RL31967, 2010, available at http://fpc.state.gov/documents/organization/105193.pdf. Debt ceilings replaced congressional approval of any loan.

16 The 2010 Tax Relief Act expected cessation of important tax reliefs and cuts of public expenditures were expected by the Budget Control Act of 2011. American Taxpayer Relief Act of 2012 was compromise which avoided the activation of this strong debt brake.

17 *Gesetz zur Änderung des Grundgesetzes (Artikel 91c, 91d, 104b, 109, 109a, 115, 143d)*, BGBl. 2009 I S. 2248, For detailed legal analyses see C. Kastrop, G. Meister-Scheufelen, M. Sudhof (eds.), *Die neuen Schuldenregeln im Grundgesetz: Zur Fortentwicklung der bundesstaatlichen Finanzbeziehungen*, Bwv – Berliner Wissenschafts-Verlag, 2010.

18 Amendment of Articles 126 and 159 of the Constitution of Swiss Confederation adopted by the National Assembly in 22. 6. 2001 and confirmed 2. 12. 2001 by popular vote.

19 Article 216(5) of *Konstytucja Rzeczypospolitej Polskiej*.

20 Amendment of Article 135 *Constitución Española*, adopted 27.9.2011.

21 For example, the *Staatschuldenauschuss* and later the *Fiskalrat* in Austria.

4. A SINGLE CURRENCY FOR THE INTEGRATION IN THE EUROPEAN UNION

The crucial task of the European Communities and of the European Union was and is the economic integration of its Member States. Basic economic freedoms are the principal legal instrument for this purpose. Numerous regulations, directives and decisions contribute to their realization. This liberalization resulted into immense trade in goods and significant movement of workforce, services and capital among the Member States.

Cross-border payments are necessary for realization of these basic economic freedoms.[22] Trade between the countries with their own currencies requires their exchange. Such exchange is, however, not for free. In addition to it, fluctuation of exchange rates causes risk to trade partners engaged in repeated, subsequent or postponed delivery. Risk coverage is expensive. Single currency shared by the extensively trading countries was and is justified with the removal of these costs and risks. Significant savings were promised with introduction of the Euro[23] and were indeed achieved.[24]

The single currency was suggested already decades ago. Exchange rates became volatile after collapse of the Bretton Woods system (1971) emulating disrupted gold standard. Exchange risks and costs for insurance thus sharply increased for intra-community trade benefiting from basic economic freedoms.

The project of the single currency accompanied the establishment of the European Union in 1993. Eleven Member States introduced the Euro as abstract currency in 1999. Sums on deposits and amounts fixed in contracts, wills, decisions and judgments were to be recalculated. Coefficients for recalculation were fixed already in 1998.[25] The Euro was represented with former banknotes and coins of the Member States for a transitional period. Troubles with replacement of cash were feared. The European Union and the Member States thus carefully prepared for it. The withdrawal of national banknotes and coins and the introduction of Euro-banknotes and Euro-coins were easier than expected. Parallel circulation of old and new banknotes and coins was thus

---

22 As demonstrated in judgment of the Court of Justice of 31.1.1984, 286/82 and 26/83 in *Luisi* and *Carbone*, ECR 1984, p. 00377.

23 Commission of the European Communities (1990): One Market, One Money: An Evaluation of the Potential Benefits and Costs of Forming and Economic and Monetary Union, European Economy 44, October. Savings were expected from 0.2–1.0% of GDP. Critical appraisal can be found in Mendizabal R., H., 'Monetary Union and the Transaction Cost Savings of a Single Currency', *Review of International Economics*, vol. 10, no. 2, pp. 263–277, 2002.

24 An analysis after the five years of the Euro in physical circulation trying to distinguish impact of the Euro on prices increases is I. Beuerlein, Fünf Jahre nach der Euro-Bargeldeinführung – War der Euro wirklich ein Teuro?, Statistisches Bundesamt, Wirtschaft und Statistik 2/2007, pp. 208–212.

25 Council Regulation (EC) No 2866/98 on the conversion rates between the euro and the currencies of the Member States adopting the Euro.

shortened for several weeks in twelve countries introducing the materialized Euro in 2002.

The Eurozone is significant part of the European Union. However, the UK and Denmark opted out and Sweden tacitly joined them after their accession. Since then, several new Member States of the European Union qualified to introduce the Euro. Introduction was smooth in all these Member States. The Eurozone comprises nineteen Member States with 340 million people in 2015.

The Euro serves as currency also in several other states. According to expectations, it has become supplementary reserve currency besides the dollar. It is widely accepted as stable currency in many other countries.

5. ORIGINAL LEGAL FRAMEWORK FOR THE EURO

The Maastricht Treaty concluded in 1992 established several crucial requirements for Member States[26] for the introduction of the single currency on their territory:

(1) independence of national central bank;
(2) convergence of inflation (within span 1.5% above three Member States with the lowest inflation);
(3) convergence of interest rates (+2% above three Member States with the lowest rates);
(4) stable exchange rate of their national currency (the participation in the European Monetary System without fluctuation beyond fixed limits);
(5) low deficit of public budgets (central, state, regional, local government plus institutions of social security and special public funds below 3% GDP); and
(6) indebtedness of such defined national government less 60% GDP.[27]

The two above mentioned fiscal requirements were confirmed later for the Member States of the Eurozone as the Stability and Growth Pact.[28]

The European Union is required to operate balanced budget.[29] It shall be noted that revenues and expenditures are limited. This supranational polity lacks power to impose taxes.

---

26 Then Article 109j of the Treaty establishing the European (Economic) Community and related Protocol on the convergence criteria referred to in Article 109j of the Treaty establishing the European Community.

27 Now Article 126 and Article 140 TFEU.

28 Resolution of the European Council on the Stability and Growth Pact Amsterdam of 17 June 1996, Regulation (EC) No 1466/97 on the strengthening of the surveillance of budgetary positions and the surveillance and coordination of economic policies, Council Regulation (EC) No 1467/97 on speeding up and clarifying the implementation of the excessive deficit procedure.

29 Article 310 paragraph 1 TFEU.

The Euro is legally required to be stable currency with low inflation.[30] The policies of the European Central Bank and central banks of the Member States of Eurozone (the Eurosystem since the Lisbon Treaty) are thus addressed with corresponding rules. Managers are independent from the Member States. These central banks are prohibited to provide money to the Member States.[31]

Legal framework for the Euro is labelled as "Economic and Monetary Union".[32] Nevertheless, the first adjective has not been clarified. Few economic policies were coordinated in reality.[33]

6. ONSET OF THE DEBT CRISIS AND ITS CAUSES

Especially German economists[34] discouraged from single currency already in its preparatory phase before 1998. Among others, it was contested whether the future zone of the single currency is optimum currency area according to theories of Robert Mundell.[35]

Several political scientists and historians admit that introduction of the Euro started in a political deal after collapse of socialist regimes in Central and Eastern Europe. Germany was allegedly allowed to unify in exchange for single currency by France desiring to curtail dominance of the Deutschmark.[36]

As mentioned, three Member States decided to retain their national currencies. Their population was suspicious or rejected the idea. Other European nations varied in their support for the single currency.[37]

The Euro was introduced in 1999 despite chronic non-compliance of many Member States with fiscal criteria.[38] Unfortunately, situation has not improved

---

30 Article 282 paragraph 2 TFEU.

31 Article 123 paragraph 1 TFEU.

32 Article 119 TFEU is introductory part of of the title VIII "Economic and monetary policy". Chapter dedicated to "economic policy" addresses prominently fiscal policy of the Member States. Economic policy beyond fiscal policy is, however, addressed with general provisions underlining joint responsibility.

33 For overview see B. Hacker, *On the Way to a Fiscal or a Stability Union? The Plans for a "Genuine" Economic and Monetary Union*, Fridrich-Ebert-Stiftung www.fes.de/ipa, 2013.

34 155 German professors of economics (initiated by M. Neumann) called in joint resolution against the introduction of the Euro in 1998. Numerous articles were published in 1997–98 in newspapers, journals and research papers. The topic was fiercely debated in thematic courses at the *Europa-Kolleg Hamburg*, I have studied in winter semester 1997/98 in post-graduate specialized programme.

35 Mundell R., 'A Theory of Optimum Currency Areas', *The American Economic Review*, Vol. 51, No. 4, pp. 657–665, 1961.

36 M. Sauga, S. Simons, Wiegrefe, *The Price of Unity: Was the Deutsche Mark Sacrificed for Reunification?*, Spiegel Online International, 30. 9. 2010, available at www.spiegel.de.

37 For overview of the developments between 1990–2012 see F. Roth, L Jonung, F. Nowak-Lehmann, *Crisis and public support for the Euro*, Vox CEPR's policy portal, 5.11.2012, available at www.voxeu.org/article/crisis-and-public-support-euro.

38 For details see C. Degenhart, *Missachtung rechtlicher Vorgaben bei der Umsetzung der Währungsunion*, pp. 85–100, in T.M.J. Möller and F.-C. Zeitler (eds.), *Europa als Rechtsgemeischaft – Währungsunion und Schuldenkrise*, Mohr Siebeck, 2012.

later. Member States were not sanctioned for excessive deficits and indebtedness. On the contrary, they achieved relaxation of rules in 2005.[39]

Economy flourished at the end of the 20th and at the beginning of the 21st centuries worldwide, including most parts of Europe. Investors were optimistic. The heavily indebted Member States using the Euro were capable to refinance their public debt with loans with significantly lower interest rates than in the past. An opportunity to reduce their indebtedness was not used. On the contrary, these states plus their municipalities, companies and individuals extended their borrowings. Economic boom was thus stimulated. Investors enjoyed high profits. Especially, real estate prices skyrocketed.

The situation reversed after the onset of global economic recession in 2007. Many countries faced serious troubles. Manufacturers and service providers suffered from decreasing demand from indebted population. Asset prices collapsed. Banks faced unpaid credits. Unemployment increased. Government revenues dropped due to decreasing wages and vanishing profits. On the contrary, public expenditures increased. Unemployed people claimed social assistance. Governments granted massive bailouts to banks, because they feared runs of creditors.

Trust of lenders disappeared in case of the heavily indebted Member States of Southern Europe. Exorbitant interest rates for refinancing of loans were asked at financial markets[40] and credit-default swaps skyrocketed. Greece has been exorbitantly indebted. Its insolvency became imminent. Insolvency of one Member State would spark (*domino effect*) troubles of the other highly indebted Member States: Portugal, Ireland, Cyprus, Spain and Italy.[41]

It was assumed that insolvency would compel such Member State to reintroduce national currency. Public debt crisis of several Member States was thus perceived as threat to the Euro.[42]

The potential collapse of the single currency would surely undermine the European Union. Reintroduction of national currencies would require restrictions of cross-border movements of payments. Necessary border controls could be misused for reintroduction of obstacles to free movement of persons, services and goods.

---

39 Presidency Conclusions – Brussels, 22 and 23 March 2005, Improving the implementation of the Stability and Growth Pact – Council Report to the European Council.

40 For the figures during onset of the crisis and related early analysis see Hagen J, Schuknecht J., Wolswijk G., *European bond spreads in the current crisis,* 21.12.2009, VOX CEPR's policy portal, www.voxeu.org/article/european-government-bond-spreads-current-crisis. Recent interest rates during 2014 are available at www.ecb.europa.eu/stats/money/long/html/index.en.html.

41 The threat of contagion (domino effect) was alleged, or rejected by numerous commentators and politicians as justification of various rescue measures or their refusal.

42 See, among others, P.J. Welfens, *Die Zukunft des Euro – Die europäische Staatschuldenkrise und ihre Überwindung*, Nicolaische Verlagsbuchhandlung GmbH, Berlin, 2012, pp. 162–173, 224–239 or P. Athanassiou, *Withdrawal and Expulsion from the EU and the EMU – Some Reflexions*, Legal Working Paper Series, No. 10, 2009, European Central Bank – Eurosystem.

It is worth to note that expulsion of any insolvent Member State as confirmed weakling from the Eurozone is hard to imagine. People would not voluntarily change the Euro for national currency while expecting its devaluation. Monetary unions broke up when their stabilized Member States decide to introduce their own stable currency.[43]

7. ALLEVIATION OF THE CRISIS AND PREVENTION OF ITS ESCALATION

Fearing the collapse of the Eurozone, leaders of the Member States and the European Union decided to assist endangered Member States with huge rescue loans. Bilateral loans were quickly followed with orchestrated action. The European Union has provided collateral for joint borrowing at financial markets known as the European Financial Stabilisation Mechanism (EFSM).[44] The European Financial Stability Facility (EFSF) was established as temporary fund for rescue loans.[45] European resources were not sufficient. The International Monetary Fund (IMF) also provided rescue loans. Finally, the European Stability Mechanism (ESM) was established as huge fund public fund besides the European Union providing rescue loans at the end in 2011.[46]

On the other hand, heavily indebted and potentially insolvent Member States of the Mediterranean have failed until now in their effort to mutualize their public debts. Various models of interstate guarantees and of "Eurobonds"

43 The Introduction of Czechoslovak *koruna* in 1919 after breakup of Austrian-Hungarian morarchy and orchestrated separation of that currency into Czech and Slovak ones in 1993 initiated by the Czech Republic, for details see J. Fidrmuc, J. Horváth, J. Fidrmuc, 'The stability of monetary unions: lessons from the breakup of Czechoslovakia', *Journal of Comparative Economics*, 1999, vol. 27, no. 4, pp. 753–781.

44 Council Regulation 407/2010 of 11 May 2010 establishing a European financial stabilisation mechanism.

45 Founded 7 June 2010, established after Framework Agreement in Luxembourg as "société anonyme" under Luxembourgish law by 17 Shareholders: Austria, Belgium, Cyprus, Estonia, Finland, France, Germany, Greece, Ireland, Italy, Luxembourg, Malta, Netherlands, Portugal, Slovakia, Slovenia and Spain. The EFSF has provided financial assistance to Ireland, Portugal and Greece. Since 1 July 2013, the EFSF may no longer engage in new financing programs or enter into new loan facility agreements. Collection of related documents is available at www.efsf.europa.eu/about/legal-documents/index.htm,.

46 Treaty establishing the European Stability Mechanism (ESM) between the Kingdom of Belgium, the Federal Republic of Germany, the Republic of Estonia, Ireland, the Hellenic Republic, the Kingdom of Spain, the French Republic, the Italian Republic, the Republic of Cyprus, the Grand Duchy of Luxembourg, Malta, the Kingdom of the Netherlands, the Republic of Austria, the Portuguese Republic, the Republic of Slovenia, the Slovak Republic and the Republic of Finland (the "euro area Member States" or "ESM Members"), signed 2. 2. 2012 and entered into force 27.9.2012.

have been discussed and proposed by the European Union.[47] Nevertheless, Northern Member States reject this idea as reward for hazard and punishment of prudency.

The control of budgetary policy of the Member States was strengthened to prevent eventual failure to honour debts endangering the single currency. The Treaty on Stability, Coordination and Governance in the Economic and Monetary Union ("the Fiscal Compact")[48] requires the Member States of the Eurozone to install and operate debt brakes. Legislation colloquially labelled as Two-pack[49] and Six-pack[50] has remodelled secondary law addressing fiscal policies and economic development of the Member States.

The debt crisis as potential currency crisis is tackled also with monetary policy. The European Central Bank and central banks of the Southern Member States became benevolent to commercial banks. Immense long-term loans have been granted to numerous banks in Southern Europe facing troubles due to collapse of real estate bubble and economic recession. These banks would collapse without such emergency liquidity assistance (ELA). Requirements for collateral for this borrowing were relaxed. Bonds of heavily indebted states are accepted.[51]

Irresponsive banking should be prevented with more stringent rules and with effective supervision. International operations are not effectively controlled by authorities of the Member States, despite harmonization of banking laws of the Member States with directives of the European Union.

---

47 Green Paper on the feasibility of introducing Stability Bonds, published 23.11.2011, COM (2011) 818 final.

48 Treaty on Stability, Coordination and Governance in the Economic and Monetary Union signed 2.3.2012 and entered into force 1.1.2013.

49 Regulation (EU) No 473/2013 of the European Parliament and of the Counicl on common provisions for monitoring and assessing draft budgetary plans and ensuring the correction of excessive deficit of the Member States in the euro area plus Regulation (EU) No 472/2013 of the European Parliament and of the Council of 21 May 2013 on the strengthening of economic and budgetary surveillance of Member States in the euro area experiencing or threatened with serious difficulties with respect to their financial stability, see also Ioannidis M., 'EU Financial Assistance Conditionality after "Two Pack"', *Zeitschrift für ausländisches öffentliches Recht und Völkerrecht*, 2013, pp. 62–104.

50 Regulation (EU) No 1175/2011 of the European Parliament amending Council Regulation (EC) No 1466/97 on the strengthening of the surveillance of budgetary positions and the surveillance and coordination of economic policies, Council Regulation (EU) No 1177/2011 amending Regulation (EC) No 1467/97 on speeding up and clarifying the implementation of the excessive deficit procedure, OJ. Regulation (EU) No 1173/2011 of the European Parliament and the Council on the effective enforcement of budgetary surveillance in the euro area, Regulation (EU) No 1176/2011 of the European Parliament and of the Council on the prevention and correction of macroeconomic imbalances plus Regulation (EU) No 1174/2011 of the European Parliament and of the Council on enforcement measures to correct excessive macroeconomic imbalances in the euro area.

51 For the development of the policy see J. Eberl, C. Weber, *ECB Collateral Criteria: A Narrative Database 2001–2013*, Ifo Working Paper No. 174, 2014, available at www.cesifo.de.

The Single Supervision Mechanism (SSM)[52] covering most important banks is already implemented by the European Union and the Member States. On the other hands, the Single Resolution Mechanism (SRM) consisting of mutual reserve fund for resolution of banks is long term task. Its finalization is unclear despite adopted legal framework.[53] At the moment it is clear where endangered banks operate.

8. POLITICAL CONSEQUENCES OF THE CRISIS

Crises cause disputes and alienation. Members of associations, shareholders and employees of companies and institutions, citizens of municipalities and nations debate about and quarrel over causes, threats and remedies. Tensions increase. Weak structures can collapse in severe crises. The debt crisis and potential currency crisis sparked serious political crisis of the European Union. Many feared – and some wished – its disintegration.

Member States assisted with rescue loans are required to introduce austerity. Budget cuts, however, curtail national economy. Lower wages result in lower spending. Demand for goods and services decreases. Manufacturers and providers incur losses, cease to pay taxes and dismiss their workers. The impact thereof on public revenues is sinister. Capacity to repay public debt is thus further compromised. Unsurprisingly, austerity measures are perceived by many as unworkable and dangerous.

Austerity measures imposed on indebted Southern Member States thus sparks opposition. Government coalitions collapse, early elections are held and populist parties strengthen their position. Politics of Northern Member States pushed to spend money for rescue loans was also not spared. Large parts of population oppose it. Various populist and Eurosceptic parties and movements emerge and grow. These parties and movements were, as expected,[54] successful in election of the European Parliament in 2014.

52 Regulation (EU) No 1022/2013 of the European Parliament and of the Council amending Regulation (EU) No 1093/2010 establishing a European Supervisory Authority (European Banking Authority) as regards the conferral of specific tasks on the European Central Bank pursuant to Council Regulation (EU) No 1024/2013, Council Regulation (EU) No 1024/2013 conferring specific tasks on the European Central Bank concerning policies relating to the prudential supervision of credit institutions.

53 Regulation (EU) No 806/2014 of the European Parliament and of the Council establishing uniform rules and a uniform procedure for the resolution of credit institutions and certain investment firms in the framework of a Single Resolution Mechanism and a Single Resolution Fund and amending Regulation (EU) No 1093/2010 plus Agreement on the Transfer and Mutualisation of Contributions to the Single Resolution Fund, agreed on 14. 5. 2014 by the Member States of the EU, not yet ratified.

54 S. Kessel, A.L.P. Pirro, *Discontent on the Move: Prospects for Populist Radical Right Parties*, pp. 14–18, in the 2014 European Parliament Elections in Times of Crisis, Intereconomics 2014, ZBW – Leibniz Information Centre for Economics, DOI: 10.1007/s10272-014-0483-1.

The debt and currency crisis reveals limits of the European Union as supranational polity which has not become a federation. The Member States have provided huge sums to the rescue funds. Therefore, they decided on their use. Certainly, variable economic performance and situation determines strength of individual Member States.

The European Commission tries to retain its authority with surveillance and control. The European Parliament is often powerless and irrelevant rubber stamp body for measures adopted by the Commission after negotiation with the Member States represented in the Council.[55]

It is worth to note that the European Union did not face similar troubles as the Member States. The Commission – presided for two terms by José Manuel Barroso since 2004 – did not collapse due the crisis as national cabinets did. There was no early election not only because law does not expect it, but also because nobody called for it. Selection of the new president of the Commission Jean-Claude Juncker as experienced negotiator confirms specific politics in supranational structure.

Nonetheless, the European Union faces considerable loss of reputation.[56] Renaissance of intergovernmental method reveals weaknesses of supranational model. Tensions among the Member States and incapacity to address the crisis without external assistance were apparent.

The debt and currency crisis has worsened relations among European nations. Southerners criticize Northerners for troubles resulting from austerity and its alleged ineffectiveness. Northerners blame Southerners for irresponsible borrowing and wider government failure to address their troubles.

There is no consensus about causes of the crisis in the European Union. Welfare model in general and its particular variants in the Member States, corruption and inefficient governance, reckless borrowing by governments and also by enterprises and individuals and hazardous lending by banks are blamed.

The design of the Eurozone without adequate economic coordination and fiscal integration necessary to mitigate different economic performance of the Member States is criticized as immediate cause of the crisis.

It shall be noted that also the other developed countries – the United States of America and Japan – suffered during last decade from economic slowdown and chronic stagnation, respectively. The debt of the United States government is comparable with heavily indebted states in the Eurozone. The public indebtedness of Japan is the highest among developed countries.

It is hard to agree on remedies without consensus about causes. Adopted remedies resulting from lengthy negotiation under considerable pressures are

---

55 F. Schimmelfennig, *Liberal Intergovernmentalism and the Euro Zone Crisis*, available at www.eup.ethz.ch/people/schimmelfennig/publications/LI_euro_crisis.pdf.

56 L. Bellier, C. Guibéléguiet, *La réputation de l'UE ternie par la crise de la dette*, Les Echos, 2.8.2012, avaialble at www.lesechos.fr.

thus also fiercely debated. Some experts, politicians and commentators criticise bail-outs as promotion of hazardous behaviour. Expansionary monetary policy is depicted as potential impulse for inflation. Others, however, claim that imposed austerity worsens situation in the Member States already suffering from economic crisis. Solidarity among the Member States and their nations consisting in rescue loans and expansive monetary policy is required.

The debt and currency crisis revealed limits of mutual understanding in multilingual European Union. People debate about its causes, consequences and remedies in spaces separated by linguistic barriers. Politicians operate also foremost in national sphere. The deliberation of national representations and representatives of the European Union continues as diplomacy, albeit with interventions of supranational authority.

Experts are capable to debate internationally. Nevertheless, their debates on national level continue. For example, German-written discourse differs significantly from English-written discourse of experts active on global level.

9. LEGAL ASPECTS OF REMEDIES AND REINTERPRETATION OF RULES

Supranational law of the European Union is enforced more effectively than international law. It is, however, weaker than federal laws in existing federations. Direct effect and primacy are well anchored in case-law,[57] but lack clear confirmation in the founding treaties.[58]

Compliance with law of the European Union is often troublesome due to weak enforcement by its own authorities. Assistance of executive and judicial authorities of the Member States is necessary in many cases. Required implementation of directives and regulations is often perfunctory.

Relative weakness of the European Union law revealed with the debt crisis.[59] Chronic incompliance with crucial requirements remained unsanctioned for decades.

Founding treaties can be amended only if all Member States achieve consensus. Signatures of premiers and ministers must be followed with parliamentary or popular approval and with ratification by the heads of the states. Similarly, many regulations, directives and decisions must be adopted unanimously in the Council. The rest requires qualified majority.

---

57 Landmark judgments 26–62 *van Gend en Loos* and 6–64, *Costa v. E.N.E.L.*

58 Declaration No. 17 concerning primacy; Annex to this Final Act the Opinion of the Council Legal Service on the primacy of EC law as set out in 11197/07 (JUR 260).

59 R. Streinz, *Rechtsprinzipien des EuGH zur Durchsetzung des Europäischen Rechts*, pp. 21–44, in Möllers T.M.J., Zeitler F.-C. (eds.), *Europa als Rechtsgemeischaft – Währungsunion und Schuldenkrise*, Mohr Siebeck, 2013.

It is not surprising that several measures adopted in situation of urgency have dubious legal framework under such conditions. The European Financial Stability Facility was established outside supranational law as private company according to Luxembourgish law. The European Financial Stability Mechanism started with secondary law hardly compatible with requirement of balanced budget set in the founding Treaties.[60] The foundation of the European Stability Mechanism with special international treaty concluded by the Member States of the Eurozone was confirmed only later with amendment to the Treaty on Functioning of the European Union.[61]

In addition, representatives of the Member States and of the institutions of the European Union and commentators supporting their decisions resort to utilitarian interpretations of rules. Refusal of them as inappropriate, inapplicable and even harmful. Provisions of the Treaty expecting the separation of budgets of the Member States and of the European Union were understood as the no-bail-out clause.[62] Rescue loans were not expected. Thresholds for public debt were expected as prevention of any demand for them.

Detailed secondary legislation was nonetheless adopted and amended for strengthening of surveillance of the Member States by institutions of the European Union. The Fiscal Compact was adopted as an additional international treaty besides the founding Treaties by most Member States.

It can be questioned whether complicated procedures of surveillance, reporting and evaluation could improve situation. Commentators are rather sceptical.[63] Imposing fines on the Member States in financial distress is intrinsically problematic. Automatized sanctions could be regretted. The requirement to amend constitutions is unusual and challenging. The Member States cannot tackle imbalance of international trade and developments in markets without interventions hardly compatible exactly with basic economic freedoms of the European Union.

The above mentioned rules on operations of the European Central Bank and central banks of the Member States were reinterpreted in the sense that purchase of bonds of highly indebted Member States facing mistrust of investors

---

60 Article 310(1) TFEU.

61 The European Council Decision of 25 March 2011 amending Article 136 of the Treaty on the Functioning of the European Union with regard to a stability mechanism for Member States whose currency is the euro (2011/199/EU), Details are analysed, among others, by A Meye-Heine, *Le TFUE et l'assistance financière à un État membre. Réflexions liées à la mise en place du MES*, Revue de l'Union Européenne, 2014, pp. 13–38.

62 The interview with German EU law professor M. Ruffert in S. Ruhkamp, Professor für Europarecht "Hilfe für Griechenland wäre Rechtsbruch", *Frankfurter Allgemeine Zeitung – Finanzen*, 23.1.2010, available www.faz.net/aktuell/finanzen/anleihen-zinsen/professor-fuer-europarecht-hilfe-fuer-griechenland-waere-rechtsbruch-1912963.html.

63 Scepticism on EU efforts to curtail public debt of the Member States with elaborate rules and mechanisms of control was expressed in R.D. Kelemen, T. Teo, 'Law, Focal Point and Fiscal Discipline in the United States and in the European Union', *American Political Science Review*, vol. 108, no. 2., 2014, pp. 355–370. Authors highlight disciplining effect of markets.

is allowed as necessary for the stabilization of currency. Emergency liquidity assistance (ELA) provided to banks which have invested in these bonds and have lost considerable sums in are also justified as necessary for stabilization of the bank sector and thus the economy.

The conditions of rescue loans, related surveillance of borrowing Member States by lenders and authorities charged by them deserve analysis, albeit their enforcement with assistance of the courts cannot be expected in most cases.

The inefficiency of several rules, vagueness and missing consensus on interpretation of other ones and the creation of complicated new rules whose applicability is questioned undermines legitimacy of entire framework for the Euro.

Legal scholars even now underline that the new Member States are obliged to introduce the Euro. It can be claimed, however, that circumstances have changed fundamentally. According to principles of international law, such changes can release from original obligation if separable from other obligation.[64] Monetary union relies now on altered rules and exists in rather different economic, political and settings.

Such interpretation was not voiced until now. Opponents of the Euro tend to delegitimize authority of the European Union in general. This approach, however, has a political parallel. The European Union ceased to push the new Member States to join the Euro. Applicants were checked rigorously. The smaller new Member States – Slovenia, Slovakia, Estonia, Latvia and Lithuania – have adopted it. On the contrary, the bigger new Member States – Poland, Czech Republic, Hungary, Romania and Bulgaria – hesitate to join.

10. JUDICIAL INVOLVEMENT IN THE CRISIS

As mentioned, judiciary is crucial for the rule of law. The Court of Justice has decisively contributed to the development of law of the European Communities as supranational legal system. The courts of Member States have largely accepted this approach.

Political controversies related to the ongoing debt crisis and eventual currency crisis thus inevitably attract judicial actions if there is legal framework for the single currency.

However, the tendency to bring these controversies before the courts is variable in the Member States. Rescue loans and other measures save the heavily indebted Member States from their insolvency. Few would complain in these countries. Complaints emerge from institutions, political parties and other

[64] Article 62 of the Vienna Convention on Law of Treaties. Nevertheless, this fundamental change can be invoked for withdrawal from treaty, e.a. from entire founding treaties of the European Union. From legal point of view, the Euro is not separable from economic liberalization.

actors. They oppose their own governments agreeing with rescue measures or approach of the institution of the European Union.

The courts in few Member States have been called to decide on cases related to the debt and eventual currency crisis. The greatest attention is duly paid to Germany.

Germany developed strong model of Rechtsstaat after the catastrophe of Nazism. The Grundgesetz is applied intensely for the control of legislation and its enforcement. Germany established strong constitutional court for this task. Its constitutional judiciary was emulated in many countries. The methodology of constitutional principles and fundamental rights developed by the Bundesverfassungsgericht is emulated abroad.

German insistence on constitutional principles and fundamental rights was and is so strong that even European integration, generally supported by the German elites and the population, was questioned if overlooked by the European institutions. Among others, German pressure contributed to consideration of the European Convention on Human Rights and the case-law of the European Court for Human Rights by the Court of Justice and to adoption of the Charter of Fundamental Rights of the European Union.

Germany contributes the greatest sums for rescue loans. Germany is prosperous thanks reformed markets and tendency to savings. German public budgets – despite non-compliance with official threshold – are perceived as the most stabilized. The interest rate of *Bundesanleihen* forms the measurement for reliability of other government bonds (spreads).[65] Germans are self-assured that the situation reflects sound national economic and fiscal policy.

Finally, Germany suffered hyperinflation ninety years ago, resulting into interwar instability leading to the Nazi regime and disastrous war. Germans thus perceive stable currency as essential for economic and social stability. The Euro is legitimate only if it will be stable for a long period of time and thus is a real successor of the Deutschmark.

The feeling of responsibility for war atrocities towards other Europeans is widely shared by German elites. Nevertheless, the preparedness to confirm it with extraordinary financial contributions to projects of European unity is vanishing.

All these factors cause significant engagement of German Bundesverfassungsgericht. This engagement is perceived as complicating in other countries as was revealed in an impatient statement of the former French minister of finance and now the director of the International Monetary Fund Christine Lagarde.[66]

---

65 Switzerland is the only country whose bonds compete with *Bundesanleihen* it their reputation. Nevertheless, German presence at international markets is bigger, see www.bloomberg.com/markets/rates-bonds/.

66 "If I hear the word Karlsruhe one more time, I'm leaving the room", K.-A. Scholz, *Karlsruhe's constitutional monastery*, analysis of Deutsche Welle 11.9.2012, www.dw.de/karlsruhes-constitutional-monastery/a-16231161-1.

The Bundesverfassungsgericht was cautious to undermine rescue measures agreed or promoted by the Bundesregierung and endorsed by the Bundestag. It accepted rescue loan to Greece and the establishment of the European Stability Mechanism.[67] Nevertheless, it underlined necessity of parliamentary approval and control over all expenditures.

Times are changing now. The Bundesverfassungsgericht requested[68] in spring 2014 the Court of Justice[69] for check of compliance of Outright Monetary Transactions (OMT). These Outrights Monetary Transactions[70] are at the moment the policy proclaimed in September 2012 by the European Central Bank to purchase without limits bonds of the Member States if rejected by investors.

The first request of the Bundesverfassungsgericht for preliminary ruling in six decades of coexistence of this court with the supranational judiciary of the European Communities shows that the court has substantial doubts about the compliance with principles of the European Union.

It shall be highlighted that the Bundesverfassungsericht declared request as necessary communication before eventual resort to rebellion against supranational law in name of core values of German constitutionalism.[71]

The courts of other Member States are asked to intervene from time to time. Nevertheless, the sole case worth to mention was a request of the Supreme Court of Ireland for preliminary ruling when deciding on complaint of deputy Pringle against establishment the European Stabilization Mechanism.[72] The Court of Justice interpreted the no-bail-clause narrowly.

We can expect that the Court of Justice would accept this policy. The request mentioned could be rejected for formal grounds because it was decided by the Council of the European Central Bank and presented by its president Mario Draghi, but not yet implemented. Even if the request for preliminary ruling is accepted, the response can be benevolent.[73]

The opinion of the advocate general delivered in January 2015[74] reveals competing inclinations within the Court of Justice. On the one hand, the European Central Bank shall enjoy considerable independence while deciding on monetary

---

67 Decision of the second senate 2 BvR – 2 BvR 987/10, 2 BvR 1485/10, 2 BvR 1099/10 of 7.9.2011.

68 Decision of the second senate 2 BvR 2728/13 of 14.1.2014.

69 Registered by the Court of justice as C-62/14 Gauweiler (deputy of German Bundestag leading group of complainants).

70 Decided by the Governing Council of the European Central Bank on 6.9.2012. The program was described in *ECB Monthly Bulletin*, September 2012, pp. 7–11, www.ecb.europa.eu/pub/pdf/mobu/mb201209en.pdf.

71 Decision of the second senate – 2 BvR 2661/06 of 6.7.2010 in *Honeywell*.

72 Judgment C-370/12, *T. Pringle v. Government of Ireland and the Attorney General* of 27.11.2012.

73 For comments on legal aspects see M. Goldmann, *Adjudicating Economics? Central Bank Independence and the Appropriate Standard of Judicial Review*, German Law Journal, vol. 15, no.2, pp. 265–280, available at www.germanlawjournal.de.

74 Opinion of AG P. Cruz-Villarón issued on 14.1.2015 accepts the OMT as unconventional and exceptional tool of monetary policy for which the ECB is competent and judiciary should be

policy. The advocate general admits lack of expertise. On the other hand, the legal framework for the Euro establishes restrictions for operations of the European Central Bank obliged to care for stable single currency. The compliance requires thus for steering of currency circulation. They shall be well explained.

It is hard to predict the incoming decision of the Court of Justice. As mentioned, judicial control of monetary policy is unprecedented at national level. I expect benevolence. It can be argued that the European Central Bank operates within its mandate for monetary policy. The Court will probably show respect for the independence of central banking of the European Union as a "sister institution" resembling in its authority and independence the Court itself. The Court could fear consequences of eventual rigorous interpretation of the rules for stability of the Eurozone, but it would surely conceal this attitude.

We can expect similar restraint of the Court of Justice in eventual future cases addressing controversial measures tackling the debt crisis of the Member States and eventual currency crisis in the Eurozone.

Debates will surely emerge whether such judicial restraint is good. This approach can cause further deterioration of legitimacy of the Euro and of the European Union. The Member States agreed and their people accepted to introduce single currency under specific conditions. Feared rebellion of the *Bundesverfassungsgericht* could be signal of such erosion of legitimacy of the supranational structure in its keystone state.

However, the Court of Justice would be swiftly accused of judicial activism if decides to intervene in measures of competent institutions of the European Union and its Member States. Many would highlight that the compliance with the rules after a decade of their ignorance could have dangerous outcomes. If amendment cannot be achieved, reinterpretation of rules can be feasible and even their ignorance would be necessary.

Doubts raised about measures aimed at alleviation of debt and currency crisis can bring new cases to the Court of Justice. The number of such causes will be low, albeit they will be of the highest political importance. Among others, the Court of Justice is expected contribute to enforcement of restrictions imposed on the Member States with the Fiscal Compact. The Court shall evaluate implementation and eventually impose heavy fines.[75]

The judiciary of the European Union can expect entire new agenda with already mentioned centralization of bank supervision.[76] Permissions, sanctions, requirements, prohibitions addressed to banks and their forced administration

---

cautious with its review. Nevertheless, principles of monetary policy and prohibition of direct financing are recalled. Eventual realization shall be carefully explained by the ECB.

75 Article 8 of the Treaty. Action of the European Commmission to the Court of Justice is expected. Financial sanctions up to 0.1% GDP can be imposed by the Court for incompliance. The article underlines relation with general provisions addressing role of judiciary.

76 Detailed analysis of judicial aspects of emerging banking union in L. Wissink, T. Duijkersloot, H. Widdershoven, 'Shifts in Competences between Member States and the EU

are rarely reviewed by courts. Decision-making is often vested to central banks. Their independence and urgency spare it from adjudication. Nevertheless, the impact of bank supervision on interests of clients, shareholders and managers cannot be denied. Therefore, judicial control cannot be entirely refused.

11. CONCLUSIONS

Recent cases brought to the Court of Justice challenging the monetary and fiscal measures adopted in the Eurozone shattered by the debt crisis of its several Member States are unprecedented. National courts have never been asked to resolve substantial controversies related to national fiscal and monetary policies.

The emergence of such cases just in the European Union deserves explanation. Firstly, the European Communities and the European Union were and are the structures governed with law, despite any weaknesses resulting from its supranational features. Secondly, the Euro was introduced according to the project formulated in legal terms. Other currencies are not subjected to similar legal framework.

However, chronic incompliance with fiscal requirements brought the Eurozone at the edge of collapse. The rescue loans and unconventional monetary policy introduced since the onset of the crisis were not expected. These measures are controversial. They assist indebted Member States at the expense of responsible Member States. Eventual inflationary trends are perceived in opposite ways by debtors and by creditors.

The compliance of these measures with the original set of rules is questionable. These rules are formulated vaguely. Original and textual[77] interpretation of these rules invoked by some is perceived as unfeasible and even dangerous for the viability of the Euro as the shared currency of nineteen Member States by others, including key persons of the European Union. The president of the European Central Bank Mario Draghi said to do "whatever it takes" to save the Euro.[78]

The approach of the Court of Justice is hard to predict. The Court of Justice is and will probably continue to be cautious whether to intervene in the fiscal and monetary policies adopted by the European Commission, the European Parliament and the Council and the European Council or by the Member States represented as political actors as well as the European Central Bank as an independent institution.

in the New Supervisory System for Credit Institutions and their Consequences for Judicial Protection', *Utrecht Law Review*, no. 5, 2014, pp. 92–115.

77 Originalism is the approach of interpretation of the US Constitution as the text was allegedly understood two centuries ago.

78 His statement of 25.7.2012 is repeatedly cited as the outline of the ECB policy during any event.

The structure of the European Union as supranational structure relying extensively on the Member States makes things more complicated. The adjudication of European Union law is realized in close cooperation with the courts of the Member States – as the Bundesverfassungsgericht – whose opinions cannot be ignored.

BIBLIOGRAPHY

Athanassiou, P., *Withdrawal and Expulsion from the EU and the EMU – Some Reflexions*, Legal Working Paper Series, No. 10, 2009, European Central Bank – Eurosystem.

Austin, D.A. and M.R. Levit, *The debt limit: history and recent increases*, Congressional Research Service Report for Congress, RL31967, 2010, available at http://fpc.state.gov/documents/organization/105193.pdf. PROEF 1

Bellier, L. and C. Guibéléguiet, La réputation de l'UE ternie par la crise de la dette, *Les Echos*, 2.8.2012, avaialble at www.lesechos.fr.

Beuerlein, I., Fünf Jahre nach der Euro-Bargeldeinführung – War der Euro wirklich ein Teuro?, Statistisches Bundesamt • *Wirtschaft und Statistik* 2/2007, pp. 208–212.

Dyson, K., *States, Debt and Power: Saints and Sinners in European History and Integration*, Oxford University Press, 2014.

Eberl, J. and C. Weber, *ECB Collateral Criteria: A Narrative Database 2001–2013*, Ifo Working Paper No. 174, 2014, available at www.cesifo.de.

Fidrmuc, J., J. Horváth and J. Fidrmuc, The stability of monetary unions: lessons from the breakup of Czechoslovakia, *Journal of Comparative Economics*, 1999, vol. 27, no. 4, pp. 753–781.

Goldmann, M., Adjudicating Economics? Central Bank Independence and the Appropriate Standard of Judicial Review, *German Law Journal*, 2014, vol. 15, no. 2, pp. 265–280, available at www.germanlawjournal.de.

Hacker, B., *On the Way to a Fiscal or a Stability Union? The Plans for a "Genuine" Economic and Monetary Union*, Fridrich-Ebert-Stiftung, 2013, available at www.fes.de/ipa, ISBN 978-3-86498-746-5.

Hagen, J., J. Schuknecht and G. Wolswijk, *European bond spreads in the current crisis*, 21. 12. 2009, VOX CEPR's policy portal, available at www.voxeu.org/article/european-government-bond-spreads-current-crisis.

Ioannidis, M., EU Financial Assistance Conditionality after "Two Pack", *Zeitschrift für ausländisches öfentliches Recht und Völkerrecht*, 2013, pp. 62–104.

Kastrop, C., G. Meister-Scheufelen and M. Sudhof (eds.), *Die neuen Schuldenregeln im Grundgesetz: Zur Fortentwicklung der bundesstaatlichen Finanzbeziehungen*, Berliner Wissenschafts-Verlag, 2010.

Kelemen, R.D. and T. Teo, Law, Focal Point and Fiscal Discipline in the United States and in the European Union, *American Political Science Review*, vol. 108, no. 2., 2014, pp. 355–370.

Kessel, S. and A.L.P. Pirro, *Discontent on the Move: Prospects for Populist Radical Right Parties, in the 2014 European Parliament Elections in Times of Crisis*, 2014, ZBW – Leibniz Information Centre for Economics, pp. 14–18 doi: 10.1007/s10272-014-0483-1.

Meye-Heine, A., Le TFUE et l'assistance financiere a un État membre. Réflexions liées a la mise en place du MES, *Revue de l'Union Européenne*, 2014, pp. 13–38.

Mendizabal, R.H., Monetary Union and the Transaction Cost Savings of a Single Currency, *Review of International Economics*, vol. 10, no. 2, pp. 263–277, 2002.

Möller, T.M.J. and F.-C. Zeitler (eds.), *Europa als Rechtsgemeischaft – Währungsunion und Schuldenkrise*, Mohr Siebeck, 2012.

Mundell, R., A Theory of Optimum Currency Areas, *The American Economic Review*, Vol. 51, No. 4, pp. 657–665, 1961.

Streinz, R., Rechtsprinzipien des EuGH zur Durchsetzung des Europäischen Rechts, pp. 21–44, in T. M. J. Möllers, F.-C. Zeitler (eds.), *Europa als Rechtsgemeischaft – Währungsunion und Schuldenkrise*, Mohr Siebeck, 2013.

Tridimas, G., "A comparison of Central Bank and Judicial Independence" in A. Marciano (Ed.), *Constitutional mythologies: New perspectives on controlling the state*" Springer, Chapter 11, pp. 155–170, New York, 2011.

Ullrich, K., *Unabhängigkeit und Verantwortlichkeit der Europäischen Zentralbank, Zentrum für Europäische Wirtschaft spolitik*, ZEW Discussion Papers, 2003, No. 03–65, available at http://hdl.handle.net/10419/23999.

Wahl, R., *Das Bundesverfassungsgericht im europäischen und internationalen Umfeld, Aus Politik und Zeitgeschichte*, B 37–38, pp. 45–54, 2001, available at www.bpb.de/apuz/26041/das-bundesverfassungs-gericht-im-europaeischen-und-internationalen-umfeld?p=all

Welfens, P.J., *Die Zukunft des Euro – Die europäische Staatschuldenkrise und ihre Überwindung*, Nicolaische Verlagsbuchhandlung GmbH, Berlin, 2012.

Wennerström, E.O., *The Rule of Law and the European Union*, Uppsala, Iustus Förlag, 2007

Winkler, R., *Administrative Justice in Europe: Th e EU Acquis, good practice and recent Developments – Working Paper submitted for the Twinning Project Support to more efficient, effective and modern operation and functioning of the Administrative Judiciary Court of the Republic of Croatia*, 2007, available at www.upravnisudrh.hr.

Wissink, L., T. Duijkersloot and H. Widdershoven, Shifts in Competences between Member States and the EU in the New Supervisory System for Credit Institutions and their Consequences for Judicial Protection, *Utrecht Law Review*, no. 5, 2014, pp. 92–115.

7. HOW CJEU'S "PRIVACY SPRING" CONSTRUED THE HUMAN RIGHTS SHIELD IN THE DIGITAL AGE

Gabriela ZANFIR*
PhD, Independent researcher

1. INTRODUCTION

The Court of Justice of the European Union (CJEU) issued two landmark decisions in April and May 2014, effectively applying Article 7 – the right to private life and Article 8 – the right to personal data protection, provided for in the Charter of Fundamental Rights of the European Union (the Charter), in order to protect the fundamental rights of the person in two different dimensions of the Surveillance Society. The first dimension opposes the individual and the state; the second one opposes the individual and private bodies. By doing so, the Court established itself as a prominent actor in the protection of fundamental rights in the digital age, not only in the EU, but also on the global stage.

In the first decision, *Digital Rights Ireland*,[2] the Court annulled Directive 2006/24/EC[3] – the "Data Retention Directive", in its entirety, arguing that its provisions run counter to both Article 7 and Article 8 of the Charter. The Data Retention Directive enshrined an obligation for telecom service providers to retain traffic data of all their clients for a period of minimum 6 months and maximum 2 years, depending on the national laws transposing the directive. While the Court found that this operation does not touch on the essence of the right to private life and the right to personal data protection, and it genuinely

---

* The author submitted this paper for publication as an independent researcher, before joining the European Data Protection Supervisor as legal officer. The views expressed here pertain solely to the author and do not engage in any way her current employer.
Email: gabriela.zanfir@pdpecho.com.

2 CJEU, Decision of the Court in joined cases C-293/12 and C-594/12 *Digital Rights Ireland* of 8 April 2014.

3 Directive 2006/24/EC of the European Parliament and of the Council of 15 March 2006 on the retention of data generated or processed in connection with the provision of publicly available electronic communications services or of public communications networks, OJ 2006 L 105, p. 54.

satisfies an objective of general interest (fight against serious crime), it is not proportionate to the purposes it pursues. Among other things, the Court observed that the directive "entails an interference with the fundamental rights of practically the entire European population"[1] and took into account the "general absence of limits"[2] from its provisions.

In the second decision, *Google v. Spain*,[3] the Court interpreted the provisions of Directive 95/46/EC[4] – the "Data Protection Directive", and Article 8 of the Charter in the sense that EU data protection law is applicable *ratione personae* to United States-based company Google Inc., due to the "inextricably link"[5] with its subsidiary Google Spain, and to the fact that it meets the criteria to be considered a "data controller". Furthermore, the Court gave effect to the right to erasure – Article 12 of the Data Protection Directive, and the right to object – Article 14 of the Data Protection Directive, so that individuals can ask the deletion of links relating to their name and which show up in the results page of the Google search engine. The implications of this decision are complex and will be analysed in detail in this paper. Two of the fundamental questions to be answered are: how many of the obligations of the data controller under EU data protection law can actually be executed by an internet search engine provider and whether there is a need to legally define different categories of data controllers.

This paper will analyse the two decisions of the Court, which represent cornerstones for the human rights protection in the digital age. It will also take into account the importance of the decisions of several constitutional courts of Member States of the EU, which found the laws transposing the Data Retention Directive unconstitutional. This approach will highlight the role of the European judiciary – by which is meant both the CJEU and the national courts acting as EU courts, in construing the coordinates of human rights protection in the digital age.

2. THE RELATIONSHIP BETWEEN INDIVIDUALS AND THE STATE IN THE DIGITAL WORLD: DIGITAL RIGHTS IRELAND

The decision of the CJEU in *Digital Rights Ireland* was already meticulously analysed by scholars.[6] The following analysis will aim at contextualizing some

---

1 *Digital Rights Ireland*, para. 56.

2 *Idem*, para. 60.

3 CJEU, Decision of the Court in Case C-131/12 *Google v. Spain* of 13 May 2014.

4 Directive 95/46/EC of the European Parliament and of the Council of 24 October 1995 on the protection of individuals with regard to the processing of personal data and on the free movement of such data, OJ 1995 L 281, p. 31.

5 *Google v. Spain*, para. 56.

6 See, for instance, E. Guild, S. Carrera, *The Political and Judicial Life of Metadata: Digital Rights Ireland and the trail of the data retention directive*, CEPS Paper in Liberty and Security

of the most important facts and findings of the Court, with a view to detect how the Court set the scene for its future case-law of defending human rights in the digital world.

2.1. PRELIMINARY OBSERVATION: THERE IS A WIDE SOCIETAL INTEREST IN PROTECTING HUMAN RIGHTS AGAINST THE BULK COLLECTION AND RETENTION OF METADATA

The two cases, which were jointly analysed by the Court, stemmed from a collective effort. This indicates a wide societal interest in defending fundamental rights threatened by the bulk collection of metadata, together with the unclearly defined access of the state to those data. Case C-293/12 is the result of an action brought by Digital Rights Ireland, an organization "dedicated to defending Civil, Human and Legal rights in a digital age",[7] to the Irish courts, challenging the legality of national legislative and administrative measures concerning the retention of data relating to electronic communications. Case C-594/12 stemmed from 11.130 applicants[8] who were seeking the annulment of national provisions that were transposing Directive 2006/24 into Austrian law. It is also noteworthy that both Courts that sent the preliminary ruling questions are constitutional courts: the Verfassungsgerichtshof (Austrian Constitutional Court) and the High Court of Ireland (which also has the competence to decide on the validity of laws in relation with the Constitution).[9]

2.2. BULK RETENTION OF METADATA TOUCHES ON THE FREEDOM OF EXPRESSION, NOT ONLY ON PRIVACY

Whenever the *Digital Rights Ireland* decision is analysed, there is one factor that usually remains in the background: the fact that the Court is ready to assess not only the infringement of Articles 7 and 8 of the Charter (the protection of private life and the protection of personal data), but also that of Article 11 – freedom of expression. In this respect, the Court affirms,

in Europe, No. 65, May 2014, available online at www.ceps.eu/book/political-and-judicial-life-metadata-digital-rights-ireland-and-trail-data-retention-directive (last time accessed on 18 November 2014); F. Boehm, M. D. Cole, 'Data Retention after the Judgment of the Court of the European Union', Munster/Luxemburg 30 June 2014, study funded by the Greens/EFSA Group in the European Parliament; J. Rauhofer, D.M. Sithigh, *The Data Retention Directive Never Existed*, SCRIPTed, 11(1), 2014.

7 See the description of the organization on its website: www.digitalrights.ie/about/ (last accessed on 18 November 2014).

8 CJEU, *Digital Rights Ireland*, para. 19.

9 Constitution of Ireland, Article 34.

> "even though (...) the directive does not permit the retention of the content of the communication or of information consulted using an electronic communications network, *it is not inconceivable that the retention of the data in question might have an effect* on the use, by subscribers or registered users, of the means of communication covered by that directive, and, consequently, *on their exercise of the freedom of expression* guaranteed by Article 11 of the Charter".[10]

Mutatis mutandis, in a case where the content of the communication or of information consulted using an electronic communication network is legally retained, the right to freedom of expression is more clearly touched upon.

The idea that collection and retention of personal data could infringe freedom of speech may not seem obvious, *prima facie*. The experience of former surveillance societies shows that, in fact, the limitation of freedom of speech was a direct consequence of ample surveillance.[11] In a study called "The Daily Fear", a psychologist who analysed the conduct of people living in the last years of communist Romania, when there was an acute problem of lack of food and heating during winter, came to the conclusion that:

> "Not only the fear of an external nature is unconsciously hidden, or, more generally, developed inside the psychological apparatus, but the society could influence such a transformation. The risks of discussing, let alone criticizing, the food and heating problems were greater than the hunger and the feeling of being cold themselves".[12]

The author explained that "the terror has as possible source the risk of expressing different opinions in a social space where only the version of the single Party had the right to exist"[13] and that "the fear of informers imposed the avoidance of certain discussions, eliminated certain subjects".[14]

In the end, the Court did not analyse the validity of Directive 2006/24/EC in the light of Article 11 of the Charter due to the fact that it had already found the directive is not compliant with Articles 7 and 8 of the Charter.[15] However, the above-mentioned paragraph of the decision shows that, in the future, the Court may engage in assessing the existence of an infringement of freedom of expression by state surveillance.

---

10 CJEU, *Digital Rights Ireland*, para. 28, emphasis added.

11 See G. Zanfir, 'Big Brother in a post-communist era. Radiography of the protection of private life in a European Romania', *Revue de Sciences Politiques*, No. 35, 2012, pp. 330–351.

12 R. Clit, 'Viața cotidiană în comunism. Frica de zi cu zi (Daily life in Communism. The Day to Day Fear)', *Psihologia socială (Social Psychology)*, Issue 12/2003, p. 180 (translated by the author).

13 Idem, p. 182 (t.a.).

14 Idem, p. 185 (t.a.).

15 CJEU, *Digital Rights Ireland*, para. 70.

2.3. CLARIFICATION ON THE DIFFERENCES IN CONTENT BETWEEN ARTICLES 7 AND 8 OF THE CHARTER

It was observed that in the case law of the CJEU, "the in-distinction of data protection and privacy has produced (and has been punctually preserved by) explicit affirmations of the close relationship linking personal data protection and privacy".[16]

Since its judgment in *Schecke*,[17] it became clear that the CJEU hesitates in differentiating between the concepts of 'respect for private life' and 'protection of personal data' – as they are protected by Articles 7 and 8 from the Charter, preferring to treat them identically at first, and then as being 'closely connected'.[18] This hesitation can be first spotted in the Opinion of AG Sharpston in *Schecke*, who literally referred to the rights "to privacy and/or to the protection of personal data".[19] In the judgment, the Court coined the notion of a right "to respect for private life with regard to the processing of personal data",[20] a symbiotic product of Articles 7 and 8 of the Charter with no clearly defined content.

Some findings of the CJEU in *Digital Rights Ireland* provide for a substantial (and much needed) differentiation between the two fundamental rights in the interpretation of the Court, which started to separately analyse the facts of the case in relation to each of the fundamental rights concerned. For instance, the Court finds that "*the retention of data for the purpose of possible access to them* by the competent national authorities (...) directly and specifically affects private life and, consequently, the rights guaranteed by Article 7 of the Charter".[21] The Court adds that "such a retention of data also falls under Article 8 of the Charter because it constitutes *the processing of personal data* within the meaning of that article and, therefore, *necessarily has to satisfy the data protection requirements arising from that article*".[22] Therefore, the Court deems that the existence of the retention of data and the access of authorities to these data touch upon private life and Article 7 of the Charter, while the fact that the retention of data represents "processing of personal data" triggers the application of Article 8 of the Charter and the data protection safeguards enshrined in the article. This approach of the Court confirms the theory that

16 G. Gonzalez Fuster, *The Emergence of Personal Data Protection as a Fundamental Right of the EU*, Springer Science and Business, Switzerland, 2014, p. 259.

17 CJEU, Judgment of the Court in Joined Cases C-92/09 *Volker und Markus Schecke* and C-93/09 *Hartmut Eifert* of 9 November 2010.

18 CJEU, Judgment of the Court in Joined Cases C-468/10 and C-469/10 *ASNEF and FECEMED* of 24 November 2011.

19 Opinion of AG Sharpston delivered on 17 June 2010 in Joined Cases C-92/09 *Volker und Markus Schecke* and C-93/09 *Hartmut Eifert*, para. 65.

20 CJEU, *Schecke*, para. 52.

21 CJEU, *Digital Rights Ireland*, para. 29, emphasis added.

22 Idem.

the right to private life is "an opacity tool" meant to be a barrier between the private life and intrusions in private life, while the right to data protection is "a transparency tool", meant to manage how personal information is used with the ultimate purpose of protecting several rights of the person, including the right to private life.[23]

This differentiation is highlighted in two subsequent paragraphs of the judgment, when the Court analyses whether the essence of the rights protected by Articles 7 and 8 was affected. The Court finds that the essence of the right to private life is not touched upon, even though the retention of data required by Directive 2006/24/EC is "a particularly serious interference"[24] with it. However, this interference "is not such as to adversely affect the essence of those rights given that (...) the directive does not permit the acquisition of knowledge of the content of the electronic communications as such".[25] *Per a contrario*, if access to the content of the retained electronic communications would be possible, the essence of the right protected by Article 7 would be affected. This statement is valuable with a view towards assessing structural surveillance of the content of electronic communications, if such facts will be brought in front of the Court.

On the other hand, the procedural nature of the right to personal data protection stems from further findings of the Court, which established that the essence of the right to personal data protection as enshrined in Article 8 is not affected, because Directive 2006/24/EC provides that "certain principles of data protection and data security must be respected by providers of publicly available electronic communications services or of public communications networks".[26] The Court added that "according to those principles, Member States are to ensure that appropriate technical and organisation measures are adopted against accidental or unlawful destruction, accidental loss or alteration of the data".[27]

AG Cruz Villalón drew an even clearer line between the two rights enshrined in Articles 7 and 8 of the Charter in his Opinion on *Digital Rights Ireland*. He stated that even if Directive 2006/24 were to be found fully compatible with Article 8 of the Charter, "in no way means that it is fully compatible with the requirements resulting from the right to privacy guaranteed by Article 7 of the Charter".[28] The AG clarified that

> "since the 'private sphere' forms the core of the 'personal sphere', it cannot be ruled out that legislation limiting the right to the protection of personal data in compliance

---

23 See S. Gutwirth and P. De Hert, "Regulating Profiling in a Democratic Constitutional State", in M. Hildebrandt and S. Gutwirth ed., *Profiling the European Citizen*, (Springer, 2008), pp. 271–303 .

24 CJEU, *Digital Rights Ireland*, para. 39.

25 Idem, para. 39.

26 Idem, para. 40.

27 Idem, para. 40.

28 Opinion of AG Cruz Villalon delivered on 12 December 2013 in Case C-293/12 *Digital Rights Ireland* and Case C-594/12 *Setlinger*, para. 60.

with Article 8 of the Charter may nevertheless be regarded as constituting a disproportionate interference with Article 7 of the Charter".[29]

The idea that personal data protection is instrumental in the protection of private life became apparent in the judgment, where the Court mentioned in one paragraph that the protection of personal data plays an *important role* "in the light of the fundamental right to respect for private life".[30]

A point to be noted is that both AG Cruz Villalón and the Court refer to a "right to privacy" in the Opinion[31] and, respectively, the judgment.[32] Both seem to link it to Article 7 and not Article 8 of the Charter, but the differentiation has some nuances – the exploration of which is not in the scope of this article.

2.4. REQUIREMENTS FOR DATA RETENTION LEGISLATION TO COMPLY WITH FUNDAMENTAL RIGHTS

The Court found that Directive 2006/24/EC does not comply with the principle of proportionality in the light of Articles 7, 8 and 52(1) of the Charter,[33] declaring it invalid. Before it reached this conclusion, the Court detailed why the provisions of the directive go beyond what is necessary to obtain the legitimate purpose of "the fight against international terrorism in order to maintain international peace and security".[34] The argumentation of the Court can be summarised in a list of requirements necessary to be met by any future legislative proposal regarding data retention. Therefore, data retention legislation must:

1. Differentiate, limit and make subject to exceptions the persons whose information is retained in the light of the objective of fighting against serious crime;[35] such limitations should be done regarding: (i) persons for whom there is no evidence capable of suggesting that their conduct might have a link, even an indirect or remote one, with serious crime and (ii) persons whose communications are subject to professional secrecy;[36]
2. Require a relationship between the data whose retention is provided for and a threat to public security;[37]

---

29 Idem, para. 61.
30 CJEU, *Digital Rights Ireland*, para. 48.
31 Idem, see, for instance, para. 26, 32, 39, 46, 49.
32 CJEU, *Digital Rights Ireland*, para. 32, 33 and 39.
33 Idem, para. 69.
34 Idem, para. 42.
35 Idem, para. 57.
36 Idem, para. 58.
37 Idem, para. 59.

3. Limit the access of national authorities to the data, by (i) laying down *objective criteria to determine the limits of the access*;[38] (ii) establishing *substantive and procedural conditions relating to the access* of the competent national authorities to the data and to their subsequent use;[39] (iii) laying down an *objective criterion* by which *the number of persons authorized to access and subsequently use the data retained is limited* to what is strictly necessary in the light of the objective pursued;[40]
4. When establishing the retention period, it should (i) make a distinction between the categories of data set out in Article 5 on the basis of their possible usefulness for the purposes pursued[41] and (ii) base the determination of the length of the retention period on objective criteria;[42]
5. Expressly require that data must be retained within the EU;[43]
6. Require irreversible destruction of the data at the end of the data retention period;[44]
7. Ensure that the way the data are processed pursuant to the data retention legislation is subject to control by an independent authority of compliance with requirements of protection and security.[45]

In the aftermath of the Court's decision in *Digital Rights Ireland*, several Constitutional Courts of the EU Member States have declared the national data retention laws transposing the Directive unconstitutional (in Romania,[46] Slovenia,[47] Austria),[48] another Constitutional Court suspended the effects of the national provisions until it will deliberate on substance (Slovakia),[49] while the CJEU radiated a case in which the European Commission sought to sanction Germany for not transposing the data retention directive.[50] In fact, even before the Court gave its decision in *Digital Rights Ireland*, several constitutional courts of EU Members States had already declared national data retention provisions unconstitutional, including the German Constitutional

38 Idem, para. 60.
39 Idem, para. 61.
40 Idem, para. 62.
41 Idem, para. 63.
42 Idem, para. 64.
43 Idem, para. 68.
44 Idem, para. 67.
45 Idem, para. 68.
46 Constitutional Court of Romania, Decision No. 440/2014 from 8 July 2014.
47 Constitutional Court of the Republic of Slovenia, Judgement U-I-65/13–19 from 3 July 2014.
48 Austrian Constitutional Court, Decision G47/2012 and others, from 27 June 2014.
49 Constitutional Court of Slovakia, Order in the Pending procedure PL. ÚS 10/2014, issued on 23 April 2014.
50 CJEU, Order of the President of the Court in Case C-329/12 *Commission v. Germany* from 5 June 2014.

Court.[51] Nevertheless, overall, most of the EU Member States still have data retention laws in force.

The legal service of the European Parliament showed in a Report[52] that even if the data retention directive is invalid, the national laws transposing it are still in the *ratione materiae* scope of EU law, considering they regulate in the field of data protection and electronic communications. Therefore, Member States must ensure that the national measures dealing with data retention in the electronic communications sector are compatible with the Charter as interpreted by the Court of Justice in the *Digital Rights Ireland* judgment.[53]

On one hand, national courts have a paramount role in adjudicating the fundamental rights of data protection and respect to private life with regard to the retention of personal data in individual cases, because they are closest to the persons seeking protection of their rights. On the other hand, constitutional courts should make sure that national measures are compatible with the Charter as interpreted by CJEU in *Digital Rights Ireland*. For instance, the decision of the Constitutional Court of Romania, which declared the national data retention law unconstitutional, started with a thorough analysis, extended on 15 paragraphs,[54] of the *Digital Rights Ireland* decision of the CJEU, before starting to apply the criteria developed by the Court in Luxemburg to the national provisions.

In conclusion, each judicial review level has a part to play in the system of protection of fundamental rights in the digital world, with the Court of Justice of the EU developing detailed criteria to determine if a national provision is compliant with the fundamental rights enshrined in Articles 7 and 8 of the Charter.

3. THE RELATIONSHIP BETWEEN INDIVIDUALS AND PRIVATE BODIES IN THE DIGITAL WORLD: GOOGLE v. SPAIN

The facts of the case before the Court of Justice oppose Google Inc., which has the headquarters in USA, to the Spanish Data Protection Authority (DPA), which issued a Decision requiring Google to de-index from the search results of its Internet search engine links connected to the name of a Spanish citizen,

---

51 For a summary of these pre-*Digital Rights Ireland* decisions, see C. Jones and B. Hayes, *The EU data retention directive, a case study in the legitimacy and effectiveness of EU counter-terrorism policy*, published within the SECILE project (Securing Europe through Counter-Terrorism: Impact, Legitimacy and Effectiveness), implemented by Statewatch.

52 Legal Opinion on Questions relating to the judgment of the Court of Justice of 8 April 2014 in Joined Cases C-293/12 and C-594/12, issued on 8 January 2015.

53 Idem, para. 78.

54 Constitutional Court of Romania, Decision 440/2014, paras. 23–38.

exercising his right to erasure of personal data. Google challenged in Court the decision of the DPA, claiming among other things that the Spanish data protection law does not apply to it. The Spanish national Court sent a question for a preliminary ruling to the CJEU, under Article 267 TFEU. At the core of the main proceedings is the request of a person – a citizen of the EU, under data protection law to have his personal data erased by a private body which processes his data and which is not located within the EU.

The ruling of the Court in *Google v. Spain* was given under the principle that Directive 95/46 must ensure "effective and complete protection" of the fundamental rights and freedoms of persons.[55] Once again, after the landmark decision annulling the Data Retention Directive, the Court has applied in an effective manner Articles 7 and 8 of the Charter.[56]

3.1. INTERNET SEARCH ENGINES ARE DATA CONTROLLERS AND THEIR ACTIVITY INVOLVES PROCESSING OF PERSONAL DATA

The most important finding of the Court in *Google v. Spain* is that Internet search engines are data controllers in the meaning of Article 2(d) of Directive 95/46/EC.

First, the Court established that the activity of Internet search engines falls under the definition of processing personal data, regardless of the fact that they carry out the same operations in respect of other types of information and do not distinguish between the latter and the personal data.[57] The Court further noted that "it is the search engine operator which determines the purposes and means of that activity and thus of the processing of personal data".[58] Consequently, the search engine must be regarded as the "controller" in respect of that processing.[59]

In this respect, the Court did not follow the Opinion of AG Jaaskinnen, who argued that even if an Internet search engine processes personal data in the sense of Article 2(b) of Directive 95/46/EC,[60] it cannot be considered as "controller" of the processing of such personal data in the sense of Article 2(d) of the Directive.[61] In his argumentation, the AG explains why he believes it is practically impossible for a search engine to be a controller, without stating what entity should be considered

55 See, for instance, para. 58 of the Judgment.

56 For other comments on the *Google v. Spain* judgment, see C. Kuner, *The Court of Justice of the EU Judgment on Data Protection and Internet Search Engines: Current Issues and Future Challenges*, Studies of the Max Planck Institute Luxembourg for International, European and Regulatory Procedural Law, Nomos/Brill 2015; I. Cofone, *Google v. Spain: A Right To Be Forgotten?*, 15 Chicago-Kent Journal of International and Comparative Law, no. 1, 2015.

57 CJEU, *Google v. Spain*, para. 28.

58 Idem, para. 33.

59 Idem, para. 33.

60 AG Jaaskinen Opinion delivered on 25 June 2013 in Case C-131/12 *Google v. Spain*, para. 75.

61 Idem, para. 100.

the controller of the personal data processing operation that he admitted is taking place. In other words, it seems that the AG considers it is possible to have a personal data processing operation existing in a void of liability: the search engine processes personal data, but it cannot be deemed liable for any unlawful processing. Such scenario cannot be valid. It should be a data protection theorem that "for each existing personal data processing operation, there is a liable data controller".[62] Otherwise, the effectiveness of data protection law will lose most of its teeth.

In the case of search engine service providers, the Court stated that their activity is capable to affect significantly and additionally the fundamental rights to privacy and data protection, compared to the activity of the publishers of the website, because it renders accessible personal data to any internet user making a search on the basis of the data subject's name, including to users who would not have found out otherwise the webpage where those data are published.[63] So holding the search engines liable for unlawful personal data processing is all the more so important.

But one should ask what is to be deemed "unlawful personal data processing" in relation to the activity of search engine providers. Indeed, if we were to expect search engines providers to comply with all the obligations of a data controller under EU data protection law, it would be impossible not to see a certain degree of unreasonableness. For instance, how can a search engine provider inform the data subjects about the details of the processing operation of their personal data, when such personal data could be generated every day, from different corners of the world? Or how can a search engine provider notify the processing operations it conducts to the national DPAs where such notifications are compulsory and strictly regulated by national law?

The fact remains that search engine providers control the processing of personal data and they must be held liable for any unlawful processing. Currently, in the EU, their activity falls under the material scope of the existing data protection laws transposing Directive 95/46/EC. But, for the sake of the effectiveness of data protection, and having regard to the great impact search engines have on private life, the question remains whether the current legal obligations of the controller need to be tailored to the reality of Internet search engines processing personal data.

3.2. "GLOBAL" TERRITORIAL SCOPE OF DIRECTIVE 95/46/EC

The Court held that the processing of personal data for the purposes of the service of a search engine such as Google Search, which is operated by an undertaking

62 This theory is developed in G. Zanfir, *Protectia datelor personale. Drepturile persoanei vizate*, C.H. Beck, Bucharest, forthcoming 2015.

63 CJEU, *Google v. Spain*, para. 36 and 38.

which has its seat in a third state, but has an establishment in a Member State of the EU, is carried out in the context of the activities of that establishment, if the latter is intended to promote and sell, in that Member State, advertising space offered by the search engine which serves to make the service offered by that engine profitable.[64]

Therefore, the Court concluded, the activity of Google Inc. and Google Spain are "inextricably linked"[65] and the directive applies to the establishment (Google Spain) of the controller (Google Inc.) on the territory of a Member State, following Article 4(1)(a) of Directive 95/46/EC.

3.3. THE RIGHT TO ERASURE APPLIES WHEN THE PROCESSING DOES NOT COMPLY WITH THE PROVISIONS OF DIRECTIVE 95/46/EC

The Court found that the individual has the right to ask for the erasure of their data, following both the right to erasure and the right to object provided for in the Directive, not only if their data are inaccurate, but whenever the processing does not comply with the provisions of the Directive. The erasure request can be made directly to the search engine.

The Court emphasized that the principles of protection laid down by the Directive are reflected also in the rights conferred on individuals whose data are the subject of processing to be informed that processing is taking place, to consult the data, to request corrections and even to object to processing in certain circumstances.[66] It further showed that the right to ask for the erasure of data does not exclusively follow the inaccurate or incomplete nature of the data being processed, but also the non-observance of the other conditions of lawfulness that are imposed by the directive upon the processing of data.[67]

The Court held that the right to object to the data processing enables account to be taken in a specific manner of all the circumstances surrounding the data subjects' particular situation.[68] In order to object to the processing and to obtain erasure, the individual may first ask the controller to erase the data, which is obliged to "duly examine" the merits of the request, and, as the case may be, end the processing. If the controller does not grant the request, the individual may bring the matter before the supervisory authority or the judicial authority, which will carry out the necessary checks.[69] In this sense, Article 29 Working Party adopted, on 26 November 2014, guidelines on the implementation of the *Google v. Spain* judgment, which contain "the common interpretation of the ruling as

64 Idem, para. 55.
65 Idem, para. 56.
66 Idem, para. 67.
67 Idem, para. 70.
68 Idem, para. 76.
69 Idem, para. 77.

well as the common criteria to be used by the data protection authorities when addressing complaints".[70]

It was further emphasized by the Court that, given the ease with which information published on a website can be replicated on other sites and the fact that the persons responsible for its publication are not always subject to EU law, effective and complete protection of data subjects could not be achieved if the data subjects had to obtain first or in parallel the erasure of the information relating to them from the publishers of the websites. Moreover, these publishers may carry their activity solely for journalistic purposes, and thus benefit from derogations under the Directive.[71]

The Court concluded that the operator of a search engine is, thus, obliged to remove from the list of results links to web pages published by third parties and containing information related to the person whose name was sought.[72]

3.4. CRITERIA FOR THE BALANCE OF RIGHTS

While the rights to private life and to personal data protection override the economic interest of the operator of a search engine,[73] a balance must be sought between the rights of the data subject and the interests of other Internet users. In this regard, the Court stated that the general rule is that Articles 7 and 8 of the Charter *override* the interests of other Internet users to have access to personal data. However, a balance between the first two and the latter must be sought.[74]

The Court also sets out criteria to be taken into account when assessing the existence of such a balance: (i) the nature of the information in question and its sensitivity for the data subject's private life and (ii) the interest of the public in having that information, an interest which may vary, in particular, according to the role played by the data subject in public life.[75]

4. CONCLUSION

With the judgment in *Google v. Spain*, the CJEU established itself as a global voice in defending fundamental rights in the digital world. The echoes of this

70 Article 29 Working Party Press Release from 26 November 2014, available here: http://ec.europa.eu/justice/data-protection/article-29/press-material/press-release/art29_press_material/20141126_wp29_press_release_ecj_de-listing.pdf (last time accessed on 11 January 2015).
71 CJEU, *Google v. Spain*, para. 84 and 85.
72 Idem, para. 88.
73 Idem, para. 81 and 97.
74 Idem, para. 81.
75 Idem, para. 81.

judgment are still being heard, several months after it was published, with Google having created an *Advisory Council on the Right to Be Forgotten* in order to "help" them "navigate this issue" of "how should one person's right to be forgotten be balanced with the public's right to information".[76] However, this endeavour was described by a EU official as being part of lobbying efforts against EU data protection rules,[77] and by data protection authorities as being a "PR war".[78] On a practical side, Google also created a special support webpage for users who want to remove links containing their names from search results[79] and decided to publish statistics on the number of requests received and the number of requests granted.[80] In addition, it sparked a debate within the USA on privacy and what does a right to be forgotten actually mean.[81]

The *Digital Rights Ireland* decision is a good example of how national courts and the Court of Justice of the EU can effectively work together for safeguarding fundamental rights in the context of bulk collection of metadata resulting from the electronic communications of citizens of the EU. As emphasized above, national courts and constitutional courts of the Member States have an important role to play in applying the criteria developed by the CJEU so attentively. The principles and safeguards set out in *Digital Rights Ireland* can prove to be very useful in a post-Snowden and post-Paris terrorist attacks era, emphasizing the role of the EU judiciary not only in adjudicating fundamental rights, but also in creating a framework for their future development.

BIBLIOGRAPHY

VOLUMES

Gonzalez Fuster, G., *The Emergence of Personal Data Protection as a Fundamental Right of the EU*, Springer Science and Business, Switzerland, 2014.

Zanfir, G., *Protectia datelor personale. Drepturile persoanei vizate*, C.H. Beck, Bucharest, 2015.

---

76 For details, see https://www.google.com/advisorycouncil/.

77 J. Fioretti, *EU official criticizes Google meetings on right to be forgotten meetings*, Reuters, published on 4 November 2014, available here: www.reuters.com/article/2014/11/04/us-google-eu-privacy-idUSKBN0IO23S20141104 (last time accessed on 11 January 2015).

78 Idem.

79 Available here https://support.google.com/websearch/troubleshooter/3111061?hl=en (last time accessed on 11 January 2015).

80 Available here: https://www.google.com/transparencyreport/removals/europeprivacy/ (last time accessed on 11 January 2015).

81 See, for instance, J. Toobin, 'The Solace of Oblivion', *The New Yorker*, 29 September 2014 Issue, available here: www.newyorker.com/magazine/2014/09/29/solace-oblivion (last time accessed on 11 January 2015); the transcript of the Diane Rehm show on The Right To Be Forgotten, from 2 January 2015, available here: http://thedianerehmshow.org/shows/2015-01-02/the_right_to_be_forgotten (last time accessed on 11 January 2015).

VOLUME CHAPTERS

Clit, R., Viata cotidiana in communism. Frica de zi cu zi (Daily life in Communism. The Day to Day Fear), *Psihologia sociala (Social Psychology)*, Issue 12/2003.

Gutwirth, S. and de Hert, P., "Regulating Profiling in a Democratic Constitutional State", in *Profiling the European Citizen*, ed. Mirelle Hildebrandt and Serge Gutwirth, (Springer, 2008), pp. 271 – 303.

RESEARCH PAPERS

Boehm, F., Cole, M.D., 'Data Retention after the Judgment of the Court of the European Union', Munster/Luxemburg 30 June 2014, study funded by the Greens/EFSA Group in the European Parliament.

Cofone, I. Google v. Spain: A Right To Be Forgotten?, *15 Chicago-Kent Journal of International and Comparative Law*, no. 1, 2015.

Guild, E., Carrera, S., 'The Political and Judicial Life of Metadata: Digital Rights Ireland and the trail of the data retention directive', CEPS Paper in Liberty and Security in Europe, No. 65, May 2014.

Jones, C. and Hayes, B., *The EU data retention directive, a case study in the legitimacy and effectiveness of EU counter-terrorism policy*, published within the SECILE project (Securing Europe through Counter-Terrorism: Impact, Legitimacy and Effectiveness), implemented by Statewatch.

Kuner, C., *The Court of Justice of the EU Judgment on Data Protection and Internet Search Engines: Current Issues and Future Challenges*, Studies of the Max Planck Institute Luxembourg for International, European and Regulatory Procedural Law, Nomos/ Brill 2015.

Rauhofer, J., Sithigh, D.M., The Data Retention Directive Never Existed, *SCRIPTed*, 11(1), 2014.

Zanfir, G., Big Brother in a post-communist era. Radiography of the protection of private life in a European Romania, *Revue de Sciences Politiques*, No. 35, 2012, pp. 330–351.

OTHER SOURCES

Fioretti, J. *EU official criticizes Google meetings on right to be forgotten meetings*, Reuters, published on 4 November 2014, available at: www.reuters.com/article/2014/11/04/us-google-eu-privacy-idUSKBN0IO23S20141104 (last time accessed on 11 January 2015).

Toobin, J., *The Solace of Oblivion*, The New Yorker, 29 September 2014, available at: www.newyorker.com/magazine/2014/09/29/solace-oblivion (last time accessed on 11 January 2015).

8. THE SUPREMACY OF THE EU LAW AS INTERPRETED BY THE POLISH CONSTITUTIONAL TRIBUNAL

Elżbieta KUŻELEWSKA*
Faculty of Law, University of Bialystok, Poland

Dariusz KUŻELEWSKI**
Faculty of Law, University of Bialystok, Poland

1. INTRODUCTION

The principle of supremacy constitutes the core and essence not only of EU law and legal order but also of the goal of European integration itself. Without the acceptance of supremacy of EU law over the laws of the Member States, it is impossible to fulfil the goals specified in the Treaties.

The principle however is not explicitly stated in the Treaties. It was "taken" from the spirit of the Treaty and clearly established by the early judgments of the European Court of Justice (*Costa v. ENEL, van Gend en Loos*). Understanding of the supremacy principle (its origin, scope and effects) varies throughout the European Union. Constitutional courts/tribunals in particular Member States have been active in a dynamic interpretation of supremacy. The debate started with famous Solange case in Germany and continued through other countries, including new members joining the Union.

The Polish Constitutional Tribunal issued three key judgments concerning the principle. Two of them came close in time but brought somehow contrary conclusions.

The first judgment of 27 April 2005 addressed the question of constitutionality of the European Arrest Warrant (EAW) regulations implemented in the Polish Code of Criminal Procedure in the light of Article 55(1) of the Constitution of the Republic of Poland. The Tribunal concluded that those implementing regulations were contrary to the Constitution which, as a rule, did not allow for the surrender of Polish citizens. As a result, the first amendment of the Polish Constitution was

* Email: ekuzelewska@gmail.com.
** Email: d.kuzelewski@uwb.edu.pl.

proceeded to satisfy the aims of the EU decision and as such, it confirmed the supremacy of the EU law over Polish law, including the Polish Constitution.

A couple of weeks later, on 11 May 2005, the Tribunal issued its judgment concerning the constitutionality of the Accession Treaty. Although the Tribunal did not find any grounds for the inconformity of the Accession Treaty to the Polish Constitution, it took another chance to widely explain the understanding of the supremacy principle and came to interesting conclusions including one stating that the collision of Community law and national constitutional norm may "in no event be resolved by assuming the supremacy of a Community norm over a constitutional norm". It further indicated three possibilities of action in case of such collision: amendment of the Constitution, modification of the EU law in question or even withdrawal from the European Union.

The question of application of the supremacy principle has been widely discussed and still causes plenty of confusion and unclearness. As if that had not been enough, the Polish Tribunal went further, when in the judgment of 16 November 2011 it confirmed its power to review constitutionality of the EU secondary laws. This is by far a very brave statement, standing against the accepted competence of the review of the EU law granted solely to the Court of Justice in Luxembourg.

This paper will analyse those judgments to provide an overview of the Polish Constitutional Tribunal's attitude towards the fundamental principle of EU law. "United in diversity" seems to fit perfectly not only as a theme of European societies, but also as a theme for legal discourse over the fundaments of the law and integration within the European Union.

2. SPECIFICITY OF THE CONSTITUTIONAL REVIEW IN POLAND

As worded in the Constitution, the Constitutional Tribunal shall adjudicate the following matters:

1. the conformity of statutes and international agreements to the Constitution;
2. the conformity of a statute to ratified international agreements whose ratification required prior consent granted by statute;
3. the conformity of legal provisions issued by central State organs to the Constitution, ratified international agreements and statutes;
4. the conformity to the Constitution of the purposes or activities of political parties;
5. complaints concerning constitutional infringements, as specified in Article 79(1).[1]

1 Article 188 of the Constitution of the Republic of Poland of 2 April 1997, OJ 1997, number 78, item 483, as amended. In addition, as provided by Article 189 of the Constitution, The

The constitutional control in Poland is therefore centralized. A single tribunal decides on the conformity of the legislation with the Constitution. There is also preventive control of the constitutionality of legislative proposals exercised by the President of the Republic of Poland who may, before signing a bill, refer it to the Constitutional Tribunal for adjudication upon its conformity to the Constitution.[2] Judgments of the Constitutional Tribunal are of universally binding application and are final (Article 190 of the Constitution).

According to Article 194 of the Constitution, the Constitutional Tribunal is composed of 15 judges chosen individually by the lower chamber of the Parliament (Sejm) for a term of office of 9 years from amongst persons distinguished by their knowledge of law. No person may be chosen for more than one term in the office. The President and Vice-President of the Constitutional Tribunal are appointed by the President of the Republic from amongst candidates proposed by the General Assembly of the Judges of the Constitutional Tribunal. As the Constitutional Tribunal Act[3] states, a judge of the Tribunal may be a person who possesses the necessary qualifications to hold the office of a judge of the Supreme Court or the Supreme Administrative Court. Candidates for the office of a judge of the Tribunal are nominated by at least 50 deputies or the Presidium of the Sejm. A resolution of the Sejm concerning the election of a judge of the Tribunal requires an absolute majority of votes in the presence of at least half of the total number of deputies.

3. THE PRIMACY OF THE EU LAW OVER NATIONAL LAW

The debates concerning the primacy principle of EU law over national law of Member States have been continuing for nearly 50 years and do not seem to be likely to come to an end. The controversies are related to the sources of the primacy rule: are they related to EU law or to constitutions of the Member States?[4] As M. Huomo-Kettunen notices, the primacy of EU law does not establish any absolute hierarchy of powers between the EU and the Member States. The principle of primacy simply expresses a rule concerning the application of law between the EU legislation and the Member States' domestic legislation. According to the principle, EU law prevails over national law, but the national law will not be declared invalid by the EU Courts. The primacy of EU

Constitutional Tribunal settles disputes over authority between central constitutional organs of the State.

2 Article 122 of the Constitution of the Republic of Poland as cited above.

3 Article 5(3,4) of the Constitutional Tribunal Act of 1 August 1997, OJ 1997, number 102, item 43, as amended.

4 S. Biernat, 'Zasada pierwszeństwa prawa unijnego po Traktacie z Lizbony' (2011), vol. XXV *Gdańskie Studia Prawnicze* 47.

law simply expresses a rule concerning the application of law in areas where the Member States have transferred their sovereign powers to the Union.[5]

Here, the next question is to be asked: whose has the final say in the situations of conflict of the norms: the EU courts or the constitutional tribunals in the Member States? The majority of the Member States' highest courts do not fully accept the primacy of EU law.[6]

Another question concerns the status of primacy rule after the Lisbon Treaty entered into force. The primacy rule was formulated neither in the Treaty on European Union (EU Treaty),[7] nor in the Treaty on the Functioning of the European Union (TFEU).[8] In 2007, the Declaration concerning primacy (No. 17) was annexed in the Final Act of the Intergovernmental Conference which adopted the Treaty of Lisbon. This Declaration refers to the earlier judicial decisions of Court of Justice of the European Union, beginning with *Costa v ENEL*.[9] Has the status of the primacy principle become less significant after the Lisbon Treaty? It is worth reminding that the primacy principle, first expressed in *Costa v ENEL* decision, was subsequently confirmed and developed in numerous CJEU decisions that followed. The primacy principle of EU/EC law was valid for several decades in judicial decisions without being formalized in the Treaties, although the Treaties were amended many times. It was commonly assumed that EC primary law consists of the Treaties, i.e. statutory law, and general principles of community law formulated by the Court of Justice of the European Union, being equivalent to treaty decisions.[10] The proposed EU Constitutional Treaty was the first (and so far the last) document clearly expressing the primacy of EU law. The rejection of this document in referenda by the French and the Dutch resulted in withdrawal of this principle from the subsequent treaty. It should be emphasized that the primacy principle (as well as the entire Constitutional Treaty) were accepted by all the EU Member States. The fact that the Treaty, as a result of the referendum failures in France and the Netherlands did not come into force, does not diminish its significance in such recognition.

During the consultations concerning the Lisbon Treaty, several Member States made it clear that they did not see the possibility to place the regulation proclaiming the principle of primacy in a Reform Treaty draft. This is the reason why the authors of a new treaty decided not to formulate the principle in it. However, it does not mean it was rejected entirely. It was expressed in the Declaration No. 17 which is not a part of the Treaties, it is not legally binding but all Member States concluding the Treaties took a stand in the Declaration

---

5 M. Huomo-Kettunen, 'Heterarchical Constitutional Structures in the European Legal Space' (2013) 6(1) *European Journal of Legal Studies* 52.

6 A. von Bogdandy, 'Doctrine of Principles' (2003) 9/03 *Jean Monnet Working Paper* 42.

7 Treaty on the European Union, OJ 2012/C 326/01, 26.10.2012.

8 Treaty on the Functioning of the European Union, OJ 2012/C 326/01, 26.10.2012.

9 ECJ 15.07.1964, C-6/64 *Flaminio Costa v E.N.E.L.*

10 *Supra* note 4, pp. 48–51.

No. 17 that it had a political significance. It declared the primacy principle valid although it was not formulated in the Treaties. The Member States probably decided to attach the Declaration to the dissemination act in order not to neglect the primacy principle. According to the Declaration, EU law has the priority, following the legal decisions of Court of Justice of the European Union. Therefore, the Declaration does not formulate the principle mentioned above, merely reminding of the Court's decisions. In the Declaration, an opinion of the Council Legal Service of 2007 was cited. This opinion refers to the legal situation established as a result of the *Costa v. ENEL* decision, when the principle of primacy was not mentioned in the Treaty. There were two reasons why the opinion of Legal Service was attached to the Declaration. First, it was a sign of its acceptance by the Member States. Secondly, its content being the support for the Member States, was to prove that the principle of primacy, as a binding EU principle expressed by Lisbon Treaty, was not the result of political settlement, but rather the result of an objective legal analysis. The fundamental principle of the EU law primacy is therefore not directly expressed in the Treaties.[11]

Even though the doctrine representatives underline that the Lisbon Treaty strengthened the primacy principle, the efforts leading to the inclusion of the principle into the primary law of the EU (as tried in the Constitutional Treaty) should be supported, as advocated among others by A. von Bogdandy.[12]

The fact that due to the objections of some Member States, the idea was given up and instead the formula of the Declaration No. 17 was used, should be regarded as specific device aiming to recognize the primacy principle *de facto*, not *de jure*.

4. THE PRINCIPLE OF SUPREMACY IN THE LIGHT OF THE POLISH CONSTITUTIONAL TRIBUNAL'S JUDICATURE

In 2005 the Polish Constitutional Tribunal issued two key judgments concerning the supremacy principle.

The first judgment of 27 April 2005 addressed the question of constitutionality of the European Arrest Warrant (EAW) and the surrender procedures between Member States regulations implemented in the Polish Code of Criminal Procedure (CCP) in the light of Article 55(1) of the Constitution of the Republic of Poland. The Tribunal concluded that those implemented

11 *Id.* pp. 54–57. Also K. Wojtyczek is in favour of the legal recognition of the Declaration no. 17 in the interpretation of EU law – K. Wojtyczek, 'Wpływ Traktatu z Lizbony na ustrój Polski' (2010) 4(99) *Przegląd Sejmowy* 29.

12 A. von Bogdandy, 'Founding Principles of EU law: A Theoretical and Doctrinal Sketch' (2010) 16(2) *European Law Journal* 99.

regulations were contrary to the Constitution which, as a rule, did not allow for the surrender of Polish citizens. "[...] The surrendering of a person prosecuted on the basis of an EAW [...], must be viewed as a form of extradition within the meaning of Article 55(1) of the Constitution".[13]

The Tribunal found that "Article 607t §1 of the CCP, insofar as it permits the surrendering of a Polish citizen to another Member State of the European Union on the basis of the European Arrest Warrant, does not conform to Article 55(1) of the Constitution".[14] However, when Poland joined the EU on 1 May 2004, it accepted the commitment to implement in full the Framework Decision of 13 June 2002. For the purpose of executing this commitment, it was primarily necessary to transfer the content of the Framework Decision into Polish legislation. The Polish legislator decided to transpose the Framework Decision as an amendment to the CCP without any accompanying amendment of the Constitution. The legislator created a terminological distinction between extradition and the surrendering of a person on the basis of an EAW (see Article 602 of the CCP).

On the one hand, the Tribunal indicated the necessity of distinction between extradition and surrender taking into account that the provisions of the Polish Constitution were adopted prior to the Framework Decision on European Arrest Warrant. The Tribunal stated that that the Polish legislator meant, in Article 55 of the Constitution, all situations of "giving" Polish citizens to other states. On the other hand, the Tribunal recognized the obligation to implement secondary EU law under Article 9 of the Polish Constitution and the provisions of Accession Treaty. However, it underlined that the national law provisions implementing the EU acts are not automatically conform to the norms of the Constitution. It also suggested the obligation to interpret domestic law consistently with the EU law. The Tribunal suggested that there must be an amendment of the national Constitution in order to apply the EAW to the Polish citizens. As a result, the first amendment of the Polish Constitution was proceeded to satisfy the aims of the EU decision and as such, it confirmed the supremacy of the EU law over the Polish law, including the Polish Constitution.[15]

Only two weeks later the Tribunal denied the supremacy of EU law in the judgment of May 11, 2005 concerning the constitutionality of the Accession Treaty.[16]

Poland became a member of the EU on 1 May 2004. The Accession Treaty was approved by the Polish citizens in a referendum on 7–8 June 2003. More than 77% of voters supported the accession.[17] The Tribunal issued the judgment

---

13 *Constitutionality of the European Arrest Warrant* – P 1/05 of 27 April 2005.

14 *Id.*

15 K. Kowalik-Bańczyk, 'Should We Polish It Up? The Polish Constitutional Tribunal and the Idea of Supremacy of EU Law' (2005) 6(10) *German Law Journal* 1360.

16 *Constitutionality of the Accession Treaty* – K 18/04, 11 May 2005.

17 See more: E. Kużelewska, A.R. Bartnicki, 'Referendum in Poland and Russia. Comparative analysis attempt' (2008) 1–2 *The International Affairs Review* 123.

as a response to a claim made by three groups of deputes of the lower chamber and submission of three motions criticizing Poland's EU membership and its conditions specified in the treaty. They did not accept the principles of Polish sovereignty and the supremacy of Constitution over other legal acts as not consistent with the Accession Treaty provisions. They argued that the Polish Constitution allowed the accession to international organizations while the EU was a supranational body. The Tribunal rejected this argument, insisting that the term "supranational organization" was not mentioned in any of the relevant legal texts. The question of transfer of competence to the EU/EC was another matter to be raised by the applicants that insisted that Poland could not act as an independent and sovereign state after its accession to the EU. According to the Tribunal, Polish sovereignty was not questioned as the Polish Constitution (Article 90) allowed transferring certain competences under very strict conditions, so losing Polish sovereignty was out of question. Polish EU membership did not infringe this article of the Polish Constitution. Yet, the Tribunal decided there would be both – rules deriving from the Polish legal system and ones set outside it. However, the Constitution has the primary position, considering both its binding nature and its functioning. The Constitution acts over any international agreement, even if the agreement was accepted by referendum.[18] The Tribunal explains that the EU law constitutes a new model of law that cannot be explained by former ideas of monism and dualism;[19]

> "The concept and model of European law created a new situation, wherein, within each Member State, autonomous legal orders co-exist and are simultaneously operative. Their interaction may not be completely described by the traditional concepts of monism and dualism regarding the relationship between domestic law and international law. The existence of the relative autonomy of both, national and Community, legal orders in no way signifies an absence of interaction between them. Furthermore, it does not exclude the possibility of a collision between regulations of Community law and the Constitution".[20]

Although the Tribunal did not find any grounds for the inconformity of the Accession Treaty with the Polish Constitution, it took another chance to widely explain the understanding of the supremacy principle and came to interesting conclusions including one stating that collision of community law and constitutional norm may "in no event be resolved by assuming the supremacy

18 *Supra* note 15, p. 1361–1365.

19 The distinction between monism and dualism is broadly described in doctrine, see e.g.: A. von Bogdandy, 'Pluralism, direct effect and ultimate say: on the relationship between international and domestic constitutional law' (2008) 6(3&4) *I•CON (International Journal of Constitutional Law)* 397–413.

20 *Constitutionality of the Accession Treaty* – K 18/04, 11 May 2005.

of a Community norm over a constitutional norm".[21] It further indicated three possibilities of action in case of such collision: amendment of the Constitution, modification of the EU law in question or even withdrawal from the European Union.

The supremacy idea was finally defeated when the Tribunal stated that these are Member States that assess if (or not) the Community institutions function according to their competences and the subsidiarity and proportionality principles. Finally, the Tribunal gave the Member States the instrument to control the Community competences.[22]

In the judgment concerning the European Arrest Warrant the Tribunal applied a different stance. At first, the Tribunal decided that in the Polish legal order the European Arrest Warrant ought to be treated as a priority for legislator. Consequently, the possibility to amend Article 55 of the Polish Constitution was suggested, if the EU law requires it. Yet, this possibility was rejected. According to the Polish Constitutional Tribunal, the primacy of the Polish Constitution over the EU law is indisputable. It could result in disobeying certain EU regulations in case they collide with the Polish Constitution. This judgment is perceived to be uncommon and odd, regarding its composition.[23]

In the last analysed judgment the Constitutional Tribunal confirmed its power to review constitutionality of the EU secondary laws.[24] This is by far a very brave statement, standing against the accepted competence of the review of the EU law granted solely to the Court of Justice in Luxembourg. The judgment concerns a constitutional complaint submitted by Ms Anna S., in which she requested the Tribunal to examine the conformity of the Council Regulation (EC) No 44/2001 of 22 December 2000 on jurisdiction and the recognition and enforcement of judgments in civil and commercial matters[25] with the Polish Constitution, in particular Article 45(1) thereof, guaranteeing the right to a fair and public hearing of her case, without undue delay, before a competent, impartial and independent court. The Tribunal did not find it unconstitutional.

The most important issue of the above judgment, however, was a decision on the cognition of the Tribunal to examine the conformity of the UE law to the Polish Constitution. Pursuant to Article 79(1) of the Constitution, a constitutional complaint may be submitted to the Tribunal to determine the conformity to the Constitution of a statute or another normative act, upon which basis, a court or organ of public administration has made a final decision on a complainant's freedoms, rights or obligations specified in the Constitution. The Tribunal established that an EU regulation was "another normative act" within the meaning of Article 79(1) of the Constitution and it might constitute

21 *Id.*
22 *Supra* note 15, p. 1364–1365.
23 *Id.*, p. 1365–1366.
24 *Right to review constitutionality of the EU secondary law* – SK 45/09 of 16 November 2011.
25 OJ L 12, 16.1.2001, p. 1, as amended.

the subject of a constitutional complaint. In the opinion of the Tribunal, not only a normative act issued by one of the organs of the Polish state, but also a legal act issued by an organ of an international organisation (primarily the acts of EU law enacted by the institutions of that organisation) is a normative act within the meaning of Article 79(1) of the Constitution.

The Polish Constitutional Tribunal also noticed and considered the possible effects of a judgment in the case of adjudication that the norms of EU secondary legislation were inconsistent with the Constitution. The Tribunal stated in the reasons of judgment of 16 November 2011 that

> "in the context of the acts of Polish law, the said nonconformity results in declaring the unconstitutional norms to be no longer legally binding (Article 190(1) and (3) of the Constitution). With regard to the acts of EU secondary legislation, such a result would be impossible, as it is not the organs of the Polish state that decide whether such acts are legally binding or not. The consequence of the ruling of the Constitutional Tribunal would be to rule out the possibility that the acts of EU secondary legislation would be applied by the organs of the Polish state and would have any legal effects in Poland. Therefore, the ruling of the Constitutional Tribunal would result in suspending the application of the unconstitutional norms of EU law in the territory of the Republic of Poland. [...] Such a consequence of the Tribunal's ruling would be difficult to reconcile with the obligations of a Member State and the principle of sincere cooperation (Article 4(3) of the TEU). The said situation could lead to proceedings against Poland conducted by the European Commission and an action brought against Poland before the Court of Justice of the European Union for the infringement of obligations under the Treaties (Articles 258–260 of the TFEU)".

The Polish Constitution shapes the internal legal order of the Republic of Poland and only normative acts of the Polish, not EU, law should be evaluated as to their conformity with the Polish Constitution. Direct application of the EU law in Poland does not prejudge the possibility of its assessment by the Constitutional Tribunal. Examination of the compatibility of the EU law with the national constitutions and, as a result, a repeal of the Union norm on the territory of a Member State, would lead to the legal chaos and deny the idea of the fulfilment of the obligations taken upon by the EU Member States.

Even though Article 79(1) of the Constitution contains the term "other normative acts" without its literal specification that it regards normative national (Polish) acts, such narrow understanding seems justified given the historical interpretation. Article 79(1) has not changed since the Constitution's enactment in 1997 when Poland was not EU member and one (internal) legal system ruled the country. As a result, at the moment of the Constitution's acceptance, when only domestic law applied on the territory of Poland, such clarification was unneeded. In 1997 we did not deal with secondary EU law and the Constitution was "tailored" for the national legal system. After Poland had joined the EU in 2004, no significant amendment of the Constitution in this regard occurred.[26]

As R. Grzeszczak rightfully points, the Tribunal has not turned with a preliminary reference to the CJEU concerning the interpretation of the EU law primacy which falls under a general tendency of rather reluctant use of this measure by the constitutional courts in other Member States. Preliminary references should pose primary instrument of the cooperation between the CJEU and national constitutional tribunals.[27] It should also be agreed with P. Bogdanowicz and P. Marcisz that national courts are not entitled to independent decisions on the invalidity of legal acts adopted by the EU institutions.[28] The acknowledgement of the Constitutional Tribunal to decide about the validity of the secondary laws of the EU constitutes violation of the obligations included in the TFEU. It means that the Tribunal extended its cognition, not to say that it "usurped" such right ignoring the fact that from the point of view of the European law, it violates the principle of primacy which may result in a suit against Poland before the CJEU.

The lack of consequence may be surprising as the Tribunal justified its decision with arguments in favour of a completely reverse attitude toward the Union's secondary law. The Tribunal stated that

> "allowing the possibility of examining the conformity of the acts of EU secondary legislation to the Constitution, what should be emphasised is the need to maintain due caution and restraint in that regard. The EU law binds all Member States. [...] What would be difficult to reconcile with that principle is granting powers to particular Member States which would allow them to declare the norms of EU law to be no longer legally binding".

The Polish Tribunal lacked the restraint which was maintained for example by the Federal Constitutional Court of Germany (FCCG) in the decision of October 22, 1986 (so-called *Solange II* case[29] and in the decision of 7 June

26 The deficit of the constitutional regulations in relationship between the EU and Poland is indicated for instance by K. Wojtyczek, 'Wpływ Traktatu z Lizbony na ustrój Polski' (2010) 4(99) *Przegląd Sejmowy* 28, as well as by M. Kruk, 'Kształtowanie konstytucyjnych zasad członkostwa państwa w Unii Europejskiej (wybrane problemy)' (2010) 4(99), *Przegląd Sejmowy* 41–42.

27 R. Grzeszczak, *Orzeczenie TK sprzeczne z prawem unijnym*, Prawo europejskie w praktyce, http://pewp.pl/index.php?option=com_content&view=article&id=100:orzeczenie-tk-sprzeczne-z-prawem-unijnym&catid=34:wymiar-sprawiedliwosci&Itemid=53. A. Kostelik-Smaza is a supporter of the use of treaty mechanisms in the first place – particularly the preliminary ruling procedure before the CJEU – to eliminate discrepancies between secondary law and the Constitution – A. Kastelik-Smaza, 'Spór o prymat prawa europejskiego po wejściu w życie Traktatu z Lizbony' (2010) 4(99) *Przegląd Sejmowy* 79–80.

28 P. Bogdanowicz, P. Marcisz, *Glosa do wyroku TK z dnia 16 listopada 2011 r., SK 45/09*, EPS 2012/9/47–52.

29 BVerfG, *Solange II*, 2 BvR 197/83.

2000 (so-called *Bananenmarktordnung* case.[30] No rulings on the merits were issued in the above cases.[31] Nevertheless, the FCCG emphasized the independent character of the Community law and rightfully assumed that it is not international law in the traditional understanding, nor it is a state law. The German Tribunal recognized the primacy of the Community law before the national law and granted the supremacy of it in case of conflict of the norms. It is realized in the form of the so-called primacy of application. In case of conflict, the court or institution is obliged to apply the Community law, not the conflicting national law.[32] Recognition of the primacy of the EU law has been however narrowed. In the *Solange I* judgment of 1974, the FCCG stated that there are parts of the constitutional laws which may not be relativized by the Community law. The identity of the constitutional order may not be contested. Such attitude was further confirmed by the *Solange II* judgment in 1986[33] and in 1993 when the Court ruled on the constitutionality of the law ratifying the EU Treaty.[34]

5. CONCLUSIONS

The Constitutional Tribunal spoke about the conformity of the primary EU law with the Polish Constitution with regards to the Accession Treaty. According to the Tribunal's ruling, the Treaty is compatible with the Constitution of the Republic of Poland. It can be concluded then, that the scope of competences transferred to the EC/EU is consistent with the constitutional provisions. The sole court entitled to hear a case concerning the invalidity of the EU act is the European Court of Justice. National courts of the Member States lack jurisdiction in this matter. According then to the EU law, a sole power to control the validity of the secondary EU laws belongs to the European Court of Justice. Based on Article 188(1) of the Polish Constitution, the Constitutional Tribunal adjudicates on the conformity of the international agreements with the Constitution. Powers of the Constitutional Tribunal in this regard are specifically significant when exercised before the final consent to be bound by the treaty is given. When the state expresses the final consent to be bound by the treaty, then according to the

30 BVerfG, *Bananenmarktordnung*, 2 BvR 1/97.

31 A. Peters, 'The Bananas Decision (2000) of the German federal Constitutional Court: Towards Reconciliation of the European Court of Justice as regards Fundamental Rights Protection in Europe' (2000) 43 *German Yearbook of International Law* 276–282.

32 R. Arnold, 'Orzecznictwo niemieckiego Federalnego Trybunału Konstytucyjnego a proces integracji europejskiej' (1999) 1 *Studia Europejskie* 99.

33 T.C. Hartley, *The Foundations of European Union Law. An Introduction to the Constitutional and Administrative Law of the European Union,* Oxford University Press 2010, p. 263.

34 K. Leonaerts, P. van Nuffel, R. Bray, *Constitutional Law of the European Union,* London 2005, p. 685; D. Halberstam, Ch. Möllers, 'The German Constitutional Court says: "Ja zu Deutschland!"' (2009) 10(8) *German Law Journal* 1241–1258.

pacta sunt servanda principle, it should in good faith perform the obligations provided by the treaty.[35]

The primacy of the EU law over the national law as regarded by the Constitutional Tribunal is not absolute and is not unconditional. Such primacy over the acts of lower rank than the Constitution is, in turn, obvious, as inevitable result of the transfer of legislative powers to the Union. Such entitlement causes the obligation to apply the law by all state organs of the Member State, including the courts. The situation is different when collision of the EU norms and the constitutional norms occurs. The national supreme law is not only the primary source of law in the national legal order but also a primary source of the primacy principle in the EU law and in this sense the limits of the primacy principle itself derive from the national constitution.[36] M. Zdanowicz has a different opinion which should be supported: the primacy principle concerns all the legal provisions of the Member States, regardless of their place in the law sources system, which includes constitutional norms.[37] W. Czapliński also underlines that if the transfer of competences was performed in accordance with the Constitution of Poland, in the areas where the Community gained the right to act, the Community law should gain absolute primacy over any norms of national law, including the norms of the Constitution.[38]

The European Court of Justice already in the judgment of 17 December 1970 stated that

> "recourse to the legal rules or concepts of national law in order to judge the validity of measures adopted by the institutions of the community would have an adverse effect on the uniformity and efficacy of community law. The validity of such measures can only be judged in the light of community law".[39]

It should be accepted that national tribunals should not have the cognition to examine the conformity of EU secondary law with national constitutions. These are Members States which should adjust to the EU law also in the matters of constitutional acts. Despite political hesitancy and number of concepts of what the EU is and what it should be, the binding force of the EU law, as well as its

35 M. Zdanowicz, *Opinia w sprawie projektu zmiany ustawy o zmianie Konstytucji Rzeczypospolitej Polskiej*, Biuro Analiz Sejmowych, Opinia Zlecona, Druk nr 3399, 2011.

36 K. Wójtowicz, 'Konstytucyjne granice pierwszeństwa prawa wspólnotowego w świetle orzecznictwa krajowych sądów konstytucyjnych', in W. Czapliński (ed.), *Prawo w XXI wieku, Księga pamiątkowa 50-lecia Instytutu Nauk Prawnych Polskiej Akademii Nauk*, Warszawa 2006, p. 1082.

37 *Supra* note 34.

38 W. Czapliński, 'Glosa do wyroku Trybunału Konstytucyjnego z 11.5.2005 r. (zgodność Traktatu akcesyjnego z Konstytucją RP) K 18/04 (Glosa nr 3)' (2005) 4 *Kwartalnik Prawa Publicznego* 210.

39 ECJ 17.12.1970, C-11/70 *Internationale Handelsgesellschaft mbH v Einfuhr- und Vorratsstelle für Getreide und Futtermittel*.

scope and influence on the national laws and on the functioning of Member States' societies, impose a conclusion that when it comes to the legal order we are dealing with an idea of federalism as a primate and irreversible direction for the EU development,[40] even if some authors rise that there are no fundamental premises conditioning the transformation of the EU into a federal state.[41] Taking into account that the EU is not a typical international organization and it appears as a specific subject, sometimes referred to as "super state", it seems justified to recognize (also in the EU *acquis communautaire*) that the principle of sovereignty of the Member States is of a secondary character and has gained a new dimension, different from the traditional understanding. It should therefore yield to the principle of primacy of the EU law.

The Polish Constitutional Tribunal avoids the preliminary reference procedure while risking issuance of controversial decisions which extend its cognition in contrary to the principles of the European law. It may be considered as specific "competence jostling" resulting from the over ambitious attitude of the Constitutional Tribunal toward its role.

As S. Dudzik and N. Półtorak note, the Tribunal seems to perceive the principle of the primacy of the Constitution as the supreme law in Poland in a conservative way. The Tribunal seems not to recognize the full consequences of Poland's accession to the EU, as well as of the recent changes within the EU itself in the field of protection of fundamental rights.[42]

BIBLIOGRAPHY

Arnold R., 'Orzecznictwo niemieckiego Federalnego Trybunału Konstytucyjnego a proces integracji europejskiej' (1999) 1 *Studia Europejskie.*

Biernat S., 'Zasada pierwszeństwa prawa unijnego po Traktacie z Lizbony' (2011), XXV *Gdańskie Studia Prawnicze.*

von Bogdandy A., 'Doctrine of Principles' (2003) 9/03 *Jean Monnet Working Paper.*

von Bogdandy A., 'Founding Principles of EU law: A Theoretical and Doctrinal Sketch' (2010) 16(2) *European Law Journal.*

---

40 See also: D.J. Meltzer, 'Member State Liability in Europe and the United States' (2006) 127 *Harvard Law School Research Paper* 1–67. According to J. Jaskiernia, the Treaty of Lisbon is a step towards realizing the vision of "federal Europe". It reinforces the federalist elements in the EU, however, it does not determine whether and when the concept of "federal Europe" would be implemented – J. Jaskiernia, 'Traktat z Lizbony a tendencje rozwojowe Unii Europejskiej' (2010) 4(99) *Przegląd Sejmowy* 166.

41 See: K. Wójtowicz, 'Poszanowanie tożsamości konstytucyjnej państw członkowskich Unii Europejskiej' (2010) 4(99) *Przegląd Sejmowy* 10.

42 S. Dudzik, N. Półtorak, "The Court of the Last Word'. Competences of the Polish Constitutional Tribunal in the Review of European Union Law' (2012) 15 *Yearbook of Polish European Studies* 257.

von Bogdandy A., 'Pluralism, direct effect and ultimate say: on the relationship between international and domestic constitutional law' (2008) 6(3&4) *I•CON Internatiuonal Journal of Constitutional Law.*

Bogdanowicz P., P. Marcisz, *Glosa do wyroku TK z dnia 16 listopada 2011 r., SK 45/09,* EPS 2012/9/47–52.

Constitution of the Republic of Poland of 2nd April 1997, Official Journal 1997, number 78, item 483.

Constitutionality of the Accession Treaty – K 18/04, May 11, 2005.

Constitutionality of the European Arrest Warrant – P 1/05 of April 27, 2005.

Czapliński W., 'Glosa do wyroku Trybunału Konstytucyjnego z 11.5.2005 r. (zgodność Traktatu akcesyjnego z Konstytucją RP) K 18/04 (Glosa nr 3)' (2005) 4 *Kwartalnik Prawa Publicznego* 210.

Dudzik S., N. Półtorak, "The Court of the Last Word'. Competences of the Polish Constitutional Tribunal in the Review of European Union Law' (2012) 15 *Yearbook of Polish European Studies.*

ECJ 15.07.1964, C – 6/64 *Flaminio Costa v E.N.E.L.*

ECJ 17.12.1970, C-11/70 *Internationale Handelsgesellschaft mbH v Einfuhr- und Vorratsstelle für Getreide und Futtermittel*

Grzeszczak R., *Orzeczenie TK sprzeczne z prawem unijnym,* Prawo europejskie w praktyce, http://pewp.pl/index.php?option=com_content&view=article&id=100:orzeczenie-tk-sprzeczne-z-prawem-unijnym&catid=34:wymiar-sprawiedliwosci&Itemid=53.

Hartley T.C., *The Foundations of European Union Law. An Introduction to the Constitutional and Administrative Law of the European Union,* Oxford University Press 2010.

Huomo-Kettunen M., 'Heterarchical Constitutional Structures in the European Legal Space'(2013) 6(1) *European Journal of Legal Studies.*

Jaskiernia J., 'Traktat z Lizbony a tendencje rozwojowe Unii Europejskiej' (2010) 4(99) *Przegląd Sejmowy.*

Kastelik-Smaza A., 'Spór o prymat prawa europejskiego po wejściu w życie Traktatu z Lizbony' (2010) 4(99)*Przegląd Sejmowy.*

Kowalik-Bańczyk K., 'Should We Polish It Up? The Polish Constitutional Tribunal and the Idea of Supremacy of EU Law', (2005) 6(10) *German Law Journal.*

Kużelewska E., A.R. Bartnicki, 'Referendum in Poland and Russia. Comparative analysis attempt' (2008) 1–2 *The International Affairs Review.*

Leonaerts K., P. van Nuffel, R. Bray, *Constitutional Law of the European Union,* London 2005, pp. 685; D. Halberstam, Ch. Möllers, 'The German Constitutional Court says: "Ja zu Deutschland!"' (2009) 10(8) *German Law Journal.*

Meltzer D.J., 'Member State Liability in Europe and the United States' (2006) 127 *Harvard Law School Research Paper* 1–67.

OJ L 12, 16.1.2001.

Peters A., 'The Bananas Decision (2000) of the German federal Constitutional Court: Towards Reconciliation of the European Court of Justice as regards Fundamental Rights Protection in Europe' (2000) 43 *German Yearbook of International Law.*

Right to review constitutionality of the EU secondary law – SK 45/09 of November 16, 2011.

The Tribunal Constitutional Act of 1st August 1997, Official Journal 1997, number 102, item 43.

Treaty on the European Union, OJ 2012/C 326/01, 26.10.2012.

Treaty on the Functioning of the European Union, OJ 2012/C 326/01, 26.10.2012.

Wojtyczek K., 'Wpływ Traktatu z Lizbony na ustrój Polski' (2010) 4(99) *Przegląd Sejmowy*.

Wojtyczek K., 'Wpływ Traktatu z Lizbony na ustrój Polski' (2010) 4(99) *Przegląd Sejmowy* 28 as well as M. Kruk, 'Kształtowanie konstytucyjnych zasad członkostwa państwa w Unii Europejskiej (wybrane problemy)' (2010) 4(99), *Przegląd Sejmowy*.

Wójtowicz K., 'Konstytucyjne granice pierwszeństwa prawa wspólnotowego w świetle orzecznictwa krajowych sądów konstytucyjnych', in W. Czapliński (ed.), *Prawo w XXI wieku, Księga pamiątkowa 50-lecia Instytutu Nauk Prawnych Polskiej Akademii Nauk*, Warszawa 2006.

Wójtowicz K., 'Poszanowanie tożsamości konstytucyjnej państw członkowskich Unii Europejskiej' (2010) 4999) *Przegląd Sejmowy*.

Zdanowicz M., *Opinia w sprawie projektu zmiany ustawy o zmianie Konstytucji Rzeczypospolitej Polskiej*, Biuro Analiz Sejmowych, Opinia Zlecona, Druk nr 3399, 2011.

9. RECEPTION OF EU LAW IN POLISH COURTS

A Case of "Teddy Bear" Law

Izabela KRAŚNICKA*
Faculty of Law, University of Białystok, Poland

1. INTRODUCTION

Czesław Miś (Czesław Teddy Bear when you translate his last name into English) is a Polish doctor of paediatrics who works at a state hospital in Nowy Sącz, a town located close to the city of Kraków in Poland.

The story of his court proceedings serves as an excellent example of and reflection on the practical application of two fundamental principles of the European Union law: supremacy and direct effect in the cases heard by the national common courts. The story should be known not only by lawyers and legal theorists. It should and has been also heard generally by the EU citizens. These citizens sometimes still believe that EU law made "out there in Brussels" is law with little or even no concrete, meaningful rights for individuals such as Kowalski in Poland or Sanchez in Spain. Moreover, the same citizens believe that Kowalski and Sanchez have limited or no chances in winning their case while battling for those limited rights in their national courts.

This paper will introduce the case, analyse the legal grounds for Czesław Miś' claims and most of all, focus on the arguments and reasoning of the Polish common courts hearing the case with specific dynamics of understanding and recognition of the EU law principles as explained by the European Court of Justice (ECJ).[1] It should serve as a comprehensive story, useful for full explanation of the principles working or not working in practice of domestic courts.[2]

---

* Email: krasnicka@uwb.edu.pl.

1 The author has chosen to quote extensively some relevant parts of the European Court of Justice's judgments for the complete understanding of rather straightforward and clear interpretation of the principles and definitions of the discussed terms and institutions.

2 The author has successfully used the story and its legal analysis while lecturing on the reception of the EU law in national courts at the School of Law at the University of Central

2. THE PRINCIPLE OF SUPREMACY, THE PRINCIPLE OF DIRECT EFFECT AND THE PRINCIPLE OF INDIRECT EFFECT OF EU LAW

The principle of supremacy (primacy)[3] and the principle of direct effect of EU law have been developed by the European Court of Justice as they are not *expressis verbis* included in the texts of the two main EU Treaties, that is the Treaty on the Functioning of the European Union[4] and the Treaty on European Union.[5] Both principles have been extensively analysed in the literature, therefore comments presented below aim to shortly summarize their significance in the ongoing, dynamic relationship between the unique legal order of the European Union and different internal legal orders of the Union's Member States.

In the famous case *Costa v. ENEL* decided in 1964, the European Court of Justice made a first clear statement on its interpretation of the principle of supremacy, as a consequence of specifics of Community (now Union) law as created by the sovereign decisions of the Member States. The Court ruled:

> "By creating a Community of unlimited duration, having its own institutions, its own personality, its own legal capacity and capacity of representation on the international plane and, more particularly, real powers stemming from a limitation of sovereignty or a transfer of powers from the states to the Community, the Member States have limited their sovereign rights and has thus created a body of law which binds both their nationals and themselves. [...]. The law stemming from the Treaty, an independent source of law, could not because of its special and original nature, be overridden by domestic legal provisions, however framed, without being deprived of its character as a Community law and without the legal basis of the Community itself being called into question".[6]

The judgment in *Costa v. ENEL* triggered a series of further ECJ decisions providing Member States with more detailed interpretation and scope of the supremacy principle which extended to supremacy of any Community norm (including secondary sources such as regulations and directives) over any national norm (including the highest, constitutional provisions). According

Lancashire. These lectures and discussions with students and faculty members of the school served as inspiration for the presented paper.

3 For the purpose of the present text, the discussion on the distinction between the concepts of "supremacy" and "primacy" is omitted and the two terms are used to describe the prevalence of EU law over national laws of Member States when conflict of norms occurs. For details on the distinction between the supremacy and primacy see for example: M. Avbelj, 'Supremacy or Primacy of EU Law – (Why) Does It Matter?', *European Law Journal*, Vol. 17, No. 6, November 2011, pp. 744–763.

4 Treaty on the Functioning of the European Union, OJ C 326, 26.10.2012, pp. 47–390.

5 Treaty on the European Union, OJ C 326, 26.10.2012, pp. 13–390.

6 ECJ 15.07.1964, C-6/64 *Flaminio Costa v E.N.E.L.*

to the Court, any collision of such norms should be resolved by providing precedence of EU law over national law.[7]

Even though the original grounds for the principle of supremacy of EU law over national law and its primacy in application if the conflict occurs were set by the European Court of Justice in 1960s and 1970s, the Court has been reminding about them and persuading their fundamental role in a number of judgments throughout the years, including the latest ones in significant cases concerning the EU Charter of Fundamental Rights.[8]

The principle of direct effect provides a guarantee for the citizens of the European Union. It is a guarantee of the effective application of the rights present in the immensity of the European legal provisions passed on the EU level and becoming binding sources of law in the Member States' legal orders. According to the principle (as originally enshrined by the European Court of Justice in the judgment of *van Gend en Loos* of 1963), not only is EU law prevailing over the national law in case of collision, but the rights and obligations deriving from this law can be directly challenged by citizens of all Member States in the national courts. The Court held:

> "The [...] Community constitutes a new legal order of international law for the benefit of which states have limited their sovereign rights, albeit within limited fields, and the subjects of which comprise not only the Member States but also their nationals. Independently of the legislation of Member States, Community law, not only imposes obligations on individuals but is also intended to confer upon them rights which become part of their legal heritage. These rights arise not only where they are expressly granted by the Treaty but also by reason of obligations which the Treaty imposes in a clearly defined way upon individuals as well as upon Member States and upon institutions of the Community".[9]

Once again, a series of further judgments gave more specific interpretation of the principle and allowed to extend its scope to the clear, sufficiently precise and unconditional norms of European Union law. Such norms may be contained in primary and secondary sources – that is in the establishing Treaties, as well as in regulations, decisions and directives passed on the EU level. The direct effect, as rule with few exceptions, applies on horizontal and

---

7 See: ECJ 13.02.1969, C-14/68 *Walt Wilhelm and others v Bundeskartellamt*, ECJ 17.12.1970, C-11/70 *Internationale Handelsgesellschaft mbH v Einfuhr- und Vorratsstelle für Getreide und Futtermittel*, ECJ 9.03.1978 C-106/77 *Amministrazione delle Finanze dello Stato v Simmenthal SpA*, ECJ 21.05.1987, C-249/85 *Albako Margarinefabrik Maria von der Linde GmbH & Co. KG v Bundesanstalt für landwirtschaftliche Marktordnung*.

8 For example: ECJ 26.02.2013, C-399/11 *Stefano Melloni v Ministerio Fiscal* where the Court reminds about the principle of primacy of EU law as an essential feature of the EU legal order.

9 ECJ 5.02.1963 C-26/62 *NV Algemene Transport- en Expeditie Onderneming van Gend & Loos v Netherlands Inland Revenue Administration*.

vertical levels, that is between individuals and between individuals and their states.[10]

The direct effect of directives became especially important as directives are specifically applicable in the national legal orders The aims established in the directives have to be achieved by Member States through a variety of implementing actions, so Member States have to take necessary measures to implement directives into their legal orders within a given deadline. As such, directives serve as instrument of harmonization of European Union law and domestic laws of the Union's members. On time and fully implemented directives sink into the national laws and thus provide rights and obligations to individuals.

The question to answer was whether individuals may benefit from the direct effect principle in case of a directive which was not implemented, not fully implemented or wrongfully implemented by a Member State. The answer from the European Court of Justice supports the rights of individuals against such situations. In *Van Duyn* case the Court decided that

> "where the Community authorities have, by directives, imposed on Member States the obligation to pursue a particular course of conduct, the useful effect of such an act would be weakened if individuals were prevented from relying on it before the national courts and if the latter were prevented from taking it into consideration as an element of Community law".[11]

The final argument and answer was given in *Ratti* case, where the Court made it particularly clear that

> "a Member State which has not adopted the implementing measures required by the directive in the prescribed period may not rely, as against individuals, on its own failure to perform the obligations which the directive entails. It follows that a national court requested by a person who has complied with the provisions of a directive not to apply a national provision incompatible with the directive not incorporated into the internal legal order of a defaulting Member State, must uphold that request if the obligation in question is unconditional and sufficiently precise. Subject to these reservations a Member State may not apply its internal law – even if provided with penal sanctions – which has not yet been adapted in compliance with the directive, to such a person after the expiration of the period fixed for its implementation".[12]

Through such judgments the European Court of Justice has been consistently reminding Member States about the existence and significance of the two

---

10 See for example: ECJ 5.04.1979, C-148/78 *Criminal proceedings against Tullio Ratti*, ECJ 8.04.1976, C-34/75 *Gabrielle Defrenne v Sabena*, ECJ 17.05.1972, C-93/71 *Orsolina Leonesio v Ministero dell'agricoltura e foreste.*

11 ECJ 4.12.1974, C-41/74 *Yvonne van Duyn v Home Office.*

12 ECJ 5.04.1979, C-148/78 *Criminal proceedings against Tullio Ratti.*

fundamental principles which symbolize the uniqueness of the EU legal order and supranational character of the Union itself.

The principle of primacy of EU law is especially difficult to be accepted by Member States in the same way and on the same level as provided by the ECJ case law. The Member States' reactions concerning the supremacy of the EU rules come through opinions of the constitutional courts or tribunals that its courts are entitled to the constitutional control of national laws. These courts have been interpreting the supremacy on multilevel dimensions, raising essential questions on the hierarchy of law and relations between the EU and national legal orders. Constitutional courts throughout the European Union participate in a constant debate with the European Court of Justice over the scope and limits of the principle, balancing between the essence of the integration, lying in the primacy of the EU laws over national laws and the essence of the independence, lying in the sovereign constitutions and their unquestionable supremacy as a source of law.[13]

Even though the European Court of Justice has issued many judgments clarifying and underlying the principle, it has never become a treaty provision through any of the modifying treaties. The last reform by the Treaty of Lisbon reached only as far as to the addition of Declaration 17 to the Treaty, stating that "in accordance with well settled case law of the Court of Justice of the European Union, the Treaties and the law adopted by the Union on the basis of the Treaties have primacy over the law of Member States, under the conditions laid down by the said case law".[14]

For the purpose of the article it is also necessary to recall the principle of indirect effect in relation with the Member States' failure to implement the directive or wrongful implementation of directive. The indirect effect has also been recognized by the ECJ in number of decisions. In 1984 the Court established the principle in a case concerning German incorrect implementation of the EU directive. The Court held that "it is for the national court to interpret and apply the legislation adopted for the implementation of the directive in conformity with the requirements of Community law, in so far as it is given discretion to do so under national law".[15] Later the Court extended the principle also to the situation where Member State failed to implement the directive at all. In such situation the national laws also have to be interpreted in the light of unimplemented directive.[16]

---

13 For the analysis of Member States attitude toward the supremacy see for example: K. Lenaerts, P. Van Nuffel, *Constitutional Law of the European Union*, Thomson Sweet & Maxwell 2005, pp. 678–700, TC Hartley, *The Foundations of European Union Law*, Oxford University Press 2010, pp. 259–286.

14 Declaration concerning primacy, Treaty on European Union, *supra*, note 5.

15 ECJ 10.04.1984, C-14/83 *Sabine von Colson and Elisabeth Kamann v Land Nordrhein-Westfalen*.

16 ECJ 13.11.1990, C-106/89 *Marleasing SA v La Comercial Internacional de Alimentacion SA*.

3. "WORKING TIME" UNDER THE POLISH LAW AND EU LAW

Back in 2004, when Poland – together with nine other countries – entered the European Union, the awareness of the EU law principles and their possible influence on everyday lives of Polish citizens was very limited. Czesław Miś' case proved that the change is necessary. The story is altogether quite complex but worth analysing to provide an example of the citizen's battle for the proper interpretation of EU law by judges deciding in national courts of the EU Member States.[17]

Doctor Miś, employed by the state (public) hospital in Nowy Sącz, realized that the calculation of his time of work, as demanded by his employee, was contrary to the provisions of the EU directive concerning certain aspects of the organization of working time.[18]

Working time and rest time of a Polish employee are regulated generally by the provisions of the Labour Code of 1974[19] and the working time of physicians falls under specific regulations – back then – under the Law on Healthcare Institutions of 1991.[20]

According to the Labour Code, working time of a Polish employee may not exceed 8 hours in a 24-hour period and an average of 40 hours in an average five-day working week. Further, an employee is entitled to at least 11 hours of uninterrupted rest in each 24-hour period (subject to some exceptions like operations to protect human life or health) and to at least 35 hours of uninterrupted rest every week including at least 11 hours of uninterrupted rest in a 24-hour period (Articles 129, 132 and 133 of the Code).

An "on-call shift" is also regulated in the Code as an obligation which may be imposed by an employer to an employee under which the latter remains on-call outside of regular working hours to provide work determined in an employment contract in the work establishment or in another place designated by the employer (Article 151^5 §1 of the Code). Night medical duty of a physician working at hospital falls under this definition. What is interesting though is that under further paragraphs, the time of an on-call shift was not counted in the working time if, during the on-call shift, the employee did not perform any work (Article 151^5 §2

17 For the purpose of this article some problems raised in the *Czesław Miś* case will be omitted as they address specifics of the Polish law. A comprehensive analysis of the regulations concerning the working time under Polish and EU law in the context of the *Dr Miś* case was published by: S. Majkowska-Szulc and M. Tomaszewska, 'Working time of physicians – commentary on judgment by the Circuit Court of Krakow of 29 December 2006 (VI Pa 445/06)', *Europejski Przegląd Sądowy (European Judicial Review)* 2007/12, pp 46–60.

18 Directive 2003/88/EC of the European Parliament and of the Council of 4 November 2003 concerning certain aspects of the organisation of working time, OJ L 299, 18.11.2003, pp. 9–19.

19 Law of 26 June 1974 on the Labour Code (OJ 2013, item 1028, as amended).

20 Law of 30 August 1991 on the Healthcare Institutions (OJ 1991, nr 91, item 408 as amended). In 2011 the Law was replaced by another act. See footnote 50.

of the Code). On the other hand, the on-call shift could not be regarded as rest time because rules for compensation for the on-call shift were provided and the employees' rights to rest could not be affected (Article 151^5 §2 and §3 of the Code). It was simply regarded as "on-call time", during which the work was or was not performed but the employee had to be ready to perform it if needed.

Working time of employees of the healthcare institutions was regulated by a separate *lex specialis* – the Law on Healthcare Institutions adopted in 1991, as an element of the economic transformation reforms introduced in Poland. Such employees were to work maximum 7 hours and 35 minutes per day and approximately 37 hours and 55 minutes per week in the average five day week (Article 32g of the Law).

Physicians employed by the healthcare institutions providing a 24 hours medical service, could be obligated by their employers to serve a "medical duty" but the time of the duty was not calculated as a working time (Article 32j of the Law).[21] It corresponded properly with the provisions of the Labour Code.

As a rule then, under the previous regulations, physicians working for the public hospital would provide a 24-hour medical duty and without any rest they continued their work for another 7 hours and 35 minutes.

The EU directive concerning certain aspects of the organization of working time[22] was adopted in 2003 and replaced an older act in the field. It originated from Article 137 of the Treaty on the European Community according to which "the Community shall support and complement the activities of the Member States in [...] improvement in particular of the working environment to protect workers' health and safety".[23]

The scope of the Directive's application is provided in the opening article along with its purpose. The law is to lay down minimum safety and health requirements for the organization of working time and applies to minimum periods of daily rest, weekly rest and annual leave, to breaks and maximum weekly working time as well as to certain aspects of night work, shift work and patterns of work. Legal definitions of the Directive leave no space for misunderstanding of the terms used in the provisions and as such "working time" means "any period during which the worker is working, at the employer's disposal and carrying out his activity or duties, in accordance with national laws and/or practice" while "rest period" means any "period which is not working time" (Article 2 of the Directive).

It was for the Member States to "take the measures necessary to ensure that every worker is entitled to a minimum daily rest period of 11 consecutive hours per 24-hour period (Article 3 of the Directive). In addition, according to the Directive, Member States take the measures necessary to ensure that, per each

21 Law of 30 August 1991 on the Healthcare Institutions before amendments introduced by the Law of 24 August 2007 on the amendments to the Law on Healthcare Institutions (OJ 2007, nr 176, item 1240).

22 *Supra*, note 18.

23 Presently Article 153 TFEU, *supra* note 4.

seven-day period, every worker is entitled to a minimum uninterrupted rest period of 24 hours plus the 11 hours' daily rest (Article 5 of the Directive). The Directive also regulates average working time of period of one week stating that "average working time for each seven-day period, including overtime, does not exceed 48 hours" (Article 6(b) of the Directive).

4. CZESŁAW MIŚ' ARGUMENTS IN THE LIGHT OF THE ECJ CASE LAW

Dr Miś was convinced that his employer demanded working time contrary to the provisions of the EU Directive. He sued the hospital as his employer (the Public Health Care Institution in Nowy Sącz) in the District Court[24] requesting 121,60 days off as compensation for his work time including medical duty time that he had served since Polish accession to the EU that is – 1 May 2004. Czesław Miś argued that, as a result of the supremacy principle, the provisions of the EU Directive should be applied directly instead of the national provisions which were contrary to the Directive. He pointed to some irrational consequences of the legal situation of physicians under the presented order. If, according to the Directive, "rest period" is any period which is not working time and "medical duty" according to Polish law is not working time, then it would have to defined as "rest period" in the light of the Directive.[25]

The plaintiff underlined that the European Court of Justice in its judgments definitely decided that medical duty should be regarded as working time. In a judgment concerning the application of the Directive to the work of doctors in primary health care teams, the Court confirmed that the scope of the Directive encompasses doctors in public health care centres (which would be the hospital employing dr Miś in the presented case). The Court also ruled that the

> "time spent on call by doctors in primary health care teams must be regarded in its entirety as working time, and where appropriate as overtime, within the meaning of Directive 93/104 concerning certain aspects of the organization of working time, if they are required to be at the health centre. If they must merely be contactable at all times when on call, only time linked to the actual provision of primary health care services must be regarded as working time".[26]

---

[24] The claim was brought to the IV Department on Labour Law of the District Court in Nowy Sacz on 14 July 2004. For the purpose of this text, the structure of Polish courts as translated into English is the following: District Court (Sąd Rejonowy), Regional Court (Sąd Okręgowy), Supreme Court (Sąd Najwyższy).

[25] See: S. Majkowska-Szulc and M. Tomaszewska, *supra* note 16, p. 47.

[26] ECJ 3.10.2000, C-303/98 *Sindicato de Médicos de Asistencia Pública (Simap) v Conselleria de Sanidad y Consumo de la Generalidad Valenciana.*

In a judgment issued couple of years later, the ECJ clearly stated that the

> "concepts of working time and rest period within the meaning of Directive 93/104 concerning certain aspects of the organization of working time may not be interpreted in accordance with the requirements of the various legislations of the Member States but constitute concepts of Community law which must be defined in accordance with objective characteristics by reference to the scheme and purpose of that directive. Only such an autonomous interpretation is capable of securing for that directive full efficacy and uniform application of those concepts in all the Member States".

The Court further argued that the Directive

> "must be interpreted as meaning that on-call duty performed by a doctor where he is required to be physically present in the hospital must be regarded as constituting in its totality working time for the purposes of that directive, even where the person concerned is permitted to rest at his place of work during the periods when his services are not required, with the result that that directive precludes legislation of a Member State which classifies as rest periods an employee's periods of inactivity in the context of such on-call duty".[27]

What is important, both judgments were issued in the preliminary reference procedures and concerned two different Member States of the European Union, namely Spain and Germany, so the questions about the application of the Directive to the medical doctors came from the practice of those Member States.

As a result, Czesław Miś argued, the medical duty during which the doctor stays at hospital for the entire time must be regarded working time.

The Directive, according to the plaintiff could be invoked against his hospital as the state hospital falls under the definition of "public body". The Court of Justice interpreted the direct effect of directives as working on vertical level only, that is when individual invokes it against a state (public) institution. The Court stated that provisions of the directive "may be relied upon by an individual against the state where that state fails to implement the directive in national law [...]". Further the Court reasoned that the horizontal application of the principle may not be used as "the directive may not of itself impose obligations on an individual and that a provision of a directive may not be relied upon as such against such a person".[28] The definition of a "public body" as "emanation of a state" also came through the ECJ jurisdiction in a case where the Court ruled that

> "unconditional and sufficiently precise provisions of a directive may be relied upon against organizations or bodies which are subject to the authority or control of

27 ECJ 9.09.2003, C-151/02 *Landeshauptstadt Kiel v Norbert Jaeger.*

28 ECJ 26.02.1986, C-152/84 *M.H. Marshall v Southampton and South-West Hampshire Area Health Authority (Teaching).* The ECJ preliminary ruling in this case concerned a claim of a British employee of a Health Authority in Great Britain. In this particular case the Court regarded the institution private and therefore the directive could not be used by the plaintiff.

the State or have special powers beyond those which result from the normal rules applicable in relations between individuals. They may in any event be relied upon against a body, whatever its legal form, which has been made responsible, pursuant to a measure adopted by the State, for providing a public service under the control of the State and has for that purpose special powers beyond those which result from the normal rules applicable in relations between individuals".[29]

5. ARGUMENTS OF THE POLISH COURTS

At the time when Dr Miś sued his employer Poland was a freshly accepted member of the European Union and the national courts just became facing the uniqueness, specificity and most importantly – consequences of the membership in their everyday work in practice.

The District Court in Nowy Sącz in its judgment of 22 November 2004 dismissed the complaint (which was in line with a motion submitted by the defendant, that is Dr Miś' employer) and ordered Czesław Miś to refund the defendant the costs of court proceedings. Two reasons served as grounds for such decision of the court. Firstly, the court decided that the defendant may not be regarded as a state or its emanation. Secondly, the court calculated that the period for the implementation of the Directive which had served as original grounds for the plaintiff's claim[30] into the national legal order had not expired yet, therefore the provisions might not be invoked and the only law applicable in this situation was the 1991 Polish Law on the Healthcare Institutions.[31]

Czesław Miś appealed to the Regional Court in Krakow and requested to revoke and remand the appealed judgment. The Regional Court in its judgment of 31 May 2005 dismissed the appeal. Interestingly, the dismissal was not based on the acceptance of the arguments of the lower court. In fact, the Regional Court stated that it was not possible to agree with any of the arguments provided by the District Court. The Regional Court argued that the state hospital can and should be defined as emanation of state because such interpretation is widely provided by the European Court of Justice in cases such as *Marshall*.[32] As to the second argument, the Regional Court corrected the calculations of the District Court and ruled that the 1993 Directive was to be implemented by 1 May 2004 and the replacing 2003 Directive was to be implemented into the Polish legal order by 2 August 2004. It

29 ECJ 12.07.1990, C-188/99 *Foster and others v British Gas.*

30 Czesław Miś used Directive 93/104/EC of 23 November 1993 concerning certain aspects of the organization of working time (OJ L 307, 13.12.1993, pp. 18–24) as original grounds for his claim. The Court noted however that this directive was replaced by the Directive 2003/88/EC of 4 November 2003 concerning certain aspects of the organization of working time (*supra*, note 18).

31 Based on: Judgment of the Supreme Court of the Republic of Poland issued on 6 June 2006, I PK 263/05 at 2.

32 *Supra*, note 28.

was therefore an admissible ground for requested compensation. The court had no doubt that the provisions of the Directive were unconditional and precise enough to constitute basis for the direct effect application. Regardless of the above, the court found that the rationality of the appeal arguments did not influence the correctness of the District Court's judgment because the plaintiff claimed for compensation in the form of the days off in return for the excessive work while completely omitting the fact that he had been paid for that work in accordance with the relevant law and internal payment regulation of the employer. As a result, Czesław Miś was not entitled to the requested compensation as, according to the Polish Labour Code, the days off are provided as compensation for the excessive work only in case when the employee was not paid for that work. The days off, on the other hand, are not granted as compensation for the night work.[33]

The final and only possibility to change the decision of the Regional Court was to use the cassation procedure before the Supreme Court which Czesław Miś decided to do and filed a cassation complaint to the Polish Supreme Court.[34] He argued that the lower courts were in breach of the law while applying the Polish provisions of the Law on Healthcare Institutions instead of the application of relevant provisions of the Directive on certain aspects on the organization of working time in accordance with the supremacy and direct effect principles. The Supreme Court issued judgment in the case on 6 June 2006 fully in favour of dr Miś' complaint by revoking and remanding the judgment. The case was to be decided once again by the Regional Court in Krakow. The Supreme Court's arguments started with the recollection of the Polish Constitutional Court's judgements concerning the conformity of the Law on Healthcare Institution with the Polish Constitution issued in 2000 in which the Court decided the law was constitutional in its provisions concerning the medical duty.[35] On the other hand however, the Constitutional Court underlined that provisions of the Europe Agreement imposed obligations on the Polish state (including all public organs of the state) to take "all necessary efforts to ensure the conformity of Poland's future law with the Community law" and the obligation was especially addressed to the "protection of the employee in their work place".[36] The Court also clearly stated that when looking for the directions of the interpretation of the Polish law

---

33 Based on: Judgment of the Supreme Court of the Republic of Poland, 6 June 2006, I PK 263/05, at 3.

34 Under the Polish legal system a party may use a special procedure to submit its case to the Supreme Court. The procedure is known as "cassation complaint" and may be defined as an "extraordinary appellate measure that a party may use to contest certain substantive judgments rendered by a second-instance court" under certain circumstances. It is to be used as a legal measure "designed to bring about uniformity of the decisions of the courts of general jurisdiction". S. Frankowski, A. Bodnar, *Introduction to Polish Law*, Kluwer Law International 2005, pp. 138–139.

35 Judgment of the Constitutional Tribunal of 24 October 2000, K 12/00.

36 Europe Agreement establishing an association between the Republic of Poland of the one part and the European Communities and their Member States, of the other part, signed in Brussels on 16 December 1991 (Official Journal 1994, Nr 11, item 38 as amended).

the priority belongs to the interpretation which allows the national provision to have the meaning closest possible to the solutions adopted in the European Union. The Supreme Court argued that if this was the Constitutional Court's position before Polish accession to the European Union, then it is even more so after 1 May 2004 when Poland became a Member of the Communities and the EU.[37] As a result, the case was sent back to the lower court for another evaluation of the plaintiffs' work time arrangements in the light of the Community law.

6. THE FINAL DECISION AND ITS CONSEQUENCES

On 29 December 2006 the Regional Court in Krakow issued the final judgment in Czesław Miś' case. Based on the recognition of the fundamental general principles of the Community law – that is direct effect and supremacy, as well as the principle of effectiveness (recalled here for the first time to remind that EU law has to take actual effect in the domestic legal orders of the Member States),[38] the court changed the appealed judgment and granted the plaintiff some time off as compensation for the wrong calculation of his working time during the requested period.[39] The court, as guided by the Supreme Court reasoning, underlined that application of the EU legal regulations requires to "respect the interpretation of the EU law provisions provided by the European Court of Justice in Luxembourg".[40] The Court widely and extensively quoted several relevant judgments of the ECJ concerning the direct effect of an unimplemented directive (*Beentjes* case of 1988,[41] *Becker* case of 1982),[42] as well as those concerning the working time regulations (*SIMAP* case[43] and *Jaeger* case).[44] The Court reached for – at the time – newest judgments and pointed to the Pfeifer case decided in 2004[45] confirming the calculation of the working time in

---

37 *Supra*, note 33, at 4 and 5.

38 See for example: P. Rott, 'The Court of Justice's Principle of Effectiveness and its Unforeseeable Impact on Private Law Relationships' in D. Leczykiewicz and S. Weatherill (eds), *The Involvement of EU Law in Private Law Relationships*, Studies of the Oxford Institute of European and Comparative Law, Hart Publishing, Oxford 2013, pp. 181–198.

39 The Court calculated the time and granted Czesław Miś total of 169 hours and 4 minutes time off work. The mathematical calculation of the time is not significant for the problems under discussion in this paper, so it will be omitted, especially that it was not the main problem in the case. The recognition of the EU law principles was confirmed and as such constituted the most important result of the entire court procedure.

40 The judgment on behalf of the Republic of Poland issued by the Regional Court in Krakow, Labour Department VI, VI Pa 445/06 at 6.

41 ECJ 20.09.1988, C-31/87 *Gebroeders Beentjes BV v State of the Netherlands.*

42 ECJ 19.01.1982, C-8/82 *Ursula Becker v Finanzamt Münster-Innenstadt.*

43 *Supra*, note 23.

44 *Supra*, note 24.

45 ECJ 5.10.2004, C-397/01 *Bernhard Pfeiffer and others v Deutsches Rotes Kreuz, Kreisverband Waldshut eV.*

accordance with the Directive and to the *Abdelkader Dellas* judgment of 2005[46] stating that duty time served at the place of work has to be calculated as working time regardless from the fact how much of the duty time was spent on actual work.[47] Doctor Miś' arguments were therefore regarded as proper understanding of the mechanisms of the EU principles.

The implications of the so-called "Miś law" (the "Teddy Bear law") were to be held in two major ways: the law was amended and the Supreme Court channelled possible compensation procedures of other doctors.

The Law on Healthcare Institutions was amended on January 1, 2008 and according to the new provision of Article 32j(2) "the duty time is calculated toward the working time" and the rules of the salary calculation for medical duties have been added and adjusted with the provisions of the Labour Code.[48]

The Supreme Court ruled soon afterwards that the doctors who had served medical duties until 1 January 2008 were not entitled to claim for additional salary compensation in cases where the employer did not provide for relevant uninterrupted rest periods as regulated by Articles 132 and 133 of the Labour Code independently from the salary paid for the duty, but such regulations were not to exclude possibility to claim compensation or redress based on general principles.[49]

Other judgments – including those issued by the lowest courts dealing with work time calculations,[50] as well as some additional opinions by the Polish Supreme Court – have been consistent in their interpretations and confirmation of the EU law principles while using the same examples of the ECJ case law and several new ones still firmly maintaining the aims of the 2003 Directive and its proper implementation in other Member States (such as the 2007 judgment in the *Jan Vorel* case).[51, 52]

It is worth to mention that the Law on Healthcare Institutions was replaced by the Law on Medical Activity which entered into force in 2011. Medical duty is now separately defined and regulated in the law, obviously as time calculated toward the working time.[53]

46 ECJ 1.12.2005, C- 14/04 *Abdelkader Dellas and others v Premier Ministre and others.*

47 *Supra*, note at 8–10 and 13.

48 Law of 24 August 2007 on the amendment of the law on health care institutions and the Law on higher education (OJ 2007, nr 176, item 1240).

49 Resolution of the Seven Judges Composition of the Supreme Court, 13 March 2008, I PZP 11/07.

50 See for instance: The judgment on behalf of the Republic of Poland issued by the District Court in Gdynia Labour Department IV, IV P 423/07.

51 ECJ 11.01.2007, C-437/05 *Jan Vorel v. Nemocnice Český Krumlov.*

52 Resolution of the Seven Judges Composition of the Supreme Court, 13 March 2008, I PZP 11/07. In fact Czesław Miś successfully sued his hospital once again for the compensation of symbolic 1 PLN for the wrong calculation of his working time in the period before 1 May 2004, that is between 1 January and 30 April 2004. See: 'Złotówka dla doktora Misia' (One zloty for doctor Miś), *Dziennik Polski* from May 30, 2008, p. R6.

53 Law of 15 April 2011 on Medical Activity (OJ 2011, number 112, item 654 as amended).

The problem of settlement of the working time during the medical duty has been subject to many other judicial decisions as the substantive Polish law issues are still to be clarified under the new law. One of the newest Supreme Court's opinions deals with the problem again, but the legal questions concern exclusively the interpretation and application of the Polish law.[54]

7. CLOSING REMARKS

It seems that with regards to the 2003 Directive, the prevalence of the supremacy and direct effect principles has been eventually fully recognized by the Polish courts on all levels of judiciary. The right of individuals to use the direct effect as guaranty of their rights listed in EU directives has been acknowledged and confirmed. The remaining problem is the one with on time implementation of other EU directives in Poland. The "Teddy Bear law" lesson however has been well learned by Polish citizens. Ironically, in the most recent cases these are patients fighting for their rights under the EU Directive on patients' rights in cross-border health care which was due to be implemented in Member States by 25 October 2013.[55] The Directive's aim was to, among others, provide clear rules and reliable information to patients regarding access and reimbursement for healthcare received in another EU country.

Polish patients, with full awareness of their rights deriving from the direct effect principle, did not resign from the cross-border health care services offered for example in Czech Republic and scheduled their treatments just days after the deadline for the directive implementation. They underwent the procedures and then requested the refund of the costs from the Polish National Health Fund. The Fund refused the reimbursement and the first claims made it to the district courts. It was once again the District Court in Krakow which on 10 June 2014 – ten years after the Polish accession to the EU and ten years after the first claim of dr Miś – granted the plaintiff a full reimbursement for the cataract surgery performed in the Czech Republic in full recognition of the principles of supremacy and direct effect of the EU law.[56]

---

54 Decision of the Supreme Court, 4 April 2014, I PK 229/13.

55 Directive 2011/24/EU of the European Parliament and of the Council of 9 March 2011 in the application of patients' rights in cross-border healthcare, OJ L 88, 04.04.2011, pp. 45–65.

56 The judgment of the District Court is subject to appeal and the National Health Fund plans to use the appellate procedure. Information is available in Polish press, for example: J. Watoła, 'Pierwszy wyrok w sprawie leczenia za granicą' (First step towards cross-border health treatment), *Gazeta Wyborcza* from 12 June 2014. Online version available at: http://wyborcza.pl/1,75478,16138852,Pierwszy_wyrok_w_sprawie_leczenia_za_granica__NFZ.html.

BIBLIOGRAPHY

BOOKS

Frankowski, S., Bodnar, A., *Introduction to Polish Law*, Kluwer Law International 2005

Hartley, T.C., *The Foundations of European Union Law*, Oxford University Press 2010

ARTICLES

Avbelj, M., 'Supremacy or Primacy of EU Law – (Why) Does It Matter?', *European Law Journal*, Vol. 17, No. 6, November 2011

Majkowska-Szulc, S. and Tomaszewska, M., 'Working time of physicians – commentary on judgment by the Circuit Court of Krakow of 29 December 2006 (VI Pa 445/06)', *Europejski Przegląd Sądowy (European Judicial Review)* 2007/12

EU CASE-LAW

ECJ 15.07.1964, C-6/64 *Flaminio Costa v. E.N.E.L.*

ECJ 5.02.1963 C-26/62 *NV Algemene Transport- en Expeditie Onderneming van Gend & Loos v. Netherlands Inland Revenue Administration*

ECJ 13.02.1969, C-14/68 *Walt Wilhelm and others v. Bundeskartellamt*

ECJ 17.12.1970, C-11/70 *Internationale Handelsgesellschaft mbH v. Einfuhr- und Vorratsstelle für Getreide und Futtermitte*

ECJ 17.05.1972, C-93/71 *Orsolina Leonesio v. Ministero dell'agricoltura e foreste*

ECJ 4.12.1974, C-41/74 *Yvonne van Duyn v. Home Office*

ECJ 8.04.1976, C-34/75 *Gabrielle Defrenne v. Sabena*

ECJ 9.03.1978 C-106/77 *Amministrazione delle Finanze dello Stato v. Simmenthal SpA*

ECJ 5.04.1979, C-148/78 *Criminal proceedings against Tullio Ratti*

ECJ 19.01.1982, C-8/82 *Ursula Becker v. Finanzamt Münster-Innenstadt*

ECJ 10.04.1984, C-14/83 *Sabine von Colson and Elisabeth Kamann v. Land Nordrhein-Westfalen*

ECJ 26.02.1986, C-152/84 *M.H. Marshall v. Southampton and South-West Hampshire Area Health Authority (Teaching)*

ECJ 21.05.1987, C-249/85 *Albako Margarinefabrik Maria von der Linde GmbH & Co. KG v. Bundesanstalt für landwirtschaftliche Marktordnung*

ECJ 20.09.1988, C-31/87 *Gebroeders Beentjes BV v. State of the Netherlands*

ECJ 13.11.1990, C-106/89 *Marleasing SA v. La Comercial Internacional de Alimentacion SA.*

ECJ 3.10.2000, C-303/98 *Sindicato de Médicos de Asistencia Pública (Simap) v. Conselleria de Sanidad y Consumo de la Generalidad Valenciana*

ECJ 9.09.2003, C-151/02 *Landeshauptstadt Kiel v. Norbert Jaeger*

ECJ 5.10.2004, C-397/01 *Bernhard Pfeiffer and others v. Deutsches Rotes Kreuz, Kreisverband Waldshut eV.*

ECJ 1.12.2005, C- 14/04 *Abdelkader Dellas and others v. Premier Ministre and others*
ECJ 11.01.2007, C-437/05 *Jan Vorel v. Nemocnice Český Krumlov*
ECJ 26.02.2013, C-399/11 *Stefano Melloni v. Ministerio Fiscal*

10. ENFORCING EUROPE'S FOUNDATIONAL VALUES IN CENTRAL AND EASTERN EUROPE

A Case in Point

Tine CARMELIET*
Johns Hopkins University School of Advanced International Studies, Washington DC

Georgia Christina KOSMIDOU**
Johns Hopkins University School of Advanced International Studies, Washington DC

1. INTRODUCTION

Ever since the inception of the EU, respect for democracy, the rule of law and human rights has constituted a corner stone of the European integration project. Indeed, the founding EU member states contemplated political and economic cooperation based on their mutual respect for the principle of liberal democracy.[1] The importance of liberal democracy can clearly be seen in the early case law of the CJEU, such as the seminal judgment *Internationale Handelsgesellschaft* proves.[2] With the entry into force of the Treaty of Lisbon, respect for democracy and the rule of law gained a newly elevated position within the Union's legal framework. In particular, the introduction of Article 2 TEU reaffirms the EU's commitment towards its foundational values, by stating that, *inter alia*, it is founded on the values of democracy, human rights and the rule of law and that these constitute a common heritage of the member states. Article 49 TEU finally also stipulates that "*any European state which respects the values referred to in*

* Email: tcarmel1@jhu.edu.
** Email: gina.kosmidou@jhu.edu.

1 For the sake of clarity, we define liberal democracy as a form of government in which representative democracy operates under the principles of liberalism by protecting the rights of the individual. It is characterised by fair, free and competitive elections between several political parties, the principle of separation of powers, respect for the rule of law and the equal protection of human rights, civil rights, liberties and political freedoms for everyone.

2 ECJ 17.12.1970, C-11/70, *Internationale Handelsgesellsaft* [1970] *ECR* 1125.

Article 2" can join the EU, and in so doing renders democratic governance and respect for human rights a *sine qua non* condition and a minimum common denominator for the member states.

However, despite the EU's renewed commitment towards its foundational values, in recent years, more and more worrying undemocratic and even authoritarian tendencies have been noticed within the European member states. While 2014 marked the 10-year anniversary of the Eastern enlargement, there is little reason to celebrate as democracy is struggling in several countries that joined the EU during the last decade.[3] Ruling leaders have tried to centralize their executive power and undermine the rule of law by breaking the constraints of the checks and balances, thereby affecting the quality and stability of the democratic regimes. Amongst them, Hungary has led the trend. Since the 2010 election of Viktor Orban and his right wing conservative party Fidesz, Hungary has been backsliding to authoritarianism. The two-thirds majority in the Hungarian parliament has empowered Fidesz to adopt legislation without the need for political compromise.[4] Various amendments to the constitution have curbed Hungary's achievements of liberal democracy. This is evident by the fact that – just to name a few – the freedom of religion, the freedom of the media, and the powers of the judiciary and the Central Bank have been restricted.[5]

Hungary is nonetheless not the only country backsliding to authoritarianism. Across Central and Eastern Europe, democratically elected leaders increasingly deploy their power to precipitate dissent, demonise opposition and media in order to tailor the political system to their needs.[6]

---

3 Opinion of the Venice Commission on the Fourth Amendment to the Fundamental Law of Hungary, available at www.venice.coe.int/webforms/documents/?pdf=CDL-AD(2013)012-e [Accessed on 31 August 2014]; K.L. Scheppele, "Hungary and the End of Politics", (2014) *(The Nation)*, available at www.thenation.com/article/179710/hungary-and-end-politics [Accessed on 31 August 2014]; B. Bugaric, "Protecting Democracy and the Rule of Law in the European Union: The Hungarian Challenge", (2013): 1–24, available at http://papers.ssrn.com/sol3/papers.cfm?abstract_id=2257935 [Accessed on 31 August 2014]; U. Sedelmeier, "Anchoring Democracy from Above? The European Union and Democratic Backsliding in Hungary and Romania after Accession", (2014) *(Journal of Common Market Studies)*, 105–121; D. Malova and B. Dolny, "The Eastern Enlargement of the European Union: Challenges to Democracy?", (2008) *(Human Affairs)* 18, 2, 67–80.

4 In April 2014, the party won a second term with 45% of the vote. However, Orban made changes to the electoral law during his first term, thereby transforming this plurality into a two-thirds parliamentary majority and allowing him to amend the constitution at his will. P. Lendvai, *Hungary. Between Democracy and Authoritarianism*, Hurst & Company, London 2013, 208–220; K.L. Scheppele, "Hungary and the End of Politics", *op. cit.*

5 In the past 4 years, Orban has tightened his grip on almost every dimension in Hungary's politics and public life: the judiciary, the central bank, the media, education and culture, not to mention the new constitution and the electoral system. K.L. Scheppele, "Hungary and the End of Politics", *op. cit.*

6 U. Sedelmeier, "Anchoring Democracy from Above? The European Union and Democratic Backsliding in Hungary and Romania after Accession", *op. cit.*, 105–121; J. Werner Mueller, "Eastern Europe Goes South", (2014) *(Foreign Affairs)*, 14–19; I. Traynor, "Eastern European

Bulgaria has become the stage for culture wars and constitutional crises.[7] Romania too is experiencing political crises and struggles to uphold the rule of law. In 2012, Victor Ponta launched a coup against President Traian Basescu, thereby imitating Hungary's Orban by openly pressuring the judiciary.[8] Respect for minorities such as the Roma poses moreover serious problems in several countries, in particular in Romania and Slovakia.[9] Finally, in the Czech Republic, corruption and abuse of power are commonplace, as President Milos Zeman demonstrated in June 2013 when he publicly defied the parliament by installing a close ally as prime minister.[10] The common thread amongst those power hungry leaders is that, while they are busy dismantling their liberal democratic political order, they are careful to maintain a democratic façade by holding regular elections and allowing political opposition. This makes it increasingly difficult for the EU to formulate a response to these undemocratic turns.

Indeed, even though the EU has perceived these developments with Argus eyes, the political pressure exerted by its leadership has not achieved the desired outcome.[11] While much attention has been focused on the nature of the political changes in these countries, less discussed is whether the EU is able to enforce its foundational values. We will therefore examine whether the EU possesses the competences to keep its member states on the democratic rails. In assessing the EU's competences, special attention will be given to the role of the European Courts. In the first part, the pitfalls of the EU's institutional framework are discussed. The analysis will however not be without engagement or commitments: where shortcomings are identified, suggestions for possible remedies are offered in the second part.

Autocrats pose New Test for Democracy", (2013) *(The Guardian)*, available at www.theguardian.com/world/2013/aug/13/eastern-europe-autocrats-return-test-democracy [Accessed on 31 August 2014].

7 J. Werner Mueller, "Eastern Europe Goes South", (2014) *(Foreign Affairs)*, 14–19.

8 This marked the beginning of a more authoritarian political identity in Romania. The end of Basescu's term in December 2014 will undoubtedly increase the political and social tension. V. Tismaneanu, "Democracy on the Brink. A Coup Attempt Fails in Romania", (2013) *(World Affairs Journal)*, 83–87.

9 J. Werner Mueller, "Eastern Europe Goes South", *op. cit.*, 14–19; I. Traynor, "Eastern European Autocrats pose New Test for Democracy", *op. cit.*

10 This act was meant to consolidate his position as a president. I. Traynor, "Eastern European Autocrats pose New Test for Democracy", *op. cit.*

11 Motion for resolution on the situation of fundamental rights: standards and practices in Hungary, European Parliament, (2013), available at www.europarl.europa.eu/sides/getDoc.do?type=REPORT&reference=A7–2013 0229&language=EN [Accessed on 31 August 2014].

2. SHORTCOMINGS OF THE EU'S INSTITUTIONAL FRAMEWORK

2.1. ARTICLE 7 TEU

Article 7 TEU is the only mechanism that allows the EU to ensure member state's compliance with its foundational values.[12] Thus, if a member state is found in serious breach of the values enlisted in Article 2 TEU, Article 7 reproaches the member state by stripping it of (some of) its political rights, such as the suspension of voting rights. While this mechanism seems *prima facie* appropriate, on further inspection, several procedural and substantive obstacles make it politically unfeasible.

2.1.1. Procedural obstacles

First, the institutional design of Article 7 renders its use as an instrument of democracy extremely cumbersome.[13] Article 7 grants the European Council the power to assess whether a member state breaches the fundamental values, subject to the democratic control by the European Parliament. Obtaining such a double majority in order to invoke Article 7 is nonetheless highly unlikely. First of all, a 4/5th majority in the European Council is rare, especially when it comes to sensitive topics such as democracy or the rule of law. Deciding to name and shame another European government is a deeply political act, which the heads of states sitting in the European Council are hesitant to take. Secondly, previous cases have proven that obtaining the parliamentary consent is problematic as well. More in particular, in the *Haider* case, in the debate to employ Article 7, a strong split occurred between the centre left and the centre right parties of the Parliament.[14] The rapid erosion of the consensus and the subsequent lifting of

---

12 The prospect of the Eastern enlargement has incentivized the member states to adopt Article 7 TEU in the Amsterdam Treaty in order to control political changes in the post-communist countries after their accession to the EU. V. Van Hüllen and T.A. Börzel, "The EU's Governance Transfer. From External Promotion to Internal protection?", (2013), available at www.sfb-governance.de/en/ISA2013/papers/ISA_2013_van_Huellen_Boerzel.pdf?1367229501 [Accessed on 31 August 2014].

13 Under the TEU, Member States may leave the EU voluntarily, but there is no legal mechanism inscribed to actually remove a country from the Union. B. Bugaric, "Protecting Democracy and the Rule of Law in the European Union: The Hungarian Challenge", *op. cit.*; V. Van Hüllen and T.A. Börzel, "The EU's Governance Transfer. From External Promotion to Internal protection?", *op. cit.*

14 The same controversy existed when France's expulsion of the Roma was discussed. J. Werner Müller, "Safeguarding Democracy Inside the EU: Brussels and the Future of the Liberal Order", (2013) *Transatlantic Academy Paper Series*, 17–18, available at www.transatlanticacademy.org/publications/safeguarding-democracy-inside-eu-brussels-and-future-liberal-order [Accessed on 31 August 2014]; M. Merlingen, C. Mudde and U. Sedelmeier,

the sanctions against the Austrian coalition government, which contained an extreme right party, showcases the weakness of this procedure.

The same controversy within the EU is noticeable when it comes to assessing Hungary's recent political developments. While the Parliament has announced its willingness to activate Article 7 if the Hungarian government refuses to take action to restore the rule of law, the European People's Party – the centre-right coalition of different European parties controlling the majority of the Parliament – clearly expressed its reluctance to employ the sanctioning mechanism on this ground. This should not cause surprise. Since Orban's party Fidesz belongs to the latter political bloc, he enjoys significant support of the European right.[15] Furthermore, while Fidesz is a right-wing party leaning towards extremism, Orban depicts his party in the international sphere as belonging to the centre right. It is therefore not surprising that Angela Merkel and Donald Tusk are unwilling to criticize a member of their own political family. The political reluctance to use Article 7 also seems to be inspired by the fear that a member state's endorsement of Article 7 against another state might backfire one day, and that the sanctions will also be applied against them.[16] The existence of such party politics is highly noxious for the protection of the European values. Today, the Parliament is dominated by governments and party affiliations, rather than by the common interest to protect Europe's liberal democracy. The operation of the Parliament thus comes down to party politics instead of the impartial protection of European values.[17] In this respect, the more significant party politics becomes, the more likely it is that political deals will be struck, and a habit of mutual indulgence of violations of the EU values amongst the member states will arise. Consequently, mindful of the procedural requirements, it is highly unlikely that a political consensus will be found, both in the Council and

---

"The Right and the Righteous? European Norms, Domestic Politics and the Sanctions against Austria", (2001) *(Journal of Common Market Studies)* 39, 1, 59–77.

15 E. Jenne and C. Mudde, "Hungary's Illiberal Turn. Can Outsiders help?", (2012) *(Journal of Democracy)* 23, 3: 147–155; V. Van Hüllen and T.A. Börzel, "The EU's Governance Transfer. From External Promotion to Internal protection?", *op. cit.*

16 V. Van Hüllen and T.A. Börzel, "The EU's Governance Transfer. From External Promotion to Internal protection?", *op. cit.*; J. Werner Müller, "Safeguarding Democracy Inside the EU: Brussels and the Future of the Liberal Order", *Transatlantic Academy Paper Series,* (2013): 17–18, available at www.transatlanticacademy.org/publications/safeguarding-democracy-inside-eu-brussels-and-future-liberal-order [Accessed on 31 August 2014]; S. Carrera, E. Guild and N. Hernanza, "The Triangular Relationship between Fundamental Rights, Democracy and the Rule of Law in the EU", (2013): 1–39, available at http://papers.ssrn.com/sol3/papers.cfm?abstract_id=2360486 [Accessed on 31 August 2014].

17 Working Document I on the situation of fundamental rights in the European Union in 2012, Committee on Civil Liberties, Justice and Home Affairs, 21 June 2013, 1–6; C. Pinelli, "Protecting the Fundamentals. Article 7 of the Treaty on the European Union and Beyond", (2012), *Fondation Européenne d'études Progressistes* 1–20, available at www.feps-europe.eu/assets/9a4619cf-1a01-4f96-8e27-f33b65337a9b/protecting%20the%20fundamentals.pdf [Accessed on 31 August 2014]. B. Bugaric, "Protecting Democracy and the Rule of Law in the European Union: The Hungarian Challenge", *op. cit.*

in the Parliament, to use Article 7 in order to halt a member state's undemocratic turn.

2.1.2. *Substantive obstacles*

The political favouritism highlights another, even more fundamental hurdle to overcome in order to invoke Article 7. The lack of a clear definition of democracy or the rule of law gives the EU an arduous task to frame a valid legal argument against Hungary's political changes. According to Article 7, there should be a *"clear risk of a serious breach by a member state of the values referred to in Article 2"*. While Article 2 is legally binding, its standards are rather imprecise and unclear.[18] Indeed, there is neither a definition, nor an operationalization of the values of democracy, the rule of law or human rights. The lack of such clarity and specification is especially problematic when a political consensus has to be reached to apply Article 7.[19] Viktor Orban has taken advantage of this loophole, by claiming that Fidesz acts with the mandate given by the Hungarian voters, since his party has obtained the parliamentary majority through free and fair elections.[20] As such, he argues that the EU must respect the member states' national identity and the resulting diversity in values and principles between the member states. Indeed, in reaction to the EU's pressure, Orban has steadily maintained that Hungary pursues values, somewhat different than those of other member states, while remaining within the spectrum of acceptable diversity.[21] Addressing the issue is all the more difficult since attempts to undermine the values of Article 2 are nowadays not undertaken with an explicit reference to authoritarian regimes. Indeed, the conventional human rights violations are not the primary problem, as dissidents are free to speak and people are free to take to the streets. The case of Hungary illustrates this problem clearly. Government spokespeople have responded to European criticisms on particular aspects of

---

18 V. Van Hüllen and T.A. Börzel, "The EU's Governance Transfer. From External Promotion to Internal protection?", *op. cit.*

19 B. Bugaric, "Protecting Democracy and the Rule of Law in the European Union: The Hungarian Challenge", *op. cit.*

20 On a recent press conference after the April 2014 elections, Orban stated that: "*an overwhelming majority was granted to us, so I think there's nothing to discuss*". It remains to be seen whether changing a constitution can be considered to be democratic when no democratic debate amongst the citizens has been held. P. Stuyvesant, "Interview with Viktor Orban: "A Majority of European leaders have lost their faith in what made Europe great", (2012) *(Frankfurter Allgemeine Zeitung)*, available at www.theoccidentalobserver.net/2012/03/interview-with-viktor-orban-a-majority-of-european-leaders-have-lost-their-faith-in-what-made-europe-great/ [Accessed on 31 August 2014]; C. Gati, 'Hungarian Rhapsodies' in *Life in the New Europe,* (2012): 65–71; E. Jenne and C. Mudde, "Hungary's Illiberal Turn. Can Outsiders help?" (2012) *(Journal of Democracy)* 23, 3: 147–155.

21 C. Pinelli, "Protecting the Fundamentals. Article 7 of the Treaty on the European Union and Beyond", (2012), *Fondation Européenne d'études Progressistes*: 1–20, available at www.feps-europe.eu/assets/9a4619cf-1a01–4f96–8e27-f33b65337a9b/protecting%20the%20fundamentals.pdf [Accessed on 31 August 2014].

their new constitutional order that such rules also exists in Greece, Germany or the United Kingdom. They fail nonetheless to mention that nowhere all those rules exist together, making the state a so-called "Frankenstate".[22]

The fact that countries like Hungary are still officially and publicly perceived as democracies makes it difficult to pinpoint their breach of the Article 2 values. Any attempt to employ Article 7 is consequently to a certain extent also perceived to be arbitrary: some member states might be targeted faster than others; which only further consolidates the member states' fear of retaliation. While Orban's attempt to frame his slide to autocracy into a European-wide *Kulturkampf* might not be entirely convincing, it is nevertheless the core reason why Article 7 is not a feasible mechanism to reproach member states.[23] The lack of a legal codification of the European post-war understanding of democracy and the rule of law allows political leaders to frame truly problematic political changes as falling within the acceptable "diversity of national values".[24] While previously the EU was considered to consist of a club of democratic countries that implicitly shared an understanding of the meaning of concepts such as "democracy" and "the rule of law", such *sous entendu* is today clearly absent.[25] Because of this controversy on the "shared" values, it is harder to find a majority of member states that want to employ Article 7 against another member state.[26] Consequently, the lack of a clear circumscription of the values enlisted in Article 2 makes the sanctions of Article 7 politically not feasible.[27]

---

22 K.L. Scheppele, "Hungary and the End of Politics", (2014) *The Nation*, available at www.thenation.com/article/179710/hungary-and-end-politics [Accessed on 31 August 2014]: "For example, as concerns the system of electoral laws, Orban combined both Germany's controversial rule for drawing electoral districts with the British highly disproportionate first past the post rules for constituency elections and topped it off with d'Hondt system for deriving proportional representation from party-list votes, a system that marginalizes small parties and bulks up plurality ones, and turns a bare plurality into a supermajority".

23 J. Werner Müller, "Safeguarding Democracy Inside the EU: Brussels and the Future of the Liberal Order", (2013), *Transatlantic Academy Paper Series*, 17–18, available at www.transatlanticacademy.org/publications/safeguarding-democracy-inside-eu-brussels-and-future-liberal-order [Accessed on 31 August 2014].

24 C. Pinelli, "Protecting the Fundamentals. Article 7 of the Treaty on the European Union and Beyond", *op. cit.*

25 B. Bugaric, "Protecting Democracy and the Rule of Law in the European Union: The Hungarian Challenge", *op. cit.*; S. Carrera, E. Guild and N. Hernanza, "The Triangular Relationship between Fundamental Rights, Democracy and the Rule of Law in the EU", (2013): 1–39, available at http://papers.ssrn.com/sol3/papers.cfm?abstract_id=2360486 [Accessed on 31 August 2014].

26 Article 7 is regarded as the "nuclear option", an ultimate measure to take against a fellow member state. J. Werner Müller, "Safeguarding Democracy Inside the EU: Brussels and the Future of the Liberal Order", (2013), *Transatlantic Academy Paper Series*, 17–18, available at www.transatlanticacademy.org/publications/safeguarding-democracy-inside-eu-brussels-and-future-liberal-order [Accessed on 31 August 2014].

27 Working Document I on the situation of fundamental rights in the European Union in 2012, Committee on Civil Liberties, Justice and Home Affairs, (2013), 1–6.

2.1.3. *Conclusion*

The unsuitability of Article 7 leads to two different findings. First of all, while the EU has many tools at its disposal to make applicant member states adopt liberal democracy by undergoing the necessary reforms, it has few appropriate instruments for changing the behaviour of their governments once they are member of the EU. Traditionally, the EU has not focused a great deal of attention on the internal enforcement of its values, as the member states formed a club of democratic countries and internalized the respect for the rule of law, human rights and democracy.[28] In this respect, the Copenhagen criteria were deemed sufficient to ensure the respect for the EU's values, as, through the carrot and stick approach, the EU employed these criteria as leverage to transform autocratic countries into liberal democracies.[29] The irony is that this conditionality, so powerful before the country joins the EU, loses much of its teeth once these countries have become members of the EU.[30]

Secondly, the controversy on Article 2 and the member states' resulting unwillingness to reproach one of their peers indicates that the problem runs deeper than only a different perception of values. Indeed, the underlying reason

---

28 V. Van Hüllen and T.A. Börzel, "The EU's Governance Transfer. From External Promotion to Internal protection?", *op. cit.*; C. Hillion, "Enlarging the European Union and deepening its fundamental rights protection", (2013), *(European Policy Analysis)* 11, 1 1–13; A. Vachudova, *Europe Undivided. Democracy, Leverage & Integration After Communism*, Oxford University Press, Oxford 2012, 63. B. Bugaric, "Protecting Democracy and the Rule of Law in the European Union: The Hungarian Challenge", *op. cit.*; G. de Burca, "Beyond the Charter: How Enlargement Has Enlarged the Human Rights Policy of the European Union", (2003) *(Fordham International Law Journal)* 27, 2, 679–714; A. Albi, "Ironies in Human Rights Protection in the EU: Pre-Accession Conditionality and Post-Accession Conundrums", (2009) *(European Law Journal)* 15, 1, 46–69.

29 D. Malova and B. Dolny, "The Eastern Enlargement of the European Union: Challenges to Democracy?", (2008) *(Human Affairs)* 18, 2, 67–80; A. Albi, "Ironies in Human Rights Protection in the EU: Pre-Accession Conditionality and Post-Accession Conundrums", (2009) *(European Law Journal)*, 15, 1, 46–69; E. Jenne and C. Mudde, "Hungary's Illiberal Turn. Can Outsiders help?" (2012) *(Journal of Democracy)* 23, 3: 147–155; A. von Bogdandy, M. Kottmann and others, "Reverse Solange – Protecting the Essence of Fundamental Rights against EU Member States", (2012) *(Common Market Law Review)* 49, 12, 489–519; A. Vachudova, *Europe Undivided. Democracy, Leverage & Integration After Communism*, Oxford University Press, Oxford 2012, 63; C. Pinelli, "Protecting the Fundamentals. Article 7 of the Treaty on the European Union and Beyond", *op. cit.*

30 A. Williams, "Enlargement of the Union and Human Rights Conditionality: A Policy of Distinction?", (2000) *(European Law Review)* 25, 1 601; A. Vachudova, *Europe Undivided. Democracy, Leverage & Integration After Communism*, Oxford University Press, Oxford 2012, 63; E. Jenne and C. Mudde, "Hungary's Illiberal Turn. Can Outsiders help?" (2012) *(Journal of Democracy)* 23, 3: 147–155; B. Bugaric, "Protecting Democracy and the Rule of Law in the European Union: The Hungarian Challenge", *op. cit.*; Working Document I on the situation of fundamental rights in the European Union in 2012, Committee on Civil Liberties, Justice and Home Affairs, 21 6 2013, 1–6; C. Hillion, "Enlarging the European Union and deepening its fundamental rights protection", (2013) *(European Policy Analysis)* 11, 1 1–13; A. Albi, "Ironies in Human Rights Protection in the EU: Pre-Accession Conditionality and Post-Accession Conundrums", (2009) *(European Law Journal)* 15, 1, 46–69.

of their hesitation seems to be that the member states do not want the EU to intervene in the internal politics of a member state. Traditionally, the EU has received a very limited mandate to act upon domestic politics that bear no immediate significance to the functioning of the EU.[31] Gradually, the EU has expanded its reach and has encroached upon the member state's sovereignty and "internal affairs", much to their dislike.[32] Advocating the use of Article 7 inevitably implies establishing a precedent, which would give the EU a more legitimate power to interfere in the countries' domestic affairs in the future.[33] It is consequently highly unlikely that the member states will invoke or support Article 7 against one of their peers.

2.2. LEGAL CREATIVITY TO PROTECT THE EUROPEAN FOUNDATIONAL VALUES

As mentioned before, Article 7 TEU is the only mechanism that explicitly provided for the protection of the values of Article 2. There are nonetheless several other instruments that the EU could use to enforce its values, albeit due to a more creative use of the European legal framework.

2.2.1. Infringement actions by the European Commission

First, the EU treaties grant the Commission, as the guardian of the treaties, the power to instigate infringement actions against member states that violate an

31 A. Albi, "Ironies in Human Rights Protection in the EU: Pre-Accession Conditionality and Post-Accession Conundrums", (2009) *(European Law Journal)* 15, 1, 46–69; C. Hillion, "Enlarging the European Union and deepening its fundamental rights protection", (2013) *(European Policy Analysis)* 11, 1 1–13; G. de Burca, "Beyond the Charter: How Enlargement Has Enlarged the Human Rights Policy of the European Union", *op. cit.*, 679–714; V. Van Hüllen and T.A. Börzel, "The EU's Governance Transfer. From External Promotion to Internal protection?", (2013), available at www.sfb-governance.de/en/ISA2013/papers/ISA_2013_van_Huellen_Boerzel.pdf?1367229501 [Accessed on 31 August 2014].

32 C. Hillion, "Enlarging the European Union and deepening its fundamental rights protection", (2013) *(European Policy Analysis)* 11, 1 1–13. G. de Burca, "Beyond the Charter: How Enlargement Has Enlarged the Human Rights Policy of the European Union", *op. cit.*, 679–714; V. Van Hüllen and T.A. Börzel, "The EU's Governance Transfer. From External Promotion to Internal protection?", (2013), available at www.sfb-governance.de/en/ISA2013/papers/ISA_2013_van_Huellen_Boerzel.pdf?1367229501 [Accessed on 31 August 2014].

33 European Parliament, Committee on Civil Liberties, Justice and Home Affairs, "Working Document I. On the situation of fundamental rights in the European Union in 2012, (2009–2014): 1–6, available at www.europarl.europa.eu/document/activities/cont/201310/20131021ATT73205/20131021ATT73205EN.pdf [Accessed on 31 August 2014]s; C. Pinelli, "Protecting the Fundamentals. Article 7 of the Treaty on the European Union and Beyond", (2012), *Fondation Européenne d'études Progressistes*, 1–20, available at www.feps-europe.eu/assets/9a4619cf-1a01-4f96-8e27-f33b65337a9b/protecting%20the%20fundamentals.pdf [Accessed on 31 August 2014]; C. Leconte, "The fragility of the EU as a community of values: lessons from the Haider affair", (2005), *(West European Politics)* 28, 3, 620–649.

obligation of EU law.[34] While this instrument enables the Commission to act at its discretion without the necessary political consensus, such infringement actions are not an appropriate legal tool to thwart precarious developments in member states.[35] The Commission may well believe that a member state breaches the values of Article 2, but basing a legal action on the 'violation of EU values' alone would give the CJEU a hard task in adjudicating the case. Indeed, the Court needs to obtain clear evidence of concrete infringements, rather than a general disrespect of Article 2.[36]

The individual character of the infringement actions is moreover emphasized by the procedure of Article 258 TFEU. Even if the Commission would instigate multiple individual infringement actions to indicate a greater concern about a member state, the CJEU is institutionally not able to discern the pattern errors if the cases are filed separately. The CJEU consists of many different panels of judges, as a consequence of which it is very likely that each infringement action against a member state is adjudicated by a different panel. This disables the judges to discern the pattern of infringements that indicate a more serious threat to Article 2.[37] Even though the Commission can try to overcome this procedural hurdle by requesting the Court to adjudicate the case in a Grand Chamber judgment, these individual actions still do not grant the Court the possibility to regard a more systematic pattern of noncompliance as an important fact in itself, without being able to rely on the evidence of any specific infringement.[38] Indeed,

---

34 Article 258 TFEU. If the European Court of Justice determines that a member state has failed to respect an obligation under the treaties, the member state can be held liable, which can constitute a basis for restitution or compensation. A violation of the obligations of the EU treaties extends not only to the treaty provisions itself, but also to secondary law, the general principles and fundamental rights, when the member state acts within the scope of Union law.

35 B. Bugaric, "Protecting Democracy and the Rule of Law in the European Union: The Hungarian Challenge", *op. cit.*; K.L. Scheppele, "What Can the European Commission Do When member States Violate Basic Principles of the European Union? The Case for Systemic Infringement Actions", (2013), 1–13, available at www.verfassungsblog.de/de/the-eu-commission-v-hungary-the-case-for-the-systemic-infringement-action/#.UrCuw406I7A [Accessed on 31 August 2014].

36 C. Pinelli, "Protecting the Fundamentals. Article 7 of the Treaty on the European Union and Beyond", *op. cit.* One qualification should be made to this statement. A recent case of the ECJ indicates that it might be possible to bring infringement actions on a broader violation of EU law. The ECJ judged that a member state's non compliance is not only related to specifically identified situations, but also to a more general practice: ECJ, 26.05.2011, C-306/08 *European Commission v Kingdom of Spain* [2011] *ECR I-04541. See also: Commission v Ireland and Others*, Commission Decision 2006/323/EC [2005] OJ 2006 L 119. M. Dawson and E. Muir, "Individual institutional and collective vigilance in protecting fundamental rights in the EU: lessons from the Roma", (2011) *(CMLReview)*, 65, 2, 764; P. Wenneras, "A new dawn for Commission enforcement under Articles 226 and 228 EC: General and Persistent (GAP) infringements, lump sums and penalty payments", (2006), *(CMLReview)*, 25, 2 48.

37 K.L. Scheppele, "What Can the European Commission Do When member States Violate Basic Principles of the European Union? The Case for Systemic Infringement Actions", *op. cit.*

38 *Ibid.*

since each individual infringement action is to be assessed on its own ground, the evidence of the connections between the individual cases would supersede the boundaries of the case that the judges have to review.

The pitfalls of this procedure have been exemplified by Commission proceedings against Hungary. In 2012, the Commission initiated three separate legal proceedings against Hungary's newly adopted laws, including a regulation that introduced an early retirement schedule for senior judges.[39] Even though it was clear that this new law was part of the broader process to reduce the independence of the judiciary and the right to a fair trial, the Commission could nevertheless only highlight the lowering of the retirement age as a violation of EU law, namely the prohibition of discrimination.[40] In its assessment, the Court consequently restricted itself to the discrimination issue, rather than analysing and tackling the broader problem of reduced judicial independence.[41] The Court ordered the Hungarian government to reinstate the judges that were forced to retire. But while the older judges were allowed to return to the judiciary, they could not be installed in their previous positions as they were already replaced by younger, pro-government judges.[42] The government moreover incentivized the judges not to return to the office, by offering them a financial compensation, as a consequence of which only a very small number of judges was reinstalled. Thus, despite the successful infringement action, most of the older judges were removed and the Hungarian courts were placed under a new, pro-regime management. This case indicates that infringement actions are not an appropriate instrument to respond to persistently non-compliant states, as chances are large that it disrespects more than just one particular EU obligation.

2.2.2. *Social pressure and issue linkage*

Finally, the EU can employ alternative instruments such as social pressure and issue linkage in order to bring the member state back on the democratic rails. Social pressure, consisting of informal meetings or public criticism and naming and shaming of non-compliant governments is an instrument that is widely used by international institutions.[43] Previous EU actions against

---

39 By lowering the retirement age from 70 to 62, the Hungarian government forced the departure of the most senior 10% of the judiciary, including one quarter of the Supreme Court justices and half of the Appeals court presidents. These judges could then be replaced by judges of the government's choice.

40 B. Bugaric, "Protecting Democracy and the Rule of Law in the European Union: The Hungarian Challenge", *op. cit.*

41 ECJ 14.12.2012, C-286/12, *Commission v Hungary* [2012] *nyr.*

42 K.L. Scheppele, "What Can the European Commission Do When member States Violate Basic Principles of the European Union? The Case for Systemic Infringement Actions", *op. cit.*

43 U. Sedelmeier, "Anchoring Democracy from Above? The European Union and Democratic Backsliding in Hungary and Romania after Accession", (2014) *(Journal of Common Market Studies)*, 105–121.

Romania and Hungary indicate that the use of social pressure is however not always very effective as a policy instrument. Indeed, its effectiveness depends largely on circumstantial factors, such as the public opinion in the country and the personality of the political leaders. For example, when Victor Ponta staged his *coup d'état* in July 2012, both the Commission President Barroso and the Council President Van Rompuy managed to obtain a commitment from Ponta to comply with measures necessary to restore the rule of law in Romania.[44] The EU's influence on Ponta was considerable, as Ponta, being relatively young, was a novice to politics and political leadership. In addition, Romania's overall positive attitude towards the EU and its desire to be recognized as a model European member state contributed to the successful exertion of social pressure. However, the EU failed to achieve greater plurality and independence of the media in Hungary through its political pressure. Orban, having a long history as former prime minister and party leader, additionally backed by the general discontent in Hungary with the EU, clearly did not feel the need to yield to the EU's pressure. The latter example showcases the circumstantial dependence of the effectiveness of such an approach.

Aside from social pressure, the EU also resorted to the mechanism of issue linkage in order to increase its leverage over its member states. Linking the non-compliance with EU law with the threat of withholding rewards for that state in another area has proven to be effective in several instances. For example, the Commission has linked breaches in the rule of law in Romania to a continued cooperation and verification monitoring, or negotiated an IMF loan with Hungary, while making it dependent on restoring the independence of the central bank.[45] Likewise, the EU has used economic sanctions under the Excessive Deficit Procedure of Article 126 TFEU in order to suspend structural funds for Hungary because it failed to meet the budget deficit limits.[46] The use of issue linkage has nonetheless several drawbacks too. First, like social pressure, its effectiveness depends largely on the circumstances. While the potential for issue linkage was high in Romania, as the country is not yet part of the Schengen area and is still subject to post-accession monitoring, not every member state has similar incentives that force it to comply with the EU law.[47] Imposing sanctions under Article 126 for other treaty violations should moreover be met with sufficient precaution. The mechanism of Article 126 is explicitly provided for economic measures, not for constitutional ones. Such improper use of Article 126, namely acting against member states under the pretext of economic

---

44 *Ibidem.*

45 *Ibidem.*

46 This article endows the Council with the competence to impose economic sanctions on a particular member state if it fails to respect the limits on the budget and public deficit. See Article 126 TFEU and Protocol 12.

47 U. Sedelmeier, "Anchoring Democracy from Above? The European Union and Democratic Backsliding in Hungary and Romania after Accession", *op. cit.*, 105–121.

sanctions, could affect Europe's legitimacy and even back fire in the longer term. Indeed, to cut funding of a non-compliant member state will affect the citizens of the country, whose living conditions can be significantly deteriorated. This will enhance and fortify the rhetoric and popularity of anti-European parties such as Fidesz and Jobbik,[48] which will reduce the incentives to comply with the European legal framework.[49]

3. POLICY RECOMMENDATIONS

3.1. IN SEARCH FOR A DEFINITION OF LIBERAL DEMOCRACY

The analysis above has showcased that due to the fundamental weaknesses in its institutional framework, the EU is unable to act against member states that disrespect its foundational values.[50] While all European states are *in abstracto* committed to the principle of liberal democracy, the devil is in the detail, as the virtues of democracy, human rights and the rule of law unite us in principle but divide us in the specifics.[51] To establish a regime and procedure for the protection of liberal democracy, be it legal or political, a common understanding needs to be developed. Below, we highlight the criterion that can be used as a starting point to extrapolate a definition of liberal democracy.

Since the EU Treaties are silent about this issue and the EU's reaction to its member states' backsliding in democratic governance is too rare and feeble to define a minimum common denominator for democracy, we seek criterion in the documents that specify and interpret liberal democracy for the accession in the EU. Indeed, the criteria set for accession – and even more specifically the

48 Jobbik is a far-right, nationalist and Eurosceptic formation that has gathered 47 seats. Although it is a political opponent of Fidesz, Jobbik hardly is a desirable partner for the liberal opposition. E. Jenne and C. Mudde, "Hungary's Illiberal Turn. Can Outsiders help?" (2012) *(Journal of Democracy)* 23, 3: 147–155.

49 I. Traynor, "Hungary Prime Minister Hits Out at EU Interference in National Day Speech", (2012), *The Guardian*, available at www.transatlanticacademy.org/publications/safeguarding-democracy-inside-eu-brussels-and-future-liberal-order [Accessed on 31 August 2014]; S. Taylor, "Orban accuses EU of colonialism", (2012), available at www.europeanvoice.com/article/2012/march/orban-accuses-eu-of-colonialism/73903.aspx [Accessed on 31 August 2014]; K. Than, "Hungary's Orban accuses Europe of 'Soviet-Style' meddling", available at www.reuters.com/article/2013/07/05/us-hungary-eu-orban-idUSBRE9640BR20130705 [Accessed on 31 August 2014]; E. Jenne and C. Mudde, "Hungary's Illiberal Turn. Can Outsiders help?" (2012) *(Journal of Democracy)* 23, 3, 147–155.

50 The European Commission proposed recently a new mechanism to strengthen the rule of law that was designed to discipline the Orban government. This new framework would provide the Commission the possibility to start enforcing the EU's requirement that all states honour the rule of law. The May 2014 European Parliament elections unfortunately prevented its implementation.

51 C. Lord, "Contested Meanings", 72.

candidate country progress reports – can give us a clearer indicator of what the members of the EU consider the lowest common denominator in terms of democratic governance to be accepted in the group of said states. To this end, we look into the relevant legal documents and the country reports for Hungary, Romania and Montenegro. These three cases were chosen because they represent (i) a Central Eastern European country that entered the EU with the massive Eastern enlargement in 2004, (ii) one of the so-called "laggards" of the 2007 accession and finally (iii) a country that is currently on its way to EU membership. In this way we aim to capture any evolution and diachronic change in the issues that the EU is focusing on to ensure democratization in its candidate countries.

When examining the country reports and common positions regarding the benchmarks, we discern a series of recurring themes.[52] First, with reference to the functioning of the national parliament, (i) the efficiency and acceleration of the legislative process, (ii) the relations between the legislative and the executive, and (iii) the reduction of the use of ordinances or emergency ordinances as legislative instruments without a clear justification for bypassing parliamentary procedure are the main sources of concern. This is because they can create instability and hinder the parliaments oversight and scrutiny over legislation. Secondly, with respect to administration, the recurrent concerns include: (i) inter-ministerial cooperation, (ii) administrative policy-making capacity building, (iii) decentralization of powers to local governments, (iv) minority rights and local government obligations, (v) the installation of mechanisms to ensure the political independence and accountability of civil servants, (vi) the creation of a career structure based on transparent promotion and assessment processes as well as (vii) the organization and functioning of the police.

Third, as concerns the judicial system, the main points of focus are: (i) speeding up court procedures, (ii) the enforcement of judicial decisions, (iii) the independence and accountability of the judiciary, (iv) publication of the court's reasoning for all their decisions, (v) simplified court procedures and the limitation of the right to appeal, (vi) immunization of the judiciary branch against the interventions of the executive, and finally (vii) corruption, as it undermines the legal system, public trust in the government and democracy

---

52 For this analysis the following documents were examined: Commission of the European Communities "Enlargement 98: Commission Report- Romania", 1998; Commission of the European Communities "Enlargement 98: Commission Report- Hungary", 1998; Commission of the European Communities "Enlargement 99: Commission Report on Hungary", 1999; Commission of the European Communities "Enlargement 99: Commission Report on Romania", Commission of the European Communities "2000 Regular Report on Romania's Progress Towards Accession", Commission of the European Communities "2001 Regular Report on Hungary's Progress Towards Accession", Commission of the European Communities "2004 Regular Report on Romania's Progress Towards Accession"; "European Union Common Position Montenegro Accession Document: Chapter 23, 2013".

in general. Related to the widespread problem of corruption were the issues of transparency and access to information. Finally, the protection of human, civil and political rights, and respect for minorities are a central point of focus in the countries reports. As such, country specific problems range from child-care institutions and child protection, adoption, trafficking of children (and generally of humans), to degrading treatment by the police, prison conditions, asylum seekers and refugees, freedom of expression, diversity of the media, homosexuality, the role of trade unions.

The recurring themes described above should not only serve an evaluation and a goal-setting purpose for the countries that are currently undergoing the accession process but are also an excellent source of inspiration for a potential definition of liberal democracy at the level of the European institutions. The positive effects of such an approach are twofold. First, it addresses the concern of candidate countries related to allowing EU Member States to hold themselves to lower standards than the ones expected from them. Secondly, it provides a pre-defined set of requirements that the member states should use to measure their performance in relation to good governance and democracy. The criterion described above consequently constitute a starting point in order to discern an operational definition of liberal democracy.

3.2. A STRONGER ROLE FOR THE CJEU

After having grappled with the main areas of interest that could provide a rough outline of what is perceived as a definition of democratic values by the EU, we assess whether the CJEU can play a part in developing an operation definition of liberal democracy. Since the Parliament and the Council are ineffective in controlling the illiberal reforms that take place in several EU member states, the CJEU remains the only guardian of the EU's foundational values. Indeed, the Court constitutes the third branch of democratic governance and despite the fact that it is a counter-majoritarian institution, it remains the key defender of democracy, the rule of law and human rights. While it cannot force governments to take action against their will, it is able to define and determine the requirements of European Union law. In doing so, it has the power to create a uniform understanding of democratic principles against which member states could subsequently be measured.[53] Indeed, the CJEU functions as the Constitutional Court of Europe that fills holes in European law and oversees a balance between integration, national rights, citizens' rights and international commitments. An adaptation of the European treaties notwithstanding, through

53 A. Dur, "Too much power to the judges", in "Key controversies in European Integration", ed. H. Zimmermann & A. Dur, (*Palgrave Macmillan*), New York, 2012, 80–85.

its case law, it is consequently the only actor capable of remedying this important gap.[54] As Tridimas notes,

> "in the EU's flawed system of governance, democracy finds solace in the judicial review of a Court which displays constitutional confidence and resolve to protect the rule of law and effective judicial protection by upholding the community law and the general legal principals emanating from the common traditions of member states".[55]

Therefore, we examine whether the Court could: (a) enhance the democratic accountability by preventing abuses of power and ensuring the protection of fundamental rights by EU institutions, (b) protect the rights of the European Polity by overseeing the respect of rule of law and democratic principles within the member states, (c) interpret and create a uniform understanding of the democratic principles.

Regarding the first function of the Court, which refers to democratic governance at the level of the Union as a whole, the CJEU can and to a great extent does enhance democratic accountability. It prevents the abuse of power and ensures the existence and respect of the checks and balances between the Union's institutions. In this way it enhances democracy by demanding a high standard of accountability by the rest of the non-elected decision-makers of the community.[56] Secondly, the Court protects and upholds the rights of the European Polity by ensuring respect for the rule of law and due process within the scope of EU law. The CJEU, when interpreting and applying the European treaties, should focus on providing legal certainty and security for the Union's citizens, with a specific emphasis on the protection of minorities, since this constitutes a distinctive feature of a liberal regime and provides the grounds for the acceptance of the majoritarian decision. In this sense, the CJEU can serve as the guardian of the rights of the European citizens within the sphere of EU actions. In the words of Judge Macini, commenting on precisely this phenomenon with respect to the CJEU:

> "when democracy advances and politics assert their claims, the judges are bound to take a pace back".[57]

Finally, the Court is able to act as the idea-giver, providing through its case law interpretations of the values and principles of liberal democracy. In doing

54 Ibid., 80–88.

55 T. Tridimas, "Terrorism and the ECJ: Empowerment and Democracy in the EC Legal Order", (2009) *(Queen Mary School of Law Legal Studies)*, 12: 1 [Accessed on 31 August 2014].

56 S. Ninatti, "How do our judges conceive of democracy? The Democratic Nature of the Community Decision-Making Process under Scrutiny of the European Court of Justice" (2003) (*NYU School of Law*), New York, 1–55.

57 A. Burleu, "Democracy and Judicial Review in the European Community" (1992) (*The University of Chicago Legal Forum*) 85.

so, it not only facilitates but also influences the debate about how these values should be understood at the Union's level. By including in its decisions relevant statements regarding its view on liberal democracy, the Court could provide suggestions to the policymakers or indicate its intentions for the direction of the future development of its relevant case law, much in the same way that the *lex ferenda* is supposed to influence and indicate the direction of international law. The CJEU, using a review of the accession criteria and benchmarks as well as the common constitutional traditions of the member states, could consequently develop through its case law and with the application of judicial activism an operational principle of liberal democracy. Such principle can be safeguarded by the Court, which would perform its function of a constitutional court. American liberal theorists, influenced by Montesquieu and Madison, have long stressed the significance of the courts to a well-functioning democracy.[58] In any case, it should be noted that much progress can be made as the CJEU is currently far from assuming such a role and due to an "asymmetry between the citizens capacity to resort to European law, the impact of the ECJ on democratization of the EU is at least in this respect marginal".[59]

4. CONCLUDING OBSERVATIONS

The European Union was founded on the assumption that all its member states constitute liberal democracies, who respect the liberal democratic order, human rights and the rule of law. It should therefore cause no surprise that the initial European treaties did not include disciplinary mechanisms to sanction member states that disrespect its foundational values. Today, the question whether there is a limit to the diversity of values and principles of political systems in European member states is no longer only of theoretical relevance, but is high on the agenda of Europe's leaders. Indeed, in recent years, several precarious political evolutions have taken place in Central and Eastern European member states, which can be interpreted as a backslide to authoritarianism.[60] The political changes in Hungary represent the most fundamental provocation to liberal democracy and the rule of law.[61] As an EU member, Hungary's present

58 Ibid., 81, 83.

59 O. Costa, "The European Court of Justice and democratic control in the European Union" (2003) (*Journal of European Public Policy*) 10, 5:740.

60 Opinion of the Venice Commission on the Fourth Amendment to the Fundamental Law of Hungary, available at www.venice.coe.int/webforms/documents/?pdf=CDL-AD(2013)012-e [Accessed on 31 August 2014]; B. Bugaric, "Protecting Democracy and the Rule of Law in the European Union: The Hungarian Challenge", *op. cit.*; D. Malova and B. Dolny, "The Eastern Enlargement of the European Union: Challenges to Democracy?", (2008) *(Human Affairs)* 18, 2, 67–80.

61 P. Lendvai, "Hungary. Between Democracy and Authoritarianism", (2013) (*Hurst & Company*) London, 208–220.

government undermines the abovementioned European norms and values from within.

The prime question that arises is consequently whether the EU can continue to turn a blind eye to this phenomenon, especially since these illiberal developments do not just undermine democracy in one of its member states, but also affect the legitimization of the Union as a whole that wants to present itself as a community of values and freedoms. Indeed, to remain on the side lines would be to legitimize Orban's challenge to European liberal democracy. Hungary is marking out once again the perilous and the all too familiar road in Europe from economic dislocation to authoritarian nationalism. As can be seen in countries like Romania and Bulgaria, this European moral crisis over basic principles has a spill over effect and is spreading beyond Hungarian borders.

The analysis above has indicated that the EU's institutional framework suffers from a structural weakness to act against member states that disrespect its foundational values. First, while Article 7 was explicitly inscribed to give the Council the power to reproach its member states, practice demonstrates that due to the rather vague values of Article 2 and the arduous institutional requirements of Article 7, it is close to impossible to find sufficient political willingness to employ the measure. Second, while a creative legal interpretation of the EU treaties grants the EU some additional assets to tackle member state non-compliance, they also have several deficiencies. As such, the infringement actions of the Commission are primarily designed to act against a specific violation of EU law, rather than against a more general tendency of disrespect. In addition, previous cases have proven that issue linkage and social pressure are not always very effective as a policy instrument.

A further exploration and definition of the values of Article 2 would give the EU a much more legitimized mandate to take action against its member states. In this respect, the CJEU, which is considered to be the prime guarantor of the EU's foundational values, could play a vital role by highlighting the necessary criterion for a liberal democracy. However, such mandate implies the existence of a complete and coherent political union, enabling the EU to enforce its values also towards its member states. If we want to protect those values, it is necessary to agree that they stand above and are independent from politics. It cannot be pluralism all the way down. As a political community, the EU has boundaries that cannot be overstepped. Where respect for human rights, the rule of law and the principle of democracy ceases to function, there Europe ends. However, if member states are not willing to contribute to such political union, the primary responsibility to protect and enforce those values will remain with the member states, and Article 2 will merely serve as a soft law mechanism, inducing but not obliging member states to live up to those values. The latter has far-reaching implications for the conception of the European integration model. From its existence, the EU has been perceived to be much more than only an economic cooperation, but has also been praised because of its area of shared prosperity, stability and peace. The refutation of such political union reduces the EU to a mere economic cooperative enterprise, without a commonly perceived democratic undertone. In any event, the current challenges to liberal democracy throughout Europe indicate that it is high time to take a common stand on the future of the European (political) Union.

BIBLIOGRAPHY

LEGISLATION AND LEGISLATIVE INSTRUMENTS

Treaty on the European Union, OJ C 236;
Treaty on the Functioning of the European Union, OJ C 326;
Charter of Fundamental Rights of the European Union, OJ C 326;
Protocol No 12 on the Excessive Deficit Procedure, OJ C 115.

CASE LAW

ECJ, Case C-306/08 *European Commission v. Kingdom of Spain* [2011] ECR I-04541;
ECJ, Case C-286/12, *Commission v. Hungary* [2012] nyr;
Commission Decision 2006/323/EC, *Commission v. Ireland and Others*, [2005] OJ 2006 L 119.

MONOGRAPHS

Andor, L., *Hungary on the road to the European Union: transition in blue,* Westport, Connecticut (2000);
Tang, H., *Winners and Losers in EU Integration: Policy issues for Central and Eastern Europe*, World Bank publications (2000);
Vachudova, A., *Europe Undivided. Democracy, Leverage & Integration After Communism,* Oxford, Oxford University Press (2012);
Lendvai, P., *Hungary. Between Democracy and Authoritarianism,* Hurst & Company, London (2013);
K. Dae Soon, *The Transition to Democracy in Hungary. Arpad Gonc and the post-communist Hungarian presidency*, Routledge (2013);

JOURNALS

Williams, A., "Enlargement of the Union and Human Rights Conditionality: A Policy of Distinction?", *(European Law Review)* 25, 1 (2000): 601–625;

Merlingen, M., C. Mudde and U. Sedelmeier, "The Right and the Righteous? European Norms, Domestic Politics and the Sanctions against Austria", *(Journal of Common Market Studies)* 39, 1 (2001): 59–77;

de Burca, G., "Beyond the Charter: How Enlargement Has Enlarged the Human Rights Policy of the European Union", *Fordham International Law Journal* 27, 2 (2003): 679–714;

Leconte, C., "The fragility of the EU as a community of values: lessons from the Haider affair", *West European Politics* 28, 3 (2005): 620–649;

Wenneras, P., "A new dawn for Commission enforcement under Articles 226 and 228 EC: General and Persistent (GAP) infringements, lump sums and penalty payments", *CMLReview*, 2, 12, (2006): 48–63;

Malova, D. and B. Dolny, "The Eastern Enlargement of the European Union: Challenges to Democracy?", *Human Affairs* 18, 2, (2008): 67–80;

Albi, A., "Ironies in Human Rights Protection in the EU: Pre-Accession Conditionality and Post-Accession Conundrums", *European Law Journal* 15, 1 (2009): 46–69;

Schopflin, G., "Democracy, Populism and the Political Crisis in Hungary", (2009), available at www.thefreelibrary.com/Democracy,+populism,+and+the+political+crisis+in+Hungary.-a0204854046;

Hockenos, P., "Central Europe's Right-Wing Populism. The EU's neoliberal economic reforms have undermined public faith in democratic politics", *The Nation* 23, 2 (2010): 18–21;

Sadurski, W., "Adding a Bite to A Bark? A story of Article 7, the EU Enlargement and Jörg Haider", 2010, available at http://papers.ssrn.com/sol3/papers.cfm?abstract_id=1531393;

Dawson, M. and E. Muir, "Individual institutional and collective vigilance in protecting fundamental rights in the EU: lessons from the Roma", *CMLReview* 25, 1, (2011): 764–803;

Blitz, B., "Evaluating Transitions: Human Rights and Qualitative Democracy in Central and Eastern Europe", *Europe-Asia Studies* (2011), 1745–1770;

Pinelli, C., "Protecting the Fundamentals. Article 7 of the Treaty on the European Union and Beyond", *Fondation Européenne d'études Progressistes* (2012): 1–20, available at www.feps-europe.eu/assets/9a4619cf-1a01-4f96-8e27-f33b65337a9b/protecting%20the%20fundamentals.pdf;

Rupnik, J., "How Things Went Wrong", *Journal of Democracy* 23, 3 (2012): 132–137;

Bankuti, M., G. Halmai and K. Lane Scheppele, "Disabling the Constitution", *Journal of Democracy* 23, 3 (2012): 138–146;

Jenne, E. and C. Mudde, "Hungary's Illiberal Turn. Can Outsiders help?" *Journal of Democracy* 23, 3 (2012): 147–155;

von Bogdandy, A., M. Kottmann and others, "Reverse Solange – Protecting the Essence of Fundamental Rights against EU Member States", *Common Market Law Review* 49, 12 (2012): 489–519;

Gati, C., "Hungarian Rhapsodies", *Life in the New Europe,* (2012): 65–71;

Kohalmi, L., "The Never-ending fight: economy and political corruption in Hungary", *Law and Economics Review* 4, 1 (2013): 67–82;

Hillion, C., "Enlarging the European Union and deepening its fundamental rights protection", *European Policy Analysis* 11, 1 (2013): 1–13;

Tismaneanu, V., "Democracy on the Brink. A Coup Attempt Fails in Romania", *World Affairs Journal* (2013), 83–87;

Atilla, A., "The Triple Crisis in Hungary: the "backsliding" of Hungarian democracy after twenty years", *Romanian Journal of Political Science* 13, 1 (2013): 1–27;

Bugaric, B., "Protecting Democracy and the Rule of Law in the European Union: The Hungarian Challenge", (2013): 1–24, available at http://papers.ssrn.com/sol3/papers.cfm?abstract_id=2257935;

Traynor, I., "Eastern European Autocrats pose New Test for Democracy", *The Guardian* (2013), available at www.theguardian.com/world/2013/aug/13/eastern-europe-autocrats-return-test-democracy;

Carrera, S., E. Guild and N. Hernanza, "The Triangular Relationship between Fundamental Rights, Democracy and the Rule of Law in the EU", (2013): 1–39, available at http://papers.ssrn.com/sol3/papers.cfm?abstract_id=2360486;

J.-W. Müller, "Safeguarding Democracy Inside the EU: Brussels and the Future of the Liberal Order", *Transatlantic Academy Paper Series,* (2013): 17–18;

Lane Scheppele, K., "What Can the European Commission Do When member States Violate Basic Principles of the European Union? The Case for Systemic Infringement Actions", (2013): 1–13, available at www.verfassungsblog.de/de/the-eu-commission-v-hungary-the-case-for-the-systemic-infringement-action/#.UrCuw406I7A;

Lane Scheppele, K., "Hungary and the End of Politics", *The Nation* (2014), available at www.thenation.com/article/179710/hungary-and-end-politics;

Werner Mueller, J. , "Eastern Europe Goes South", *Foreign Affairs* (2014), 14–19;

Sedelmeier, U., "Anchoring Democracy from Above? The European Union and Democratic Backsliding in Hungary and Romania after Accession", *Journal of Common Market Studies* (2014), 105–121;

Tomini, L., "Reassessing Democratic Consolidation in Central and Eastern Europe and the Role of the EU", *Europe-Asia Studies* (2014), 859–891;

Coman, R., "Quo Vadis Judicial Reforms? The Quest for Judicial Independence in Central and Eastern Europe", *Europe-Asia Studies* (2014), 892–924.

Traynor, I., "Hungary Prime Minister Hits Out at EU Interference in National Day Speech", Guardian, 15 March 2012. www.transatlanticacademy.org/publications/safeguarding-democracy-inside-eu-brussels-and-future-liberal-order;

Taylor, S., "Orban accuses EU of colonioalism", 2012, available at www.europeanvoice.com/article/2012/march/orban-accuses-eu-of-colonialism/73903.aspx;

Than, K., "Hungary's Orban accuses Europe of 'Soviet-Style' meddling", available at www.reuters.com/article/2013/07/05/us-hungary-eu-orban-idUSBRE9640BR20130705;

Stuyvesant, P., "Interview with Viktor Orban: "A Majority of European leaders have lost their faith in what made Europe great", *Frankfurter Allgemeine Zeitung,* 2012, available at www.theoccidentalobserver.net/2012/03/interview-with-viktor-orban-a-majority-of-european-leaders-have-lost-their-faith-in-what-made-europe-great/.

MISCELLANY (REPORTS – SPEECHES – WEBSITES)

European Parliament, Committee on Civil Liberties, Justice and Home Affairs, "Working Document I. On the situation of fundamental rights in the European Union in

2012, (2009–2014): 1–6, available at www.europarl.europa.eu/document/activities/cont/201310/20131021ATT73205/20131021ATT73205EN.pdf;
Opinion of the Venice Commission on the Fourth Amendment to the Fundamental Law of Hungary, www.venice.coe.int/webforms/documents/?pdf=CDL-AD(2013)012-e;
Motion for resolution on the situation of fundamental rights: standards and practices in Hungary, European Parliament, July 2013, available at www.europarl.europa.eu/sides/getDoc.do?type=REPORT&reference=A7-2013-0229&language=EN;
Jose Manual Duaro Barroso, State of the Union 2012, Plenary Session of the European Parliament, Strasbourg 2012, available at http://europa.eu/rapid/press-release_SPEECH-12-596_en.html;

PART TWO

THE EUROPEAN COURT OF HUMAN RIGHTS

11. PROTOCOL 16 TO THE ECHR

A Convenient Tool for Judicial Dialogue and Better Domestic Implementation of the Convention?

Władysław Jóźwicki*
Adam Mickiewicz University in Poznań, Poland

1. INTRODUCTION

"The only thing to do with good advice is pass it on. It is never any use to oneself", Oscar Wilde once noticed.[1] Good advice might be worth passing on rather than practicable for oneself out of demand of an effort, self-restraint and commitment on the part of an agent or maybe even more because of its usual lack of any utility whatsoever. Nevertheless, sharing an advice not just passing it on, especially by a well respected person or entity, with authority in certain field, and when it comes together with explanation and reasoning behind it, might amount to an element of important thought exchange, which enhances agreement and cooperation rather than resistance and concurrence.

This text shall be an attempt at analysing and assessing the newly adopted Protocol No. 16[2] (further: Protocol 16 or Protocol) to the Convention for the Protection of Human Rights and Fundamental Freedoms[3] (further: European Convention of Human Rights; European Convention; Convention or ECHR) and the advisory opinion (further: AO) mechanism, which it introduces in the light of the recent discussion over the reform of the Strasbourg human rights protection system as well as in the light of some fundamental principles underlying this system. Of course the Protocol is not yet in force and, if at all,

---

* Email: wjozwi@amu.edu.pl.

1 What has been already cited in the context of the Protocol 16: K. Dzehtsiarou, N. O'Meara, 'Advisory jurisdiction and the European Court of Human Rights: a magic bullet for dialogue and docket-control?' (2014) Vol. 34, No. 3, *Legal Studies*, p. 444.

2 *Protocol No. 16 to the Convention for the Protection of Human Rights and Fundamental Freedoms*, CETS No. 214.

3 *Convention for the Protection of Human Rights and Fundamental Freedoms*, CETS No. 5 with later amendments.

most likely it will not be in any near future. Therefore the argument below shall not be detailed when it comes to procedures or possible practices that could develop only with actual application of the Protocol. The text will focus on an attempt at identifying some week and strong sides of this document in the light of its main goals, which place it among endeavours aimed at enhancing the long term effectiveness and efficiency of the Strasburg human rights protection system. To do so, it will be necessary to present some background knowledge on the development of the Protocol as well as some essential information on what kind of regulations it introduces together with, if necessary for the argument developed in this text, some brief comments on their rationale and consequences. This will lead to conclusions on the possible chances, which the Protocol opens for the amendment of the system of the Convention as well as on some of its weak sides, which may lead it to have limited, if any, significance.

2. PROTOCOL 16 – BACKGROUND

The development of the Protocol is one of the effects of a long-lasting debate over the reform of the Strasbourg human rights protection system, which has been going on for almost the past decade and a half. The debate concentrated mostly on the effectiveness or rather lack of it of the individual application mechanism which became particularly visible at the turn of the millennia and later on. As many have argued and repeated almost *ad nauseam*, the Court in Strasbourg became a victim of its own success,[4] which resulted in a significant increase of the number of individual applications lodged to the Court, what eventually led to a serious caseload crisis. Many debates and initiatives have been since undertaken to deal with this problem in the course oriented around the Interlaken, Izmir and Brighton conferences.[5] Many more or less successful developments have been already introduced to the Strasbourg mechanism to tackle the problem. The most important examples would probably be the Protocol 14[6] and the pilot judgment procedure. A lot has been said and written

---

4 See for example L.R. Helfer, 'Redesigning the European Court of Human Rights: Embeddedness as a Deep Structural Principle of the European Human Rights Regime' (2008), *EJIL (European Journal of International Law)*, vol. 19 no. 1.

5 For more see for example: *Reforming the European Convention on Human Rights: Interlaken, Izmir, Brighton and Beyond. A Compilation of Instruments and Texts Relating to the Ongoing Reform of the ECHR*, Directorate General Human Rights and Rule of Law Council of Europe, 2014 [www.coe.int/t/dghl/standardsetting/cddh/reformechr/Publications/Compilation%20 ReformECHR2014_en.pdf] [accessed: 10 January 2015]; Compare as well for example: J.P. Rui, 'The Interlaken, Izmir and Brighton Declarations: Towards a Paradigm Shift in the Strasbourg Court's Interpretation of the European Convention of Human Rights?' (2013), *Nordic Journal of Human Rights (NJHR)*, vol. 31 no. 1.

6 *Protocol No. 14 to the Convention for the Protection of Human Rights and Fundamental Freedoms amending the control system of the Convention*, CETS No. 194.

on those issues,[7] they will be thus left aside this text's argument. Here, the focus will be solely put on the Protocol 16 and the new AO mechanism, which so far has not been that widely commented on.

Probably the first explicit and official proposition to extend the Courts' jurisdiction to give AOs, which led to the development of the Protocol 16, dates back to the report to the Committee of Ministers (further: CoM) of the Group of Wise Persons, which was set up under Action Plan, that was adopted at the Third Summit of Heads of State and Government of the Member States of the Council of Europe held in Warsaw (16–17 May 2005).[8] The Report stated *inter alia*

> "that it would be useful to introduce a system under which the national courts could apply to the Court for advisory opinions on legal questions relating to interpretation of the Convention and the protocols thereto. This is an innovation which would foster dialogue between courts and enhance the Court's 'constitutional' role".[9]

Afterwards a firm proposition to develop AO mechanism found its place in the Brighton Declaration in April 2012. The Declaration confirmed that:

> "the interaction between the Court and national authorities could be strengthened by the introduction into the Convention of a further power of the Court, which States Parties could optionally accept, to deliver advisory opinions upon request on the interpretation of the Convention in the context of a specific case at domestic level, without prejudice to the non-binding character of the opinions for the other States Parties".[10]

As it is quite clear, the mere dialogue between the courts is not what was at stake here. The development of the Protocol was aimed to be one of the elements of a wider reform of the European Convention system in the light of the mentioned above caseload problem. It was a part of the wider process of enhancing the domestic implementation of the rights and freedoms guaranteed

---

7 See for example S. Besson (ed.), *La Cour européenne des droits de l'homme après le Protocole 14: premier bilan et perspectives = The European Court of Human Rights after Protocol 14: preliminary assessment and perspectives*, Genève: Schulthess, 2011; D. Haider, *The Pilot-Judgment Procedure of the European Court of Human Rights*, Leiden: Martinus Nijhoff Publishers, 2013.

8 *Nota bene* the discussion over introducing AOs to the Strasbourg system can be traced back even to the 1970s, when it was finally considered to be inconsistent with the system's nature. Compare: M. O'Boyle, 'The legitimacy of Strasbourg review: time for a reality check?' in: *Mélanges en l'honneur de Jean-Paul Costa. La conscience des droits*, Dalloz: Paris 2011; K. Dzehtsiarou, N. O'Meara, *supra* note 1, p. 451.

9 *Report of the Group of Wise Persons to the Committee of Ministers*, 979*bis* meeting, CM(2006)203, para. 81 [https://wcd.coe.int/ViewDoc.jsp?id=1063779] [accessed: 10 January 2015].

10 *High Level Conference on the Future of the European Court of Human Rights, Brighton Declaration* adopted on 19 and 20 April 2012, para. 12d [www.echr.coe.int/Documents/2012_Brighton_FinalDeclaration_ENG.pdf] [accessed: 10 January 2015].

by the Convention.[11] All in all, it is explicitly declared in the Preamble to the Protocol itself, which claims that: "Considering that the extension of the Court's competence to give advisory opinions will further enhance the interaction between the Court and national authorities and thereby reinforce implementation of the Convention, in accordance with the principle of subsidiarity". The subsidiarity principle guiding the whole reform of the ECHR process links the Protocol 16 with another not yet in force additional Protocol to the Convention, namely Protocol No. 15,[12] which among other perhaps less significant novelties, introduces to the very text of the Convention the principle of subsidiarity as well as the margin of appreciation, which so far have not been there present. The context of parallel, opened for signature only about three months earlier, Protocol 15 should be bore in mind when examining Protocol 16, it will, however, be left aside in this text.

Protocol 16 has been opened for signature on 2 October 2013 in Strasbourg. At the moment, after more than a year, it has been signed by 16 state-parties to the Convention[13] with no reservations by any of them (*nota bene* possibility of reservations to the Protocol is excluded by its Article 9). According to its Article 8, it is necessary for ten High Contracting Parties to have expressed their consent to be bound by it for the Protocol to enter into force. So far, none of the signatories have done so. At the margin one can notice that it is a novelty when it comes to procedure-changing protocols to the Convention. As Björg Thorarensen notices: "Previous procedural amendments related to the Court's jurisdiction have, as a rule, required the ratification of all States Parties when it comes to Protocols amending the procedure before the Court".[14] The lack of such

---

11 See for example: D. Spielman, "Judgments of the European Court of Human Rights Effects and Implementation" Keynote Speech at *Conference at the Paulinerkirche Göttingen Georg-August-University, Göttingen 20 September 2013*, p. 4 and 7 [www.echr.coe.int/Documents/Speech_20130920_Spielmann_Gottingen_ENG.pdf] [accessed: 10 January 2015].

12 *Protocol No. 15 amending the Convention for the Protection of Human Rights and Fundamental Freedoms*, CETS No. 213. Protocol 15 seems to be more attractive to the parties to the Convention than the 16. It has been so far (state at 1 January 2015) signed by 39 High Contracting Parties and ratified by 10 of them.

13 Namely (state at 10 February 2015): Albania (24 November 2014) Armenia (2 October 2013), Estonia (17 February 2014), Finland (2 October 2013), France (2 October 2013), Georgia (19 June 2014), Italy (2 October 2013), Lithuania (10 June 2014), Netherlands (7 November 2013), Norway (27 June 2014), Romania (14 October 2014) San Marino (2 October 2013), Slovakia (2 October 2013), Slovenia (2 October 2013) and Ukraine (20 June 2014).

14 B. Thorarensen, 'The Advisory Jurisdiction of the ECtHR under Protocol No. 16: Enhancing Domestic Implementation of Human Rights or a Symbolic Step?' paper submitted in relation to the Conference *Shifting Centers of Gravity in European Human Rights Protection* in Reykjavik (6–7 March 2014), p. 7; The mentioned in the *Explanatory Report to the Protocol 16* para. 30 [http://conventions.coe.int/Treaty/en/reports/html/214.htm] [accessed: 10 January 2015] Protocol No. 9 (CETS No. 140) should not count as an exception, as it did not involve strictly jurisdictional issues. Protocol 9 was adopted in 1990 and enabled persons, non-governmental organisations and groups of individuals, which have lodged the complaint with the Commission to bring a case before the Court. This protocol was optional and came

a demand can be understandable in the light of the nature of the AO mechanism and its flexibility, which shall be described later on in this text. It may, on the other hand, lead to some serious doubts from the systemic perspective, especially in the light of the European Union (further: EU) joining the Convention, which also shall be addressed further in this text.

Finally one has to notice that advisory opinion by the European Court of Human Rights (further: ECtHR) is not as such an alien institution to the Strasbourg system. It has been introduced to it with the Protocol No. 2 to the Convention[15] from 1963 and is now incorporated into Articles 47–49 of the ECHR. This institution, however, diametrically differs from the one proposed in Protocol 16. So far, it is only the CoM that is competent to address the Court with the request for "advisory opinions on legal questions concerning the interpretation of the Convention and the protocols thereto" (Article 47[1] of the Convention). It is, however, crucial to remember that those requests may not "deal with any question relating to the content or scope of the rights or freedoms defined in Section I of the Convention and the Protocols thereto, or with any other question which the Court or the Committee of Ministers might have to consider in consequence of any such proceedings as could be instituted in accordance with the Convention" (Article 47[2] of the Convention). Very narrow scope of this procedure was probably the main reason for its very rare application and lack of significance.[16]

3. THE NEW ADVISORY OPINION MECHANISM – BASIC CHARACTERISTICS

The scope of AO under Protocol 16 is exactly opposite to the one under Articles 47–49 of the Convention. The Protocol is aimed at increasing domestic implementation of the Strasbourg human rights protection standards accordingly to the mentioned above fundamental principle of subsidiarity.

into force after ten ratifications in 1994. Following reform of the Court and entry into force of Protocol No. 11 (CETS No. 155) in 1998 made Protocol 9 of little practical significance.

15 *Protocol No. 2 to the Convention for the Protection of Human Rights and Fundamental Freedoms, conferring upon the European Court of Human Rights competence to give advisory opinions*, CETS No. 44.

16 So far two such opinions have been issued by the ECtHR and both of them concerned questions relating to judges appointment procedures: 1) Advisory opinion on certain legal questions concerning the lists of candidates submitted with a view to the election of judges to the European Court of Human Rights from 12 February 2008; 2) Advisory opinion on certain legal questions concerning the lists of candidates submitted with a view to the election of judges to the European Court of Human Rights no. 2 of 22 January 2010. On 2 June 2004 the Court has also issued a Decision on the competence of the Court to give an advisory opinion. See also B. Rainey, E. Wicks, C. Ovey, *The European Convention on Human Rights*, Oxford University Press: Oxford 2014 (6th edition), pp. 49–51; For more see for example K. Dzehtsiarou, N. O'Meara, *supra* note 1, 8, pp. 446–448.

Therefore the procedure is aimed at answering only "questions of principle relating to the interpretation or application of the rights and freedoms defined in the Convention or the protocols thereto" (Article 1[1] of Protocol 16). Only such questions may be submitted to the Grand Chamber (further: GCh) of the ECtHR and it is only the GCh that is competent to issue AOs in this procedure (Article 2[2] of Protocol 16).

This places the AO on the very apex of the Strasbourg system, in a sense that it may concern only matters of fundamental importance from the perspective of the rights and freedoms protected by the Convention, as well as that it can be issued only by the highest authority of the Court. Some doubts may arise though over what does it exactly mean that the matter of AO needs to reflect "questions of principle". Similarly, referral to the GCh of the ECHR according to Article 43(2) of the Convention is possible only in cases rising "serious question affecting the interpretation or application of the Convention or the protocols thereto, or a serious issue of general importance". As the Explanatory report (para. 9) to the Protocol admits, Article 43(2) was inspirational while drafting the Protocol. The scope of actual similarity of approach of the Court to "questions of principle" as different or equivalent to "serious questions" will have to develop in practice. According to the Protocol, panel of five judges of the GCh (similarly as in the cases of referral to the GCh) will decide whether to accept the request for an advisory opinion or not (Article 2[1] of the Protocol 16). The dialogical character of the AO is reflected in an obligation of the panel to give reasons for refusal to accept the request (Article 2[1] of the Protocol), which obligation is absent in the referral to the GCh under Article 43(2) procedure.[17] Those issues shall be addressed in a little more detail later on in this text.

Only highest courts and tribunals of the parties to the Protocol are allowed to request AO in this procedure (Article 1[1] of the Protocol). What needs to be underlined though, is that they are not obliged to do so, which is clear from the word "may" used in this article. The courts and tribunals are also free to withdraw their request.[18] No later than at the time of depositing its instrument of ratification, acceptance or approval, each state-party will also have to declare, which of their courts or tribunals shall be competent to address the ECtHR with requests for AO (Article 10 of the Protocol). This declaration can be modified at any later stage. This leaves the parties to the Protocol a free hand in deciding between their main courts and tribunals – which of them is, or which of them are the most appropriate for such a role. This flexibility again seems to well reflect

---

17 *Nota bene* obligation to give reasons at this stage was not obvious from the beginning. Also the ECtHR itself opted for discretion in this field augmenting that such a flexibility would not increase unnecessarily the workload of the Court. See: *Reflection Paper on the Proposal to Extend the Court's Advisory Jurisdiction*, para. 36 [www.coe.int/t/dgi/brighton-conference/documents/Court-Advisory-opinions_en.pdf] [accessed: 10 January 2015].

18 *Explanatory Report to the Protocol 16*, *supra* note 14, para. 7.

the European legal diversity.[19] Openness to modifications of the declaration enables as well to reflect any changes that may occur in the domestic systems after certain state becomes bound by the Protocol. It is left with no doubt, however, that the states are not free to choose any other kind of an institution than highest courts and tribunals for the sake of the Protocol 16 procedure.

As the Protocol states, the opinions shall not be binding to anyone, including the referring court or tribunal (Article 5 of the Protocol). The domestic courts or tribunals will be free to decide on the effects of the opinion in domestic proceedings, including those which led it to request for the opinion.

Opinions under Protocol 16 may not be issued on abstract basis. According to the Protocol, appropriate courts or tribunals of state-parties may seek an opinion only in the context of a case pending before them (Article 1[2] of the Protocol). This particular-case-related context seems to strengthen reasonableness of the nonbinding effect of the opinions. The opinions, as it has been said, may refer only to matters of principle regarding Convention rights and freedoms' interpretation and application. In concrete cases domestic courts or tribunals seem to be much better positioned to asses whether the principles referred to by the Strasbourg Court really fit and should be applied in each particular case. The non-abstract character of the AOs seems also to reflect well the main purpose of the Protocol – to strengthen the domestic implementation of the Convention and thus make the Strasbourg system more effective and less overloaded. Paul Gragl rightly notices that

> "the examination of purely contrived cases would not only draw on Strasbourg's judicial resources (which already are extremely occupied with the existing backlog of cases), but could also prove detrimental to the coherence of the Court's case law, if an abstract or hypothetical legal issue becomes 'concrete', but not in the same manner as envisaged in the Court's judgment, and thus causes ambiguous legal consequences in the form of contradicting decisions".[20]

The Protocol seems to be laconic or maybe even silent about effects of the opinions. The real direct and indirect effects of the AOs will probably be possible to see and assess only after the Protocol enters into force and some practice develops. However, according to the Explanatory Report to the Protocol, individual application under Article 34 of the Convention subsequent to the "proceedings in which an advisory opinion of the Court has effectively been

---

19 The diversity of the domestic legal regimes makes it sometimes very problematic which of their courts or tribunals actually is the highest in certain category of cases. Just to mention for example Austrian Asylum Court, German Finance Court or the British Court of Appeal. Compare: P. Gragl, '(Judicial) Love is Not a One-Way Street: The EU Preliminary Reference Procedure as a Model for ECtHR Advisory Opinions under Draft Protocol No. 16' (2013) 38, *European Law Review*, p. 232.

20 P. Gragl, *supra* note 19, p. 238.

followed, it is expected that such elements of the application that rate to the issues addressed in the advisory opinion would be declared inadmissible or struck down".[21] So, if the domestic court or tribunal will follow the AO, there will be no more possibility of the party involved in the case on the domestic level to seek redress in Strasbourg in the individual application procedure under Article 34 of the Convention. This consequence is clearly connected to the increase of domestic implementation and subsidiarity strengthening principles guiding the development of the Protocol. Some doubts from the perspective of an individual may, however, arise, especially that the party to the domestic proceedings does not automatically become party to the AO proceedings. According to Article 3 of the Protocol, only the high contracting party to which the requesting court or tribunal pertains, as well as The Council of Europe Commissioner for Human Rights, will have automatic right to submit written comments and take part in the hearing. Other contracting parties, as well as persons (including parties to the domestic proceedings), may, but do not have to be invited by the Court, in the interest of the proper administration of justice, to submit their comments or take part in the hearing.[22]

After the Protocol 16 enters into force, even not binding AOs shall become a part of Court's jurisprudence. Even if the very text of the Protocol might again leave some doubts about that, it is made clear in the Explanatory report. As we read in it: "Advisory opinions under this Protocol would have no direct effect on other later applications. They would, however, form part of the case-law of the Court, alongside its judgments and decisions. The interpretation of the Convention and the Protocols thereto contained in such advisory opinions would be analogous in its effect to the interpretative elements set out by the Court in judgments and decisions".[23]

It seems thus possible for the Court to take the AOs into consideration in its future judgments not only on the mentioned earlier admissibility basis. It seems to be possible for the Court to do so in all other cases to which the interpretation of certain right or freedom provided in the opinion would be relevant. This seems to be also possible even in cases of applications against those parties to the Convention, which at the moment would still not be party to the Protocol. The fact that the opinions would cover only questions of principle regarding interpretation and application of the rights and freedoms defined in the Convention and Protocols thereto, and that they would be issued by Grand Chamber, seems to raise their rank and increase the possible impact of the opinions on future jurisprudence of the Court. The opinions are not binding in the same way as the judgments of the ECtHR are not binding to

21 *Explanatory Report to the Protocol 16 supra* note 14, 18, para. 26.

22 The possibility of participation of the party to the domestic proceedings in the AO procedure indeed mirrors the situation concerning third parties interventions under Article 36(2) of the Convention. See: *Explanatory Report to the Protocol 16, supra* note 14, 18, 21, para. 9.

23 *Explanatory report..., supra* note 14, 18, 21, 22, para. 27.

anyone else than the parties to a certain case. As it is well known, the ECtHR is not a common-law-kind precedence Court and its judgments bind only *inter partes* (according to Article 46 of the Convention). Nevertheless, what can be labelled as "orientation effect" of the Court's case law should not to be underestimated.[24] The Court needs to care about consistency of its jurisprudence and about coherent application of the Convention. Therefore it often refers to its own previous judgments and basing on it, builds its argument in new cases. The judgments have therefore wider than only *inter partes* effects under Article 46. Paul Gragl is probably right when he says that "the ECHR's Grand Chamber represents the constitutional formation of the Court and is entrusted to ensure the overall coherence of its case law (...)".[25] Leaving it at the moment, we shall go back to this later on in this text.

It is possible to sum up this part of the text by stating that the main intended function of the AO mechanism under Protocol 16 was "not only to strengthen the judicial dialogue between the domestic courts and Strasbourg, but also to emphasize the Contracting Parties' primary responsibility to protect human rights, thus relieving the ECtHR from further surges in individual applications."[26] This places the development of the Protocol in line with other elements of the latest Court's reform process. The new AO mechanism is therefore not designed as dialogical tool aimed simply at increasing exchange of opinions between courts or at enhancing in human rights jurisprudence within the ECHR system, a very popular in past years concept known as judicial "cross-fertilization".[27] The AO mechanism is mostly supposed to be another tool to decrease the caseload in the ECtHR and to improve control of the docket through improvement of the domestic implementation of Convention rights and freedoms standards, as well as introducing another decreasing mechanism of the number of individual applications lodged to the Court.

3. PROTOCOL 16 AND THE CHANCES IT OPENS

As it is clearly visible, the AO opinion mechanism designed in the Protocol 16 is a very flexible procedure. It invites state parties rather than obliges them to participate in this thought exchange process with the ECtHR on the

---

24 See G. Ress, 'The Effect of Decisions and Judgments of the European Court of Human Rights in the Domestic Legal Order' (2005) 40, *Texas International Law Journal*, p. 374 and following, compare as well: R. Degener, L. Garlicki, 'Art. 46 [moc obowiązująca oraz wykonanie wyroków]' in L. Garlicki (ed.), *Konwencja o Ochronie Praw Człowieka i Podstawowych Wolności. Komentarz do artykułów 19–59*, Warszawa: C.H. Beck, 2011, p. 361.

25 P. Gragl, *supra* note 19, 20, p. 238.

26 P. Gragl, *supra* note 19, 20, 25, p. 230.

27 See for example F.G. Jacobs, "Judicial Dialogue and the Cross-Fertilization of Legal Systems: The European Court of Justice", (2003) 38 *Texas International Law Journal (TILJ)*.

interpretation and application of the Convention rights and freedoms. It also leaves a lot of discretion on their side whether to do so, as well on how and when to do so, which may make them more willing to use the procedure and apply the results. "It is possible, (...), that the national court would feel 'ownership' of the issue and hopefully show a high degree of willingness to implement the opinion even though it were non-binding, since it decided to refer the question for an opinion in the first place".[28] Those soft solutions may determine some strength of the mechanism rather than its weakness.

3.1. A STEP TOWARDS ENHANCING DOMESTIC IMPLEMENTATION OF THE ECHR

Parties to the Protocol are free to choose highest, but not 'the highest' courts or tribunals of their own as competent to issue requests for AOs.[29] That opens to them a possibility to choose more than just one apex court in their system but more of the highest courts, which would be, regarding each states' legal system particularity, most appropriate to request opinions. This openness to requests from all the appropriate domestic highest courts or tribunals reflects well the goal of the procedure to more effectively implement the Convention in domestic orders. The AO procedure opens a broader scope of implementation of the Convention rights and freedoms as interpreted by the ECtHR than it is available through the judgments issued in the individual application procedure. If highest courts or tribunals of a particular state come to doubt whether rights and freedoms guaranteed by the Convention of a party involved in proceedings in front of them are threatened, they will be free to clarify that at the very source. And there will be no difference if the rights or freedoms would be compromised on the basis of individual or systemic factors. Even if, as many argue, the ECtHR develops in the direction of becoming a constitutional or *quasi*-constitutional court,[30] it is not yet one even though the Court repeatedly refers to the Convention as to "a constitutional instrument of European public

[28] B. Thorarensen, *supra* note 14, p. 11.

[29] It remains, however, open if the definition of the highest courts or tribunals remains entirely on the side of the state parties to the Protocol, which is what the wording of the Protocol seems to suggest. As some argue, the Court might come up with the autonomous interpretation of the concept of highest courts or tribunals and thus make the declaration by the parties under Article 10 of the Protocol not to have constitutive but informative character. Compare in this context: A. Paprocka, M. Ziółkowski, 'Opinie doradcze w świetle Protokołu nr 16 do Europejskiej Konwencji Praw Człowieka' (2014), *Europejski Przegląd Sądowy (EPS)*, vol. 10, p. 17–18; For some criticism over the scope of the subjects competent to launch AO procedure under Protocol 16 see for example: K. Dzehtsiarou, N. O'Meara, *supra* note 1, 8, 16, pp. 462–463; A. Ploszka, 'Nowa opinia doradcza Europejskiego Trybunału Praw Człowieka' (2013) *Państwo i Prawo (PiP)*, vol. 10, pp. 97–99.

[30] See for example S. Greer, L. Wildhaber, 'Revisiting the Debate about "constitutionalising" the European Court of Human Rights', (2012) *Human Rights Law Review (HRLR)*, vol. 12(4);

order (*ordre public*)".[31] As it has been said above, *de lege lata*, the ECtHR's judgments are binding *inter partes*. The Court has no authority to eliminate laws from domestic orders, even if those laws are grounds for violations of the Convention rights or freedoms. Domestic courts, on the other hand, especially the constitutional courts, often have such powers and are competent to eliminate from their domestic systems certain laws and regulations when they come to a conclusion over their unconstitutionality or other incoherence with higher norms.

In the individual application procedure the ECtHR analyses particular interferences with individual rights and freedoms. Practically, it rarely questions the general – legal – basis of infringements (also for pilot judgments procedure it is necessary for many prerequisites to be met, which limits the scope of application of this method). With Protocol 16's entry into force, the domestic highest courts and tribunals might and probably would request the ECtHR's opinion mostly in such cases in front of them when they would have doubts about the legal basis of the alleged infringements. It is hardly possible that they would bother with launching the AO procedure in order not to examine the law but some factual or procedural problems within domestic application of laws leading to alleged infringements. In issues relating to general problems, after having received answers from the ECtHR, they would be able to undertake steps within their capacities to eliminate the regulations incompatible with the ECHR human rights protection standards as interpreted by the ECtHR. Of course this would depend on their willingness to do so, which may be problematic even without presupposing bad will on their side. Such a possibility however, based on a division of competences: ECtHR to interpret the Convention and determine understanding of the rights and freedoms guaranteed in it and the domestic highest courts and tribunals to implement human rights protection standards accordingly to their capacities, including those related to adopting general means in their respective domestic systems, seems to be the greatest promise that the Protocol brings.

3.2. A STEP TOWARDS MORE HARMONIOUS AND UP-TO-DATE INTERPRETATION OF THE CONVENTION

Even though the AOs under the Protocol 16 after its entry into force will not be binding, they will become a part of the Court's jurisprudence. They will be issued by the GCh and cover "questions of principle" which correlates with the character of the GCh's activity under Article 43(2) of the Convention. Basing

L. Wildhaber, 'A Constitutional Future for the European Court of Human Rights' (2002) *Human Rights Law Journal (HRLJ)*, vol. 23.

31 *Loizidou v. Turkey* (Preliminary Objections) Application no. 15318/89 (1995), para. 75. See as well for example *Al-Skeini and Others v. the United Kingdom* [GC] Application no. 55721/07 (2011), para. 141.

on this, the AOs may play a role similar to other Grand Chamber judgments. The Court's jurisprudence is first and foremost aimed at maintaining individual justice in individual cases. This can, however, be effective only when it is consistent and based on coherent interpretation of the Convention. It makes the Court's case law to have, as it has been said earlier, "orienting" or even precedential character.[32]

This also leads to the emergence of more general implementation obligations on the side of parties to the Convention than only those stemming from Article 46 of the Convention. Parties to the Convention should also take into consideration verdicts in cases to which they were not parties and undertake general means aimed at implementing to their own legal systems the Convention rights and freedoms as interpreted in the ECtHR's case law.[33] To quote the Interlaken Declaration, the State Parties to the Convention should commit themselves "to taking into account the Court's developing case-law, also with a view to considering the conclusions to be drawn from a judgment finding a violation of the Convention by another State, where the same problem of principle exists within their own legal system".[34] The practice shows that states indeed tend to make legislative and other changes following decisions or judgments against them, as well as to amend their laws or practices following judgments in cases to which they have not been a party in order to comply with the obligation upon them to secure rights and freedoms guaranteed in the Convention according to Article 1 of the Convention.[35]

Not all of the judgments of the ECtHR are of equal significance when it comes to matters of interpretation or application of the Convention. Certain hierarchy of the ECtHR's jurisprudence stems mostly from the Court's practice. Some judgments weigh more than others. This becomes especially visible when the Court changes its earlier jurisprudence. As Hanneke Senden argues, the activities of the ECtHR and their constitutional or individual dimension are not exclusive but are a matter of certain balance spread mostly between character of adjudication in chambers and in Grand Chamber.

> "In the current situation constitutional justice is most visible in the functioning of the Grand Chamber. (...) It is up to the Grand Chamber to determine whether it is

---

32 See for example L. Wildhaber, 'Precedent in the European Court of Human Rights' in: P. Mahoney, H. Petzold (eds.), *Protecting Human Rights: The European Perspective*, Köln: Karl Heymanns Verlag, 2000.

33 A. Bodnar, 'Res Interpretata: Legal Effect of the European Court of Human Rights' Judgments for other States Than Those Which Were Party to the Proceedings' in: Y. Haeck and E. Brems (eds.) *Human Rights and Civil Liberties in the 21st Century*, Dordrecht: Springer, 2014.

34 *High Level Conference on the Future of the European Court of Human Rights Interlaken Declaration* from 19 February 2010, para. B.4.c [www.coe.int/t/dgi/hr-natimplement/Source/interlaken_declaration_en.pdf] [accessed: 15 January 2015].

35 Compare: D. Harris, M. O'Boyle, Warbrick, *Law of the European Convention of Human Rights*, Oxford University Press: Oxford 2014 (3rd edition), pp. 34–35.

> necessary to overrule a previous precedent. The function of the Grand Chamber is to ensure uniformity and to decide the most complex and controversial cases."[36]

What would be the possible role of the AOs? No matter that non-binding, they would still be expressions of the ECtHR's Grand Chamber view on questions of principle regarding interpretation and application of the Convention rights and freedoms. As Ada Paprocka and Michał Ziółkowski argue, typical "questions of principle" on the basis of Article 1(1) of the Protocol, would be those regarding: 1) new and unresolved issues in the process of interpretation and application of the Convention, 2) inconsistencies in the ECtHR's jurisprudence, 3) current view on a question reflected in the ECtHR's jurisprudence before, but not recently verified, which raises doubts in the light of the Convention being a living instrument.[37] This may lead to a conclusion that concrete and not binding character of the AOs does not undermine their interpretational character, and that those interpretations would be relevant to all the parties to the Convention and their courts and tribunals in the same way as the so far Court's jurisprudence. Comparable significance of the AOs as the Court's leading judgments fostering harmonious interpretation of the Convention rights minimal standards and thus ensuring the effective protection of those rights and freedoms is well reflected in the Court's Reflection Paper on the AO procedure.[38]

Additionally, the obligation on the side of the panel of five judges of the GCh to provide decisions of non-acceptance of the AO request might play *mutatis mutandis* some role in further developing of understanding of Article 43(2) and the "serious question" criterion. So far, the meaning of the "serious question" could be reconstructed only on the basis of the cases accepted and further analysed by the Grand Chamber, as well as on the mere assessment of cases not accepted for re-examination, which are being left with no reasoning behind such a decision by the panel. Paul Gragl argues even that

> "referring to the principles already enshrined in Luxembourg's jurisprudence, Strasbourg could thus develop its own *acte clair* and *acte éclairé* doctrines on when to accept or to refuse questions for advisory opinions and therewith provide the domestic courts with illustrative guidelines on questions requiring further judicial elucidation and which questions have already been sufficiently expounded".[39]

We have to remember though that "when applying the criteria, the different purposes of the procedure under this Protocol and that under Article 43(2) of the

---

36 H. Senden, *Interpretation of Fundamental Rights in a Multilevel Legal System. An analysis of the European Court of Human Rights and the Court of Justice of the European Union*, Intersentia: Antwerp 2011, p. 19.

37 A. Paprocka, M. Ziółkowski, *supra* note 29, pp. 20–21.

38 *Reflection Paper on the Proposal to Extend the Court's Advisory Jurisdiction*, *supra* note 17, para. 5.

39 P. Gragl, *supra* note 19, 20, 25, 26, p. 247.

Convention will have to be taken into account. Interpretation of the definition will be a matter for the Court when deciding whether to accept a request for an advisory opinion".[40]

What seems to be quite certain is that the dialogical character of the AO mechanism, demanding all actors to give reasoning at all stages of the procedure (as well as allowing judges of the GCh to present their dissenting or concurring opinions), creates a space for a deepened reflection on the Convention and the rights and freedoms guaranteed in it through judicial dialogue and thought exchange. The non-binding character of the AOs may even with time become inviting to the Court to formulate perhaps more far reaching arguments than it would do in its ordinary proceedings. This, on the other hand, might weaken the more general effects of the AOs which have been mentioned above. At the moment however, it is probably too early to make any clear predictions in that matter. Nonetheless, Kanstantsin Dzehtsiarou and Noreen O'Meara are probably right when they point out that the AOs (if the GCh finally has an opportunity to issue them) will have to be dealt with a high delicacy and caution because "situations could arise in which the ECtHR's nurturing of dialogue with highest national courts in the context of advisory opinions could prove delicate and require sensitive handling".[41] This seems to be right despite the *per se* less confrontational character of advisory procedures like this one, where the state is not a party of a dispute and needs not to defend itself against charges, as it is the case in individual application procedure.[42]

The non-binding character of the AOs does not have to result in the lack of compliance by the state parties with the opinions by the GCh. Paul Gragl rightly notices that

> "the contracting parties to the Convention are (...) generally quite eager to comply with Strasbourg's judgments, as the most recent statistics demonstrate, (...) especially given the non-coercive methods of enforcing Strasbourg's judgments. In case of non-compliance with their obligations under Article 46(1) ECHR, the most severe consequences the contracting parties might face are the examination of their behaviour by the Committee of Ministers (Article 46(2) ECHR) and subsequent peer pressure, and, if they persist in violating Convention rights, referral of the case to the ECtHR, political pressure from the other Contracting Parties, (...) and – in the most extreme case of non-compliance – suspension from their rights of representation in or expulsion from the Council of Europe (Articles 3 and 8 Statute of the Council of Europe)".[43]

If the Court in the AO procedure follows the same patterns which led it to have such a high authority in its current status, there seems to be no reason why AOs would be less respected by the state parties than the ordinary jurisprudence of

40 *Explanatory Report to the Protocol 16*, *supra* note 14, 18, 21, 22, 23, para. 9.

41 K. Dzehtsiarou, N. O'Meara, *supra* note 1, 8, 16, 29, p. 468.

42 Compare: J.C. Schmid: 'Advisory Opinions on Human Rights: Moving Beyond a Pyrrhic Victory' (2006) *Duke Journal of Comparative & International Law (DJC&IL)*, vol. 2, p. 415.

43 P. Gragl, *supra* note 19, 20, 25, 26, 39, p. 245.

the Court, even though the AOs would be non-binding. The earlier mentioned 'ownership' issue may only reinforce this effect.

The second biggest chance that the Protocol seems to bring is an increase in harmonious interpretation of the Convention, by introducing, other than only individual application procedure, a possibility to react to questions and doubts regarding understanding of the Convention rights and freedoms, which may be earlier spotted and addressed by the GCh of the ECtHR, after they appear in domestic proceedings. The AO mechanism may become a tool to provide more harmonious interpretation of the Convention especially in the aspects which are not yet clear or which demand new approach, what would be revealed already at the stage of domestic proceedings. The AO procedure might become a mechanism of early warning about systemic violations, even before they reach Strasbourg level through individual applications, hence the AO procedure may become a platform to deal with them in cooperation between the ECtHR and domestic courts and tribunals according to their competences.

4. PROTOCOL 16 AND ITS DRAWBACKS

Having highlighted some potential advantages and chances that the Protocol 16 opens, it is now necessary to give attention to some crucial – according to the author – drawbacks and week sides of the AO procedure, as it is designed in the Protocol 16. Only then it will be possible to draw some general conclusions about this institution.

4.1. ECtHR – VICTIM OF ITS SUCCESS REVISITED?

One of the main, if not simply the main reason behind the introduction of the Protocol, was dealing with the workload problems at the ECtHR. Nevertheless, if the AO procedure starts to operate and operates well, hence gains more popularity reflected with increase of the amount of the requests for the AOs, it may again lead to a well-known paradox of the Strasbourg court becoming a victim of its own success.[44] It seems rather not likely that the procedure becomes so popular, as the example of the preliminary reference procedure to the Court of Justice of the European Union (further: CJEU) might suggest, because of some vital differences between these mechanisms ingrained in natures of CJEU and ECtHR.[45]

44 Another thing is that the main case flow to the Strasbourg concern "clone cases" which lead to repetitive and monotonous findings of similar violations. Those would, however, fall out of the scope of the AOs, which may diminish the supposed case flow diminishing effect of the Protocol. For more see: K. Dzehtsiarou, N. O'Meara, *supra* note 1, 8, 16, 29, 41, pp. 457–461.

45 Compare: K. Dzehtsiarou, N. O'Meara, *supra* note 1, 8, 16, 29, 41, 44, p. 461; A. Paprocka, M. Ziółkowski, *supra* note 29, 37, p. 15; L.A. Sicilianos, 'L'élargissement de la compétence consultative de la Cour européenne des droits de l'homme – À propos du Protocole no 16

Nonetheless, Kanstantsin Dzehtsiarou and Noreen O'Meara rightly spot one of the primary concerns about the procedure, which "is the capacity of the Grand Chamber to handle the acceptance and delivery of advisory opinions while maintaining its modest adjudicatory case-load."[46] In 2012 the GCh accepted seven cases for referral under Article 43 of the ECHR,[47] in 2013 it did so in ten cases.[48] We also have to remember about the relinquishment cases in front of the GCh according to Article 30 of the Convention. There have not been many of those either. In more general terms, the GCh delivers around 30 judgments *per annum*. Despite this tiny number of cases, it takes the GCh usually a lot of time to adjudicate on them. Of course the cases in front of the GCh are not easy ones. They concern complex "serious questions affecting the interpretation or application of the Convention" and thus demand a lot of attention and time. The AOs are not going to be easy either. They will concern similarly complex "questions of principle relating to the interpretation or application of the rights and freedoms defined in the Convention and Protocols". Additionally, as it has been explained earlier, the panel of five judges of the GCh that decides upon accepting or not a request for the AO will be supposed to give reasoning in a situation of not accepting the request, which is not demanded in the Article 43 procedure. The AOs may therefore significantly increase the workload of the GCh and might lead to the increase of the backlog, even if they do not become as popular as the advocates of this mechanism would like them to, or as, perhaps not the best in this context, example of the preliminary references to the CJEU might suggest.

More than that, the ordinary case flow to the ECtHR does not have to decrease with the introduction of the AO procedure. It is not obvious that the domestic courts and tribunals would follow the opinions, which they would be provided with by the GCh and even if they would be willing to do so (on the basis presented earlier), it is not certain whether they would do it in a satisfactory to the ECtHR way. But even if domestic courts or tribunals would do so in the frames of their capacities, it does not have to mean that the problem will always be eliminated from their domestic legal systems and that it will not concern other subjects in a similar way and on similar basis, but handled differently in different proceedings. In addition, not all the highest courts may be in power to adopt general solutions to systemic problems, which surface in the proceedings. More than that, even if the AOs would be followed by the domestic courts or

à la Convention européenne des droits de l'homme', (2014) *Revue Trimestrielle des droits de l'homme*, vol. 97, p. 14.

46 K. Dzehtsiarou, N. O'Meara, *supra* note 1, 8, 16, 29, 41, 44, 45, p. 468.

47 European Court of Human Rights, *Annual Report 2012*, Registry of the European Court of Human Rights, Strasbourg 2013, p. 61 [www.echr.coe.int/Documents/Annual_report_2012_ENG.pdf] [accessed: 10 January 2015].

48 European Court of Human Rights, *Annual Report 2013*, Registry of the European Court of Human Rights, Strasbourg 2014, pp. 50–51 [www.echr.coe.int/Documents/Annual_report_2013_ENG.pdf] [accessed: 10 January 2015].

tribunals properly, even in the systemic way, this still does not have to prevent the parties to those proceedings from lodging an application. Of course, in such situation the application would be declared inadmissible or struck down, as it has been described earlier in this text. Nevertheless, the application would still be lodged and still would have to be dealt with by the ECtHR.

4.2. THE OPTIONAL AND NONBINDING CHARACTER OF THE AOs AND SOME PRACTICAL CONCERNS

As it has been explained, requests for an AO by the domestic courts or tribunals are not obligatory. Neither are the AOs binding for the issuing court or tribunal or to anyone else. Of course that does not mean that after having been given, the AOs would have no effect whatsoever. This issue has been addressed in the earlier parts of this text.

One has to notice, however, that no priority is given to AO requests in the proceedings of the ECtHR. The text of the Protocol is silent about any such priority. The Explanatory Report makes it clear, that any prioritization in the AO procedure is left entirely to the Court itself to decide, as it is with respect to all other proceedings.[49] The priority policy of the Court may cover AOs because of the nature and scope of the requests. As Paul Gragl rightly points out,[50] this would place AO in the II priority category, which is described by the Court's Priority Policy Paper as:

> "Applications raising questions capable of having an impact on the effectiveness of the Convention system (in particular a structural or endemic situation that the Court has not yet examined, pilot-judgment procedure) or applications raising an important question of general interest (in particular a serious question capable of having major implications for domestic legal systems or for the European system) (...)."[51]

Only one category of cases is considered to have higher priority than this, namely: "Urgent applications (in particular risk to life or health of the applicant, other circumstances linked to the personal or family situation of the applicant, particularly where the well-being of a child is at issue, application of Rule 39 of the Rules of Court)".[52] If the Court would be willing and able to prioritize the AOs and indeed give its opinions quickly, will, however, be possible to know only with time and practice development. Especially, if there are many requests

---

49 *Explanatory Report*, *supra* note 14, 18, 21, 22, 23, 40, para. 17.

50 P. Gragl, *supra* note 19, 20, 25, 26, 39, 43, p. 239.

51 European Court of Human Rights, *The Courts Priority Policy* [www.echr.coe.int/Documents/Priority_policy_ENG.pdf] [accessed: 10 January 2015], p. 2.

52 *Ibidem*, p. 2.

pending in front of the Court, the time to receive an opinion might lead to delays resulting in lengthening the domestic proceedings significantly.[53]

Let us then imagine domestic highest courts or tribunals, which are about to make a decision whether to request the Strasbourg Court for the AO or not. Such a domestic court or tribunal, as being one of the highest courts or tribunals of a particular state, would face an important dilemma. If it is one of the highest courts or tribunals, the domestic proceedings have presumably already been going on for a long time. Of course how lengthy the proceedings have already been, would depend on each and every one legal system of the parties' to the Convention and their efficiency. It is, however, well known how many problems parties to the Convention have had with the length of their proceedings in the light of Article 6 of the Convention. But even in the most efficient systems cases do not reach their highest courts or tribunals immediately. Each court therefore would have to ask itself if it is really worthy to request the OA, even though it is not bound to do so, and that it will not be bound with the response, especially that, at least at the beginning of the AO mechanism operation after entry into force of Protocol 16, it will not be possible to estimate how long it would take for the GCh to respond, if at all it decides to respond rather then to reject the request. Additionally, the preparation of a well-reasoned request, and such an obligation is put on the requesting court or tribunal, needs to take some time. Finally, the request might also lead to a response on questions of principle relating to interpretation and application of the rights and freedoms guaranteed by the Convention, but being not relevant to the particular case. Such a possibility is encompassed in the Protocol 16 mechanism and was mentioned earlier in this text.

Therefore, the request for an AO might significantly lengthen domestic proceedings (which already are not short) and not give any guarantees that

53 At the margin when it comes to prioritization of the proceedings, one has to notice as well that if a request for an advisory opinion would concern a question already arisen in the individual application procedure (under Article 34 of the Convention) it is not certain which of the proceedings should be given a priority (the present in the Draft Explanatory Report prioritization of the individual application has been deleted from the final version of the Report, leaving the question open for the Court to decide in future practice). Another problem, which Paul Gragl rightly points out is a situation in which "the ECtHR had already decided the case submitted under Article 34 ECHR at that time [and] it would be required to answer the questions raised in an advisory opinion in an identical fashion, in order to guarantee the coherent interpretation and application of the Convention rights. The main drawback in this scenario is that only the judgment in the regular Article 34 ECHR procedure would be binding; Strasbourg's legal expertise given in its advisory opinion would indeed provide guidance how to adjudicate a concrete case, but it would still be optional for the domestic court to act in compliance with it. This means in conclusion that, even though parallel proceedings may not endanger the coherence of the ECtHR's jurisprudence, they might lead to incoherent implementation within the legal orders of the high contracting parties, as the same or comparable cases could lead, on the one hand, to binding judgments (via individual applications), and, on the other hand, non-binding advisory opinions". (P. Gragl, *supra* note 19, 20, 25, 26, 39, 43, 50, p. 242).

the opinion will at all be received or, whether it will be of use to the particular case. Such concerns may lead highest courts and tribunals of the parties to the Protocol to be very reluctant to request for the AOs. That may solve the new version of the ECtHR being victim of its new success conundrum problem, which was mentioned earlier. It may, however, lead the AO procedure to be very rarely applied and thus less significant as a tool to enhance the domestic implementation of the Convention standards or to enhance the harmonious interpretation of the Convention. It also creates a threat to an individual right to a hearing within a reasonable time in domestic proceedings. Björg Thorarensen rightly notices that

> "[t]he general aim of Protocol No. 16, to create a dialogue between the European Court of Human Rights and national courts to enhance harmonisation and strengthen the image of the Strasbourg Court as a constitutional court, is perhaps too costly, compromising individual procedural guarantees. It must not be forgotten that the interests of the individual may have greater weight than the benefits of legal harmonization".[54]

4.3. PROTOCOL 16 AND THE EU

The specificity of the AO mechanism under Protocol 16 ingrained in the nature and particularity of the Strasbourg human rights protection system, makes it different from other – at the first glance similar – procedures known from domestic or international jurisdictions.[55] Probably the most obvious association, which might come to mind and which have been mentioned earlier in this text, is the one with the preliminary reference procedure in the CJEU under Article 267 of the Treaty on Functioning of European Union (further: TFEU).[56] Despite the first association, both procedures differ significantly. At least since the time of the Report of the Group of Wise Persons, it has been clear that the preliminary reference to CJEU is not a role model for the Protocol 16. Authors of the Report admit that

> "the introduction of a preliminary ruling mechanism on the model of that existing in the European Union was discussed. However, the Group reached the conclusion

---

54 B. Thorarensen, *supra* note 14, 28, p. 14.

55 The most interesting in this context international examples might be the Inter-American Court of Human Rights or the International Court of Justice. For more about that see for example: J.M. Pasqualucci, 'Advisory Practice of the Inter-American Court of Human Rights: Contributing to the Evolution of International Human Rights Law' (2002) *Stanford Journal of International Law (SJIL)*, vol. 38:241; K. Dzehtsiarou, N. O'Meara, *supra* note 1, 8, 16, 29, 41, 44, 45, 46, p. 449–451; Also other courts may serve an interesting comparison like the EFTA Court or others. For more see: B. Thorarensen, *supra* note 14, 28, 54, pp. 3–4.

56 *Treaty on the Functioning of the European Union (Consolidated Version)*, OJ C 326, 12 October 2012.

> that the EU system is unsuitable for transposition to the Council of Europe. The preliminary ruling mechanism represents an alternative model to the judicial control established by the Convention, which requires domestic remedies to be exhausted. The combination of the two systems would create significant legal and practical problems and would considerably increase the Court's workload".[57]

Exhaustive comparison of these two mechanisms is out of the scope of this text.[58]

Nevertheless, while examining Protocol 16 and trying to assess its possible significance, it is necessary to take under consideration the European Union as a future party to the Convention, even though the association process has recently become even more turbulent than it used to be.[59] The AO procedure was supposed to serve enhancement of the dialogue between the ECHR and domestic highest courts and tribunals but eventually also with the CJEU.[60] European Union's notion of the AO procedure, especially the one recently expressed by the CJEU in its opinion on the EU's accession to the ECHR, is therefore not to be omitted. The Opinion 2/13 issued by the CJEU on 18 December 2014 is highly critical about the draft agreement on the accession[61] and the CJEU concluded that for numerous reasons the draft agreement is not compatible with the EU law. The agreement and the opinion in whole their complexities are out of the scope of this text.[62] Some parts of the Opinion however, directly address Protocol 16 and the AO mechanism it introduces in the context of its compatibility with the EU law. The comments presented below shall therefore be limited only to those issues.

According to the CJEU, the possibility of the highest courts and tribunals of parties to the Convention and Protocol 16 to request AOs on questions of principle relating to the interpretation or application of the rights and freedoms guaranteed by the ECHR or the protocols thereto, interferes with the obligation

57 *Report of the Group of Wise Persons...*, *supra* note 9, para. 80.

58 For more in this matter see especially: P. Gragl, *supra* note 19, 20, 25, 26, 39, 43, 50, 53.

59 For more about the process of the EU accession to the ECHR and some problems and dilemmas relating to it see for example: P. Gragl, *The Accession of the European Union to the European Convention on Human Rights*, Hart Publishing: Oxford 2011, V. Kosta, N. Skouratis, V.P. Tzevelekos (eds.), *The EU Accession to the ECHR*, Oxford and Portland, Oregon: Hart Publishing, 2014.

60 See: *Reflection Paper on the Proposal to Extend the Court's Advisory Jurisdiction*, *supra* note 17, 38, para. 10.

61 For the *Draft revised agreement on the accession of the European Union to the Convention for the Protection of Human Rights and Fundamental Freedoms* see: [www.coe.int/t/dghl/standardsetting/hrpolicy/Accession/Meeting_reports/47_1%282013%29008rev2_EN.pdf] [accessed: 10 January 2015].

62 For more on those issues see for example: P. Gragl, 'The Reasonableness of Jealousy: *Opinion 2/13* and the UE Accession to the ECHR', forthcoming in W. Benedek, F. Benoit-Rohmer, W. Karl, M. Nowak (eds.), *European Yearbook on Human Rights* 2015 [https://www.academia.edu/10671511/The_Reasonableness_of_Jealousy_Opinion_2_13_and_EU_Accession_to_the_ECHR] [accessed: 10 February 2015].

on the part of EU Member States' highest courts and tribunals (and of course all the EU Member States are parties to the Convention) to submit a request to that end to the Court of Justice in a preliminary ruling procedure under Article 267 TFEU.[63] After the EU joins the Convention, the latter will become part of the EU law. The problem identified by the CJEU concerns thus the sphere of those rights guaranteed by the Convention, which correspond to those secured by the Charter of Fundamental Rights of the EU (further: Charter).[64]

Requests for the AO by the EU Member States could also, according to the CJEU, trigger the procedure of the prior involvement of the Court of Justice (if the issue at stake justifies it) which eventually might lead to circumvention of the preliminary reference procedure, which procedure is according to the CJEU the key stone of the judicial system of the EU as established by the Treaties.[65] In the prior involvement procedure, as it has been drafted in the agreement on the EU joining the Convention, the CJEU does not see itself to be capable to rule on interpretation of legal provisions contained in acts of the EU institutions, bodies, offices or agencies, but just to rule on their validity.[66] In the preliminary reference procedure the CJEU is capable to do both – rule on interpretation and on validity of the EU law.

For those reasons the CJEU concluded: "By failing to make any provision in respect of the relationship between the mechanism established by Protocol No 16 and the preliminary ruling procedure provided for in Article 267 TFEU, the agreement envisaged is liable adversely to affect the autonomy and effectiveness of the latter procedure".[67]

In political terms Martin Scheinin may be right when he argues that introduction by the Council of Europe Member States of the Protocol 16 AO mechanism – a kind of a parallel preliminary reference procedure but to the ECtHR instead than to CJEU – in matters which are at the same time substantive EU law issues "coming just after a complicated accession agreement has been carefully drafted and negotiated with the EU is a sign of profound disloyalty towards the EU".[68]

Protocol 16 has been opened to signature already after the draft agreement has been reached. The agreement thus does not imply that the EU after it joins the

---

63 Court of Justice of the European Union, *Opinion 2/13 of the Court (Full Court)* from 18 December 2014, para. 196 [http://curia.europa.eu/juris/document/document.jsf?text=&docid=160882&pageIndex=0&doclang=en&mode=lst&dir=&occ=first&part=1&cid=40247] [accessed: 25 January 2015].

64 *Charter of Fundamental Rights of the European Union*, OJ C 364/1 from 18 December 2000.

65 *Opinion 2/13 of the Court (Full Court)* from 18 December 2014, *supra* note 63, paras. 176 and 198.

66 See *Draft revised agreement...*, *supra* note 61, para. 66.

67 *Opinion 2/13 of the Court (Full Court)* from 18 December 2014, *supra* note 63, 65, para. 199.

68 M. Scheinin, 'CJEU Opinion 2/13 – Three Mitigating Circumstances' in: *Verfassungsblog. On Matters Constitutional* [www.verfassungsblog.de/cjeu-opinion-213-three-mitigating-circumstances/#.VLoWetKG-So] [accessed: 20 January 2015].

ECHR would also join Protocol 16. As it has been said however, the mechanism was designed with intention to encompass all the parties to the Convention. Even if it does not happen that all the parties to the Convention including the EU would also sign and ratify the Protocol, after the Protocol's entry into force (with ten ratifications) it will embrace all the parties to the Convention, because of the general effects of the AOs, which have been described earlier in this text. The EU seems to be reluctant towards the Protocol, even if it itself would not become a party to it but only its Member States would do so. It is transparent in the CJEU's opinion and arguments risen in it about the preliminary reference procedure circumventing effect ingrained it the Protocol.

Basing on the checklist proposed by Steve Peers, of what needs to be done in amending the EU accession to the ECHR process, in relation to Protocol 16 it would be necessary to ensure that "any use of Protocol 16 ECHR by national courts cannot undermine the EU preliminary ruling system, presumably by ruling out the use of Protocol 16 where the EU law issues are involved".[69] This might lead to undermining the whole AO mechanism and creating inequality between the parties to the Convention.

It is possible, however, to claim that Protocol 16 indeed is not contrary to the EU law and that the CJEU objections towards it are indeed unfounded.[70] Perhaps some more moderate means might be sufficient to solve the Protocol 16 problem in relation to the EU law, especially when it comes together with the prior involvement procedure problem, by allowing the CJEU (through revising delicately the accession agreement in this matter) to rule on interpretation, not just validity of the EU law in the prior involvement procedure. As some argue though, such a possibility is already present in the Draft Accession Agreement, if it is not read in a very literal way, and it is indeed possible to be interpreted from the current Article 3(6) of the Agreement.[71] Even if it would be right, the CJEU's

69 S. Peers, 'The CJEU and EU's accession to the ECHR: a clear and present danger to human right protection' in: *EU Law Analysis: The insight into EU law developments* [http://eulawanalysis.blogspot.com/2014/12/the-cjeu-and-eus-accession-to-echr.html] [accessed: 15 January 2015].

70 Paul Gragl argues that: "In completely determined cases such as *Melloni* (...) [a]rticle 267(3) TFEU would always take precedence over national law and thus also over any posterior international agreement (such as Protocol No. 16) that has been ratified by the Member States, thereby ensuring the proper functioning and effectiveness of the preliminary ruling procedure. (...) And even if the Member States should fail to comply with this provision, the Commission could, *ultima ratio*, argue that they compromised the attainment of the objectives of the Union Treaties (Article 4(3) TEU), (...) and consequently initiate infringement proceedings against them, as they did in the *Mox Plant* case. (...) In merely partially determined scenarios such as *Åkerberg Fransson*, and cases completely outside the scope of EU law, conversely, the Member State courts have of course retained their right to submit such a request for an advisory opinion to the ECtHR. Precluding them from submitting such questions to the ECtHR under these circumstances would amount to an extension of the EU's competences and thus be in violation of Article 6(2) second sentence TEU." (P. Gragl, *supra* note 62, p. 10–11).

71 For more see: P. Gragl, *supra* note 62 and 70, pp. 13–14.

opinion seems to reflect the Luxemburg Court's approach to the Protocol and express the attitude which may comprise also the EU's notion of more political kind towards the accession to the ECHR process as such, as well as to the Protocol 16 and the mechanism it introduces. If the works on the EU joining the Convention will go in the direction sketched in the Opinion, the AO mechanism might become one of their victims.

5. CONCLUSION

Björg Thorarensen is probably right when she states that "it would be unrealistic to expect that Protocol No. 16 will have a significant impact on the implementation of the Convention in the States Parties to the ECHR, though it may be of value in exceptional circumstances".[72] If this Protocol might be a step towards the long debated constitutionalisation of the ECHR, it is certainly not sufficient one and without being accompanied with other steps in the same direction, it may remain more of a symbolic rather than a real step.[73] In the context of this book, which concerns also questions of democratic legitimacy of the judicial process, it is possible to invoke Björg Thorarensen once more, when she notes that

> "[t]he fact that the Court has slowly and gradually assumed the role of a constitutional court for Europe, without having being defined as such through the democratic processes of the States Parties, has raised questions regarding its legitimacy, the role of the national constitutional legislature and judiciary and ultimately the sovereignty of member states".[74]

Kanstantsin Dzehtsiarou and Noreen O'Meara also notice that

> "[t]he authority of the ECtHR and its relationships with Contracting Parties are increasingly under the legal and political spotlight. (...) It is too early to tell whether the Brighton process will prove to be a watershed moment for the Court. While efforts to reform it have progressed in recent years, these have often been overshadowed by attacks on the Court's constitutional legitimacy (...)".[75]

For such a transformation of the Strasbourg Court – so it becomes a constitutional court for Europe – a political will of parties to the Convention, as well as of the parties-to-be, would be necessary. Such a will seems, however, to be absent. The Protocol 16 may therefore, in a limited scope, serve as harmonious interpretation enhancer, early warning mechanism, means to fill in the gaps in

72 B. Thorarensen, *supra* note 14, 28, 54, 55, p. 15.
73 B. Thorarensen, *supra* note 14, 28, 54, 55, 72, p. 15.
74 B. Thorarensen, *supra* note 14, 28, 54, 55, 72, 73, p. 14.
75 K. Dzehtsiarou, N. O'Meara, *supra* note 1, 8, 16, 29, 41, 44, 45, 46, 55, p. 468.

the ECtHR jurisprudence, or perhaps – but even more unlikely than all the other mentioned effects – as a provider of some training grounds for new developments by the ECtHR. Which of those ways, if any, would be followed, will depend a lot on the actual operation of the AO procedure resulting from strategies and attitudes chosen both – by the requesting courts and tribunals, as well as by the ECtHR itself after it, if at all, enters into force. The Protocol seems, however, not to be a golden tool to heal the Strasbourg's diseases of docket control and improving efficiency of the Strasbourg human rights protection system. Additionally, its potential significance seems to be seriously weakened by the CJEU's opinion on the EU's accession to the ECHR draft agreement, which includes the Protocol 16 advisory opinion mechanism seen to be contrary to the EU law.

As a result, it seems rather unlikely that the Protocol will achieve its main goals – the more procedural and pragmatic ones, like reducing the case flow to ECtHR as well as those more systemic or substantive ones, like enhancing the domestic implementation of the Convention or strengthening the Strasbourg Court's constitutional character.

BIBLIOGRAPHY

BOOKS AND ARTICLES

Besson, S. (ed.), *La Cour européenne des droits de l'homme après le Protocole 14: premier bilan et perspectives = The European Court of Human Rights after Protocol 14: preliminary assessment and perspectives*, Geneve: Schulthess, 2011; D. Haider, *The Pilot-Judgment Procedure of the European Court of Human Rights*, Leiden: Martinus Nijhoff Publishers, 2013

Bodnar, A., 'Res Interpretata: Legal Effect of the European Court of Human Rights' Judgments for other States Than Those Which Were Party to the Proceedings' in: Y. Haeck and E. Brems (eds.) *Human Rights and Civil Liberties in the 21st Century*, Dordrecht: Springer, 2014

Degener, R. and L. Garlicki, 'Art. 46 [moc obowiązująca oraz wykonanie wyroków]' in L. Garlicki (ed.), *Konwencja o Ochronie Praw Człowieka i Podstawowych Wolności. Komentarz do artykułów 19–59*, Warszawa: C. H. Beck, 2011

Dzehtsiarou, K. and N. O'Meara, 'Advisory jurisdiction and the European Court of Human Rights: a magic bullet for dialogue and docket-control?' (2014) Vol. 34, No. 3, *Legal Studies*

Gragl, P., *The Accession of the European Union to the European Convention on Human Rights*, Hart Publishing: Oxford 2011

Gragl, P., '(Judicial) Love is Not a One-Way Street: The EU Preliminary Reference Procedure as a Model for ECtHR Advisory Opinions under Draft Protocol No. 16' (2013) 38, *European Law Review*

Greer, S. and L. Wildhaber, 'Revisiting the Debate about "constitutionalising" the European Court of Human Rights', (2012) *Human Rights Law Review (HRLR)*, vol. 12(4)

Harris, D., M. O'Boyle, Warbrick, C., *Law of the European Convention of Human Rights*, Oxford University Press: Oxford 2014 (3rd edition)

Helfer, L.R., 'Redesigning the European Court of Human Rights: Embeddedness as a Deep Structural Principle of the European Human Rights Regime' (2008), *EJIL (European Journal of International Law)*, vol. 19 no. 1

Jacobs, F.G., "Judicial Dialogue and the Cross-Fertilization of Legal Systems: The European Court of Justice", (2003) 38 *Texas International Law Journal (TILJ)*

Kosta, V., N. Skouratis, V.P. Tzevelekos (eds.), *The EU Accession to the ECHR*, Oxford and Portland, Oregon: Hart Publishing, 2014

M. O'Boyle, 'The legitimacy of Strasbourg review: time for a reality check?' in: *Mélanges en l'honneur de Jean-Paul Costa. La conscience des droits*, Dalloz: Paris 2011

Paprocka, A. and M. Ziółkowski, 'Opinie doradcze w świetle Protokołu nr 16 do Europejskiej Konwencji Praw Człowieka' (2014), *Europejski Przegląd Sądowy (EPS)*, vol. 1

Pasqualucci, J.M., 'Advisory Practice of the Inter-American Court of Human Rights: Contributing to the Evolution of International Human Rights Law' (2002) *Stanford Journal of International Law (SJIL)*, vol. 38:241

Ploszka, A., 'Nowa opinia doradcza Europejskiego Trybunału Praw Człowieka' (2013) *Państwo i Prawo (PiP)*, vol. 10

Rainey, B., E. Wicks and C. Ovey, *The European Convention on Human Rights*, Oxford University Press: Oxford 2014 (6th edition)

Ress, G., 'The Effect of Decisions and Judgments of the European Court of Human Rights in the Domestic Legal Order' (2005) 40, *Texas International Law Journal*

Rui, J.P., 'The Interlaken, Izmir and Brighton Declarations: Towards a Paradigm Shift in the Strasbourg Court's Interpretation of the European Convention of Human Rights?' (2013), *Nordic Journal of Human Rights (NJHR)*, vol. 31 no. 1

Senden, H., *Interpretation of Fundamental Rights in a Multilevel Legal System. An analysis of the European Court of Human Rights and the Court of Justice of the European Union*, Intersentia: Antwerp 2011

Schmid, J.C., 'Advisory Opinions on Human Rights: Moving Beyond a Pyrrhic Victory' (2006) *Duke Journal of Comparative & International Law (DJC&IL)*, vol. 2

Sicilianos, L.A., 'L'élargissement de la compétence consultative de la Cour européenne des droits de l'homme – A propos du Protocole n° 16 à la Convention européenne des droits de l'homme', (2014) *Revue Trimestrielle des droits de l'homme*, vol. 97

Wildhaber, L., 'A Constitutional Future for the European Court of Human Rights' (2002) *Human Rights Law Journal (HRLJ)*, vol. 23

Wildhaber, L., 'Precedent in the European Court of Human Rights' in: P. Mahoney, H. Petzold (eds.), *Protecting Human Rights: The European Perspective*, Köln: Karl Heymanns Verlag, 2000

LEGAL ACTS

Charter of Fundamental Rights of the European Union, OJ C 364/1, 18 December 2000

Convention for the Protection of Human Rights and Fundamental Freedoms, CETS No. 5 with later amendments

Protocol No. 2 to the Convention for the Protection of Human Rights and Fundamental Freedoms, conferring upon the European Court of Human Rights competence to give advisory opinions, CETS No. 44

Protocol No. 9 to the Convention for the Protection of Human Rights and Fundamental Freedoms, CETS No. 140

Protocol No. 11 to the Convention for the Protection of Human Rights and Fundamental Freedoms, restructuring the control machinery established thereby, CETS No. 155

Protocol No. 14 to the Convention for the Protection of Human Rights and Fundamental Freedoms amending the control system of the Convention, CETS No. 194

Protocol No. 15 amending the Convention for the Protection of Human Rights and Fundamental Freedoms, CETS No. 213

Protocol No. 16 to the Convention for the Protection of Human Rights and Fundamental Freedoms, CETS No. 214

Treaty on the Functioning of the European Union (Consolidated Version), OJ C 326, 12 October 2012

CASE LAW

Loizidou v. Turkey (Preliminary Objections) Application no. 15318/89 (1995), ECtHR

Al-Skeini and Others v. the United Kingdom, [GC] Application no. 55721/07 (2011), ECtHR

Advisory opinion on certain legal questions concerning the lists of candidates submitted with a view to the election of judges to the European Court of Human Rights from 12 February 2008, ECtHR

Advisory opinion on certain legal questions concerning the lists of candidates submitted with a view to the election of judges to the European Court of Human Rights no. 2 from 22 January 2010, ECtHR

Decision on the competence of the Court to give an advisory opinion from 2 June 2004, ECtHR

Opinion 2/13 of the Court (Full Court) from 18 December 2014, CJEU

OTHER

Draft revised agreement on the accession of the European Union to the Convention for the Protection of Human Rights and Fundamental Freedoms, [www.coe.int/t/dghl/standardsetting/hrpolicy/Accession/Meeting_reports/47_1%282013%29008rev2_EN.pdf], [accessed: 10 January 2015]

European Court of Human Rights, *Annual Report 2012*, Registry of the European Court of Human Rights, Strasbourg 2013, [www.echr.coe.int/Documents/Annual_report_2012_ENG.pdf], [accessed: 10 January 2015]

European Court of Human Rights, *Annual Report 2013*, Registry of the European Court of Human Rights, Strasbourg 2014, [www.echr.coe.int/Documents/Annual_report_2013_ENG.pdf], [accessed: 10 January 2015]

European Court of Human Rights, *The Courts Priority Policy* [www.echr.coe.int/Documents/Priority_policy_ENG.pdf], [accessed: 10 January 2015]

Explanatory Report to the Protocol 16 [http://conventions.coe.int/Treaty/en/reports/html/214.htm], [accessed: 10 January 2015]

Gragl, P., 'The Reasonableness of Jealousy: *Opinion 2/13* and the UE Accession to the ECHR', forthcoming in W. Benedek, F. Benoit-Rohmer, W. Karl, M. Nowak (eds.), *European Yearbook on Human Rights* 2015, [https://www.academia.edu/10671511/The_Reasonableness_of_Jealousy_Opinion_2_13_and_EU_Accession_to_the_ECHR], [accessed: 10 February 2015]

High Level Conference on the Future of the European Court of Human Rights Interlaken Declaration from 19 February 2010, [www.coe.int/t/dgi/hr-natimplement/Source/interlaken_declaration_en.pdf], [accessed: 15 January 2015]

High Level Conference on the Future of the European Court of Human Rights, Brighton Declaration adopted on 19 and 20 April 2012, [www.echr.coe.int/Documents/2012_Brighton_FinalDeclaration_ENG.pdf], [accessed: 10 January 2015]

Peers, S., 'The CJEU and EU's accession to the ECHR: a clear and present danger to human right protection' in: *EU Law Analysis: The insight into EU law developments*, [http://eulawanalysis.blogspot.com/2014/12/the-cjeu-and-eus-accession-to-echr.html], [accessed: 15 January 2015]

Reflection Paper on the Proposal to Extend the Court's Advisory Jurisdiction, [www.coe.int/t/dgi/brighton-conference/documents/Court-Advisory-opinions_en.pdf], [accessed: 10 January 2015]

Reforming the European Convention on Human Rights: Interlaken, Izmir, Brighton and Beyond. A Compilation of Instruments and Texts Relating to the Ongoing Reform of the ECHR, Directorate General Human Rights and Rule of Law Council of Europe, 2014 [www.coe.int/t/dghl/standardsetting/cddh/reformechr/Publications/Compilation%20ReformECHR2014_en.pdf], [accessed: 10 January 2015]

Report of the Group of Wise Persons to the Committee of Ministers, 979*bis* meeting, CM(2006)203, para. 81, [https://wcd.coe.int/ViewDoc.jsp?id=1063779], [accessed: 10 January 2015]

Scheinin, M., 'CJEU Opinion 2/13 – Three Mitigating Circumstances' in: *Verfassungsblog. On Matters Constitutional* [www.verfassungsblog.de/cjeu-opinion-213-three-mitigatingcircumstances/#.VLoWetKG-So], [accessed: 20 January 2015]

Spielman, D., "Judgments of the European Court of Human Rights Effects and Implementation" Keynote Speech at *Conference at the Paulinerkirche Göttingen Georg-August-University, Göttingen 20 September 2013*, p. 4 and 7, [www.echr.coe.int/Documents/Speech_20130920_Spielmann_Gottingen_ENG.pdf], [accessed: 10 January 2015]

Thorarensen, B., 'The Advisory Jurisdiction of the ECtHR under Protocol No. 16: Enhancing Domestic Implementation of Human Rights or a Symbolic Step?' paper submitted in relation to the Conference *Shifting Centers of Gravity in European Human Rights Protection* in Reykjavik (6–7 March 2014)

12. THE EU'S PARLIAMENTARY REPRESENTATION IN THE LIGHT OF THE STRASBOURG COURT'S *SEJDIĆ* AND *ZORNIĆ* STANDARDS

Is there Tendency for a New Parliamentary Order in the EU?

Fisnik Korenica*
PhD in Law, Vrije Universiteit Brussel
Research Fellow at FRC Research Group, Vrije Universiteit Brussel
Lecturer at the University of Prishtina, Kosovo

Dren Doli**
PhD candidate, Faculty of Law, University of Hamburg
Lecturer at the University of Prishtina, Kosovo

1. INTRODUCTION

The electoral system of the European Union (EU) has yet a lot to demonstrate: it is not merely a multifaceted system of divergent values but also a unique system of law that has the ability to produce several democratic ramifications at the level of the right to vote under the European Convention on Human Rights' (the Convention, ECHR) standards. This chapter, therefore, discusses the electoral system of the EU from the perspective of the conceptual standards deriving from the European Court of Human Rights' (Strasbourg Court, ECtHR) seminal cases *Sejdić & Finci* and *Zornić*. With the note that the EU is not a contracting party to the Convention, this chapter merely tries to delineate some fundamental and abstract collisions which the current system of elections in the EU may face with the Convention law.

As a primary note, it is worth considering Schleicher. He argues that '[t]he reason why EU leaders have repeatedly increased the powers of the

---

* Email: fisnik@legalpoliticalstudies.org.
** Email: dren.doli@legalpoliticalstudies.org.

European Parliament (EP) is clear. Giving power to a directly-elected body was considered a way to cure the "democratic deficit," or the *perceived inability* of European citizens to influence EU decision-making.'[1] The democratic deficit in the EU is not simply a reflection of the 'common sense' (political) maturity of the governments of the EU member states. It is also a consequence of the constitutional model concerning the electoral system in the EU which both the Treaties and the EU legislation designate. Tackling this issue from the perspective of the Strasbourg Court's case-law and standards on voting rights and prohibition on discrimination would provide guidance on how to reduce the democratic deficit from the perspective of human rights.

To note, the EP elections are another set of electoral democracy within the EU and its Member States. Turning out to vote in the EP elections is a separate democratic demonstration of EU citizens independently from the elections in their home countries. From the perspective of the democratic deficit, turn out in these elections is a part of the challenges that the EU and Member States must address. For example, Kumm shows evidence that there is a continual decrease of voter turnout in direct elections to the EP, which is also lower than the voter turnout in the national elections in those countries.[2] Kumm's evidence basically demonstrates that due to the lower level of effective outputs which the EU elections have compared to the national elections, constituencies trust more and turn out more in their national elections compared to the EP elections. In itself, this evidence may also suggest that EP elections are still seen by the constituency as basically national elections for their state's seats in the EP. This perception – which often is a result of the way the national political parties frame the EP elections – also reflects the constitutional ramifications which the present electoral model for the EP demonstrates. By contrast, adding upon this, Hix *et al.* essentially argue that with the increase of powers of the European Parliament, Euro parties have seen a constant boost in their party cohesion around EU topics. This illustrates that with a stronger EP there is always a stronger possibility for the political parties to become better interconnected and uniformly representative of the 'people' of the EU.[3]

As a basic inquiry, to demonstrate the complex nature of the electoral system of the EU from a supranational constitutional perspective, the EP Committee on Constitutional Affairs has compellingly argued that:

---

1 D. Schleicher, 'What if Europe Held an Election and No One Cared?' (2011) 52 *Harvard International Law Review*, p. 112 [emphasis added].

2 M. Kumm, 'To Be a European Citizen? The Absence of Constitutional Patriotism and the Constitutional Treaty' (2005) 11 *Colum. J. Eur. L. (Columbia Journal of European Law)* 481, 512.

3 S. Hix, A.G. Noury and G. Roland, *Democratic Politics in the European Parliament*, Cambridge University Press, Cambridge 2007, p. 104.

> 'Parliament's electoral system is a compromise between the democratic principle of equality ('one man one vote') and the international law principle of equality among states [...]'[4]

It should therefore be noted that a constitutional characteristic of the European electoral system is that it is grounded in a model of double-facet parity: it is the 'one' that balances the equal treatment of the right to vote with the equality of Member States as sovereign agents of the EU. This model of balancing the positions of Member States with the full-fledge equality of EU citizens' capacity to vote seems to be rather complex and conflicting considered from a human rights point of view. The nature of this balance, one needs to mention, may seriously harm the intended objectives of a democratic electoral system which the EU should aim to reach.

Taking the above into account, this chapter will discuss the EU's electoral system within the context of the Convention's standards on the right to vote and the prohibition of discrimination from the perspective of the ECtHR *Sejdić & Finci* and *Zornić* cases. The latter represent very recent and sound examples of new conceptual directions which the Strasbourg Court has given to the right to vote and prohibition of discrimination in governing systems involving power-sharing mechanisms. Although the EU is not perfectly well-situated to be compared with these two landmark cases, it still needs to be said that these two cases provide new conceptual developments from the perspective of Strasbourg's jurisdiction which may play a role in the reshaping of the EU's electoral system, in particular after the EU's accession to the ECHR.

This chapter first examines the EU electoral system from the perspective of its share of burden with the Member States, and the main guiding procedural principles shaping this relationship. It then continues to examine whether these two landmark cases may remodel the EP from a parliament of the EU Member States' peoples to a parliament of EU people. Next, it offers a section that scrutinizes the context and scope of the right to vote under the EU Treaties' institutional structure, and after that, another section on the EU electoral specifics and their perspective from the two landmark cases concerned. The chapter concludes with some closing remarks and forthcoming perspectives on this topic.

4 Committee on Constitutional Affairs 'REPORT on a proposal for a modification of the Act concerning the election of the Members of the European Parliament by direct universal suffrage of 20 September 1976', 2011, (2009/2134(INI)), No. A7-0176/2011.

2. EU'S CONSTITUTIONAL ARCHITECTURE WITH REGARD TO PARLIAMENTARY REPRESENTATION

The European Union has a largely complex parliamentary representation system, both in the context of the articulation of the right to vote and the nature of the institution that is thought to perform the parliamentary representation function, the European Parliament. On a declaratory level, the Treaty on the European Union (TEU), in Article 10(1) reads: 'The functioning of the Union shall be founded on representative democracy.' It is therefore generally maintained that the EU Treaties try to set up – by declaring this principle – two broad-scope intentions: first, to proclaim the nature of the Union as founded on a representative democracy, as a basic means of democratic governance, and, second, to instil legitimacy of the Union by providing a facet of credibility that rests on popular interests. Regrettably, none of these two intentions are practically present within the constitutional context of the EU, as the latter's model of parliamentary democracy is not only limited in scope but also in the degree with which it tries to implement its mission.

The European Union's Parliament, namely the European Parliament, is the body established by the Treaties to serve this declaratory target. Article 14(2) TEU – to this purpose – establishes that:

> 'The European Parliament shall be composed of representatives of the Union's citizens. They shall not exceed seven hundred and fifty in number, plus the President. Representation of citizens shall be degressively proportional, with a minimum threshold of six members per Member State.'

In general, therefore, the European Parliament is established as an institution to represent the citizens of the Union – not individually the people of the Union or the peoples of the Union Member States. It seems that the Masters of the EU Treaties intentionally omitted to define whether the EP is an institution representing the Union's 'people' or 'peoples', as that would then have led to the question of whether there is an 'EU people' at all (as explained *infra*). Nevertheless, naming the EP as the institution that represents the Union's citizens is a rather important declaratory aspect which indicates the fact that the EP stands as the bottom of the Union's representative democracy. Such declaratory aspect, one should note, amounts to a constitutional principle that may perhaps serve as the foundation for the Union's constitutional legitimacy to govern as a democratically elected and controlled entity.

To note, Article 14(2) TEU makes it explicit that the maximum number of representatives – namely Members of the European Parliament (MEPs) – at the EP is established numerically, therefore changes in the Union's census will not change those numbers. However, it is important to note that each Member State of the Union serves simultaneously as an electoral constituency for the EP, with an explicit number of MEPs which it may elect as its representatives in the EP. The system of EU Member States' constituencies and the number of their representatives within the EP is regulated with the 'degressive proportionality' formula, which is the principal blueprint that indicates the nature of the Union's electoral system. Such blueprint also designates the Union's nature of parliamentary representation, as it establishes that citizens' votes are counted and represented within the EP: on the basis of each Member States' individualities and asymmetrical positions.

Is there a uniform electoral law in the EU? Article 223(1) of the Treaty on the Functioning of the European Union (TFEU) – to this purpose – tries to establish that:

> 'The European Parliament shall draw up a proposal to lay down the provisions necessary for the election of its Members by direct universal suffrage in accordance with a uniform procedure in all Member States or in accordance with principles common to all Member States.'

The above provision sets a baseline rule on the duty to establish a uniform electoral system to serve the Union's direct universal suffrage for the election of the EP. In concretizing this basic obligation under the TFEU, the Council Decision 2002/772/EC in Article 1 establishes that:

1. In each Member State, members of the European Parliament shall be elected on the basis of proportional representation, using the list system or the single transferable vote.
2. Member States may authorise voting based on a preferential list system in accordance with the procedure they adopt.
3. Elections shall be by direct universal suffrage and shall be free and secret.[5]

Two observations can therefore be drawn from a synchronized analysis of the TFEU obligation deconstructed above and the Council Decision referred to previously. First, that the concept of a 'uniform' electoral system, under Article 223(1) TFEU, tries to establish only the minimal guarantees and procedures which the Union's electoral system should embark. Such a minimum standard does not seem to fulfil the role of a true uniform electoral system which TFEU aims to ascertain. Second, 'uniform' electoral system in this regard is written to refer merely to the general electoral formula which every Member State should apply for the EP elections, that is, the 'proportional' electoral system, yet again with the opportunity to choose among list system and/or single

---

5 2002/772/EC, Euratom: Council Decision of 25 June 2002 and 23 September 2002, Article 1(2).

transferable vote system.[6] The nature, scope and contents of this 'proportional' electoral system are left to the Member States' discretion and preference. Therefore, 'uniformity' in the context of Article 223(1) TFEU does not appear to be a predictable standard as regarding the Union's electoral system. Two additional provisions of the Council Decision concerned support this argument, as follows:

Council Decision 2002/772/EC in Article 1(3) reads:

> In accordance with its specific national situation, each Member State may establish constituencies for elections to the European Parliament or subdivide its electoral area in a different manner, without generally affecting the proportional nature of the voting system.

In addition to the above clause, Council Decision 2002/772/EC in Article 2B (8) also establishes that:

> Subject to the provisions of this Act, the electoral procedure shall be governed in each Member State by its national provisions. These national provisions, which may if appropriate take account of the specific situation in the Member States, shall not affect the essentially proportional nature of the voting system.

This said, with regard to the Council Decision of 2002, Member States enjoy rather broad discretion as regards the organization of proportional electoral model which they should apply to elect their MEPs for the EP. Thus, Member States decide themselves individually on the territorial definition of their zones, whether to opt for the list system or the single transferable vote system, or whether to establish – and methods to set up – a preferential voting based on a preferential list system. In deciding which approach to adopt, the EU Member States enjoy broad discretion which they exercise by implementing the so-called 'degressively proportional' electoral system wherein they become represented in the EP on the basis of internal procedural autonomy as regards the electoral mechanics they decide on.

On the other hand, to note, Article 10(3) TEU establishes that '[e]very citizen shall have the right to participate in the democratic life of the Union.' Whether such right relates to the entire concept of electing a fully-fledged legislature under the Convention terms seems debatable and not elucidated by the above-mentioned provision. To examine whether that right can be enjoyed equally in practice by EU Member States citizens', one needs to examine the mechanics and effects of the Union citizens' vote in the decision-making structures of the Union and its 'legislature'. An additional general clause is provided in Article 10(4) TEU

---

6 See a wealthy journal article on this, at: D.M. Farrell and R. Scully 'Electing the European Parliament: How uniform are 'uniform' electoral systems?' (2005) 43 *Journal of Common Market Studies*, pp. 969–984.

which establishes that '[p]olitical parties at European level contribute to forming European political awareness and to expressing the will of citizens of the Union.'[7] Whether this treaty provision speaks for an effective expression of the citizens will – and its effects both with regard to the legislation and government decision-making processes – needs be further analysed in the context of the Convention standards.

3. A NOTE ON THE CONCEPT OF PARLIAMENTARY REPRESENTATION IN THE LIGHT OF *SEJDIĆ* AND *ZORNIĆ*: EUROPEAN PARLIAMENT OF THE EU PEOPLE OR EUROPEAN PARLIAMENT OF THE EU MEMBER STATES *PEOPLES*

The reason why the (very recent) *Zornić* and *Sejdić* & F*inci* cases are relevant to the EU is simple to address. The latter aims to be part of the European Convention regime, and the ECtHR interpretations will be relevant if not detrimental to the EU parliamentary representation, but not only. The extent to which both decisions will impact the limits of the right to vote, as well as the concept of the legislator within the EU, are only few dimensions which this chapter tends to unfold.

To begin with, the ECtHR in both cases holds that the provisions of the Constitution of Bosnia and Herzegovina guaranteeing that '... only persons declaring affiliation with a "constituent people" (Bosniacs, Croats and Serbs) are entitled to run ...' for the House of Peoples of Bosnia and Herzegovina and to stand for the election to the Presidency '... amount[s] to a discriminatory difference in treatment in breach of Article 14 taken in conjunction with Article 3 of Protocol No. 1 and Article 1 of Protocol No. 12'.[8] According to the Court, the only noted difference between the *Sejdić* & F*inci* case, on the one hand, and *Zornić* case, on the other, is that in the former the applicants were declared Roma and Jewish origin while in the latter the applicant (Zornić) refused to declare her affiliation, except her Bosnian citizenship.

The Court in *Zornić* case therefore reiterates that:

> '... identical constitutional provisions have already been found to amount to a discriminatory difference in treatment in breach of Article 14 taken in conjunction with Article 3 of Protocol No. 1 in *Sejdić & Finci* (ibid., §50). Accordingly, and for

[7] See on this an interesting chapter, at: J. Thomassen 'Empirical research into political representation: Failing democracy or failing models?' in K. M. Jennings, and Th. Mann, (eds), *Elections at Home and Abroad: Essays in Honor of Warren E. Miller*, University of Michigan Press, Ann Arbor 1994, pp. 237–265.

[8] ECtHR, 15.7. 2014, *Zornić v. Bosnia and Herzegovina* [2014], paras. 30, 32 and 36.

> the detailed reasons elaborated in *Sejdić & Finci* (§§47–49), the Court concludes that there has been a violation of Article 14 taken in conjunction with Article 3 of Protocol No. 1 and a violation of Article 1 of Protocol No. 12 resulting from the applicant's continued ineligibility to stand for election to the House of Peoples of Bosnia and Herzegovina.'[9]

In addition the Court goes on to rule that:

> 'The lack of a declaration of affiliation by the present applicant with a "constituent people" also renders her ineligible to stand for election to the Presidency. An identical constitutional precondition has already been found to amount to a discriminatory difference in treatment in breach of Article 14 taken in conjunction with Article 3 of Protocol No. 1 and Article 1 of Protocol No. 12 as regards the House of Peoples [...] and, moreover, the notions of discrimination prohibited by Article 14 and by Article 1 of Protocol No. 12 are to be interpreted in the same manner [...]. In *Sejdić & Finci* (ibid., §56) the Court has already found that the constitutional provisions which rendered the applicants ineligible for election to the Presidency were discriminatory and in breach of Article 1 of Protocol No. 12. The Court does not see any reason to depart from that jurisprudence in the present case.[10]

The Court in both cases highlights that eligibility to stand for elections linked to the ethnicity rather than citizenship as a requirement amounts to discrimination and is in breach of the relevant articles of the Convention law. However, before offering a perspective of the anticipated impact of the ECtHR cases within the EU, firstly, it is worth scrutinizing the model of the EU parliamentary representation, and secondly – to analyse it in the light of the human rights standards established in the *Sejdić* and *Zornić* cases.

A basic question relating to the model of parliamentary representation in the EU is whether the European Parliament serves as a parliament of the EU 'people' or of the EU Member States' 'peoples'.

Our basic proposition here relies in the assumption that European Parliament cannot be the representative of the EU people unless the EU electoral system consents the election of the MEP directly by the people of the EU regardless of the territorial, residency and citizenship requirements.

From the EU constitutional perspective, there is no definite answer which could help solve this dilemma, as long as the question requests an empirical answer rather than a legal one. However, to the extent possible, there are still some constitutional issues which may provide guidance on this issue. To start this discussion, it is worth quoting the now-amended provision of the 1976 Act on Direct Elections in the Union, which, in Article 1[11] reads that:

---

9 ECtHR, 15.7. 2014, *Zornić v. Bosnia and Herzegovina* [2014], para. 32.

10 ECtHR, 15.7. 2014, *Zornić v. Bosnia and Herzegovina* [2014], para. 36.

11 Formally titled as: Act concerning the election of the representatives of the Assembly by direct universal suffrage, 8.10.1976, OJ L 278/5.

'The **representatives** in the Assembly of the **peoples** of the **States** brought together in the Community shall be elected by direct universal suffrage.'[12]

It was the intention of the 1976 Act to note down, that the European Parliament is a parliament of EU Member States' peoples and there exists no EU people as such. Although this provision was later amended, the constitutional dilemma on the EU people or peoples still continues to remain in the background of the constitutional democracy of the EU.

The core problem still remains with 'proportional digression' formula, which explicitly refuses to ensure the equality of the vote among the citizens of EU. To that aim, this system requires that EU Member States serve as the legal and political constituencies for the European Parliament. This builds a practice in which the European Parliament is composed of representatives from each Member State constituency, therefore placing emphasis on the Member States' constituencies rather than an EU-wide constituency independent of the Member States' divisions and control.[13] This said, a second more important definition is provided by Article 2(2) of Council Directive 93/109/EC,[14] which establishes that:

'"electoral territory" means the territory of a Member State in which, in accordance with the above Act and, within that framework, in accordance with the electoral law of that Member State, members of the European Parliament are elected by the people of that Member State'.

The above provision seems to suggest that – electorally speaking – citizens of the individual Member States' elect their own (Member State) representatives to the European Parliament. Therefore, the European Parliament – due to the nature of the constitutional design of the electoral system – seems to be controlled by the representatives of the individual Member States' peoples rather than controlled by the EU people on a self-governing basis. This model of dividing the electoral territory of the EU on the basis of Member States' territories and consequently their constituents – while omitting that a citizen from e.g. Germany votes for a French candidate (as part of the Europe-wide political party list) – designs the EP as a vertical representative structure reflecting individual Member States' constituencies vote preferences.

---

12 Emphasis added.

13 *Cf*: Hix *et al* note that '[l]eft-right politics explains an overwhelming proportion of voting in the European Parliament. In contrast, national interests, independent of national party positions, have very little systematic influence on voting in the European Parliament.' See: S. Hix, A.G. Noury and G. Roland, *Democratic Politics in the European Parliament*, Cambridge University Press, Cambridge 2007, pp. 180–81.

14 Adopted on 6 December 1993, referred to as the second directive on electoral law on the European Parliament Elections.

This said, the current legal framework on elections in the EU seems to suggest that the EP functions more as a representative democracy of the individual Member States' constituencies gathered in a common body, rather than as a common-sense representation body reflecting the common will of the EU people.

Hix in this regard – from an empirical perspective – proposes that

> '[t]he problem is that European Parliament elections actually have very little to do with "Europe"! [...] Instead, voters, the media, and national parties treat European Parliament elections as just another set of domestic elections, where the dominant issue is how well national governments have performed.'[15]

Hix's conclusions seem to support that the above-mentioned EU constitutional argument is also reflected in how citizens perceive the EP elections. On the other hand, Burson-Marsteller evidence suggests that when EU citizens answer opinion polls for EP elections they think of national elections. Their perception and model of thought in this regard reflects their national electoral will, a lens through which they see the EP members as well.[16] Therefore, there is little dilemma on the nature of the EP from the perspective of voters' perception on Election Day (this does not reflect the MEPs behaviour post-elections). Whether this perception is induced solely by the EU constitutional arrangements is yet another claim which falls outside the scope of the present chapter to elucidate.

However, adding upon the latter argument – Walczak argues that

> 'even if voters more frequently rely on their attitudes towards EU integration in casting a ballot, the extent to which the party of their choice will represent them on this issue will vary. So, even if considerations regarding EU integration have begun to guide voters in their party choice [...] significant differences can be observed with regard to how voters are represented on this issue and, ultimately, in the extent to which their vote can influence the direction of integration.'[17]

This said, the party structure in the EP is argued to centre upon their national politics rather than EU politics, something that is thought to have also been preconditioned from the model of the electoral system.

Before appraising these arguments through the lens of the Strasbourg Court's standards, it is worth mentioning that the latter has recognized a rather wide

---

15 S. Hix, *What's Wrong with the European Union and How to Fix It*, Polity Press, Cambridge 2008, p. 79.

16 Burson-Marsteller, *Predict'09 Methodology*, 4 June 2009, http://burson-marsteller.de/en/2009/06/final-european-election-prediction-epp-to-win-and-centre-right-to-retain-power/ (last visited 9 December 2015).

17 A. Walczak and W. van der Brug, 'Representation in the European Parliament: Factors affecting the attitude congruence of voters and candidates in the EP elections' (2012) 14 *European Union Politics*, pp. 3–22, p. 18.

margin of appreciation to High Contracting Parties regarding the models of electoral systems to which they apply.[18] It is therefore not the intention to argue that Strasbourg Court will not recognize a wide margin of appreciation to the EU (compared to the States) with regard to its electoral system; instead the aim is to reflect on potential conceptual clashes which one may observe if the above arguments were situated within the discussion of *Sejdić & Finci* and *Zornić*.

As noted above, in the *Sejdić & Finci* and *Zornić* cases the Court (ECtHR) has concluded that the condition which requires the candidates for elections in Bosnia and Herzegovina to demonstrate their affiliation with a 'constituent people'[19] – which in the Bosnia case refers to three major ethnic community peoples – violates both the right to vote and prohibition of discrimination under the Convention.

Observing that the EU's electoral system makes it a condition to register for EP elections within a certain Member State – and to apply within its constituency elections for the EP – it is apparent that it seeks a sort of affiliation between the candidate and the Member State concerned in order to reach the EP. This hidden affiliation – which is not formally made a condition for ineligibility – likely falls within the prohibitions of the *Zornić* and *Sejdić* cases, as without such affiliation, a candidate would not be capable of running for EP elections. Even the provisions of the Charter of the Fundamental Rights of the European Union guaranteeing the right of the Union citizens to vote and to stand for elections under the same conditions as the citizens of the particular state, seem not helpful.[20]

Therefore, in line with these two Strasbourg cases, it may be suggested that this virtual – if not legal – link to eligibility which a citizen needs to maintain through belonging to a certain Member State's constituency and electoral system to apply and be elected for the EP runs counter to the Strasbourg's prohibition of affiliation to a certain constituency or people as a condition to be a candidate for elections. If correct, the argument here calls the EU to advance from '*EU people's concept*' to an '*EU people concept*' to better stand within the limits of the Strasbourg's concept of the right to vote without discrimination.

A further examination of the Court decisions reveals the limits of the right to vote and of the concept of legislature within the Convention and its protocols.

The meaning of the right to vote under the Convention system is rather complex and multifaceted from the perspective of the end user. This – combined with the electoral architecture of the EU – may become rather interesting but also problematic in the context of the EU's legislative configuration. Even more, the obligation – emanating from the Article 53 of the Charter of the Fundamental

---

18 ECtHR. 15.7. 2014, *Zornić v. Bosnia and Herzegovina* [2014], para. 26.

19 ECtHR, 15.7.2014, *Zornić v. Bosnia and Herzegovina* [2014], para. 30.

20 Charter of Fundamental Rights of the European Union, OJ, 2000/C 364/01, available at: www.europarl.europa.eu/charter/pdf/text_en.pdf, article 39.

Rights of the European Union – to fashion the meaning and the scope of the rights akin to the Conventional law, except accession, is yet another wing of internal pressure within the EU.[21] The Strasbourg Court's landmark cases *Sejdić & Finci v. Bosnia & Herzegovina* and *Zornić v. Bosnia and Herzegovina* are two highlighted benchmarks that may make this interface methodically appealing. The Strasbourg Court, in both cases, has enlightened the interface between the right to vote and prohibition of discrimination in electoral systems of democracy that provide for complex power-sharing institutional structures, such as that of Bosnia and Herzegovina. To the extent that both cases' conceptual meanings remain untouched, both of these cases are particularly significant in connection with the EU's compatibility with the Convention's standards on the right to vote and prohibition of discrimination.

To repeat, the Court in *Sejdić* considered whether the claimants' ineligibility to stand for the House of the People and the Presidency of Bosnia and Herzegovina violates Article 3 of Protocol No. 1 and the prohibition of discrimination (as an annexed violation to the former) under the Convention system. In *Sejdić & Finci*, for that reason, 'the Court concludes that the applicants' continued ineligibility to stand for election to the House of Peoples of Bosnia and Herzegovina lacks an objective and reasonable justification and has therefore breached Article 14 taken in conjunction with Article 3 of Protocol No. 1.'[22] Article 3 of Protocol No. 1 of the Convention, which the claimant alleged as violated by Bosnia and Herzegovina, reads:

> The High Contracting Parties shall hold free elections at reasonable intervals by secret ballot, under conditions which will ensure the free expression of the opinion of the people in the choice of the **legislature.**[23]

In this light, Article 3 of Protocol 1 basically does provide for a broader protection than merely the right to vote, a system of protection that covers the integrity of the entire electoral system.

To that extent and for the purposes of Article 3 of Protocol 1 – both in the light of *Sejdić* and *Zornić* – the interpretation of the term 'legislature' is of high importance, which is the objective to which the right to vote must align. Deconstructing the meaning of the 'legislature' concept under the Convention system becomes highly important for the context under which Article 3 of

---

21 See Charter of Fundamental Rights of the European Union, OJ, 2000/C 364/01, available at: www.europarl.europa.eu/charter/pdf/text_en.pdf, Article 52, para 3. '3. In so far as this Charter contains rights which correspond to rights guaranteed by the Convention for the Protection of Human Rights and Fundamental Freedoms, the meaning and scope of those rights shall be the same as those laid down by the said Convention. This provision shall not prevent Union law providing more extensive protection'.

22 ECtHR, 2.12.2009, *Sejdic and Finci v. Bosnia and Herzegovina* [2009], para. 50;.

23 Emphasis added.

Protocol 1 should apply upon the EU parliamentary representation, respectively the EU's 'legislature'.

Although *Sejdić & Finci* and EU parliamentary representation do not operate under identical legal conditions, they still engage with the same comparable criteria at the conceptual level. Therefore, one needs to deconstruct the concept of 'legislature' in both cases in order to observe if comparable criteria may make the EU relevant under *Sejdić & Finic*. In *Sejdić & Finic*, the Court set forth three tests to consider whether a certain institution is capable of falling within the reach of Article 3 of Protocol No. 1 of the Convention (which may concurrently stand in the scope of Article 14 of the Convention, afterward). First, whether it has a 'wide' function with regard to the passing of legislation, namely a constituent role in the legislative procedure. Second, whether it has a constituent function with regard to the determination of sources of financing of government expenditures (budget designing function), and third, whether it has a constituent competence in concluding international treaties.[24]

The first issue in this regard is whether the term 'legislature' should be taken for granted as referring to the national parliament of a High Contracting Party. Similarly, applied to the EU context, the questions turns on to be whether the European Parliament should be understood as the only institution falling within the concept of 'legislature' under Article 3 of Protocol 1. To this purpose, for example, the Strasbourg Court had already and compellingly ruled in *Mathieu-Mohin & Clerfayt v. Belgium* that the term legislature 'has to be interpreted in the light of the constitutional structure of the State in question.'[25] This means that it should not be taken for granted that *only* national parliaments fall within the reach of the concept of 'legislature', as the Court takes into account domestic constitutional structures that are sometimes incomparable in every contracting state. Instead, the Court applies a substantive test to assess whether a certain institution falls within the reach of 'legislature' by considering the scope of the competences of such an institution and comparing them to the common-sense legislative competences. That being the case, the Court is not satisfied if the EU was to argue that its only 'legislature' is the European Parliament, instead it would insist the inclusion of institutions assigned with common legislative competences by the EU Treaties. To that aim, in *Mathews*,[26] the Court moreover has established that the European Parliament falls within the concept of 'legislature' under Article 3 of Protocol 1.

However, whether there are other institutions which fall within the scope of 'legislature' still to still be considered: that being a signal which then leads to the question of whether there is an electoral system in place that allows for its compliance with Article 3 of Protocol 1. To this purpose – one should note

[24] ECtHR, 2.12.2009, *Sejdic and Finci v. Bosnia and Herzegovina* [2009], para. 41.

[25] ECtHR, 2.03.1987, *Mathieu-Mohin and Clerfayt v. Belgium* [1987], Series A, No. 113, para. 53.

[26] ECtHR, 18.02.1999, *Matthews v. The United Kingdom* [1999], para. 63 and 64.

– Article 14(1) TEU establishes that: 'The European Parliament shall, jointly with the Council, exercise legislative and budgetary functions.' Therefore, if the Strasbourg Court would substantively apply the *Sejdić & Finic* test on 'legislature' to the Article 14(1) TEU, then both European Parliament and the Council would fall within the domain of its concept of 'legislature'. This would further be supported by the mere fact that Article 14(1) TEU makes the Council a constituent institution in law-making and budgetary planning, which are two of the three criteria the Court applies to frame the scope of 'legislature' from the perspective of *Sejdić and Finic*. One should mention here that even *Mathews* would not contradict this finding. The Court in *Mathews* has simply ruled that the European Parliament falls within the scope of 'legislature' but has not established whether there are other EU institutions which possess that attribute. This said, it is highly likely that the Strasbourg Court should recognize the Council as falling within the scope of 'legislature' for the purposes of Article 3 of Protocol 1.

The question that needs be posed, at this level, is whether the Council – if it is recognized as falling within the scope of 'legislature' – fulfils the criteria of Article 3 of Protocol 1 which request that a fair and free electoral system should choose the legislature by ballot. The Council is not directly elected by the people, however, it stems from the indirect choice of the national parliaments through their national governments, the latter representing the EU Member States in the Council. To rationalize this, Article 10(2) TEU notes that:

> 'Citizens are directly represented at Union level in the European Parliament. Member States are represented in the European Council by their Heads of State or Government and in the Council by their governments, themselves democratically accountable either to their national Parliaments, or to their citizens.'

Article 10(2) TEU tries to neutralize the above criticism (which may contravene Article 3 of Protocol 1) by establishing that the European Council and the Council members are indirectly elected by their national parliaments or their citizens, therefore circuitously by some means kept accountable to their states' people. This means that the EU Treaties try to legitimize the fact that the members of the Council or the European Council are not directly elected. Two issues need be raised in this regard.

First, although the Council and European Council members are somehow elected under indirect model of elections, they are nevertheless elected to their own governments as national institutions. Their election or indirect election as member of government or head of state or government has not been intended or designed to serve the needs of the Council or has not been designed for purposes of the European Council. In addition, according to Article 47 TEU, the EU has a distinct legal personality from its Member States, therefore, the national elections in its Member States may not serve in filling the democratic needs of an organization which has its own legal personality and system of governance. This said, the election of heads of governments or states and government ministers is not done for purposes of the Council as the legislature for Article 3 of Protocol 1.

Second, the more problematic aspect of this – in light of *Sejdić & Finci* and *Zornić* – is that there are blocking criteria regarding the eligibility to stand for the Council or European Council even if both bodies were considered to fall within the scope of 'legislature'. To explain this, as an example, would it be possible for a German citizen to stand for the position of Council or European Council seat of Italy? In general and theoretically not, as domestic constitutional rules for heads of states and governments but also ministers, usually make non-citizens ineligible to stand for such positions. This said, a German citizen would be ineligible – because of his/her nationality – to stand for any of the seats of the Council and European Council except that of Germany. This practice certainly stands in the line of ineligibility to stand for a position within one of the institutions of EU 'legislature' because of national citizenship. Such practice amounts to a comparable – notionally, identical – situation to the *Sejdić & Finci* and *Zornić* cases' prohibitions.

Therefore, even if the Council would be considered as enjoying a democratically indirectly elected status in the context of the EU's 'legislature' under Article 3 of Protocol 1, still the criteria via which eligibility to stand for it in the context of the right to vote demonstrate that it is likely that appointment as a candidate to the Council and European Council violates the right to vote and prohibition of discrimination in the light of the *Sejdić & Finci* and *Zornić* cases.

4. THRESHOLDS ON EU PARLIAMENT AND 'REGRESSIVE PROPORTIONALITY' MODEL OF ELECTORAL SYSTEM: IS THERE AN OBJECTIVE SYSTEM OF ELECTORAL CRITERIA?

Although there are some fundamental criteria upon which the EU's 'uniform' electoral rules are grounded, there are numerous divergent rules on the basis of which EU Member States demonstrate their procedural autonomy in the EU electoral system. Fortin-Rittberger & Rittberger support this by arguing that 'EU member states exhibit significant differences in electoral formulas, district magnitudes, and the structure of ballots.'[27]

As explained above, the EU Member States are worn with certain discretion on several aspects of the organization of the electoral system of the EU.[28] The

27 J. Fortin-Rittberger and B. Rittberger 'Do electoral rules matter? Explaining national differences in women's representation in the European Parliament' (2014), *European Union Politics*, published online 26 March 2014, p. 7.

28 See e.g.: J. Fortin-Rittberger and B. Rittberger 'Do electoral rules matter? Explaining national differences in women's representation in the European Parliament' (2014), *European Union Politics*, published online 26 March 2014, p. 7; See also the impact of divergent rules in EP

following may be some of the representative examples: a) although generally proportional, Member States use different models of counting votes (some Member States use D'Hondt system, Germany uses Sainte-Laguë/Schepers system, Luxembourg uses 'Hagenbach-Bischoff' system, and so on);[29] b) those states which opt for the preferential voting system, do have divergent criteria for the management of votes: some offer closed lists some open lists;[30] c) the management of vacant seats is also divergent among states;[31] d) the minimum age for the right to vote and to be a candidate for the European Parliament is also different across all Member States (as an example the minimum age to run for EP in Germany is 18 whereas in Belgium it is 21);[32] e) some Member States have their entire territory as a single electoral zone for the EP whereas some others have divided their territory into many electoral zones for the EP elections;[33] f) some Member States have established higher thresholds whereas some have established lower thresholds for parties competing for the EP elections (within the margins allowed by Article 14(2) TEU). 'Of the 28 Member States, 15 have established an electoral threshold for the allocations of seats in the EP. The thresholds mostly vary between 3% and 5%.'[34]

A final 'variable to be taken into consideration for its marked ability to effect expected disproportionality is the number of available seats: the smaller this number, the greater the implicit disproportionality in the electoral system.'[35] Counting on these differences, the EU electoral system – as Emanuele notes – 'represents a proportional system with variable geometry and 28 national variants. This produces chaos of formulas and election thresholds that, in turn, offer different incentives and constraints in the various national contexts.'[36] This said, there are a number of electoral mechanics which are devised on the basis

elections, at: P. Norris, *Electoral Engineering. Voting Rules and Political Behavior*, Cambridge University Press, New York 2004.

29 Directorate General for Internal Policies, Policy Department C: Citizens' Rights and Constitutional Affairs, *The European elections: EU legislation, national provisions and civic participation*. Study for the AFCO Committee, p. 15.

30 The European elections: EU legislation, national provisions and civic participation, p. 15.

31 The European elections: EU legislation, national provisions and civic participation, p. 15/6.

32 The European elections: EU legislation, national provisions and civic participation, p. 17.

33 The European elections: EU legislation, national provisions and civic participation, p. 17.

34 E.M. Poptcheva, *Electoral thresholds in European elections Developments in Germany* European Parliament Research Service, Briefing, 27/02/2014, available at: www.europarl.europa.eu/RegData/bibliotheque/briefing/2013/130606/LDM_BRI(2013)130606_REV2_EN.pdf, p. 2.

35 V. Emanuele, 'Proportional representation with variable-geometry: Here is how to vote in the 28 member states', p. 38, in L. DeSio, V. Emanuele and N. Maggini (eds), *The European Parliament Elections of 2014*, Centro Italiano Studi Elettorali-Italian Center for Electoral Studies) (CISE), Rome 2014, available at: http://eprints.luiss.it/1344/1/EUROPEAN_PARLIAMENT_ELECTION_2014_DE_SIO_EMANUELE_MAGGINI.pdf.

36 V. Emanuele, 'Proportional representation with variable-geometry: Here is how to vote in the 28 member states', pp. 37–42, in L. DeSio, V. Emanuele and N. Maggini (eds), *The European Parliament Elections of 2014*, Centro Italiano Studi Elettorali-Italian Center for Electoral Studies) (CISE), Rome 2014, available at: http://eprints.luiss.it/1344/1/EUROPEAN_PARLIAMENT_ELECTION_2014_DE_SIO_EMANUELE_MAGGINI.pdf, p. 38.

of Member State-preferences and discretion, therefore seriously harming the 'uniform' nature of the electoral system for the EP which the Treaties endeavour to institute. Hix & Hagemann make this statistically relevant, by demonstrating that:

> 'Eleven member states, who elect 286 MEPs (36 percent), already use relatively small districts. Eight member states, who together elect 188 MEPs (24 percent), use medium-sized districts. And, eight member states, who elect 311 MEPs (40 percent), use large districts. Meanwhile, 18 member states, who elect 318 MEPs (41 percent), use either fully-open or semi-open ballots, while the remaining 9 member states, who elect 467 MEPs (59 percent), use a closed-ballot structure. Put another way, 267 MEPs (34 percent) are already elected in relatively small districts and under some form of preferential voting, while 260 MEPs (33 percent) are elected in large districts under a closed-ballot structure.'[37]

It is therefore basically argued that '[t]he choice of formula impacts the proportionality of the system – the closeness of the relationship between votes and seats – from the most proportional Sainte-Lague to the least proportional d'Hondt.'[38] On the other hand, as Fortin-Rittberger & Rittberger note, '[e]lectoral formulas, district magnitude, and the number of MEPs each country elects have significant consequences for the resulting proportionality of seat attribution: proportionality is constrained in the case of countries having only a handful of seats to fill.'[39] This said, the nature and degree of proportionality system varies greatly among EU Member States and is subject to their internal discretion on its scope. Therefore, in essence, the relationship between the citizens' votes and their power of representation in the EP is rather well based on the design of electoral mechanics which their Member States shape. Hix & Hagemann, by confirming this reality, argue compellingly that:

> 'These results consequently suggest that the design of the electoral system used in European Parliament elections is one of the main reasons why citizens in Ireland, Malta, Luxembourg, Italy and Finland feel considerably more engaged in the process of electing their MEPs than citizens in Germany, Portugal, Greece, Poland and The Netherlands.'[40]

---

37 S. Hix and S. Hagemann, 'Could changing the electoral rules fix European parliament elections?', Politique Européenne 2/2009 (no. 28), p. 37–52, www.cairn.info/revue-politique-europeenne-2009-2-page-37.htm, p. 44.

38 Referring to Gallagher, 1992; Lijphart, 1986, at: J. Fortin-Rittberger and B. Rittberger,, 'Do electoral rules matter? Explaining national differences in women's representation in the European Parliament' (2014), *European Union Politics*, published online 26 March 2014, p. 7.

39 J. Fortin-Rittberger and B. Rittberger, 'Do electoral rules matter? Explaining national differences in women's representation in the European Parliament' (2014), *European Union Politics*, published online 26 March 2014, p. 9, referring to Katz, 1997 & Lijphart, 1986.

40 S. Hix and S. Hagemann, 'Could changing the electoral rules fix European parliament elections?', Politique Européenne 2/2009 (no. 28), p. 37–52, www.cairn.info/revue-politique-europeenne-2009-2-page-37.htm, p. 49.

The question therefore is whether these differences – internal to the EU legal order – amount for an electoral system which does not provide the right to vote under an equal treatment standard. In this regard, the Court has previously ruled in *Mathieu-Mohin and Clerfayt v. Belgium* that 'the phrase "conditions which will ensure the free expression of the opinion of the people in the choice of the legislature" implies essentially [...] the principle of equality of treatment of all citizens in the exercise of their right to vote and their right to stand for election.'[41] To examine the concept of 'equality' which the latter case refers to, the Court has in effect ruled in *Zornić* and *Sejdić & Finci* cases that electoral systems which provide for application of subjective criteria – instead of objective criteria – contravene Article 3 of Protocol 1 and the principle of prohibition of discrimination under the Convention system.[42] Such subjective criteria, in the light of *Zornić* and *Sejdić & Finci* cases may be the duty of a candidate to declare affiliation to a certain constituent people as precondition to stand for elections. In this regard, it is not the intention of this chapter to argue that if the *Zornić* standard would apply to the EU, the latter would appear to violate the Convention. Instead, the intention is to open a debate on the possible directions which *Zornić* and *Sejdić & Finci* cases may lead the debate on the EU's compliance with the Convention electoral standards. One such absolute example – rather distinct when compared against the criteria of *Zornić* and *Sejdić & Finci* cases – is the case of Luxembourg which has an electoral rule prohibiting electoral lists with majority of non-Luxembourg candidates for the EP elections.[43] This clearly makes it ineligible for a majority of EU non-Luxembourg citizens to stand within the same electoral list as a matter of the electoral prohibitions, clearly contrary to the *Zornić* and *Sejdić & Finci* cases principles on the rules on ineligibility to stand for elections.

In this light, the question is whether the different mechanics, which each EU Member State chooses on the design of its electoral system with regard to the election to the EP, amounts to subjective criteria which leave room for dissimilar treatment of citizens among different EU Member States. From a legal perspective, the 'degressively proportional' electoral system which the EU Treaties establish in itself promotes subjective criteria to be applied by the Member States – 'subjective' meaning EU Member State-specific criteria, not criteria applying on all EU Member States from an equal objective perspective. On the other hand, the individual regulation of the EU Member States' electoral systems seems to amount to quite a large-scale variation among their citizens' relative voting power which makes the electoral system of the EU rather well structured on multi-individualized perspectives. This argued, the differences between the EU Member States' electoral mechanics regarding the election of the EP seem to precondition rather high practical chances for divergent positions of

41 ECtHR, 2.3.1987, *Mathieu-Mohin and Clerfayt v. Belgium* [1987], Series A, No. 113, para. 54.

42 ECtHR, 15.7.2014, *Zornić v. Bosnia and Herzegovina* [2014], para. 31.

43 The European elections: EU legislation, national provisions and civic participation, p. 17.

voters on basis of the fact whether they electorally belonged to Member State X or Y. This being the case, it seems that EU citizens' affiliation to a certain Member State electoral rules for the EP elections amounts to a subjective affiliation which citizens of other Member States may not be able to enjoy. Lacking 'uniform objective criteria' upon which the mechanics of the Member States electoral systems function seems to amount to a tendency to contravene the standards established by *Zornić* and *Sejdić & Finci* cases. Such an objective set of standards would need to ensure that citizens in Member State X compared to all citizens of other Member States are not found in an unequal position or disadvantaged position because his/her Member State regulated its electoral system on the basis of its individual desire. Lacking uniformity in the objective sense, therefore, seems to contravene the *Zornić* and *Sejdić & Finci* cases – at least conceptual – standards.

5. CONCLUDING REMARKS AND A GENERAL FORTHCOMING OUTLOOK

It seems likely that the current set up of electoral rules in the EU may perhaps be in breach of the Convention's standards on the right to vote and prohibition of discrimination. This chapter concludes that if the Convention standards were to be applied – conceptually speaking – to a firmer degree, they would lead to a change in the nature of representation of international organizations, including the EU. This said, it is concluded that the EU – as basically an international (supranational) organization – is not perfectly formed to be compared within the same boundaries of the electoral standards of states, as there are several organizational and functional principles which make the EU unable to fulfil the Convention standards on elections compared to state contracting parties of the Convention. However, after the EU accedes to the ECHR, it will need to carefully consider its alignment with the Convention electoral standards as, sooner or later, there will be the need to gradually transform the electoral system into one that better supports the human rights of EU citizens. Such a development would mark the gradual transformation of international organizations' electoral rules – including the nature of their legislatures. Hence *Zornić* and *Sejdić & Finci* cases may prove of significant importance for the global law maturity as well.

Observing that the current electoral system of the EU is rather contrary to the Convention standards on the right to vote and prohibition of discrimination, one needs to consider the forthcoming reforms which it needs to introduce. Some have made efforts to propose several reforms of the current electoral system of the EU – not for human rights reasons, as may be the intention of this chapter – but rather for political and policy reasons. To narrow the gap of democratic deficit which the current EU electoral system exhibits, Schleicher, for instance, proposes that the EU may choose to adhere to a 'double threshold' electoral system. That means that '[i]n order for a party to get an MEP elected from any member state, the party would have to: (1) receive a certain percentage in the member state; and (2) receive a certain percentage in a set number of other EU member states. For instance, in order to receive representation in the French delegation to the EP, a party would have to receive, say, five percent of the French vote, and three percent of the vote in at least seven other EU member states'.[44] The EP Committee on Constitutional Affairs, from its own perspective, has also proposed something similar, as following:

> '[...] an additional 25 MEPs be elected by a single constituency formed of the whole territory of the European Union; transnational lists would be composed of candidates drawn from at least one third of the States, and may ensure an adequate gender representation; each elector would be enabled to cast one vote for the EU-wide list in addition to their vote for the national or regional list: voting for the EU constituency would be in accordance with the closed list proportional system; and seats would be allocated without a minimum threshold in accordance with the D'Hondt method; further, proposes that an electoral authority be established at EU level in order to regulate the conduct and to verify the result of the election taking place from the EU-wide list'.[45]

Bardi *et al* – to this purpose – note that '[t]he proposed transnational constituency could foster closer party co-operation at the EU level, by promoting genuine transnational campaigning and EU-level party programmes.'[46] These two proposed reforms may certainly lower the likelihood for the EU electoral system to contravene the Convention standards discussed above, however, they would not directly reform the system to the degree requested by those standards. Briefly, it is proposed that to align the EU Treaties with the Convention standards, three far-reaching reforms need be undertaken: first, to transform the Council into a normal legislature – although likely not practicable – with no rules on ineligibility based on nationality or affiliation to a certain EU Member State; second, to remove the rules on ineligibility for national citizenship – except that for EU citizenship – for anyone willing to stand for a position within the EP or Council; and, third, to transform the electoral system into one wherein not Member States' peoples, but EU people are electorally preconditioned to become represented in the EP. This may be done

44 D. Schleicher, 'What if Europe Held an Election and No One Cared?' (2011) 52, *Harvard International Law Journal*, p. 116.

45 Committee on Constitutional Affairs (2011) 'REPORT on a proposal for a modification of the Act concerning the election of the Members of the European Parliament by direct universal suffrage of 20 September 1976' (2009/2134(INI)), No. A7-0176/2011, point 2.

46 L. Bardi (et al) '*How to Create a Transnational Party System: A study prepared in the framework of the European Union Democracy Observatory for the European Parliament (AFCO Committee)*', EUDO Report 2010/2. European Union Democracy Observatory (EUDO), Robert Schuman Centre for Advanced Studies, European University Institute. Florence: Italy, 2010, p. 104.

by establishing a common EU (single) constituency not grounded on Member States' individual territories. These reforms may produce large consequences for the current EU treaties' framework; therefore very little chances exist to align the EU electoral system with the *Zornić* and *Sejdić & Finci* cases conceptual standards.

BIBLIOGRAPHY

BOOKS, EDITED VOLUMES AND ARTICLES IN JOURNALS

Bardi, L. (et al) 'How to Create a Transnational Party System: A study prepared in the framework of the European Union Democracy Observatory for the European Parliament (AFCO Committee)', *EUDO Report 2010/2.* European Union Democracy Observatory (EUDO), Robert Schuman Centre for Advanced Studies, European University Institute. Florence: Italy, 2010.

Burson-Marsteller, Predict'09 Methodology, June 4 2009, http://burson-marsteller.de/en/2009/06/final-european-election-prediction-epp-to-win-and-centre-right-to-retain-power/ (last visited Dec. 9, 2015).

Committee on Constitutional Affairs (2011) 'REPORT on a proposal for a modification of the Act concerning the election of the Members of the European Parliament by direct universal suffrage of 20 September 1976' (2009/2134(INI)), No. A7-0176/2011.

Committee on Constitutional Affairs 'REPORT on a proposal for a modification of the Act concerning the election of the Members of the European Parliament by direct universal suffrage of 20 September 1976', 2011, (2009/2134(INI)), No. A7-0176/2011.

Directorate General for Internal Policies, Policy Department C: Citizens' Rights and Constitutional Affairs, *The European elections: EU legislation, national provisions and civic participation*. Study for the AFCO Committee.

Emanuele, V., 'Proportional representation with variable-geometry: Here is how to vote in the 28 member states', in L. DeSio, V. Emanuele and N. Maggini (eds), *The European Parliament Elections of 2014*, Centro Italiano Studi Elettorali-Italian Center for Electoral Studies) (CISE), Rome 2014, available at: http://eprints.luiss.it/1344/1/EUROPEAN_PARLIAMENT_ELECTION_2014_DE_SIO_EMANUELE_MAGGINI.pdf.

Farrell, D.M. and R. Scully 'Electing the European Parliament: How uniform are 'uniform' electoral systems?' (2005) 43 *Journal of Common Market Studies*, pp. 969-984.

Fortin-Rittberger, J. and B. Rittberger 'Do electoral rules matter? Explaining national differences in women's representation in the European Parliament' (2014), *European Union Politics*, published online 26 March 2014.

Hix, S., A.G. Noury and G. Roland, *Democratic Politics in the European Parliament*, Cambridge University Press, Cambridge 2007.

Hix, S., *What's Wrong with the European Union and How to Fix It*, Polity Press, Cambridge 2008.

Hix, S. and S. Hagemann, 'Could changing the electoral rules fix European parliament elections?', *Politique Européenne* 2/2009 (no. 28), p. 37–52, URL: www.cairn.info/revue-politique-europeenne-2009-2-page-37.htm.

Kumm, M., 'To Be a European Citizen? The Absence of Constitutional Patriotism and the Constitutional Treaty' (2005) 11 *Colum. J. Eur. L. (Columbia Journal of European Law)* 481, 512.

Norris, P., *Electoral Engineering. Voting Rules and Political Behavior*, Cambridge University Press, New York 2004.

Poptcheva, E.M., *Electoral thresholds in European elections. Developments in Germany*, European Parliament Research Service, Briefing, 27/02/2014, available at: www.europarl.europa.eu/RegData/bibliotheque/briefing/2013/130606/LDM_BRI(2013)130606_REV2_EN.pdf.

Schleicher, D., 'What if Europe Held an Election and No One Cared?' (2011) 52 *Harvard International Law Review*, pp. 109–161.

Thomassen, J. 'Empirical research into political representation: Failing democracy or failing models?' in K.M. Jennings and Th. Mann (eds), *Elections at Home and Abroad: Essays in Honor of Warren E. Miller*, University of Michigan Press, Ann Arbor 1994.

Walczak, A., and W. van der Brug, 'Representation in the European Parliament: Factors affecting the attitude congruence of voters and candidates in the EP elections' (2012) 14 *European Union Politics*, pp. 3–22.

OFFICIAL DOCUMENTS, LEGISLATION AND JUDGMENTS

Charter of Fundamental Rights of the European Union, Official Journal of the European Communities, 2000/C 364/01, available at: www.europarl.europa.eu/charter/pdf/text_en.pdf.

Act concerning the election of the representatives of the Assembly by direct universal suffrage, OJ 8.10.1976, No. L 278/5.

Council Decision of 25 June 2002 and 23 September 2002, Euratom: 2002/772/EC.

Council Directive 93/ 109/EC, Second directive on electoral law on the European Parliament Elections, adopted on 6 December 1993.

ECtHR, 2.12.2009, *Sejdic and Finci v. Bosnia and Herzegovina* [2009].

ECtHR, 15.7. 2014, *Zornić v. Bosnia and Herzegovina* [2014].

ECtHR, 2.03.1987, *Mathieu-Mohin and Clerfayt v. Belgium* [1987], Series A, No. 113.

13. THE EUROPEAN CONCEPT OF A FAIR TRIAL AND THE LEGAL ADMISSIBILITY OF ASSESSORS IN THE POLISH JUDICIAL SYSTEM

Karol PACHNIK*
Siedlce University of Natural Sciences and Humanities
Attorney-at-law

Jakub KRAJEWSKI**
Attorney-at-law

1. INTRODUCTION

Across several European legal systems we can see an ongoing struggle to develop both efficient and legitimate way to promote and evaluate new judges. This legal procedure is to ensure that the staff needs of the judiciary system are satisfied, but at the same time it seeks the opportunity to select those of the candidates for a full nominated judge who – during acting as a temporary judge – failed to prove their practical adjudicating skills. In order to carry out this task, different systems established different institutions, i.e. a temporary judge, a lay judge, an assistant judge or an assessor.

Each of them differs slightly from the other, but all of them were argued not to meet the standards of a fair trial put forward by the European Convention on Human Rights.

2. THE POSITION OF AN ASSESSOR IN POLISH COMMON COURTS

With the idea of reintroducing the position of a temporary judge in the Polish judicial system[1] comes the question of the constitutionality of this legal

* Email: karol.pachnik@uph.edu.pl.
** Email: jakub.maciej.krajewski@gmail.com.

construct and its compliance with the European concept of a fair trial laid down in the European Convention on Human Rights,[2] especially its Article 6.

Knowing that a temporary judge position – as proposed – is in fact a fixed resurrection of a previous office – the general court assessor, one has to keep in mind the prohibitions put forward both by the European and the domestic judicial institutions.

The institution of the assessor (assistant judge) in general courts has been revoked from the Polish legal system on the basis of the Polish Constitutional Tribunal judgment of 24 October 2007,[3] as it was found not to be in compliance with the standards of a fair trial upheld by the Polish Constitution.

Assessors were candidates for the office of district court judge who, under the 2001 Law on the Organisation of Common Courts,[4] had to work for a minimum of three years as an assessor in a district court on completion of their training and examinations.

The decision of the Constitutional Tribunal removed the assessors from general courts, leaving the same office in administrative courts. Although the legal practice in administrative courts has also changed, the legal position of an assessor in these special courts is more independent then the one the assessors in general courts have ever had. Later in this article the authors will argue for the possibility of non-judge adjudicators that is coherent with the standpoint put forward by the European courts in numerous decisions. The decisions that hold the European standard today.

Analysing the institution of an assessor one has to remember that the European Court of Human Rights (ECtHR, the Court) had previously taken it under the scope of its proceedings.

In the case *Henryk Urban and Ryszard Urban v. Poland,*[5] the ECtHR has found the office of an assessor in Polish courts not to meet the standards of a fair trial. The reason for that is that assessors could be removed from their office by the decision of the Ministry of Justice and thus were given no adequate guarantees protecting them against the arbitrary exercise of that power by the Minister.

In the given case the applicants were objecting to the fact that their case had been decided by assessor, and not by a judge. In their objection, the applicants referred in particular to the Constitutional Tribunal's leading judgment of 24 October 2007 on the status of assessors. It held that section 135 para 1 of the

---

1 On the aims of the new statutory project, cf. Waldemar Szmidt, "W drodze po koronę", *Na Wokandzie*, 3 February 2014, http://nawokandzie.ms.gov.pl/numer-19/dobre-praktyki/w-drodze-po-korone.html.

2 European Convention for the Protection of Human Rights and Fundamental Freedoms, as amended by Protocols Nos. 11 and 14, 4 November 1950, ETS 5.

3 Judgment of 24 October 2007, SK 7/06, Exercise of Judicial Power by Assistant Judges, (OTK ZU 2007, No. 9A, item 108).

4 *Journal of Laws* No. 98, item 1070, as amended.

5 Case no. 23614/08, §§16–25.

2001 Act on the Organisation of Common Courts was not constitutional mainly because assessors did not enjoy the necessary guarantees of independence from the Minister of Justice. Notably, assessors could be appointed and removed by the Minister. The Constitutional Tribunal ordered that the provision at issue should be repealed 18 months after delivery of its judgment.[6]

Delivering a sentence that was based on Article 6(1) of the European Convention on Human Rights, the ECtHR referred to the domestic decision (the Constitutional Tribunal's judgment of 24 October 2007) acknowledging a violation of a constitutional provision identical to Article 6 of the ECHR.

What is important for the sake of this article, in their judgments both the ECtHR and the Constitutional Tribunal of the Republic of Poland did not exclude the possibility that assessors or similar officers could possess judicial powers, as long as they had the needed guarantees of independence. Even with the constraints of international standards, the courts signalled the ongoing possibility of adjudication by persons other than judges. The main condition that was to be met by any future office other than an office of a judge, was the guarantee of independence in delivering the decision.

Still, in the applicants' case the assessor had lacked independence, as she could have been removed by the Minister of Justice at any time during her term of office and there had been no solid guarantees preventing the arbitrary exercise of that power by the Minister.

The ECtHR has also stressed that this could not have been rectified on appeal by the Regional Court even if the appeal court was composed of a professional judge. Even if a higher court is "independent", this cannot by itself make up for the lack of independence of the lower court, unless the higher court were to address the specific issue of independence in its decision. This was not the case since even after the judgment of the Constitutional Tribunal, an appeal based on the unconstitutional status of assessors had been doomed to fail as the revoked act had remained legally binding for a period of time after the judgment.

The revised case shows the standpoint of the European judiciary when analysing the standards of a fair trial. It shows them not as they are commonly seen, as an understanding of the principles of the courts procedural conduct – the "adversarial" principle, equality of arms, the presumption of innocence.[7] Instead, it reaches out to the position of the adjudicator within the branches of power and checks whether the adjudicators who are to deliver the verdict can form a truly independent and impartial tribunal. Stressing these systematic guarantees may sometimes seem to go overboard, especially for practicing lawyers. This is often the effect of a lack of outside perspective. Studies show that temporary judges – who assessors in fact

---

6 English version of the judgment is available at the Constitutional Tribunal's website: http://trybunal.gov.pl/fileadmin/content/omowienia/SK_7_06_GB.pdf.

7 D. Vitkauskas, G.v Diko, (2012) *Protecting the right to a fair trial under the European Convention on Human Rights. Council of Europe human rights handbooks*, Strasbourg, p. 44.

were – have more points of influence than permanent judges.[8] Apart from regular influence from colleagues and the general public comes the strong influence from the other branches, especially the executive branch. One has to remember that the influence does not always have to be conscious, but it nevertheless takes place.

3. STANDARDS OF A FAIR TRIAL

Deriving the standards of a fair trail from Article 6(1) of the European Convention on Human Rights can be achieved properly by the proper interpretation and finding the coherent ideas in numerous ECtHR's decisions.

In the interpretation of the ECtHR, the notion of independence is mostly referred to as the independence from the executive branch. The European Court has noted that it is a violation of Article 6(1) if the hearing and deciding upon a case is done by a court which is formed even with only one person that is put into office strictly on the basis of a ministerial administrative decision. This was the subject of the ECtHR's ruling in *Woś v. Poland*.[9]

In the Court's decision *Brudnicka v. Poland*[10] the ECtHR has stressed that when analysing the impartiality of the adjudicators, one has to thoroughly examine the procedure of the nomination and the duration of the term as they are the key factors that prevent any unwanted influence from the executive.

Also in the case *Cambell and Fell v. The United Kingdom*[11] when determining whether a body can be considered to be "independent" from the executive, the ECtHR looked carefully at the manner of appointment of justices and the duration of their term of office. The second safeguard of the fair trial was the existence of guarantees against outside pressures. The Court also stressed the importance of the appearance of independence, as well towards the general public, as to the participants of the trial.

Those same issues were revised by the Court in the case of *Langborger v. Sweden*.[12] The ECtHR upheld its previous standpoint and elaborated on the question of appearance of impartiality. The Court drew a distinction between a subjective conviction of a given judge in a given case which the judge is entitled to when delivering the sentence, and an objective appearance throughout the trial aimed at ascertaining there is no legitimate doubt in the impartiality and independence.

This triad – terms of appointing, guarantees against pressure and objective appearance – was established and repeated in other numerous cases, i.e. case of

---

8 L. Baum, (2008) *Judges and their audiences. A perspective on judicial behavior*, Princeton University Press.

9 Case no. 22860/02, §94.

10 Case no. 54723/00.

11 Case no. 7819/77; 7878/77.

12 Case no. 11179/84.

Bryan v. The United Kingdom[13], case of *Coeme and others v. Belgium*.[14] In each of them there was a visible concern of the ECtHR about the objective impartial appearance of the courts that would build up the confidence which the courts in a democratic society must inspire in the public and, above all, as far as criminal proceedings are concerned, in the accused.

In the case *Benthem v. Holand*,[15] apart from coming up with the criteria for "dispute" that Article 6(1) refers to, the ECtHR has delivered a decision that a civil servant is not impartial even if the adjudicatory act issued by him was judicial in its character.

As we will later on turn to the problem of terms of office that is characteristic for all temporary judges, assessors including, the ECtHR has issued a decision that sheds light on what is the standard in this matter. According to the European Court, a temporary judge is independent only if he cannot be easily removed from office during his term. This standpoint is held both in *Zand v. Austria*[16] and *Sramek v. Austria*.[17]

One has to also note that the position of temporary judges is not only the problem of a Polish judicial system. For instance the United Kingdom, and the Judiciary of Scotland in particular, use temporary judges in the Court of Session and the High Court of Justiciary.[18] Those countries as well have been keen observers of the evolution of standards for fair trial and took action whenever the position of a temporary judge was in question.[19]

The notion of right to a fair trial understood as the right to be judged by an independent tribunal was the object of proceedings of the Court of Justice of the European Union (CJEU).

The CJEU examined the notion of judicial impartiality when deciding upon the competence to address a prejudicial question to the CJEU and the right to trial in a reasonable time.

Interpreting Article 6(1) of the European Convention on Human Rights in conjunction with Article 14 of the International Covenant on Civil and Political Rights, which the EU is bound to honour, the CJEU in a judgment on the case *Graham J. Wilson v. Ordre des avocats du barreau de Luxembourg*[20] ruled that the idea of judicial impartiality and independence consists of two elements:

1. the external one which entails protection from the influences of others; and

13 Case no. 19178/91.
14 Case nos. 32492/96, 32547/96, 32548/96.
15 Case no. 8848/80.
16 Case no. 7360/76, §80.
17 Case no. 8790/79.
18 For detailed information: www.scotland-judiciary.org.uk/55/0/Temporary-Judges.
19 See: www.heraldscotland.com/sport/spl/aberdeen/temporary-judges-told-to-avoid-criminal-trials-1.77465.
20 Case no. C-506/04.

2. the internal one that expresses the adversarial character and the equality of arms before the court.

In a number of similar rulings the CJEU uphold this position (i.e. *Köllensperger and Atzwanger*,[21] *Abrahamsson and Anderson*).[22]

As it was put in these and many other judicial decisions, the minimal threshold of guarantees of independence comes with the irremovability from office during the term the adjudicator was appointed to.[23]

What is notable as well, the CJEU acknowledged that the adjudicator, who is not an appointed judge, should exercise the same or strongly similar position as a judge for the whole duration of his mandate.[24]

Notably the CJEU has admitted that the there are situations where the non-judicial adjudicator can be removed from office, but with the restriction that he has to undergo rigorous procedure beforehand. This would prevent the executive branch to easily intervene in adjudicative proceedings.[25]

Having laid down the European standards one ought to remember that a similar standard has been developed at an international level as well.

For instance, the United Nations Commission on Human Rights (UNCHR) in the commentary to Article 14 of the International Covenant on Civil and Political Rights has argued that the only way to ensure independence and impartiality of judges and other adjudicators is to set up a proper procedure of appointing them for office (best without the involvement of the government), a stable terms of promotion, preventing the possibility of their impeachment before the term they were appointed for.[26]

As one can see, Poland is obviously not the only country struggling with the implementation of the fair trial standards while addressing the efficiency needs of the judicial system. For example, the Latvian Constitutional Court in the judgment of 5 November 2004,[27] has also addressed this problem on the grounds of the statues regulating the organization of the courts. The problem concerned Article 75 of the Law on Judicial Power in the following wording:

> "In case of a vacancy or the temporary absence of a judge of a District (city) court, the Minister of Justice may, for a period not exceeding two years, assign a judge of another District (city) court, a judge emeritus, a judge of a regional court or **a lay**

21 Case no. C 103/97.
22 Case no. C 407/98.
23 On irrevocability also see combined cases C 9/97 and C 118/97 – *Jokela* and *Pitkäranta*.
24 See: C-259/04 *Elizabeth Florence Emanuel v. Continental Shelf* 128 Ltd.
25 See: C-53/03 *Synetairismos Farmakopoion Aitolias & Akarnanias (Syfait) v. GlaxoSmithKline plc and GlaxoSmithKline AEVE*.
26 General Comment No. 13: Equality before the courts and the right to a fair and public hearing by an independent court established by law (Art. 14):. 13/04/84. CCPR General Comment No. 13. (General Comments).
27 Case no. 2004-04-01 available in English at: www.satv.tiesa.gov.lv/upload/2004-04-01E.rtf.

judge, who meets the requirements for the nomination of a candidate for a judge of a district (city) court as set out in Article 52 of this Law, if such person has given written consent to fulfil the duties of a judge of a District (city) court."

The position of the lay judge acting in place of a professional judge was the biggest concern. The Constitutional Court had to take into consideration that the procedure under which the Minister of Justice charges the lay judge with the duty of substituting the judge of the particular District (city) may cause suspicion on the potential dependence of the appointed judge from the executive power, as well as create doubt on the legitimacy of the decisions adopted by him.

The Constitutional Court of Latvia took into account both the internal legal system of Latvia and Article 6 of the Convention and found the procedure (in accordance with which the Minister of Justice may assign a lay judge to the office of a judge) does not comply with the concept of independent court, incorporated in the Satversme (Constitution of Latvia) and the Convention and runs contrary to Articles 84 and 92 of the Satversme.

The Court stressed that the guarantees with regard to the period of authority of the judge do not suffice, as the judge may become easily influenced. It was taken into consideration that Article 75 of the Law on Judicial Power allows the Minister of Justice on his own discretion to appoint the lay judge to the office of the judge for the period shorter than two years.

One can easily point out that these are the same concerns put forward by the ECtHR in the cases cited above, which rather constitutes evidence of shared standard of a fair trial. Despite the ongoing problems with temporary judges across a variety of national legal systems, new countries tend to implement the institution in their judicial organization. For example Japan introduced it to its legal system in 2009 and a research on the legal and social results of this change has already begun.[28]

4. AMENDING THE ORGANISATION OF COURTS

After this brief reconstruction of the fair trial standard that is prevailing in the European judiciary system the authors will try to describe its impact on their domestic (Polish) judiciary system with the special inclusion of assessors both in general and administrative courts.

As it was said in the previous sections of the article, the ground rules for the current Polish legal system standard concerning the admissibility of an assessor's office has been laid down by the Polish Constitutional Tribunal in the judgment

[28] See: www.law.columbia.edu/media_inquiries/news_events/2008/november2008/saiban_in.

of 24 October 2007. The direct consequence of that was the amendment of the Law of 27 July 2001 on the Organisation of Common Courts.

Taking that into account, the Supreme Court of the Republic of Poland has also ruled that the impartiality of an assessor in general courts has no real guarantees since he is appointed by the Minister who is empowered with the right to prolong the *votum*.[29]

The changed act was considered unconstitutional as there was too much possible influence from the Minister of Justice on the non-judge adjudicator. Therefore the act had to be modified so that the general courts could continue with their proceedings without the objection that they would be unconstitutional.

This ruling of the Polish Constitutional Court prompted a debate both within the practice and academia. Most of the judges in the general courts expressed concern for the future practice and efficiency of the judicial system. The main line of argument was, if only the justices nominated by the President can perform the role of the judge in trial, the ongoing cases that are already long, are going to take even more time with every recess that a court takes. The never-ending trails cannot be considered fair either.[30]

Some of the members of the judiciary proposed a number of solutions. For instance, that a junior judge-assessor in the beginning years of his office would perform the role of a judge within the courts of appeal where he would learn and be supervised by senior judges.[31] This kind of solution is rather implausible because it does not address the problem in the first place (the triad of conditions set above).

The other suggested route was to enable assessors to judge only the lesser offense cases. This idea will also not stand. The Polish Constitution requires that if a person is to be found guilty of crime, the sentence has to be delivered by a full nominated judge. The time where the lesser offenses were in fact not considered a source of criminal liability and could be adjudicated by the executive branch is long gone, which is also an achievement of the Constitutional Tribunal of the Republic of Poland.

Part of the academic society went in the other direction. Some saw the decision of the Constitutional Tribunal as inconsequent as it denied all the parties who were sentenced by assessors the right to a new trial based on Article 190(4) of the Polish Constitution.[32] Since the main problem is to grant the citizens the right to a fair trial, no matter the consequences for the court's

---

29 H. Gajewski, 'The gloss to the Supreme Court's Resolution (7) – VI KZP 2/81', *Państwo i Prawo* 1983 (5) p. 145.

30 S. Polański (2008) 'The gloss to the Polish Constitutional Tribunal judgment of 24 October 2007, case no. SK 7/06', *Gdańskie Studia.Prawnicze.Prz.Orz.* (3). 197–209.

31 J. Tylewicz (2007) 'Problem z asesorami', *Prokurator* (3/4), 75–80.

32 Wiącek M., (2008) 'The gloss to Polish Constitutional Tribunal judgment of 24 October 2007, case no. SK 7/06', *Przegląd Sejmowy* 2 (85), 224.

efficiency, the right solution should be to give the parties the opportunity to revise their case in front a nominated judge. Others argued even, that withholding of the implementation of the Constitutional Tribunal's judgment has no rational grounds and the state of violating the Constitution should not be ignored for another 18 months.[33]

5. REGULATIONS ON ASSESSORS IN POLISH ADMINISTRATIVE COURTS – POSSIBLE SOLUTIONS

Arguments concerning the assessors in common courts do not seem to address the Law of 25 July 2002 on the Organisation of Administrative Courts,[34] that has not been amended due to the same verdict of the Polish Constitutional Tribunal. Although that judgment did not concern the mentioned act, the act – to this day – contains regulations concerning assessors and the range of their possible empowerment. Also there are no legislative initiatives being put forward in order to change that.

The rules of rational legislation or – as it is being put in the Polish literature – the dogma of the rational legislator, presupposes that if the act has not been modified, then it is a conscious conduct as the act is still considered by the legislator as constitutional.

The ongoing judicial practice did not follow the path of reasoning that was put forward here. Despite the fact that Articles 10 and 26 are still part of the Law of 25 July 2002 on the Organisation of Administrative Courts, the practice after the judgment of the Constitutional Tribunal changed rapidly.

Although on the grounds of the mentioned act, one can still be appointed to the office of an assessor in an administrative court if only that person meets the requirements put forward in Article 26 of the discussed act. One of the possible "paths" on the way of becoming an assessor in an administrative court is in fact holding a position of a judge in a general court. This definitely does not pose any objections from the standpoint presented in the justification of the Constitutional Tribunal's judgment. Still, all other requirements mention an office that has no adjudicating function such as an attorney or a public prosecutor. This is the reason why the Supreme Administrative Court dismissed the general possibility of appointing assessors in administrative courts.

In its verdict of 23 November 2009,[35] the Court stood on the position that, since the position of an assessor in an administrative court is very similar to the

33 Czarny P., (2008) 'Gloss to the Judgment of the Constitutional Tribunal of October 24, 2007 (Act Call No SK 7/06)', *Przegląd Sejmowy* 2 (85), 237.

34 *Journal of Laws* No. 153, item 1269, as amended.

35 Case no. I OSK 277/09.

one of an assessor in general courts, the judgment of the Constitutional Tribunal should apply to administrative courts as well.[36] This sentence did not address the vital differences between the assessors in both common and administrative courts. The authors evaluate this critically as both institutions cannot be treated equally, especially since the decision of the Constitutional Tribunal concerns only the Law of 27 July 2001 on the Organisation of Common Courts.

The verdict led to the practice found in administrative courts today. Although there have been no changes in the Law of 25 July 2002 on the Organisation of Administrative Courts, the assessors are not being appointed. The authors stand on the position that this practice is both ineffective and legally invalid.

First of all, an assessor in an administrative court is not subject to any direct influence from the executive. Only the President of the Supreme Administrative Court has the power to appoint assessors. The administrative court's assessor is also not irremovable. He or she can be put down from office by the President of the Supreme Administrative Court. There is also a prescribed term of office. The President of the Supreme Administrative Court may – with the approval of the Council of Judges – appoint an assessor to an Voivodship Administrative Court to act as a temporary judge for up to five years. The assessor acts under the tutorship of a consultant judge, who also prepares their evaluation.

Although not totally independent, they are being considered as judges when it comes to delivering a sentence. The Supreme Administrative Court stood by this position in a number of cases, i.e. the judgment from 16 October 2006.[37]

6. CONCLUSION

As we can see, the time limitations to the office of a temporary judge do not necessary diminish the fact that during his term, he is independent. The assessors in Polish administrative courts benefit from this kind of independence. Their judicial decisions cannot be corrected and their evaluation is being done *ex post*. That being said these transparent limitations do not deprive the assessors if the independence from the executive or other members of the judiciary.

According to the authors, the presented legal regulation on assessors in administrative courts is admissible in the Polish legal system

The statutory requirements of administrative courts meet – in opinion of the authors – the European standards for adjudicators and fair trial that were given in the beginning parts of the article. Especially, the fact that the assessor is being appointed by the officer of the judiciary (President of the Supreme Administrative Court) guarantees him the independence. The legal path of appointing temporary judges should not be dismissed as it enables the judiciary

36 Text available at http://orzeczenia.nsa.gov.pl.

37 Case no. I OSK 1341/05.

system to find the best candidates for full nominated judges. The model that we find in Polish administrative courts proves both efficient and safe from any influence. As such it could be a starting point in developing regulations on the office of a temporary judge in other legal systems.

BIBLIOGRAPHY

BOOKS AND ARTICLES

Baum L., (2008) *Judges and their audiences. A perspective on judicial behavior*, Princeton University Press

Czarny P., (2008) Gloss to the Judgment of the Constitutional Tribunal of October 24, 2007 (Act Call No SK 7/06), *Przegląd Sejmowy* 2 (85), 237

Gajewski H., The gloss to the Supreme Court's Resolution (7) – VI KZP 2/81, *Państwo i Prawo* 1983 (5), p. 145

Polański S., (2008) The gloss to the Polish Constitutional Tribunal judgment of 24 October 2007, case no. SK 7/06 *Gdańskie Studia Prawnicze.Prz.Orz.* (3). 197–209

Tylewicz J., (2007) Problem z asesorami, *Prokurator* (3/4), 75–80

Vitkauskas D., Diko G., (2012) *Protecting the Right to a Fair Trial under the European Convention on Human Rights.* Council of Europe human rights handbooks, Strasbourg, p. 44

Wiącek M., (2008) The gloss to Polish Constitutional Tribunal judgment of 24 October 2007, case no. SK 7/06, *Przegląd Sejmowy* 2 (85), p. 224

LEGAL ACTS

The 2001 Law on the Organisation of Common Courts, *Journal of Laws* No. 98, item 1070, as amended

The 2002 Law on the Organisation of Administrative Courts, *Journal of Laws* No. 153, item 1269, as amended

The European Convention for the Protection of Human Rights and Fundamental Freedoms, as amended by Protocols Nos. 11 and 14, 4 November 1950, ETS 5

CASE-LAW (IN ORDER OF CITATION)

ECtHR Case no. 23614/08, §§16–25 *Henryk Urban and Ryszard Urban v. Poland*

ECtHR Case no. 22860/02, §94 *Woś v. Poland*

ECtHR Case no. 54723/00 *Brudnicka v. Poland*

ECtHR Case no. 7819/77; 7878/77 *Cambell and Fell v. The United Kingdom*

ECtHR Case no. 11179/84 *Langborger v. Sweden*

ECtHR Case no. 19178/91 *Coëme and others v. Belgium*

ECtHR Case nos. 32492/96, 32547/96, 32548/96 *Bryan v. The United Kingdom*

ECtHR Case no. 8848/80 *Benthem v. Holland*
ECtHR Case no. 7360/76, §80 *Raport Zand v. Austria*
ECtHR Case no. 8790/79 *Sramek v. Austria*
ECJ Case no. C-506/04 *Graham J. Wilson v. Ordre des avocats du barreau de Luxembourg*
ECJ Case no. C 103/97 *Köllensperger and Atzwanger*
ECJ Case no. C 407/98 *Abrahamsson and Anderson*
ECJ C-259/04 *Elizabeth Florence Emanuel v. Continental Shelf 128 Ltd*
ECJ C-53/03 *Synetairismos Farmakopoion Aitolias & Akarnanias (Syfait) v. GlaxoSmithKline plc and GlaxoSmithKline AEVE*
PCT Judgment of 24 October 2007, SK 7/06, Exercise of Judicial Power by Assistant Judges, (OTK ZU 2007, No. 9A, item 108)
The Republic of Latvia Constitutional Court Judgment from November 5, 2004, Case no. 2004-04-01 available in English at: www.satv.tiesa.gov.lv/upload/2004-04-01E.rtf
The Supreme Administrative Court, judgment from 23.11.2009 r., Case no. I OSK 277/09
The Supreme Administrative Court, judgment from 16.10.2006 r., Case no. I OSK 1341/05

INTERNET SOURCES

http://nawokandzie.ms.gov.pl/numer-19/dobre-praktyki/w-drodze-po-korone.html
http://trybunal.gov.pl/fileadmin/content/omowienia/SK_7_06_GB.pdf
www.scotland-judiciary.org.uk/55/0/Temporary-Judges
www.heraldscotland.com/sport/spl/aberdeen/temporary-judges-told-to-avoid-criminal-trials-1.77465

www.ingramcontent.com/pod-product-compliance
Ingram Content Group UK Ltd.
Pitfield, Milton Keynes, MK11 3LW, UK
UKHW051922100926
8556IPUK00021B/1316

9 781780 683164